Territory, State and Nationalism

Anglo-Iraqi Policy Toward the Kurdish

National Movement, 1918-1932

ADEL SOHEIL

Adel Soheil 2018

Förlag: BoD-Books on Demand, Stockholm, Sverige

ISBN: 9789117855132

To My Parents

Contents

Introduction

Following the dismantlement of the Ottoman Empire after WW 1, the Allied powers forged individual states with no particular considerations to their ethnic, religious and social characteristics introducing an artificial state system into the Middle East. One of these countries was Iraq, which was created by the British through the unification of the three former Ottoman *Wilayats* (provinces) of Baghdad, Basra and Mosul. However, Britain did not employ direct rule in Iraq and was obliged to compromise with the U.S. non-annexation policy strongly advocated by President Wilson. The U.S. entry into WW1 against the Central Powers led to the Allied powers' victory. Based on this contribution and its anti-colonial policy, the U.S. supported non-annexation of the former colonies and dependent territories of the German and the Ottoman Empires and stressed the principle of self-determination and set about to establish a mandate system under the supervision of the League of Nations.

However, this policy did not rest on any "Wilsonian idealism" but was rather guided by Wilson's realism. As this study will illustrate later, Wilson conditioned his approval of Iraq being under British mandate to the latter's approval of the open door policy, i.e. equal political and economic opportunities for the U.S. and especially to have access to Iraq's oil. On the other hand, Wilson's concept of self-determination, which at the time had gained currency among the populations of the former Ottoman Empire, gave impetus to the national sentiments already ignited among the Kurds as well as the Arabs. However, the concept of national self-determination as a legal status was applied only in certain East European countries and was not really meant to be applied on countries in the Middle East.

1

According to the treaty of Sèvres, concluded on August 10, 1920, between the victorious Allied powers and the Ottoman Empire (Turkey), the Kurds were entitled to an independent national state. But it was never realized partly due to the Kemalist military progress and subsequent British abandonment of the idea and partly due to the reluctance on the part of the Iraqi government to accommodate Kurdish wishes and instead to incorporate them into the structure of the nascent Iraqi state.

The aim of this book is hence to examine the policy of the British and Iraqi political elites with the objective to create a homogeneous nation-state in Iraq from the time of king Faisal I's installation in Iraq by the British in 1921 until the end of the mandate period in 1932. In doing so prominence is given to some Iraqi personalities in carrying out this policy. These were ex-Ottoman officers who participated in the famous Arab revolt of Hijaz under Emir Faisal and returned to Iraq when the latter ascended the throne there in 1921 to constitute his closest entourage such as Nuri al-Sa'id, Jafar al-'Askari and Jamil al-Mifa'i (he joined the government later, in 1930). Others, included Abdul Muhsin al-Saa'dun, who embarked on a political career and served as Prime Minister four terms, and Sati al-Husri, who was Director General of Education from 1921 to 1927. These Sunni Arab personalities who occupied leading positions in several Iraqi governments were actually the new ruling elite of the country. This is of course not to diminish the forceful role of the British decision making in Iraq during the mandate period. Previous studies, despite their valuable information, have either belittled the role of these key figures or have mentioned them only in passing. By highlighting the actions of these men, often motivated by Arab nationalism, and by the idea of welding together different ethnic and religious groups into a cohesive Iraqi nation in a country that not even today has become a nation, this study will hopefully contribute to a better understanding of the factors that hampered, or fostered if there were any, the trajectory of nation-state formation in Iraq.

As the largest ethnic group in the country, the Kurds with a distinct cultural and linguistic identity rejected this policy of ethnic homogenization and struggled for their national and cultural rights. However, unlike later Sunni Arab dominant groups, particularly during the reign of the Ba'thists from 1968 to 2003, who resorted to extreme measures and terror such as intensive Arabization, mass expulsion, and genocide of the Kurds in order

2

to create a homogeneous nation-state, the rulers of the mandate period refrained from employing such methods. Although they also used military force in suppressing the Kurdish national movement, they sought primarily to incorporate the Kurdish region into the newly created Iraqi state and to impose cultural assimilation on the Kurds. Moreover, the British who as the mandatory power were obligated to supervise the implementation of minority rights in Iraq were reluctant to use extreme violence. Overall, the relations between the Anglo-Iraqi Authorities and the Kurds were characterized by hostilities and mistrust and on several occasions resulted in open armed conflicts.

At the threshold of the occupation of Iraq, nationalism had been for decades a powerful political force in Europe with a pervasive influence on the peoples of the Middle East, among them the Kurds and the Arabs. Kurdish as well as Arab nationalists claimed to act in the name of their peoples for their national rights and many of them laid down their lives for their cause. In Iraq, Arab nationalists, in the government alongside King Faisal, despite their cooperation with the British to consolidate the Iraqi state, wanted independence and the end of the mandate rule. Those outside the government, largely consisting of Shiites, desired also independence, but without any foreign rule. On the other hand, the Kurdish national movement under the leadership of Shaikh Mahmud Barzanji and later the Barzanis, strongly inspired by the principle of national self-determination, struggled against the Anglo-Iraqi authorities in order to set up an autonomous government of their own, preferably under the auspices of Great Britain, refusing subjugation to the dominant Arab rulers. This study provides then a historical background of Kurdish and Arab nationalism and their development since their inceptions until the end of the mandate period. Finally, since this study concerns principally the Anglo-Iraqi policy toward the Kurdish national movement, emphasis will therefore be put on significant features of this movement.

1

Nation and Nationalism

The prevailing belief among scholars of the modernist school is that nation and nationalism are modern phenomena, developing in Europe during the nineteenth and twentieth centuries. Anthony Smith summarizes the modernist perspective as follows: Nation and nationalism appeared in the last centuries, in the wake of the French Revolution, and they are regarded as the product of the specifically modern processes of capitalism, industrialism, bureaucracy, mass communications and secularism. [1]

Thus, the modern social structure provided the context for the emergence of nation and nationalism. Eric Hobsbawm states that the nation is a changeable social entity which "belongs exclusively to a particular, and historically recent, period. It is a social entity only insofar as it relates to a certain kind of modern territorial state, the "nation-state", and it is pointless to discuss nation and nationality except insofar as both relate to it."[2] In short, in his opinion nationalism precedes nations, and nations do not create states and nationalism, but the other way around.[3] In addition, Hobsbawm focuses on components such as artefacts, inventions[4] and

---

[1] Anthon D. Smith, *Nations and Nationalism in a Global Era* (Oxford: Blackwell, 1995) , p. 29.
[2] E.J.Hobsbawm, *Nation and Nationalism since 1780: Programme, Myth and Reality* (Cambridge: Cambridge University Press, 1990), pp.9-10
[3] Ibid., p. 10.
[4] By invention Hobsbawm refers to the inventing of tradition in the process of nation- building. He uses the term "invented traditions" in a broader sense to mean "a set of practices normally governed by overtly or tacitly accepted rules and of a ritual or symbolic nature, which seek to inculcate certain values and norms of behaviour by repetition, which automatically implies continuity with the past." See idem. The Invention of Traditions (Cambridge, 1983) p.1

4

"social engineering" that contribute to nation-building and refers in this connection to Gellner:

> Nations as a natural, God –giving way of classifying men, as an inherent though long-delayed political destiny, are a myth; nationalism, which sometimes takes pre-existing cultures and turns them into nations, sometimes invents them, and often obliterates pre-existing cultures: *that* is a reality. [5]

Based on the assumption that prior to the modern time no explicit link between nation and state-territorial organization existed, Hobsbawm again refers to Gellner and uses the term nationalism in the same sense as defined by him, that is to imply "primarily a principle which holds that the political and national unit should be congruent." [6]According to Gellner, due to the relationship between power and culture, nation and nationalism cannot emerge in agrarian societies. A common denominator of such societies is that the ruling class is composed of a small minority of the population, namely, warriors, priests, clerics, administrators and burghers, and is firmly divorced from the large majority of direct agricultural producers, or peasants, who generally have "inward-turned lives", and are connected to their localities by economic necessities rather than political prescription. This horizontally stratified ruling minority emphasizes cultural differentiation rather than cultural homogeneity. In fact, the state in agrarian society, consist of, two kinds of political units; local self-governing communities and large empires, is more interested in, and benefit more from, extracting taxes and maintaining peace than in imposing cultural homogeneity between its subjects at the lower social stratum.

Thus, in agro-literate societies "the two potential partners, culture and power, destined for each other according to nationalist theory, *neither* has much inclination for the other in the conditions prevailing in the agrarian age." [7] On the other hand, in industrial societies the relationship between

---

[5] Ernest Gellner, *Nation and Nationalism* (New York, Cornell University Press, 1983), pp. 48-49.
[6] Ibid., p.1.
[7] Ibid., pp. 9-13. The idea of nationalism is originally developed in Gellner's *Thought and Change* (London, 1964), pp.147-178.

power and culture is fundamentally different; "A high culture pervades the whole of society, defines it, and needs to be sustained by the polity. *That is the secret of nationalism.*" [8] According to Gellner, hence, nation only can exist in industrial societies where the means for the homogenization of culture are available. He holds that "nation can be defined only in terms of the age of nationalism, rather than, as you might expect, the other way around...Rather, when general social conditions make for standardized, homogeneous, centrally sustained high cultures, prevailing entire populations and not just elite minorities." [9] Similar to Hobsbawm, he takes the view that "it is nationalism which engenders nations, and not the other way around." [10]

Miroslav Hroch and the Three-Phase Model of the Development of Nationalism

A path-breaking comparative analysis of national movements with the aspiration of establishing national states has been done by Miroslav Hroch. Hroch's concern is the study of the social basis of the national movements of mainly oppressed and non-dominant East European nationalities. However, since the development of the national movements of the peoples of the Ottoman Empire in some important aspects are similar to the East European ones, it would also be appropriate to use Hroch's three-stage process for this study.

According to Hroch, during Phase A (the period of scholarly interest), the beginning of the national revival, groups of people or individuals and, above all, intellectuals felt affinity for and interest in the study of the

---

[8] Ibid., p.18.
[9] Ibid., p. 55.
[10] Ibid. However, Hobsbawm underlines at the same time the fact that Gellner's perspective of modernization is from above that is a perspective which only pays attention to the behavior and action of the political and cultural elite for a certain movement rather than the sentiments, wills and needs of the ordinary people, who constitute the object of the elite's action and propaganda. Hobsbawm, (1990), pp.10-11. He points out that national identification of these people can shift in any time even within quite a short period of time.

language, culture, and history of the oppressed nation. Characteristic of this phase was the lack of will and interest on the part of the individuals for any organized political or social activity, and they did not even attempt to mount a patriotic agitation. They remained at the personal level of their agitation without any considerable influence on the people and were isolated from each other. They were motivated by patriotism of the "Enlightenment type" in that their affection and interest was confined to solely acquiring more knowledge about the region of their residence.[11]

This phase, Phase B, which he labels (the period of patriotic agitation) is the most important period for the formation of small nations. It was during this phase that the agitation of the patriots influenced and mobilized a great portion of the oppressed nationality in order to obtain nationalist ends. Language and establishment of various associations and networks occupied a central role in this phase. Hroch maintains that the national agitation was not destined to succeed in all cases and the transition of Phase B into Phase C was not certain, and in a number of cases, this transition did not take place. The transition from one Phase to the other did not occur at one stroke: "between the manifestations of scholarly interest, on the one hand, and the mass diffusion of patriotic attitudes, on the other, there lie an epoch which was decisive for the actual formation of the small nation, an epoch characterized by active patriotic agitation: the fermentation-process of national consciousness"[12]

In the concluding Phase, Phase C, (the rise of mass national movement), the national consciousness became the concern of the masses and the national movement was solid organized over the whole territory. In addition, nationalist programs normally achieved mass support and a basic level of vertical social mobility was created.[13]

Hobsbawm stresses the significance of the transition of Phase B to Phase C for the chronology of the national movements. In Europe the

---

[11] Miroslav Hroch, *Social Preconditions of National Revival in Europe* (Cambridge, 1985), p.23.
[12] Ibid. pp.22.24.
[13] Ibid. p.23.

transition sometimes takes place before the establishment of a national state, and perhaps as a consequence of this establishment, it frequently takes place afterwards. On the other hand, in the so-called Third World, sometimes it does not occur even then.[14]

Although Hroch's study focuses on the development of non-dominant nations in Central and Eastern Europe during the nineteenth century, he argues that the nation was the product of a long and complicated process of historical development in Europe. He traces the development of some of the "fully-formed" state-nations in Western Europe back to the Middle Ages.In these countries the early modern state developed under the domination of one ethnic culture, either in absolutist form or in a representative-state system.[15] For this reason his approach has been criticized to be close to primordialism. However, he contends that such critical views basically stem from misconceptions of his approach and explains that he does not perceive the nations as "eternal categories" and that he has employed the term "revival" in "metaphorical sense."[16]

Print-capitalism and National Consciousness

Similar to Hroch, Benedict Anderson attaches a crucial role to national consciousness in the creation of modern nations. According to Anderson, the print-languages laid the foundation for the national consciousness in three ways. First, they "created a unified field of exchange and communication below Latin and above the spoken vernaculars." Second, print-capitalism gave "a new fixity to language... which helped to build that image of antiquity so central to the subjective idea of the nation." Third, print-capitalism "created languages-of-power of a kind different from the older administrative vernaculars." In other words, what, in a positive sense, made the modern nations, or as Anderson calls them, the

---

[14] Hobsbawm, (1990), p. 12.

[15] Miroslav Hroch, *From National Movement to the Fully-Formed Nation*: *The Nation-building Process in Europe*, New Left Review (1/198, 1993), P.2.

[16] Miroslav Hroch, *Real and Constructed: the Nature of the Nation,* in J.A.Hall (ed.), The *State of the Nation: Ernest Gellner and the Theory of Nationalism* (Cambridge: Cambridge University Press, 1998), p. 94.

new communities, imaginable was "a half- fortuitous, but explosive, interaction between a system of production and productive relations (capitalism), a technology of communications (print), and the fatality of human linguistic diversity."[17]

Regarding the evolution of the national language and its crucial role in the formation of the modern concept of nation-building, Benedict Anderson stresses the fact that printed literature, print-capitalism, and its dissemination alongside the wide range growth of literacy, commerce, industry and communications, which were characteristic of the nineteenth century "created powerful new impulses for vernacular linguistic unification within the dynastic realm."[18] Consequently, for instance, the Maronites and Copts, many of them educated at Beirut's American College (founded in 1866) and the Jesuit College of St. Joseph (founded in 1875) played a major role in the revival of classical Arabic and the spread of Arab nationalism. In addition, the emergence of a lively vernacular press in Istanbul in the 1870s marked the birth of Turkish nationalism. This implied the rejection of "Ottoman", which was a dynastic language of officialdom of the Empire consisting of Turkish, Persian and Arabic elements.[19]

Central in the modernist approach to the theme of nation and nationalism is that these concepts are perceived as modernist phenomena, that is, as products of a dynamic historical process which has emerged during the industrialization era, contrasting the primordialist perception of the nation formation in the *longue durée*. However, it is worth noting that despite this fact, it does not imply that affection for a language or the sense of belonging to a certain group or region did not exist before.

Anthony D. Smith, although he concedes that nationalism as an ideology and a movement is a quite recent phenomenon, dating from the late eighteenth century, he traces the growth of national sentiments back to

---

[17] Benedict Anderson, *Imagined Communities: Reflections on the Origin and Spread of Nationalism* (London: Verso, 2006), pp.42-54

[18] Ibid., pp. 77.78.

[19] Ibid., 75.

the fifteenth and sixteenth centuries in many states of Western Europe.[20] He makes a distinction between ethnic communities, which he calls *ethnie* (using the French term) and modern ones, the nations. He defines the nation as "a named human population, which shares myths and memories, a mass public culture, a designated homeland, economic unity and equal rights and duties for all members"[21],whereas he ascribes *ethnie* the following main attributes: a collective proper name, a myth of common ancestry, one or more differentiating elements of common culture, shared historical memories, association with a specific "homeland", and sense of solidarity for significant sectors of the population. [22]

Nation and *ethnie*, Smith points out, are both "forms of collective cultural identity that may coexist or compete with each other...within the boundaries of the political community of the nation."They are "part of a wider ethno-cultural family of collective identities and aspirations." This explains why nationalists "appeal to culture and symbolic repertoires within the antecedent populations with whom they claim a deep cultural continuity."[23]

Thus, the modern nations, as mass phenomena can be seen as politicized, territorialized forms of *ethnies*. Their existence is due to a long and complex development of pre-existing collective cultural identities and particularly of *ethnie*. Smith, however, clarifies that not all *ethnies* have evolved into modern nations; many earlier *ethnies* disappeared or were absorbed by others or fell apart, while some of these *ethnies* have survived

---

[20] Smith, (1995), p. 38. Despite this fact, Smith, contends that the "modern nation" absorbs many features of pre-modern *ethnie* and "owes much to the
general model of ethnicity which has survived in many areas until the dawn of the 'modern area'." See Idem, *The Ethnic origins of Nations* (Oxford: Blackwell, 1986), p. 18. In his book *Nations before Nationalism* (Chapel Hill, 1982) John A. Armstrong, employs a similar approach to the development of national identity. However, he traces the emergence of group identification, or the 'nation' further back to the ancient civilizations such as the Egyptian and the Mesopotamian.
[21] Smith, (1995) , pp.56-57.
[22] Anthony D. Smith, *National Identity* (London, 1991), p.21.
[23] Anthony D. Smith, *Nation and Nationalism: Theory, Ideology, History* (Cambridge, 2001), p. 58.

from pre-modern periods and often constituted the foundation for the rise of modern nations and nationalist movements.[24]

On the other hand, other factors of particular importance in the trajectory of nation-building were the administrative, the capitalist and the educational revolutions, which led to territorial integration as well as to political and cultural homogenization that occurred during the transition from feudalism to capitalism. In addition, the need for the standardization and centralization of political and cultural lives were more and more regarded as prerequisites of success of the state-making process. Alongside this process, a strong national consciousness developed.[25]

The Principle of Nationality

As has been noted, the promoters of the modernist paradigm such as Gellner, Hobsbawm, Hroch and Anderson dismiss the premise that nations are natural, eternal and rooted in ancient times and contend that nations are modern phenomena of the nineteenth and twentieth centuries. Hobsbawm stipulates that "the basic characteristic of the modern nation and everything connected with it is its modernity"[26], and in order to grasp the meaning of

---

[24] Smith, (1995), p. 57. Hobsbawm also makes reference to earlier ethnic identities which he calls popular proto-nationalism. He maintains that ethnicity "in the Herodotean sense" was, is, and can draw together peoples from large territories, without a polity, into something which he labels proto-nationalism. For instance, he refers to the case of the Kurds, the Somalis, the Jews, and the Basques. However, he claims that such ethnicities lack historical relation to what is essential to the modern nation, i.e. the creation of nation-state. Hobsbawm (1990), p. 64. Hobsbawm suggests, according to Smith, that proto-nationalism cannot develop politically, and hence, cannot form the basis for the modern nation. Smith argues that Hobsbawm disregards the possibility that these "proto-national bonds" are the very ethnic links that he rejects as a basis for formation of modern nations. See Anthony, D. Smith, *Nationalism and Modernism, A Critical Survey of Recent Theories of Nations and Nationalism*, (London: Routledge, 1998), pp.127-128. On the other hand, Hobsbawm argues that in some Eastern European countries there existed something like proto-nationalism, but "paradoxically" it evolved into conservatism rather than national rebellion. See idem, *The Age of Revolution: Europe 1789-1848* (London, 1973), p. 176.

[25] Smith, (1995), pp. 87-91.

[26] Hobsbawm, (1990), p. 18.

the modern concept of "the nation" he refers to its use during the Age of Revolution, and particularly referred to as "the principle of nationality" since the 1830s. At that time, the time of the French Revolution, which sowed the seeds of the modern nation -building, the political aspect of the nation was a more important factor than the cultural and linguistic factors. It regarded the nation as a body of citizens whose collective sovereignty entitled them to a state as their political expression. Thus, the equation nation= state = people, and especially sovereign people, linked nation to territory, since states were now delineated along territorial lines.[27]

However, during the period from 1830 to 1880, Europe went through a dramatic change. Based on the national principle Germany and Italy emerged as two great powers which altered the European balance of power. At the same time, a number of small countries in southeast Europe, which had seceded from the Ottoman Empire and elsewhere achieved their independence and claimed to be recognized on the basis of the same principle. The problem that arose was the question which of the many European peoples acknowledged a "nationality" would acquire a state and which of the many existing states would enjoy the status of "nation"? [28]

It was widely accepted by "the serious thinkers of the subject", of the liberal era, that the "principle of nationality" would only be applied to nations of a required size. According to this "threshold principle" and Giuseppe Mazzini, the father of the Italian nationalism, and the proponent of the "principle of nationality", small nationalities that did not fulfill the condition of the threshold could not become independent. Nations had to be viable culturally and especially economically in order to be eligible for self-determination. Thus, the "principle of nationality" and self-determination were implemented in a completely different sense by Mazzini and Woodrow Wilson. Based on the latter's formulation of these principles twenty-seven states (including the Irish Free State) were created in Europe at the peace treaties after World War 1.

National movements were also considered to be movements of unifying

---

[27] Ibid., pp. 18-19.
[28] Ibid., p. 23.

nations. It was expected that small, and especially small and backward nationalities, would benefit from being absorbed into greater nations and hence make their contribution to humanity. An inevitable consequence of this view was that some of smaller nationalities and languages would disappear. This apparently conflicted with definitions of nations as based on ethnicity, language or common history.[29] This also certainly was irreconcilable with the concept of self-determination as put in the French Revolution's Declaration of Rights of 1795 "each people is independent and sovereign, whatever the number of individuals who compose it and the extent of the territory it occupies. This sovereignty is inalienable". [30]

Contrary to the pre-modern era, the modern national states, which ruled over the people directly and within a strictly defined territory, decided in "turning subjects into citizens" through democratization of politics. This implied that the citizens were given "a stake in the country and thereby made the state to some extent 'our own'." It was vital for states and regimes to claim loyalty, which they placed at the top of their political agenda, of their citizens. However, the state legitimacy lacked solid ground since not all nationalities constituting the 'nation' were willing to be absorbed into the dominant nation or to be eliminated by it. The failure of the state was reinforced by the very process of modernization since it implied a homogenization and standardization of its different nationalities, basically by means of a written 'national language'. The primary schools became effective vehicles in this process as they disseminated the image and the heritage of the 'nation' and instilled attachment to it. The governments were thus "plainly engaged in a conscious and deliberated ideological engineering." Consequently, nationalist movements, based on culture and language, opposed this kind of state policy and laid dawn political programs which they endeavored to carry out. [31]

In Iraq, during the process of nation-building, Iraqi governments as well as King Faisal (1921-1933) pursued a policy of negligence vis-à-vis

---

[29] Ibid., pp. 31-34.
[30] Ibid., p. 19.
[31] Ibid., pp. 83-92.

different ethnic and religious minorities in the country. Their efforts, backed by the mandatory power, were to create a nationally homogeneous nation-state from a heterogeneous population. The Kurds with a distinct culture and language and as the larger ethnic component in Iraq, formulated aspirations for national self-determination, but as this study will show they inevitably came into conflict with the incorporation program envisaged by the Anglo-Iraqi authorities.

2

Nation-State Formation in Iraq: Politicization and Homogenization of Ethnic Groups

The question what is responsible for the emergence of nationalism and nation-state formation has been answered by prominent scholars on the subject previously mentioned in this study. However, the rise of modern nation-states in Europe and its proliferation in the rest of world followed two different trajectories. While the nation-states in Western Europe came about after the decline of absolutism, in other regions in the world there were different causal mechanisms at work; West Europeans influenced the model of nation-states as standard.[32]

Iraq-created after the collapse of the Ottoman Empire, through the unification of the three former Ottoman provinces of Basra, Baghdad and Mosul, after World War 1- came under the auspices of the British as the mandatory authority. The British action of adding of Mosul province to the Iraqi state was to secure their hold on its oilfields and to change the preponderance of the Shiites in the country, given that the majority of the population of the province were Sunni Kurds, as well as to decrease Turkey's influence in the region.

The creation of modern Iraq commenced once the British proclaimed the Hashemite Faisal of Hijaz, the leader of the Arab Revolt against the Ottoman Empire, as the king of Iraq. He, together with the ex-Sharifian officers who joined him in the Revolt, became the de facto power holder

---

[32] Andreas Wimmer, *Nationalist Exclusion and Ethnic Conflict: Shadows of Modernity* (Cambridge: Cambridge University Press, 2002) p. 74.

in the nascent Iraqi state, albeit, under the British administration, 1923-1932. Being the fervent advocates of pan-Arab nationalism, they dominated the Iraqi politics both during the mandate (1921 to 1932) and the monarchy (1932-1958). During this period, almost half of the premier positions were occupied by them, and the rest by the old Ottoman bureaucratic families (10 percent) or by the Sunni notables of Baghdad (30 percent). Out of the twenty-three individuals who held office of the premiers, four were of Shiites, the rest Sunni Arabs (10) or almost entirely Arabized Kurdo-Arabs (1), Turko-Arabs (1), Seljuq-Arabs (2), Circassians (1), or Kurds (3), all were completely Sunni.[33]

Iraq, which was ruled by Britain under the League of Nations, was expected to acquire the necessary attributes of statehood and be legitimize by its population. However, during the period the Sunni Arab elite were in power (1923-1932), there was nothing that signified political cohesion or the feeling of national identity. According to Longrigg and Stokes during this period:

> There were the deep divisions within Iraqi society (urban-tribe, Kurd-Arab, Sunni-Shia) and the widely various stages of evolution reached by different elements in the population, from the cultured intelligentsia to the mass illiteracy of the tribesmen…there was an uncompromising national character, uncorrected by previous experience in public life, and by its extreme individualism ill-adapted for the workings for any real democracy, yet intolerant of other forms of government.[34]

During the 1920s the idea of an Arab nation, as was intended by the Sunni Arab rulers to constitute the foundation upon which the Iraqi nation-state would be established, lacked any serious base of support, even among the Arabs of the country. Yet, the new ruling elite endeavored to meld together people from different ethnic groups and different religions into a conscious Arab nation in order to stand up against European powers and to protect the Arab heritage. Thus, the army, a unified administration and schools were crucial tools with which the nation-building project would be

---

[33] Ibid., pp.173-174.
[34] Stephen Hemsley Longrigg and Frank Stokes. *Iraq.* (London: E. Benn,1958), p.90.

realized. Accordingly, Saati al-Husry, the founder of modern Pan-Arab ideology, was appointed as head of the education system, the army introduced universal conscription, and a unified administration of the country by Baghdad-trained officials, eventually ended the indirect rule system that existed for centuries.[35]

Wimmer argues that:

> Unlike the Young Turks, still adherents of an imperial ideology, the new regime envisioned the compulsory assimilation of the different minorities-in fact the large majority of the population-into the main stream of Arabism and, implicitly, Sunni Islam, which was regarded as the centerpiece of the nation's cultural heritage and its foremost contribution to world history.[36]

The assimilation policy adopted by the Arab elite in Iraq as an instrument of nation-building proved to be a failure; it alienated the ethnic non-Arab groups, particularly the Kurds. However, on the other hand, as Fred H. Lawson maintains, the central administration in Baghdad was at the time strong enough to exercise considerable influence on the management of the domestic policy during the mandate years, and quotes Roger Owen in this respect as he observes that, "already by the early 1920s the most politically active groups within both the Shi'i and Kurdish populations had accepted the realities of the new order and focused their attention on trying to exert pressure on the power centre in Baghdad".[37]

As for the Kurds, they undertook political activities to resist the Anglo-Iraqi policy of ignorance against them; to not accommodate their political and cultural demands, and to instead pursue a policy of Arabization and homogenization of the various ethnic groups in the country. The state of affairs thus prevalent in Iraq during the mandate period, demonstrate the fact that the process of creating a nation-state and its consolidation politicized the Kurdish national movement further. This was in the sense that nationalist feelings among the Kurds gained huge momentum, and took hold on Kurds from other social strata than only the tribal Shaikhs and

---

[35] Ibid., pp-174-175.

[36] Ibid. p. 175.

[37] Fred H. Lawson, *Constructing International Relations in the Arab World* (Stanford, California, Stanford University Press, 2006)p. 69-70.

their adherents, particularly during the few years preceded Iraq's independence, as this study will show in another chapter.

The policy of ethnic exclusion that the dominant Sunni Arabs in power adopted to build a nation-state in Iraq serves as an example "to illustrate how introducing the nation-state model into a heterogeneous society politicizes notions of ethnic belonging in a pervasive and divisive way leading to a compartmentalization of the polity along ethnic lines."[38]

It serves also as a demonstration that in the process of the "unsuccessful"[39] nation-state formation during the mandate period, and for that matter, in the period up to the end of the Baath rule in 2003, homogeneity as a necessary component for nation building was never achieved. The Arab elite, strove to eradicate ethnic, cultural and linguistic differences primarily by means of Arabization, thereby the Kurds would be integrated in a single Iraqi national structure. Thus, they neglected Kurdish national demands; in addition, that they as well frequently deployed military violence to suppress their grievances and rebellions. The political structure within which the Anglo-Iraqi authorities operated allowed for a discriminatory treatment of the Kurds. As Wimmer argues under such circumstances:

> state resources are then viewed as collective goods exclusively available to those belonging to the 'right' ethnic group. The unequal discrimination of infrastructure projects over different regions, … is then perceived as ethnic discrimination, because the state apparatus is dominated by an ethnic group

---

[38] Wimmer, (2002), p.173.

[39] Wimmer contends that studying the case of a "successful" nation-building, in Turkey indicates that melding different ethnic and tribal identities (the Kurdish being an exception) in the Turkish nation, resulted in a cultural compromise, providing "sufficient collective goods" to dissolve ethnic groups, thereby preventing their politicization.Ibid.p.67.
Karl Deutsch has also worked out a model for a successful nation-building. According to this model national homogeneity and social mobilisation are two necessary components for integrative policies. The process of assimilation and mobilization leads to "complementarity of social communication", an imperative criterion for nation formation. See Karl, W. Deutsch, *Nationalism and Social Communication: An Inquiry into the Formation of the Nationality*, (Cambridge:Mass:The M.I.T.Press,1966)

that excludes one's own from its nationalist discourse. People are thus brought to rally on the basis of their ethnic membership and to launch a struggle to be recommended as a *Staatsvolk* in their own right, and to be represented by 'their own people' in the bureaucracy.[40]

Indeed, it was the British who laid the foundation of ethnic discrimination in Iraq as they created state institutions through which allowing only the Arab Sunni to exercise power under their guidance. As mandatory power the British were to fulfill their commitments vis-a´-vis both the Iraqi people and the League of Nations and prove under the new international order that came into being after WW1, that they were "the closest friend of the Arab people". Moreover, they set about trying to form an Arab government and give it all moral and material support to succeed. A note from the Middle East Department of the Colonia Office to the Cabinet confirmed this strategy as it stated that Britain's:

> Whole course of action has been deeply committed us to the creation and support of an independent Arab State in the whole area [of Iraq], and to the rendering of such advice and assistance as may be required to enable such a state to pass through the initial difficulties of its existence... We have committed ourselves to the support of a particular form of government, viz., that of a constitutional monarchy under King Faisal... We have undertaken, under the auspices of the League of Nations and in the eyes of the world, to do our best to make this regime a success.[41]

As this study will show, Britain remained faithful in their commitment to reinforce the new Arab elite headed by King Faisal. The choice to install Faisal as King of Iraq was made taking into account two main factors. The first was that he was regarded by the British to be a moderate figure who would be able to oppose the Iraqi nationalists who demanded the total withdrawal of the British from Iraq, and the second that he was an ardent advocate of Iraq's unity, even that he at the same time was a promoter of pan-Arabism. As indicated in the above-mentioned note, for the British it was vital that a unified Arab state be established in Iraq that

---

[40] Ibid.,pp.68-69.
[41] Quoted in Toby Dodge, *Inventing Iraq: The Failure of National Building and a History Denied* (London: C. Hurst &Co.2003), p. 17.

integrated all ethnic groups. The coercive policy the Anglo-Iraqi authorities pursued against the Kurds during the mandate period left the latter with no choice but to frequently recourse to armed struggle. The ultimate goal of the Kurdish national movement thus became to dissociate themselves from the Arab dominance and form their own government. A powerful driving force behind the Kurdish national movement was the principle of self-determination, according to which nationalities severed at the time from collapsed empires had the right to attain independent statehood.

3

National Self-Determination: Its Meaning and Its Interpretation by Great Powers

The concept of self-determination was among the key philosophical issues during the Age of Enlightenment. Some of the philosophers of this age, such as Rousseau and Kant, although they approached the relationship between the subjects and the rulers in different ways, they endorsed the values of democratic principle and advocated for government reforms in order to enhance the rights of the people against the authority of the government. They contended that people as rational human beings should have the right of choice even when it is limited. Rousseau, for instance, maintained that the legitimacy of the authority of the state over subjects should only derive from a social contract with them. The government imposes obligations on the subjects as well as granting them their rights. Exercising any kinds of power over the subjects, thus, should only occur with their consent. The focal point in this contract is that the authority of the ruler is conditioned and hence obliges him to carry out his duties. Society, according to Kant, was made for men, not men for society; a ruler should treat the subjects as an end, not as a means. For Kant, Rousseau and other prominent theorists of social contract and natural law, such as Grotius, concepts like freedom of choice, social contract and priority of men were the most persistent qualities of these theories.[42]

People's desire for freedom and liberty, and their radical demands such as participation in political life and self-determination evolved from the

---

[42] George H. Sabine, A *History of Political Theory* (London, 1966), pp.428-432.

seventeenth and eighteenth centuries' social, philosophical and political thoughts.

During the French Revolution, the radical demands expressed in new principles such as *"Liberté, égalité, fraternité"* contributed to the overthrow of the absolute monarchy in France. The revolution marked a period of radical social and political upheaval that permeated not only French society, but also the whole of Europe for a long time.

Brownlie points out in his essay that the French Revolution, among other things, underscored principles of equality and government by the consent of the people. Humanity, as the decree of the constituent assembly in May 1790 declared, forms a single unity, and from then on *"les droits des peoples"* constituted a principle in the cultural and political life in Europe and elsewhere. [43]

Furthermore, the French constitution maintains that the French people are entitled to "the Rights of man and principles of national sovereignty as defined by the Declaration of 1789" and recognizes the "free determination of peoples."[44]

The concept of self-determination as a principle was a product of the Western condition of the eighteenth and nineteenth centuries. Due to the extension of the European influence throughout the world, Western political idea inevitably spread among the nations outside Europe. The basic premise of the idea of self-determination was the right to the free determination of peoples. Oppressed peoples should have the right to be free and choose their own governments and reject all kinds of alien domination.

The right to self-determination was first proclaimed by Lenin during the First World War. Lenin's approach to the theme of national self-determination was, of course, materialistic and believed that this struggle

---

[43] Ian Brownlie, *An Essay in the History of the Principle of Self-Determination,* p. 92, in C.H. Alexandrowicz.(ed.), Grotian Society Papers,
Studies in the History of the Law of Nations, (The Hague, 1970).
[44] Eyassu Gayim, *The Principle of Self-Determination: A Philosophical, Historical and Legal Approach.* (Uppsala University,1987), p. 24.

was a class struggle and as long as the capitalist system existed, the abolition of the national or other kinds of political oppression was impossible since this "requires the abolition of class, i.e. the introduction of socialism." Lenin, thus, considered the struggle of the oppressed nations against the oppressors as a necessary step toward a classless society and finally the establishment of socialism.[45]

Despite the fact that Lenin was conscious that nationalism was connected with the rise of the middle class to power and that the nation-state was a political system typical to the capitalism era, he did not condemn all forms of national movements. He distinguished between nations in the advanced capitalist countries in the West and in colonial countries such as the whole of Asia "where bourgeois nationalism had yet hardly begun its appearance should be encouraged."[46]

However, as Hans Kohn argues, by his declaration of the principle of national self-determination, Lenin hoped on the eve of the October Revolution to gain the cooperation first of the non-Russian nationalities in the Russian Empire, which he restored on a new basis, and then peoples outside the Empire. From the inception of his revolutionary movement, Lenin's focus was on Asia, where he had observed the significance of the new nationalist movements even before 1914.[47]

At the same moment, political parties in England, France and Germany were divided into two belligerent political blocks. Their positions to the war aims can in sum be described as the advocates of the Old Diplomacy and the New Diplomacy. Each of these antagonist blocks followed a war

---

[45] Alfred Cobban, *National Self-Determination*, (London: Oxford University Press, 1945), p. 103.

[46] Ibid., p. 103. Smith points out that Hobsbawm also distinguishes between two kinds of European and non-European nationalism. However, he describes the first as a "democratic mass political nationalism of the "great nation" based on the idea of French Revolution and the second, from 1870 to 1914, as "a narrow ethnic or linguistic nationalism, a small-nationality reaction to the obsolete polities of the Ottoman." See Smith, (1995), p. 11.

[47] Hans Kohn, (1958), *The United Nations and National Self-Determination*, The Review of Politics, vol. 20, No. 4.Twentieth Anniversary Issue pp.275-288. , p. 528.

aims policy which was irreconcilable to the other block. For instance, the exponents of the Old Diplomacy or the forces of order were keen on their decision to follow a traditional policy and method characterized by annexations, secret diplomacy, protectorates, and spheres of influence. In contrast, the exponents of the New Diplomacy or the forces of movement agreed on a common program of war aims, which supported the idea of non-annexation and open diplomacy.[48]

This polarization of the political parties and movements was accompanied with broad political unrest and disorder, especially among the left-wing and the radical movements of Central Europe. Following the publication of the secret treaties[49] by the Bolsheviks, the Allies risked losing the fragile credibility they had with the left-wing movements in their countries. The danger that Lenin could be regarded as the leader of the forces of movement, especially in Central Europe, was the chief reason which urged President Wilson to explicitly adopt the principle of national self-determination. [50]Wilson's declaration of his fourteen points, a master plan for world peace, was embraced by the leftist parties and the radicals who saw their ideas reflected in Wilson fourteen points.[51]

One of the main causes for the enunciation and application of Wilson's fourteen points was, hence, "deeply affected by consideration of wartime strategy and diplomacy."[52] However, in light of the evolution of the idea

---

[48]Arno J. Mayer, *Political Origins of the New Diplomacy, 1917-1918* (New Haven: Yale University Press, 1959), pp-3-7.

[49] The most important of these secret treaties relevant to this study was the Sykes-Picot agreement of 1916 concluded by the French diplomat Francois Georges-Picot and the British Sir Mark Sykes. For more information about this agreement see p. 27 and p. 43of this study.

[50] Klaus Schwabe, *Woodrow Wilson and the Revolutionary Germany, and Peacemaking 1918-1919: Missionary Diplomacy and Realities of Power* (Chapel Hill, 1985), p. 18.

[51] Ibid., p. 9. In Germany, for instance, lefties-liberals saw similarities between their political war program and that of Wilson's. Like Wilson they too advocated the "Open Door" doctrine and were against the threat of the Bolsheviks to the political and economic order in the world. P. 392.

[52] Allen Lynch, *Woodrow Wilson and the Principle of National Self-Determination: A Reconsideration*, Review of International Studies, (April,

of self-determination in Europe, it is then consistent to hold, in conformity with Hroch, that the principle of self-determination was not "invented" by Lenin or Wilson, but should be seen as a historical phenomenon and as the final stage of European national development.[53]

The United States had not the slightest interest or any ambition to enter the war. It stuck to its tradition of neutrality and non-intervention. When the war broke out Wilson was persistent in his position that the United States had absolutely "no part in making" the war. Wilson's attitudes were not only clear and explicitly expressed to the domestic public, but were even known to the European powers at war.[54]

In his reply to the Allied and the Central Powers addressed to the Senate on January 22, 1917, a little more than two months before the United States entered the war against Germany[55],Wilson appealed for a settlement of the conflict; that the peace "must be a peace without victory...Victory would mean peace forced upon the loser, a victor's terms imposed upon the vanquished." He spoke of rejection of the policy of balance of power, and supported "government by the consent of the governed" and freedom of the sea. [56]This notable speech was described by Wilson as firm "America's principles." These were later leading principles both for the settlement of

---

2002), p.419. However, Michla Pomerance points out that the Principle of self-determination as Wilson conceived it, was generated not only as a result of the wartime development, but it was " an imprecise amalgam of several strands of thought, some long associated in his mind with the notion of "self-government" ... but all imbued with general sprit of democracy ("consent of the governed") Michla Pomerance, *Self-Determination in Law and Practice: The New Doctrine in the United Nations* (The Hague, Nijhoff, 1982), p. 1.

[53] Miroslav Hroch, p.298. *National Self-Determination from a Historical Perspective*, Canadian Slavinic Papers/ Revue Canadienne des Slavistes, vol. 37, (1995), pp.283-299.

[54] Thomas A. Bailey, *Woodrow Wilson and the Lost Peace* (New York, 1944), pp.22-23

[55] The United States entered the war following the German violation of international law by waging a submarine war against it and Britain, sinking *Lusitania* on May 7, 1915, killing 1, 198 persons, 128 of whom were American citizens.

[56]Quoted in Seth, P. Tillman, *Anglo-American Relations at the Peace conference of 1919* (Princeton, New Jersey, 1961), p. 15.

the conflict as well as for the Peace Conference of Paris.

The British government welcomed Wilson's statement, which was considered to be similar to theirs with regards to war aims. However, Lloyd George, the British Prime Minister, commented that Wilson's speech affirmed that Germany must pay indemnity, that its colonies must be submitted later to the Peace Conference and that Mesopotamia should be separated from "blasting tyranny of the Turk." [57]

Woodrow Wilson's Fourteen Points

In the meantime, and among other things, as a consequence of the Bolsheviks exposure of the secret Treaty of Sykes-Picot in November 1917, the British Prime Minister was under heavy domestic pressure, above all from the radicals and trade unionists, for a declaration of liberal and moderate war aims. The Bolsheviks, who had seized power in November added to this pressure when they feverishly launched a peace policy; they issued a peace decree on November 8 and invited the Allies to participate in a peace conference in order to end the war in all fronts. [58] In a significant speech delivered on January 5, 1918, in London before the representatives of the trade unions, Lloyd George focused on crucial political and territorial issues such as settlement of territorial questions in the war based on self-determination for the peoples of Austria-Hungary. As to the Ottoman Empire, he spoke of the "integrity of the national Turkey", but with internationalized straits and that Arabia, Armenia, Mesopotamia, Palestine and Syria must be entitled to "recognition of their separate national conditions." [59]

Wilson delivered his memorable speech on January 8, 1918, in Congress, presenting his fourteen points. The most important were: Point 1 called for "open covenant, openly arrived at"; Point 2, "absolute freedom navigation upon the sea, outside territorial waters…" point 3, "removal of

---

[57] Ibid.

[58] Martin Laurence W., *Peace without Victory: Woodrow Wilson and the British Liberals* (New Haven, Yale University, 1958 p. 146.

[59] Tillman, (1961), pp.24-27.

economic barriers and establishment of equalities of trade conditions; point 4, that national armament should be reduced " to the lowest point consisted with domestic safety" point 5, for an " imperial adjustment of all colonial claims," implying that "the interests of the population concerned must have equal weight with the equitable claims of the governments whose title is to be determined", Point 10 was about "free opportunity of autonomous development "for the peoples of Austria-Hungary, and point 12 was for a "secure sovereignty for the Turkish portion of the Ottoman Empire and an "absolutely unmolested opportunity of autonomous development" for the non- Turkish nationalities and internationalization of the straits. Another important point was, "A general association of nations must be formed under specific covenant for the purpose of affording mutual guarantees of political independence and territorial integrity to great and small states alike." [60] Wilson concluded his fourteen points address by stating, "An evident principle runs through the whole programme I have outlined...
It is the principle of justice to all peoples and nationalities, and their right to live on equal terms of liberty and safety with one another."[61]

Despite the fact that there were some differences in the declarations of Wilson and Lloyd George, such as the creation of a League of Nations, which was central to Wilson's peace program while Lloyd George had only mentioned it *en passant*, there were as well considerably many similar points which could serve as a political platform upon which they could construct a viable peace program. Among the salient points they generally agreed on were: the principle of self-determination and equal justice under the law; the integrity of Turkey; self-determination of the Arabs and

---

[60] Ibid., pp. 28-29. Concerning the Ottoman Empire, Wilson was relying on a group called Inquiry, which was composed of students from foreign affairs and functioned as his personal staff. They supplied Wilson with data they collated especially about Turkey's condition. See John A. DeNovo, *American Interests and Policies in the Middle East 1900-1939* (Minnesota: Minnesota, University Press, 1963) p. 111.
[61] Throntveit Trygvne, (2011), *The Fable of the Fourteen Points: Woodrow Wilson and National Self-Determination.* Diplomatic History 35 (3), pp. 445-481.

Armenians; the German colonies and finally the establishment of an international organization for keeping peace.[62]

On February 11, 1918, Wilson decided to make the self-determination as an "imperative principle of action" to be applied with regards to the Germany's war policy. He addressed the Congress that:

> There shall be no annexations, *no contributions*, *no punitive damages* ... Self-determination is not a mere phrase. It is an imperative principle of action which statement will henceforth ignore at their peril ... Every territorial settlement involved in this war must be made in the interest and for the benefit of the populations concerned, and not as a part of any mere adjustment or compromise of claims amongst rival State.[63]

On November 4, the Allied powers' proposed terms were formally approved by the Supreme War Council. They were accepted by Wilson on November 5 and presented by a note to Germany. On November 11, Germany signed the Armistice with the Allies and the United State. Germany had thus accepted the war terms, which were referred to as the pre-Armistice contract based on Wilson's fourteen points. [64]

Despite the tension and disagreement between the United States and Great Britain throughout the war which seemed to be irreconcilable, they were pragmatic enough to submit to the reality of the time and look for common solutions that guaranteed their interests. The Armistice was certainly an important achievement in Anglo-American relations before the Paris Peace Conference, where they put their best efforts together in forging a new diplomacy and reconstructing a new world order.

---

[62] Ibid., p 31.
[63] Quoted in John Maynard Keynes, C.B. *The Economic Consequences of the Peace* (London, 1919), p.57.
[64] Tillman, (1961), p. 51.

4

Forging a New World Order: Anglo -American Program for the Middle East

Preconference Preparation

Great Britain's preparation for the peace settlement with regards to non-European territorial questions was focused on the fate of the Ottoman Empire and the distribution of Germany's colonial possessions. One of the significant issues that the British were concerned with in their preparations was the role the principle of self-determination would play outside Europe. As for the Ottoman Empire, Lloyd George had stated that Great Britain's intention was not to "deprive Turkey of its capital, or of the rich and renowned lands of Asia Minor, and Thrace, which are predominantly Turkish in race." President Wilson had suggested in his speech of the fourteen points, that "The Turkish portion of the present Ottoman Empire should be assured a secure sovereignty."

It was generally believed that since a peace with no annexations was promised, the states created from the previous Ottoman territories and the German colonies should be placed under the control of a mandatory power on behalf of the Allies or the proposed League of Nations. Thus, Arnold Joseph Toynbee, who served as a British delegate at the Peace Conference, prepared his most important report, "The Peace Settlement for Turkey and the Arabian Peninsula", which was submitted on November 21, 1918. Great Britain was obsessed with retaining control of the route to its Indian Empire and wanted to prevent France and Italy from becoming major factors in the Middle East. Great Britain's preoccupation at the peace negotiation, hence, was to persuade France and Italy to renounce their claims under secret treaties, while it preserved the control of the Middle East without any overt annexations.[65]

The report Toynbee prepared embodied fourteen aims of British policy in the area once under the control of the Ottomans. They were inter alia: 1- European Turkey and Anatolia: Sovereign independence (the balance of advantage, as regards Constantinople, remaining in doubt), 5-Armenia: Independence, with equal rights for all nationalities, and with assistance of an outside power for a term of years, 6-Arab Countries in General: Maintenance of existing British possessions, protectorates, and treaties, widest local independence compatible with this; widest extension of British Trucial system to independent Arab States,... , 7-Arab Federation: Desirable, but without prejudice to 6., 11-Mesopotamia: Independence, with British administrative assistance (subject to limitation of period and function), 12- Kurdistan: Same desiderata as in Mesopotamia.[66]

According to Toynbee, Lloyd George regarding the fate of the Ottoman Empire had thought aloud, "Mesopotamia ... yes ... oil… irrigation... we... must have Mesopotamia; Palestine... Holland...

Zionism... we must have Palestine; Syria... h´m... what is in Syria. Let the French have that." [67]

However, achieving these goals presupposed that Great Britain circumvented its obligations under the secret treaties. Toynbee proposed to do this by arriving at artful interpretations of the agreements themselves. The common assumption among most British officials was that the local peoples would certainly choose Great Britain as their mandatory power, or at worst the United States. Thus, Toynbee "hoped that by giving each Allied power an equal opportunity to be chosen as a mandatory state the equilibrium of power could be maintained in form, while in substance

---

[65] Erik Goldstein, *Winning the Peace: British Diplomatic Strategy: Peace Planning, and the Paris Peace Conference 1916-1920* (Oxford, 1991), pp.151-154.

[66] Ibid., pp. 154-155.

[67] Jonathan M. Nielson, *American Historians in War and Peace: Patriotism, Diplomacy, and the Paris Peace Conference, 1918-1919* (Dublin, 2012), p.100.

France and Italy would be excluded from the region." For the British the Sykes-Picot agreement constituted a key stumbling block in reaching a deal with France, which insisted upon the strict implementation of its terms and refused to abandon its claims to territory promised under the agreement. Lord Curzon, the Acting Foreign Secretary, referred to Sykes-Picot as "that wretched Agreement", and General Jan Smuts, a member of the Eastern Committee, regarded it as a "millstone" around the British neck.[68]

Since there was no decision on a wholesale annexation of the Middle East, the British seemed very much likely to offset France's claims, as Toynbee had suggested, by advocating a policy of self-determination. The members of the Eastern Committee [69]had firm conviction that in case the peoples of the Ottoman Empire were given a choice they would entirely favor Britain as the mandatory power. Curzon stated that:

> If we cannot get out of our difficulties in any other way we ought to play self-Determination for all it is worth wherever we are involved in difficulties with the French, the Arabs, or anybody else, and leave the case to be settled by that final argument knowing in the bottom of our hearts that we are more likely to benefit from it Itan[sic] anybody else.[70]

General Smuts was truly acquainted with the reality and doubted that all peoples would prefer to be ruled by the British if they were given a choice. He was instead in favor of bringing in the League of Nations.

Smuts was of the opinion that "by giving the territories in question to the League for supervision, Britain would maintain some degree of leverage over whatever state became responsible for the day to day

---

[68] Goldstein, (1991), pp.154-158.

[69] The Eastern Committee was formed and met nine times in November and December 1918, to outline resolutions on British policy in order to support British negotiators. The P.I.D. (Political Intelligence Department), also
played a significant role in the evolution of the British negotiating plan with the regards to the Middle East. See Erik Goldstein, *The Foreign Office and Political Intelligence 1918-1920*, Review of International Studies, Vol.14, No. 4. October, 1988, pp. 275-288.

[70] Goldstein, (1991), pp.158-159.

administration."[71] However, on November 29, 1918, France worked out a program which was delivered to the French ambassador in Washington. The French program included several aims such as reparation of war damages resulting from the German aggression, suspension of all war time secret treaties, and setting up a League of Nations. [72]The state department and Wilson rejected the French program, arguing that prior to the Peace Conference no program procedure was accepted. Instead of formulating a program both Wilson and Lloyd George were more eager to pursue their policy for reconstructing Europe and the Middle East.

Franco-British Settlement of the Mosul Question

Along the same line, in a conference in London on December 1-3, 1918, the Allied premiers and Foreign Ministers met to discuss the agenda of the Peace Conference and the problems that they had to wrestle with. One of the main issues of this meeting was the Franco-British settlement of the Mosul *Wilayat*. Weeks before the opening of the Peace Conference of Paris, Great Britain strengthened its position in the Near East at the cost of French claims. Lloyd George succeeded in forcing Georges Clemenceau, the French prime minister, to give up the French plan for the occupation and administration of Mosul *Wilayat*. This important cession on the part of France occurred due to several factors. Among them were, Lloyd George turning the overwhelming British military preponderance in the Near East to the best account in bargaining with Clemenceau, and the fact that the French were faced with unforeseen difficulties in Syria.When Clemenceau asked Lloyd George in London to give his approval to the French position in Syria and Cilicia, the latter "made demands for certain places which he thought to be included in the British zone of influence, namely Mosul."[73]

When Clemenceau returned to Paris he urged for a deliberation in favor of these British claims, which finally ended in the memorandum of

---

[71] Ibid., p. 160.

[72] Bailey, (1994), p. 141.

[73] Henry H. Cumming, *Franco-British Rivalry in the Post-War Near East: The Decline of French Influence* (Oxford, 1938), p. 59

February 15, 1919, according to which France formally sanctioned those changes. This change implied placing France in an unfavorable position in the Near East and later became the subject of an excessive amount of conjecture in the French Parliament.

On June 25, 1920, Arestide Briand, who was Prime Minister at the time of the signing of the Sykes-Picot agreement, emphasized the fact that "the accord gave France an important *monnaie d´ échange*" and asked the chamber what had become of that now "having abandoned Mosul and its zone, having abandoned Palestine, which is now purely under English mandate, what have we received in compensation?." Even André Tardieu, minister of the liberated regions, attacked Clemenceau for the loss of Mosul and its supposed oil deposits.[74] He then argued that the loss of Mosul and Palestine might be attributed to following circumstances:

1-France was to obtain by the exchange her part of the Mosul oil (the 25 per cent, formerly owned by Germany), (2) Great Britain was to support France unconditionally at the Peace Conference on the basis of the secret treaties; (3) the mandates once established, the French mandates for the zone defined in the Sykes-Picot accord (including Syria, with Damascus and Aleppo, Alexandretta, and Beirut) would be supported.[75]

On the contrary, when the question of the Near East was again reviewed in parliament on July 28, 1920, the senator Victor Bérard supported Clemenceau's 'wise' policy in reducing French responsibility in the Near East and was critical toward futile French expenditures in Syria. Concerning the "Frenchness" of Clemenceau's diplomacy and in connection to the question of Mosul and Kurdistan he maintained:

In 1916, we had Syria, Celicia, Mesopotamia, a part of Kurdistan, and our international share of Palestine. Now, when we reopened the accords in 1919, we saw that M. Clemenceau had abandoned *en route* Mesopotamia and Kurdistan, by giving Mosul to the English, and that he had also abandoned Palestine by transforming it from an international land into an English land.

---

[74] Ibid.
[75] Ibid., p.65.

And he argued:

and I do not hesitate to say that the day when M. Clemenceau abandoned Mosul, Palestine, Kurdistan, in order to have Metz and Strasbourg without plebiscite, the Saar basin, occupation of Rhineland, complete security and coal without advance payment, he fashioned a great French policy. (great applause).[76]

Thus, when the Peace Conference was convened, France had lost vast territories, Emir Faisal had imposed his authority in Syria and hundreds of thousands of British troops were in control of areas that were pledged by their government to their French allies.[77]

In a meeting with the Inquiry held on December 10, President Wilson presented his view by persisting that the leading principle for the Conference should be the respect of the will of the people against their leaders otherwise, there might occur "another breakup of the world, and when such a breakup comes, it would not be a war but a cataclysm." He spoke of the establishment of a League of Nations as the only international organization with ability and legal authority to guarantee "political independence and territorial integrity" as well as security to stand as a sharp contrast to the balance of power politics.[78] Wilson's statement certainly indicates that he, just before the Peace Conference, wanted to take the role of the unchallenged leader of a liberal and progressive movement of Europe who contemplated to achieve his goal, namely forging a new world order by all means possible. As he pointed out to the members of the Inquiry "agreeably if we can, disagreeably if necessary" and as a true pacifist he denounced any cooperation with Great Britain as the world's sea patrol which he described as "militaristic propaganda." Some other significant points which were not mentioned in Wilson's formulations of his peace program were discussed in a private meeting

---

[76] Ibid., p. 66.
[77] Ibid., p.67.
[78] Tillman, (1961), p. 61.

with Lloyd George and Balfour, the British foreign secretary, at 10 Downing Street. At this meeting, there seemed to be an Anglo-American understanding that the setting up of the League of Nations should be given precedence while the freedom of the sea was to be postponed until the League was a reality.[79]

The Paris Peace Conference

During the first week of the Peace Conference, the Council of Ten, commonly referred to as the Supreme Council, was busy discussing procedures and how to reach decisions. The Supreme Council consisted of Lloyd George, Clemenceau, Wilson and the Italian Prime Minister Orlando; each one accompanied by their foreign secretary. To these were added two Japanese per recommendation of Lloyd George. But as the process of the negotiations was terminated at the end of March the meetings were held only between the heads of the governments as a Council of Four.[80] From the start of the negotiations, Wilson proposed that the establishment of the League of Nations should be dealt with first, but without any fixed schedule for discussing it. Clemenceau demanded that a formal League of Nations should be set up, but was not accepted. There seemed to be a divergence of views between Lloyd George and Wilson to whether to deal with questions pertaining to Europe first or colonial problems. While Lloyd George preferred to give priority for discussing the Dominions demand on German colonies, Wilson was recalling the critical situation in Europe, emphasizing immediate solutions to remedy European crises.[81]

Territorial settlements were central from the beginning of the Peace Conference for the great powers. In mid-January 1919, a joint committee of experts on territorial problems was built to inform the Conference directly instead of their national delegates. During the work of the committees, a

---

[79] Ibid., p. 67
[80] Margaret McMillan, *Peace Makers, Sex Month that Changed the World* (London, 2003) p. 64.
[81] Tillman, (1961), p. 76.

mutual understanding and consultation procedure evolved between the expert commissions of the United States and Great Britain. These experts were instructed to formulate frontier proposals for the new states of South-Eastern Europe based on national and ethnographic principles rather than political ones. Contrary to the French and Italian colleagues, Wilson and Lloyd George received the "objective" reports of these expert commissions without questioning them, which constituted the basis for their decisions on frontier matters. Although the Anglo-American powers were by no means interested in territorial settlements of this part of Europe, they realized the importance of its stability for the rest of the world.

There was no formal or detailed plan procedure for the work of the Supreme Council in advance. They often developed their own routine during the course of the conference depending, above all else, on reports from their expert commissions. [82] A reasonable explanation might be that Wilson already had a peace program outlined and declared before his arrival in Paris which was known by the peacemakers. He needed only to be at the Conference to implement it without being obliged to circumscribe his freedom of action by binding himself to unfavorable routines, and also to restrict the influence of Clemenceau as a head of the Conference who was eagerly attempting to counterweight the Anglo-Saxon influences.

However, as mentioned above, there was a consensus between Wilson and Lloyd George with respect to the trusteeship principle, which they had supported in their pronouncement on war aims. In regards to Wilson's fourteen points outlined in the Copp-Lippmann Memorandum of October 1918, the fifth point was defined as follows:

It would seem as if the principle involved in this preposition is that a colonial power acts not as owner of its colonies, but as trustee for the natives and for the interest of the society of the nations, that the terms on which the colonial administration is conducted are a matter of international concern and may legitimately be the subject of international inquiry and that the peace conference

---

[82] Ibid., pp. 83-84.

may, therefore, write a code of colonial conduct binding upon all powers.[83]

The Mandates System

President Wilson: *it is delightful to be made*
Aware of such community of thought and counsel in
approaching the high and difficult task now awaiting us.
Lloyd George: *the ideals of our two countries in regard to*
international reconstruction are fundamentally the same....[84]

The idea of the Mandates system came into being as a reaction to the colonial policy adopted by the colonialists. The colonial rivals during the 18th century were France and Great Britain. Great Britain lost the thirteen American colonies between 1756 and 1815 but gained Canada, India and small colonies from France and thus by the beginning of the 19th century was the only great colonial power. During this period of colonial enterprise they employed the principle of exclusion and monopoly in their colonial trade policies.

The treatment of the natives of these colonies and especially the slave trade provoked reactions from theologians, philosophers and politicians, who harbored humanitarian and liberal ideas and advocated a just and humane treatment of the inhabitants of these colonies. Consequently, the French Revolution abolished the slave trade in its colonies. Likewise, in Great Britain and elsewhere, many philanthropic societies were established in order to forbid slavery and protect the native populations. From 1830 onwards, as a result of these anti-slavery movements, a series of legislative measures were taken against colonial slave trade, which compelled the colonialists to take the humanitarian aspects of the subjected population into consideration. Concluding treaties and agreements with the tribal chiefs and indigenous states became a usual and significant form of "protectorate." [85]

---

[83] Tillman, (1961), pp. 86-87.

[84] Ibid., p.37.

[85] *The Mandates System: Origins-principles-Application* (Geneva, League of Nations, April 1945)

As another colonial power, Germany was a rival to the European powers in Central Africa, entered the colonial enterprise later and obtained its African colonies between 1884 and 1885. Germany advocated the open door policy, or equal economic opportunity, in all its territories, except in South Africa, which constituted the basis of the Conference of Berlin, leading to the Act of 1885.[86] The provision of the second paragraph of the fifth article of the Act provides "protection to persons and property of foreigners, and to engage that there will be no differential treatment of foreigners as to settlement or access to market". [87]Some of the principles of the Berlin Act, which appealed to the well-being of the natives and stipulated economic equality between the members of international community, later evolved to make the basis upon which the mandates system was set up. For instance, article 6 of the Act affirms that:

> All the Powers exercising sovereign rights or influence in the aforesaid territories bind themselves to watch over the preservation of the native tribes, and to care for the improvement of the conditions of their moral and material well-being, and to help in suppressing slavery, and especially the slave trade.

The ultimate goal for these powers, the article maintains, was "instructing the natives and bringing home to them the blessings of civilization." Thus, colonial doctrine embodied moral obligations both in theory and practice to implement the idea of tutelage and trusteeship in order to help the natives to reach a degree of development so that they could stand by themselves. The recognition of Cuba by the United States in 1898 and the announcement of the American Senate in letting the Philippines establish "a government suitable to the wants and conditions of the inhabitants ...to prepare them for local self-government..." in 1899 should be seen in this light. The mandatory idea was also implemented in some special cases around the world often with short duration; in 1860, France intervened in Lebanon to protect the Christian population there on account of a mandate

---

[86] Benjamin Gerig, *The Open Door and the Mandates System:A Study of Economic Equality before and since the Establishment of the Mandates System*' (London: Allen & Unwin,1930), p. 30.
[87] Ibid., p. 80.

from the great powers. In connection with the crisis in Morocco the United States proposed a mandate be entrusted to Spain and France for dealing with the Moroccan forces and ensuring equality of commercial treatment and the principle of the open door. Furthermore, some countries of the Dominions were entrusted by the British government to administrate some territories inhabited by "backward races."[88] In England, as early as 1915, the idea of tutelage of backward peoples was in circulation among liberal and labor movements that acted in favor of equal economic opportunity in the colonies. In April 1916, Philip Kerr, later to become Lloyd George's personal secretary, proposed the idea of trusteeship for the backward peoples by advanced peoples. In 1917, the Labour Party discussed the question of the tutelage, and in February 1918 the inter-Allied and Labour and Socialist Conference suggested international trusteeship under the auspices of a League of Nations. In 1918, the Labour Party took the leading role in the trusteeship movement. [89]

Benjamin Gerig traces the mandatory idea back to the General Act of Algeciras, signed on April 7, 1906. According to him, during the war a group of individuals interested in international politics were dealing with problems related to the war and working to find solutions to them. These were known as the Round Table Group[90] who issued a magazine with the same title and often with anonymous articles written by reliable authors, most of whom were from the British Empire. The magazine appeared all over the world. Among the members of this group were such individuals as Philip Kerr and General Jan Smuts, who worked out a scheme of international colonial administration based on the Algeciras plan. Smuts' plan contained observations regarding the protection of the natives and insurance for the implementation of the open door principle, which was presented by him as a document in December 1918 entitled "The League

---

[88] *The Mandates System*, (1945), pp. 9-12.
[89] Tillman, (1961), p. 86.
[90] On other activities of this group see for instance Erik Goldstein, (1998) *The Round Table and the New Europe*, The Round Table:The Commonwealth Journal of International Affairs, 78,346, 177-189,DOI:10.1080/00358539808454413.

of Nations: A Practical Suggestion."[91]

In his plan Smuts outlined broadly an international mandates system submitted to the League of Nations. According to him since the collapse of the empires in Central and Eastern Europe as well as in the Near East were unavoidable, it was necessary to create a League of Nations, which would become "the reversionary in the broadest sense of these empires, and clothed with the right of ultimate disposal in accordance with certain fundamental principles." These fundamental principles, he argued, were "No annexations and the self-determination of nations."[92] The mandate would be applied to former territories belonging to Turkey, Russia and Austria-Hungary and the implementation of the principle of self-determination concerning states and territories depending on their degree of development with no direct authority exercised by the League, but by the mandatory state whose degree of their authorities and administration should be decided and regulated by the League. In other words, the mandatory would be "subject to the supervision and ultimate control of the League."[93]

Consequently, his plan provided the right to the territories and subjected peoples to appeal to the League in case of any authoritative abuse by the mandatory power. Another significant point in the plan was that the mandatory was obliged to guarantee the application of the open door policy and use their military forces only for domestic purposes in accordance with the League's regulation. Smuts' plan was confined only to the territories of Eastern Europe and to the Near East, which the Peace Conference had to determine their futures, whereas the German colonies "inhabited by barbarians" could not stand by themselves and thus, the idea of self-determination in the European sense for their part was "impracticable."[94] Robert Lansing, Wilson's secretary of state, noted later that the principle of self-determination did not apply to "races, peoples, or communities whose state of barbarism or ignorance deprive them of the capacity to

---

[91] Gerig , (1938), p. 115.

[92] Elie Kedourie, *Nationalism* (London: Hutchinson, 1960), p. 135.

[93] *The Mandates System*, (1945), p 17.

[94] Tillman, (1961), p 88.

choose intelligently their political affiliations." He was convinced of the "danger of putting such ideas into the minds of certain races," which was bound to "create trouble in many lands and to "breed discontent, disorder and rebellion."[95] Wilson did not exclude the non-European peoples from the right of self-determination as a matter of principle. He anticipated that under the supervision of a benevolent tutelage of a "civilized" power these peoples would attain self-determination.[96]

Japan, France and the Dominions all advocated an annexation policy. Orlando and Clemenceau, although they sympathized with the mandate principle, shared the opinions of Britain that certain exemptions should be applied. As for France, the possession of colonies implied power and hence, manpower, vital to France to defend itself against its enemy, Germany. It would as well guarantee a sort of balance of power if there were colonies in Asia and Africa, but if France was entrusted with mandates that would imply restrictions to recruiting native soldiers for defense purposes in case of war.[97]

France's fear of being exposed to a possible German aggression in the future was the main motive behind its anti-Germany political behavior at the Peace Conference. Clemenceau's main concern during the peace settlement was to provide security to France: "how to protect France against another German aggression, something which all of France believed was possible."[98]

On January 29, the Supreme Council decided on a fundamental issue, the mandates system, based on General Smuts' formula which was approved by Wilson and, with some changes, became Article 22[99] of the

---

[95] Erez Manela, *Wilsonian Moment: Self Determination and the International Origins of Anticolonial Nationalism* (Oxford, 2007), p. 25.
[96] Ibid.
[97] Margaret, (2003), pp. 109-110.
[98] Zara Steiner, *Lights that failed: European International History 1919-1933* (Oxford: Oxford University Press, 2005), p.32.
[99] Actually, the Covenant of the League of Nations was embodied in the Treaty of Versailles signed by Germany; it sanctioned international law to a mandates system that specifically permitted the partition of the Ottoman Empire. Article 22 of the Covenant stipulated, "Certain communities formerly belonged to the

League of Nations.The Smuts plan proposed that the German and Turkish colonies should not be restored, but entrusted to the tutelage of "advanced nations" as a "sacred trust of civilization" and it divided the mandates into three categories based on their stage of development, geography and economic conditions.The first category (Class A mandates) were states belonging to the Turkish Empire. They had to have reached a stage of development and their independence would be "provisionally recognized subject to the rendering of administration advice and assistance" by a mandatory until they could stand by themselves; the second (Class B mandates) were colonies in Central Africa belonging to Germany and were deemed to be at a stage that necessitated mandatory supervision for the administration. The third category (Class C mandates) were territories such as Southwest Africa and the Island of the South Pacific, and were "owing to the sparseness of their populations, or their small size, or their remoteness from central of civilization" to be "administered under the laws of the mandatory state as integral portions thereof" [100]

The United States and Britain envisaged a settlement in the Middle East within the framework of a new world order settlement based on the League of Nations. However, this policy inevitably conflicted with the secret treaties concluded during the war by the Allies. Even before the exposure of the secret treaties by late 1917 by the Bolsheviks, the United States had been aware that countries such as Great Britain, France, Russia and Italy had been contemplating to carve the Ottoman Empire into spheres of influence.[101] As has been noted, the most important of these secret treaties

---

Turkish Empire have reached a stage of development where their existence as independent nations can be previously recognized subject to the rendering administrative advice and assistance by the Mandatory until such time they are able to stand alone". Quoted in Eugene Rogan L., *The Fall of the Ottomans: the Great War in the Middle East 1914-1920* (London: Allen Lane, 2015), pp. 391-392.

[100] Ibid, pp. 93-94 See also Leonard V. Smith, *Empires at the Paris Peace Conference*, in, Robert Gerwarth and Erez Manela (eds.), *Empires at War: 1911.1923*, (Oxford, 2004), pp.254-277.

[101] DeNovo, (1963), p. 111.

was the Sykes-Picot Agreement of May 16, 1916, concluded between Francois George-Picot and Sir Mark Sykes, the French and British diplomats. According to the agreement, inter alia, the British and French governments were ready to recognize and protect an independent Arab state or a confederation of Arab states after the war, dividing the Arab provinces of the Ottoman Empire into zones of influence. According to the agreement the Mosul *Wilayat* was allocated to France, thereby Kurdistan was partitioned one more time. The main objective of the agreement was creating a buffer state under French protection between Russian territories in the north and a British protected Mesopotamia in the south.[102] This rendered the negotiation of the Paris Peace Conference on Middle East territorial and administrative issues January-June 1919, more complex.

The Allies had to decide on important issues such as Turkey's boundaries in case it remained as an independent entity, the possibility of implementating the principle of self-determination when the non-Turkish areas were detached from the Empire, and finally on their future role in this area. The Allied powers were confronted with an intricate political situation- their traditional secret treaties, balance of power, the new political order, and self-determination in the Middle East. As for the British they had to stick to their commitment to the Arabs on the one hand and the promises of national self-determination on the other. When these basic issues were discussed in the Council of Ten, Wilson called for the mandates system as an alternative to the old-fashioned annexation. Clemenceau and Lloyd George opposed this arrangement, yet the latter, announced his acceptance of the mandate principle for all Turkish areas captured by Great Britain.[103]

On January 20, 1919, Lloyd George, speaking before the representatives of powers, stated that the "doctrine of a mandatory for all conquests in the late Turkish Empire and in the German colonies" had now been accepted. However, he asserted the recognition of the facts that the mandates should be applicable to countries civilized, but not yet organized,

---

[102] A. T. Wilson, *Loyalties, Mesopotamia 1914-1917* (London: Oxford University press, 1930), p. 153.
[103] DeNovo, (1963), pp.110-115.

such as Arabia, where "a century might elapse before the people could be properly organized" and that mandates should be applicable only to conquered parts either of the Turkish Empire or the German Empire.[104] On January 30, after further discussion, the Council of Ten agreed to adopt the draft resolution by which Armenia, Syria, Mesopotamia, Palestine and Arabia should be detached from Turkey and be entrusted to mandatories.[105] Lloyd George then decided to detach another territory from Turkey to be added to the draft resolution, namely Kurdistan:

> ... He [Lloyd George] did not realize that it was separate. He thought Mesopotamia and Armenia would cover it but he was now informed that it did not. He referred to Kurdistan, which was between Mesopotamia and Armenia... [106]

As the meeting was terminated the Supreme Council decided to agree to this important resolution:

> ... the Allied and Association Powers are agreed that Armenia, Syria, Mesopotamia and Kurdistan, Palestine and Arabia, must be completely severed from the Turkish Empire. This is without prejudice to the settlement of other parts of the Turkish Empire.[107]

The British decision to add Kurdistan to the list of territories severed from Turkey had been taken with the consideration that an independent Kurdish state under British supervision would prevent Turkey from retaining its hegemony in the region between Armenia and Mesopotamia. Moreover, it would secure a British control of the Mosul *Wilayat*, and provide a buffer zone for that oil-rich province. Arnold Wilson, Acting Civil Commissioner in Mesopotamia, recounted that the Kurds, in January 1919, had established a local government through tribal leaders under British guidance, stating "We were charged with the foundation of an

---

[104] Cumming, (1961), p.70.
[105] DeNovo, (1963), p. 115.
[106] Cumming,(1938), p. 71.
[107] Ibid., p. 72.

independent Southern Kurdish state under British auspices" Wilson's opinion was however that the best solution was to incorporate Kurdistan into Mesopotamia as an autonomous province.[108]

Alongside its policy for Turkey, Great Britain attempted to convince the United States to undertake responsibility by accepting a mandate for Armenia and the Anatolia-strait. Having no imperial ambitions the United States was deemed reliable as mandatory with no intention to dominate in the region. An American involvement in the mandate question would imply, from Britain's point of view, an American protection of Britain's strategic straits by preventing the southward spread of Bolshevism as well as considerably reducing its imperial resources. But France was suspicious of Great Britain's policy that the idea of the mandate for the United States was to oust France from Anatolia as its rival.[109]

At the same time, during the course of negotiations of the Turkish territories, the Turkish delegation at the Peace Conference, by appealing to Wilson's principle of self-determination, attempted to maintain territorial integrity of the Ottoman Empire. It was rejected by the Council of Four, which on June 21 replied that it "Wishes well to the Turkish people, and admires their excellent qualities. But they cannot admit that among these qualities are to be counted capacity to rule over alien races." Satisfied with this reply, President Wilson wished the return of the Turkish delegation to their country because "They had exhibited complete absence of common sense" and "a total misunderstanding of the West."[110] The United States

---

[108] Paul C. Helmreich, *From Paris to Sevres: The Partition of the Ottoman Empire at the Peace Conference of 1919-1920* (Ohio: State University Press, 1974). P.27.

[109] On the question of Great Britain's plan for Constantinople and the European Turkey, See Erik Goldstein, *The Eastern Question:The Last Phase,* in Dockrill, M.L. and Fisher John (eds.), *Paris Peace Conference 1919: Peace Without Victory?* (New York, N.Y.: Palgrave, 2001), pp.146-149.

[110] Tillman, (1961), pp. 367-369. Despite the fact that Great Britain supported an American mandate it was at the same time anxious that American presence in that area would imply threat to their interests. This anxious is expressed in Lloyd George's reply to Curzon on a possible American mandate for Palestine, "As regards Palestine, he had been in favour to entrusting that to the United States originally, but had changed his mind. It would involve placing an absolute new

started to collate reports from two investigative groups in order to know to what extent the native Armenians and Levant Arabs were willing to accept mandatory.

Faisal's Position: Aspirations for Arab Unity

Before the arrival of the King-Crane Commission in Jaffa, on June 10, 1919, Faisal convened a meeting with the Syrian notables in Damascus. He gave an encouraging version of his participation in the negotiations with the great powers at the Paris Conference. He stated that his policy rested on two main principles: that the Arab countries should not be divided between the European powers and that the Hejaz, Mesopotamia and Syria, at the present moment, should have their own identities pending an appropriate time to be united under a single Arab government even if the Arab nation, the *umma*, was one. When the notables gave Faisal's policy their approval, he stressed the importance of the organization of Arab opinion that would be appreciated at the Peace Conference, particularly by the Americans. On July 2, a National Assembly, under the name of the General Syrian Congress, opened its session in Damascus. Among the resolutions this congress adopted were the demand for recognition of an independent Syria (including Palestine, and Lebanon), with Faisal as King, abrogation of the Sykes-Picot agreement and the Balfour Declaration, and renunciation of the mandate, although it was accepted to have foreign assistance for a limited period, first choice being given to the United States and second to Great Britain. The demand for full independence for Syria and the rejection of the implementation of the Zionist program in "Southern Syria" was based on the:

> Principles proclaimed by President Wilson in condemnation of secret treaties ... The lofty principles proclaimed by President Wilson encourage us to believe that the determining consideration in the settlement of our own future will be the real desire of our people; and that we may look to President Wilson and the liberal American nation, who are known for their sincere and generous

---

and crude power in the middle of our complicated interests in Egypt, Arabia, and Mesopotamia." See Helmreich,(1974), p. 14.

46

sympathy with the aspirations of weak nations, for help in the fulfillment of our hopes.[111]

During the tour of the King- Crane Commission, Faisal and the Arabs made their utmost efforts to give the impression that they were disgusted by the French rule and admired the American system of government. On July 9 Faisal dispatched a telegram to President Wilson to inform him that:

> There is no doubt that after the arrival of your honourable commission and the statements made to its expressing unreservedly the true desires and aspirations, the people and particularly myself have incurred as a matter of course the risk of terrible strong current against us. I earnestly beg you not to leave me between the pawns of the devourers... [112]

Overall, Faisal was convinced that in case the Arabs were granted independence "the natural influences of race, language and interests" would soon unite the various Arab groups into one people. The great powers would have supplied them with "open internal frontiers, common railways and telegraphs, and uniform system of education. "As early as January 1, 1919, in a memorandum, Faisal explained that the aim of the Arab nationalist movement was "to unite the Arab eventually into one nation."[113]

According to the King-Crane Commission's report on July 10, there were strong anti-French feelings in Syria, and the United States was preferred as mandatory first and Great Britain as second choice. However, public opinion in the United States did not support any American involvement in international affairs. On November 30, 1920 the Senate rejected the Allied request for the United States to accept the mandate on the grounds that it was against its isolationist policy and that the idea was inappropriate bearing in mind that the United States had rejected

---

[111] Laurence Evans, *United States Policy and the Partition of Turkey 1914-1924* (Baltimore: The John Hopkins Press, 1965), pp. 151-152.

[112] Ibid., P. 155.

[113] Harry N. Howard, *An American Inquiry in the Middle East: The King-Crane Commission* (Beirut, 1963), pp.22-23.

membership in the League of Nations.[114]

Indeed, the U.S. as a contributor to the victory of the Allied powers was concerned in having a share of the spoils of the war. In November 1920, Secretary of State Bainbridge Colby, maintained that the U.S. had full and equal rights in the mandate and declared:

> Such powers as the Allied and Associated nations may enjoy or wield, in the determination of the governmental status of the mandated areas, accrued to them as a direct result of the war against the Central Powers. The United States, as a participant in that conflict and as a contributor to its successful issue, cannot consider any of the associated powers ... debarred from the discussion of any of its consequences, or from participation in the rights and privileges secured under the mandates provided for in the treaties of peace.

By this declaration, the U.S. asserted that its claim and position to the open door was justified and that it would be guaranteed the same rights as the Allies in the mandates as well as the same rights in the decision process of those mandates. In addition, in order to safeguard its rights and privileges, the United States government wanted to participate in the creation of the mandate system. The State Department asked to study the draft before it was subject to the League's considerations since, according to Colby, the U.S. was "undoubtedly" one of the powers which was considerably interested in the terms of the mandates. [115]At the Paris Peace Conference, President Wilson attempted to prevent the division of the former colonies of the German and the Ottoman empires into economically exclusive spheres of influence. When the delegates of the Conference discussed the issue of the partition of the territorial spoils, the American delegation demanded the application of the principle of the open door for investment, which was endorsed by others. As for the ownership of the former enemies

---

[114] DeNovo, (1963), pp. 118-123. Under the Treaty of Sèrves Armenia was recognized as independent state but it was left alone without protection to the Turkish nationalism of Mustafa Kemal. See Tillman, p. 375.

[115] Quoted in Annie Tracy Samuel (2014) *The Open Door and U.S. policy in Iraq between the World Wars.* Diplomatic History, 38 (5): 926-952. doi: 10.1093/dh/dhu033 931.

in Africa and the Middle East, "the open door principle was embodied in Article 22 of the Covenant of the League of Nations, which, in setting forth the basic principles on which these lands were to be ruled, prohibited the governing powers from discriminating against the commercial interests of other states."[116] As the open door was accepted in the following negotiations, the United States anticipated unrestricted enterprise in the Middle East, particularly in the oilfields of Iraq.[117]

---

[116] William Stivers, *Supremacy and Oil, Iraq: Turkey, and the Anglo-American World Order, 1918- 1930* (Cornell University Press, Ithaca and London, 1982). pp. 46-47. With regards to the open door, Stivers explains that this principle was adopted in the Covenant of League only to comprise the African mandates, albeit it was possible to be applied to the Ottoman Empire as well. During the meeting of the Council of Four the issue was discussed by Wilson, Lloyd George, and Clemenceau, and had been acknowledged during the negotiation of the Mandates Commission which was responsible to create terms and conditions for each territory when the time came to conclude the agreement.
[117] Ibid., p. 47.

5

The Emergence of Arab Nationalism:
Arab Nationalism before 1914

The Tanzimat Reforms

During the period of 1839 to 1876 the Ottoman society underwent its most radical reform of the nineteenth century as the Tanzimat reforms embodied in two royal decrees were carried out. The first one was promulgated in 1839, and was known as Hatti-Sharif of Gulhane. This decree provided some administration reforms such as the abolition of tax farming, the standardization of military conscription and included measures for the elimination of corruption. The second decree known as Hatt-i-Humayan was proclaimed in 1856. This decree postulated in a more explicit manner than the previous on the total equality of the subjects of different creeds of the Ottoman Empire with regards to military services, equal opportunities for state employment and entrance to state schools. The reform occurred at a time when the territorial integrity of the Empire was threatened by the intensified national movements in its European provinces. By the abolition of obstacles separating the Muslims from non-Muslims, who were divided alongside their religious or national affiliations, the reforms intended to weld them together with a spirit of community and thereby replace the *Millet* affiliation. This would imply the superiority of the Muslims, by a concept of Ottomanism and regarding all subjects as common Ottoman citizens. The modernization reform expressed by the two above mentioned decrees thus, marked a serious rapture with the old Ottoman values and traditions.

The impact of this change was seen in the increased relationship between Egypt and Europe during the reign of one of Muhammad Ali's sons, Said (1856-1863) which resulted in the emergence of new bureaucrats elite trained in Europe or in institutions modeled on European style. These could fill the administrative positions in order to conduct the specialized state activities with its increased diversity.[118]

One of most outstanding reformers was Rifa'a al-Tahtawi (1801-1873) who played a great role in the orientation of the cultural life in Egypt. His contribution consisted of supervising the translation of more than 2000 works from foreign languages into Arabic and writing several books.[119]

Another prominent figure for this period was Abd al-Rahman al-Kawakibi, (1854-1902). He placed a great emphasis on features like language and ethnicity as core components in his political orientation. The distinguishing characteristic of al-Kawakibi was that he employed nationalism as an instrument in his political agitation a fact that had a significant impact on the situation in the Arab provinces of the Ottoman Empire.[120] Regarding the Arabs as the only people who had the legitimacy of representing Islam, Tibi argues that he can "accurately be described as an important pioneer of Arab nationalism."[121] Al-Kawakibi attributed the glorious Islamic civilization exclusively to the Arabs who, according to him, were the only protectors of Islam, urging Abdul Hamid to abandon his claim to the caliphate, and asserting that the Arabs were the

---

[118] William Cleveland. *A History of the Modern Middle* East (West view Press, 1994), pp.79-82. In fact, Egypt established its close relations with the West after the invasion of Napoleon Bonaparte of the country in 1789. The Egyptian ruler, Muhammad Ali (1805-1848), sent young Egyptians as students to Europe and built a modern army and navy by the assistant of the French instructors. He also tried through a nucleus of a nascent modern intelligentsia to popularize European science and revive Arabic culture and reform Egyptian society. See Hans Kohn, *The Age of Nationalism, The First Era of Global History* (New York: Harpers & Brothers, 1962), p. 82.

[119] Ibid., pp.88.90.

[120] Ibid., p.121.

[121] Bassam Tibi, *Arab Nationalism: Between Islam and the Nation-State* (New York: St. Martin Press, 1997), p.93.

true representatives of this title.[122]

According to Choueiri an important feature of al-Kawakibi's thought was that he stressed the political aspects of the national revival and thus was "an important link in the transition from cultural to political Arabism."[123]

The Missionaries Work and their Contribution to Revival of Cultural Awareness.

Due to the invasion of Syria in 1831, by Muhammad Ali's armies under the leadership of his son Ibrahim Pasha the great Syria underwent significant social and cultural changes, causing the early emergence of the Arab national movement. Furthermore, Ibrahim Pasha carried out reforms, which included the school and education domain, and encouraged establishing a school system for boys modeled on the one his father had established in Egypt. It was necessary then to bring the American mission's printing-press from Malta to Beirut.

Muhammad Ali's expedition to Syria and the reforms conducted by his son were short lived, lasting just nine years from 1831 to 1840. However, despite the failure of realizing the reform program the impact of Ibrahim Pasha's period as far as the revival of national Arabic concerned was enough, Tibi argues, to create a divergence between the Arabs and the Ottomans.[124]

It is interesting to note in this connection that the main objective of the missionaries was to convert the Muslims, and they, especially the American missionaries, soon realized how effective it was to teach the gospel message to the Muslims and translate the scriptures in their vernacular language. The activities of the Missionaries, without being their intention, contributed to the Arab literary renaissance and hence to the intellectual foundation for modern Arab nationalism.[125] Thus, acquiring a

---

[122] Cleveland, (1994), p.121.

[123] Yousef M. Choueiri *Arab Nationalism,: A History, Nation and State in the Arab World* (Blackwell Publishers, 2000), pp. 84-86.

[124] Tibi, (1997), pp.96-99

[125] DeNovo, (1963), p.13.

new national identity "pushed religious identity, formerly the substance of the Arabs' loyalty to the Ottoman Empire, into the background."[126]

An outstanding figure of great importance for the literary life of this period was Nasif Yaziji. At the time of the evacuation of Syria from Ibrahim Pasha's troops in 1840 and his forced exile, he already had a great literary production mainly in verse, owing to his excellent skill in the Arabic language. He wrote books on grammar, logic, rhetoric and prosody. These books were intended for use in schools, especially in American ones, but became appreciated teaching books in the science of Arabic and were employed by a wide range of schools and teachers.

Another prominent figure was Butrus al-Bustani, a contemporary of Yaziji, who was also born in Lebanon. Like Yaziji he cooperated with the American missionaries. One of his major works was a dictionary of the Arabic language which was printed in 1870, called *Muhit al-Muhit* (Circumference of the Ocean). His second major work was an Arabic encyclopaedia. However, al-Bustani's productions were not confined only to literal or language; he also published political reviews such as *al- Jinan* (The Paradises) with its conspicuous motto: (Hubb al-watan min al-iman) *Patriotism is an Article of Faith,* which was a novelty for the Arab cultural nationalism at the time. Furthermore, in 1847, al-Bustani a nd Yaziji in a joint effort founded the *Society of Arts and Science* (Jamiyyat al-Adab w´al-Ulum) which was unique in its kind not only in Syria but also in the whole of the Arab world. They also established the *Syrian Scientific Society* (al-Jam´iya al-Ilmiya al-Suriya) in 1857 which, contrary to the previous society, embodied members from a variety of religions such as Muslims, Christians and Druze.[127] The efforts of al-Bustani and others concerning Arabic cultural revival mixed with political and scientific thought of the time brought into existence a unique intellectual atmosphere among the Arab literarily circles in Beirut. In this city, between the 1860s and 1870s, literarily clubs and scientific societies functioned as centers for

---

[126] Tibi, (1997), p.100.

[127] George Antonius, *The Arab Awakening: The Story of The Arab National Movement* (London, 1938), pp.45-53.

political and literary debates.

Central to this literary Renaissance known as *al-nahdah*, (the awakening), was the Arabic language which contributed to enhance the awareness of the Arabs about their cultural identity. As the reign of Sultan Abdull-Hamid II (1878-1909) continued its repressive policy toward the Christians and Muslim Arabs the Beirut literary societies, shifted the focus of the debates to topics such as the shared heritage of the Arabs and replacing religious bonds by communal loyalties among the Arab speakers. Thus, the notion of patriotism, and the sense of belonging to a distinct territorial entity became familiar at this time.[128]

Yet, at this stage, Arab nationalism emerged due to the activities of the linguists and intellectuals, and manifested itself as literary renaissance not based on political theories. The reason was that at the time, Tibi points out, "neither the subjective nor the objective conditions for a political movement existed in the Middle East in the nineteenth century… the early Arab nationalists confined themselves to emphasizing the existence of an independent Arab cultural nation without demanding a national state."[129]

Arab Nationalism under the Young Turks, 1908-1914

The idea of Arab Nationalism as including all Arabic-speaking territories emerged in Syria and Iraq. But at this stage, the aim of the Arab nationalists, was not the overthrowing of the caliphate or the establishment of complete independence. The idea of achieving total independence from the Turks began to take shape after the Young Turk revolution in 1908.[130] During the last decades of the Tanzimat[131] a new group of westernized intellectuals and bureaucrats known as Young Ottomans emerged. Although this group was influenced by the progress of the European societies and endeavored to incorporate its achievements they did not

---

[128] Cleveland, (1994), p. 123.

[129] Tibi, p. 104.

[130] Hisham B. Sharabi, *Nationalism and Revolution in the Arab World: The Middle East and North Africa* (New York 1966), p. 9.

[131] For a detailed account on the Tanzimat reforms see for instance, Roderic H. Davidson, *Reform in the Ottoman Empire 1856-1976* (Princeton, 1963), ch.2.

intend to replace the Islamic model of state and society by a European one. For the Young Ottomans, the Islamic tradition was the source for any democratic government. This was based on the Islamic tradition of consultation between the absolutist ruler and his ministers and was not modeled on European democratic procedures.[132]

The seizure of power by Sultan Abdull-Hamid put an end to the movement of the Young Ottomans, but then another movement made itself felt, that of the Young Turks, mainly consisting of an exiled community, civic servants and students and army officers stationed in Ottoman Europe. Their secret society *Ittihad ve terakki cemiyeti,* known as the Committee of Union and Progress (CUP), was founded in 1889, the intent of which was to force Sultan Abdul-Hamid to restore the constitutional form of government. In doing so, the Young Turks, whose patriotism derived from the tenet of Ottomanism, induced a group of officers from the third army stationed in Salonika to conduct a revolt in summer 1908, demanding Abdul Hamid to restore the constitution. Fearing a mutiny within the army, the Sultan complied with the demand of the Young Turks and declared in July 1908, that the constitution was once again restored.[133]

Consequently, a new hope was infused into communities of Arabs, Muslims and Christians all over the empire, believing that the constitution would provide them with treatment on an equal footing as the Turks. As a result, the first Arab society was established known as *al-Ikha al-Arabi al-Uthmani*, the Ottoman Arab Fraternity, on September 2 of the same year. The main principle of this society was to protect the constitution, ensure the loyalty of the peoples of the empire to the Sultan and grant the Arabs their rights as well as to promote their education in Arabic..[134]

However, due to the emancipation of all of the European provinces of the empire followed by the ceding of the province of Libya to Italy, a shift in the policy of the CUP occurred, marked by increased centralization policy and making Turkish the language of communication and

---

[132] Cleveland, (1994), p. 83.
[133] Ibid.,pp.127-128.
[134] Antonius, (1938), p.102.

government.[135] As the Young Turks succeeded in putting down a Hamidian counter-coup in 1909 and were in power, their nationalist ideology, the Turanism, became very much in evident. [136]Braune points out that after the loss of the Ottoman provinces in Europe and Tripoli the Young Turks inclined "toward an authoritarian Turkish nationalism. Obscure theories constructed from the researches of the French historian Leon Cahun made 'Turan the place of origin of the Turks in Central Asia, and the pre-Islamic Turkish homeland became the focal point of history in the writing of the authors Halide Edib and the poet-philosopher Ziya Gökalp."[137]

As the Young Turks stiffened their policy against other ethnic non-Turkish communities, the Society of Arab-Ottoman Brotherhood was banned and *al-Muntada al-Adabi* (The Literary Club), which was built in Constantinople in 1908 by western-educated Arab intellectuals, could not escape the same destiny. As a reaction, the Arab nationalists were forced to choose underground activities and defend their rights against the centralization and Turkification policy of the Young Turks. In this connection, T.E.Lawrence writes:

> ... the Arabs had tasted freedom: they could not change their ideas as quickly as their conduct; and the stiffer spirits among them were not easily to be put down. They read Turkish papers, putting `Arab` for `Turk` in the patriotic exhortations. Suppression charged them with unhealthy violence. Deprived of constitutional outlets they became revolutionary. The Arab societies went underground, and changed from liberal clubs into conspiracies, the Akhua, the Arab mother society, was publicly dissolved. It was replaced in Mesopotamia by the dangerous Ahad, a very secret brotherhood, limited almost entirely to Arab officers in the Turkish army, who swore to acquire the military knowledge of their masters, and to turn it against them, in the service of the

---

[135] Choueiri, (2000), p. 88.

[136] Tibi, (1997), p. 108. See also Cleveland (1994), pp 127-128 in spring 1909 a counter-coup occurred against the new government by common soldiers and theological students. They protested against the influence of Europeanized army officers and demanded to restore the *shariah*. This counter-coup was put down and Adbul Hamid was sent to Salonika and was replaced by his younger brother, Mehmet V (1909- 1919).

[137] Quoted inTibi, (1997), pp.108-109.

Arab people, when the moment of the
rebellion came.[138]

Jam'iyyat al-'Ahd (The Society of the Covenant) was established in
Constantinople in 1909 and composed only of Arab officers under the
leadership of the Egyptian Aziz Ali al-Misri. According to Hartman "al
Misri had noticed from his own experience of the Committee of Union and
Progress that the army was more capable of effective action than civilian
politicians." The society *al-Ahd*, with its 315 officers in 1914, together
with *al-Fatat* were the most influential political secret societies. Branches
of the *al-Ahd* were founded in Mosul and Baghdad by Taha al-Hashimi of
Baghdadi origin. His brother, Yasin al-Hashimi, headed a branch in Mosul,
which included a number of Iraqi army officers who, like him, were to play
a prominent political role in the future of the Iraqi government. Both of
these branches initiated cooperation with the Reform Society of Basra,
where Muzahim al-Pachechi headed a smaller branch of the *al-Ahd*.[139]
One of the main points of the *al-Ahd's* program was autonomy for
the Arab countries, forming a unity similar to the Austro-Hungarian
Empire.[140] After WW1 the society regrouped and many of its founders,
among them the Iraqi ex-Ottoman officers who had joined the revolt of
Sharif of Mecca, returned to Iraq with Faisal to hold prestigious positions
in the politics of the country.

Societies with distinct Arab national aims were *al-Fatat*, and *al-Ahd*.
However, none of these societies espoused openly separation or
independence, what the Arab nationalists before 1914 endeavored to
achieve was preservation of their cultural identity and acquisition of their
rights within the political framework of the Ottoman Empire.[141]

Bernard Lewis argues that:

---

[138] T.E.Lawrence, *Seven Pillars of Wisdom: A Triumph* (New York, 1935), p. 46.
[139] Charles Tripp, *A History of Iraq* (Cambridge University Press, 2000), p. 28.
[140] Nadmi, W.J.O.,*The Political, Social and Intellectual Roots of the Iraqi
Independence Movement of 1920* (Durham University, 1974). P.142.
[141] C. Ernest Dawn, *From Ottomanism to Arabism, Essay on Origins of Arab
Nationalism* (University of Illinois Press, 1973), pp. 151-152.

... Until the impact of European political ideas, the Arab subjects of the Ottoman Empire, though well aware of their separate linguistic and cultural identity and of the historic memoires attached to them, had no conception of a separate Arab state and no serious desire to part from the Turks. ... So alien was the idea of a territorial nation-state that Arabic has no word for Arabia, and Turkish, until modern times, lacked a word for Turkey. The Turks now use a word of European origin, the Arabs make do with an expression meaning the peninsula of the Arabs.[142]

Elie Kedourie points out that Turkey of course is not the only country whose name has been invented and resuscitated fairly recently, Iraq:

a name with associations going back to the early Islamic conquest of the Sassanid Empire, was chosen by Arab nationalists for another successor state of the Ottoman Empire as an evocation of past and a promise of future Arab glory.[143]

In fact, before WW1 the majority of the Arab population did not desire total secession from the Empire and those minorities who were grouped in oppositional societies demanded improvement of their social and political situations within the Empire.[144] These demands were expressed in the Arab Congress of Paris in 1913 officially convoked on the initiative of the Decentralization Party, although it appeared, that it was actually organized and supported by the secret Young Arab group.[145] The Congress articulated its demands through its organizers for the political and cultural rights of the Arabs, making Arabic the official language in the Arab provinces, and for administrative reforms and decentralization within the Ottoman Empire.[146]

The C.U.P who were in power at the time first agreed with these

---

[142] Bernard Lewis, *The Middle East and the West* (London, 1964), p.73

[143] Eli Kedourie, (ed.), *Nationalism in Asia and Africa* (London, Weidenfeld & Nicolson, 1970), pp. 49-50.

[144]Adeed Dawisha, *Iraq: A Political History from Independence to Occupation* (Princeton University Press, 2009), p. 33.

[145] Francesco Gabrieli, *The Arab Revival*. (London, 1961), p. 53.

[146] Adeed Dawisha, *Arab Nationalism In the Twentieth Century: From Triumph to Despair* (Princeton University Press, 2003), p.33.

demands but the subsequent months demonstrated, that they were not sincere with their promises refusing to ratify the agreement except on the subject of Arabic, which according to a governmental decree would be the medium in primary and secondary schools, Turkish still remained the medium of teaching in secondary schools in provincial capitals.[147]

Thus, the "Pan-Turanian Young Turks" disregarded Arab demand for self-determination, a principle they had previously agreed upon.[148] In 1914 the Ottoman authorities who suspected the activities of the secret society of *al-Ahd* acted against it in the three Iraqi provinces, but most of its members managed to escape arrest and some were obliged to exile to Egypt and Arabia.[149] The prominent members of the Arab national movement were incarcerated and then executed in 1915 and 1916 such as the chairman of the Congress of Paris al-Zahrawi and other important participants.[150]

The Arab Revolt of 1916

The grievance of the Arab nation culminated in the famous Arab Revolt of 1916 led by Sharif Husain ibn Ali, the Emir of Mecca. Cleveland argues that Sharif Husain was the most suitable person to lead the revolt against the Ottoman Empire, since as the Empire had entered into the war on the side of the Central Powers the sultan-caliph proclaimed jihad against the Entente spurred among the Muslims anti-British sentiment along the Britain-Indian route as well as inside India.[151] Sharif Husain was also urged by the Turks to proclaim the call for a holy war in order to induce the Arabs to fight against the Entente. However, the Sharif, refused to do so and the Turks, irked by his recalcitrance, contemplated his arrest and deportation as well as replacing him with a more venerable grand Sharif.[152]

By bringing Sharif Husain in as the guardian of the two holy cities of

---

[147] Antonius, (1938), pp 14-116.
[148] Tibi, (1997), p.113.
[149] Tripp, (2000), p. 29.
[150] Tibi, (1997), p.113.
[151] Cleveland, (1994), p.147.
[152] Antonius, (1939), p.144.

Mecca and Medina, on the side of the Entente, Britain thought they, could counteract the prominent position of the Ottoman sultan as the caliph of the Islamic *umma*.[153]

In early 1915 the societies *al-Ahd* and *al-Fatat* commenced cooperation and laid down a plan for a general revolt against the Ottomans. Syria was chosen to be the center of the revolt, where Arab soldiers were stationed at the time. Since the revolt was planned to reach the Arabian Peninsula the societies entrusted the Sharif of Mecca with its leadership. Faisal, as his father's emissary, was then sent to Damascus in March 1915, and met members of *al-Ahd* and *al-Fatat,* as a result a protocol was drawn up defining the condition on which the revolt against the Turks would be conducted. [154]The protocol is known as Damascus protocol, and it constituted the basis for the Anglo-Arab negotiation and therefore deserves to be quoted in full:

"The recognition by Great Britain of the independence of the Arab countries lying within the following frontiers:

North: The line Mersin: Adana to parallel 37 degree N. and thence along the line Birejik-Urfa-Midiat-Jazirat (Ibn Umar)-Amadia to the Persian frontier;
East: The Persian frontier down to the Persian Gulf;
South: The Indian Ocean (with the exclusion of Aden, whose status was to be maintained);
West: The Red Sea and the Mediterranean Sea back to Mersin. The abolition of all exceptional privileges granted to foreigners under the capitulations.
The conclusion of a defensive alliance between Great Britain and the future independent of Arab states.
The grant of economic preference to Great Britain.[155]

Then, on July 14, 1915, Husain, initiated negotiations by exchanging letters with Sir Henry McMahon, the British High Commissioner in Cairo, known as the

---

[153] Cleveland, (1994), p.147.
[154] Eliezer Tauber, *The Formation of Modern Iraq and Syria* (Ilford: Frank Cass, 1995), p.5. See also Zeine N. Zeine, *The Emergence of Arab nationalism, With a Background study of Arab-Turkish Relations in the Near East* (New York: Karavan Books, 1966), pp. 116-117.
[155] Antonius, (1939), pp. 157-158.

Husain-McMahon correspondence through which Husain undertook to launch a revolt against the Ottomans. As a *quid pro quo* he would obtain British support for establishing an Arab state. In a letter to Husain on August 30, 1915, McMahon conformed Lord Kitchener's[156] message in which he had pledged, on behalf of His Majesty's Government, even the restoration of the caliphate headed by "An Arab of true race." [157]Yet, in his negotiation with Britain, Husain, did not give any particular weight to the subject of the caliphate, showing more concern for the boundaries of the future Arab state,which constituted a stumbling block in their negotiation.[158]

Having made reservation on each other's demands Husain and McMahon agreed to postpone the negotiation of the future of these territories until the end of the war. McMahon seemed satisfied with this arrangement, he pledged then that "Great Britain is prepared to recognize and uphold the independence of the Arabs in all regions lying within the frontiers proposed by the Sharif of Mecca."[159]

The Arab Revolt took place in June 1916 under the command of Sharif Husain's son Emir Faisal accompanied by some British military advisers among them Captain T. E. Lawrence and a group of ex-Ottoman officers.

---

[156] W.W. Gottlieb, notes that as back as November 1912, Arab from the Lebanon and Damascus had asked the British for assistance in their struggle Against theTurks.A delegate from Syrian notable have asked Lord Kitchener, the High-Commissioner in Cairo, for the annexation of their country to Egypt. According to authoritative evidence, Kitchener anticipated "that if Turkey were ranged against Britain, as she must be as the Ally of Germany...
Arab co-operation would be clearly useful as a means of discouraging Jihad [the Holy War]... and of thwarting German ambition in the Middle East" W.W.Gottlieb, *Studies in the Secret Diplomacy during the First World War* (London, 1957), p. 199.
[157] Elie Kedourie, *England and the Middle East: The Destruction of the Ottoman Empire 1914-1921* (Dowes & Dowes, 1956), p. 52. For more detail about the issue of Caliphate and Husayn position to it see Dawn's *From Ottomanism to Arabism,* pp 40-46.
[158] Dawn, (1973), p.40.
[159] Cleveland, (1994), p. 149.

[160]These officers together with those individuals who were involved in the Sharif of Mecca's revolt in Hijaz against the Ottoman Empire, known as Sharifians, constituted the backbone of the Arab revolt. [161]A large number of the Arab army officers organized the Bedouin tribes in the war against the Ottomans. The majority of the army officers were of Iraqi origin, who had served in the Ottoman army and, had either been former prisoners of war in India and released by Britain to serve the Sharifians, or they had come voluntarily to join the revolt.[162] Some of the British Arab friends such as Nuri al-Said, Muzahim al-Pachachi, and Ali Jawdat also contributed in the recruitment of army officers to use their military knowledge in the service of the Arab cause. Out of forty six officers who in two rounds arrived in Hijaz in 1916, thirty one were Iraqi officers, among them Nuri al-Said and Jamil al-Midfai.[163]

As noted earlier, these military officers occupied several significant political positions in Iraq, which was realized due to the fact that they attended one of the few military schools in the Arab provinces of the Ottoman Empire situated in Baghdad. After obtaining an introduction to military life at these schools, the officers were given the opportunity for social and political progress non-existent for Arabs in other part of the Ottoman Empire. It is believed that those who attained the military college in Istanbul came from families of modest means. Talib Mushtaq, a son of an Ottoman bureaucrat, maintains:

> ... As for the poor families they made their sons attend the military school in Baghdad so that it might lead to their completing their higher studies in the Military College in Istanbul and graduate as officers in the Ottoman army.[164]

---

[160] Ibid.,p.153.

[161] David Pool, *From Elit to Class: The Transformation of Iraqi political Leadership,* in Abbas Kelidar (ed.) *The Integration of Modern Iraq* (New York, 1979), p. 63.

[162] Zeine N. Zeine, *The Struggle for Arab Independence, Western Diplomacy and the Rise and Fall of Faisal's Kingdom in Syria* (New York: Caravan Books, 1977), p.16.

[163] Nadmi, (1974), p. 152.

[164] Pool, (1979), pp. 65-68.

When Faisal ascended the throne of Iraq in 1921, these officers as his entourage not only held prestigious positions in government, but were also generously rewarded for their services in the Arab Revolt. The British Intelligence Report, February 1st 1922, indicated that the Iraqi Council of Ministers instructed the Ministry of Defense, for the purpose of pension and seniority, to double the period of service in the Arab army of the Hijaz for the officers drafted before the overthrow of King Faisal's kingdom in Syria in July 1920. Among the officers who first benefited from this decision were Jafar al-Askary and Nuri al-Said, both of whom were promoted, the latter, Minister of Defense, to colonel, and the former became first a lieutenant and two years later advanced to the same ministerial position.[165]

However, Istanbul was not only a destination where goal oriented Iraqis chose to secure their advancement in society, but was also a place where the "Iraqis first became acquainted with Arabism, having left the confines of their provincial backwater. Of these, the officers constituted the overwhelming majority, playing a vital role in the development of Arab consciousness before the First World War, and an instrumental part in the Arab Revolt of their particularism, modeling themselves upon the Young Turks as a 'Young Arab'antitheses to the Unionists and the policy of Turkification."[166]

A great number of these officers became politicians or occupied positions in the public service, and their participation in the revolt paved the way for position and success. Out of fourteen premiers between 1922 and 1932, nine were ex-Ottoman officers among them Nuri al-Said, Jafar al-Askary, and Yasin al- Hashimi, and thirty-two of fifty-six were possible Cabinet Ministers two of them, Jamil Midfai and Ali Jawdat, held office as premiers after the independence of Iraq. Through their positions as the ruling elite in the Iraqi government, they endeavored to impose Arab

---

[165] Abbas Kadhim, *Reclaiming Iraq, the 1920 Revolution and the Founding of the Modern State* (Austin: University of Texas Press, 2012), p. 153.
[166] Paul P.J. Hemphill, *The Formation of Iraqi Army, 1921-1933*, in Abbas kelidar (ed.) *The Integration of Modern Iraq* (London: Croom Helm, 1979), p. 91

nationalism upon the nascent Iraqi state and bring into being a homogeneous nation with an Arab identity by identifying with the Arab revolt.[167]

Since the military college in Istanbul was modeled on German staff training and organized by Germans, the Germanophilia ideas had a great influence upon these officers. For them nationalist integration was feasible through militarism, hence, Germany as a model appealed to them. Sati al-Husri, the Arab nationalist and ideologue, who became the Director General of Education during the mandate period, was also an ardent adherent of Germanophilia and attempted to instill Arab nationalism into students through the education system.[168] As Phebe Marr points out Husri was also "an early advocate of military exercise in the school system and conscription, a cherished aim of Iraqi nationalists all through the mandate." Husri claimed "that general military service is one of the most important means of teaching social education and increasing a spirit of a unity and discipline in the individuals of the nation."[169]

Tibi summarizes the "politicisation"of the second phase of the Arab national movement i.e. the second phase in 1920 by this quotation of Anis al-sayigh:

> The national movement was largely a political movement in the narrow sense... it was a right-wing conservative movement... which had been adjusted to the needs of a particular leadership and was monopolized by traditional politicians who were usually either rich feudalists or their agents. They saw their own interests as being the interests of the homeland and excluded workers, peasants and the middle classes from the power they were

---

[167] Ibid. pp. 91-92.

[168] Peter Wien, *Iraqi Arab Nationalism: Authoritarian, Totalitarian, and Pro-fascist Inclinations, 1932- 1941,* (Routledge, 2006), p. 9. See also *Simon. S. Revaa: The Education of an Iraqi Ottoman Army Officer* in Rashid Khalidi, Lisa Anderson, Muhammad Muslih, and Simon S. Reeva (eds.), *The Origins of Arab Nationalism,* (New York: Columbia University Press, 1991), pp. 151-167.

[169] Phebe Marr, *The Development of a Nationalist Ideology in Iraq 1920- 1941,* The Muslim World, Vol. 75, 1985, p. 91.

able to gain for themselves for a third century.[170]

It is within this context that we can consider, based on Hroch's three phase model described in chapter one, that in the Arab national movement a transition from Phase A to Phase B occurred. Decisive factors for this transition have been activities among Arab intellectuals and literati for the revival of Arab culture and tradition alongside efforts to increase the awareness of social and historical attributes of the Arabs.

However, these activities have been carried out at the local level and as personal initiatives with the aim of improving the condition of the Arabs within the Ottoman Empire. This phase evolved into Phase B, which was characterized by patriotic agitations, carried out for the most part by army officers and members of secret societies, as well as by organized political movements for national self-determination and territorial separation from the Empire.

---

[170] Tibi, (1997), pp. 115-116.

6

The Emergence of Kurdish Nationalism

Within the modern discourse of nation and nationalism as we have already outlined in the previous chapters there are two major bodies of thought on the emergence and evolution of the nation and nationalism among European scholars; the primordialist and the modernist, also called the constructive. Concerning the origins of the Kurdish nationalism, there is a similar approach to this question. Kurdish primordialists mainly trace the origins of Kurdish nationalism back to 1597, the year the *Sharafname* was written by the Kurdish *mir* (prince), Sharaf Khan Bitlisi (1543-1603), a medieval Kurdish historian and poet.[171]

During the 15th and 16th centuries, the Ottoman Empire, due to its weakness, lost its hold over its vast territories. This, combined with the failure of the Safavid in co-opting the Kurds, gave rise to the establishment of semi-independent or "autonomous mini-states", *emirates* (principalities), in the late 16th century. It was thanks to these favorable political and cultural circumstances that the *Sharafname* could be

---

[171] Abbas vali states that most Kurdish nationalists are primordialist. For them the Kurdish nation is a "primordial entity", a natural formation rooted in the nature of every Kurd, defining the identity of people and community throughout history". This perception of the concept of Kurdish nation, according to Vali, is prevailed both in "nationalist political circles" and in "established trend in nationalist scholarship which conveniently identifies nation identity with human nature, as a quality inherent in human individual, defining his/her social and political existence." Abbas Vali, *"Genealogies of the Kurds: Constructions of Nation and National Identity in Kurdish Historical Writing. In Abbas Vali (ed.) Essays on the Origins of Kurdish Nationalism*, (Costa Mesa, Mezda publisher, 2003), pp.59-60.

written.[172] According to Hassanpour, Sharaf Khan wrote his *Sharafname* since, until then, no historian "in no epoch and time had recounted the situation of the governors (volat) of Kurdistan and their circumstances", so he intended to "write a book about the description of their conditions and a compilation about their manners… so that the story of the magnificent families of Kurdistan would not remain under the veil of secrecy and denial."[173] Although the *Sharafname* deals with some distinctive features of the Kurdish society such as language, politics, tribalism and ethnicity, it stresses mainly the stories of different Kurdish dynasties that existed during the reign of the Safavid and the Ottoman Empires. The *Sharafname* is written in Persian and consists of four parts or (sahife) that are entirely devoted to the Kurdish dynasties. Typically, these dynasties enjoyed the status of royalty (Saltanat) or Emirs and governors (omara va hokkam).

Hassanpours interprets Sharaf Khan's employment of the concept of "independent rule" (*hokomat be esteqlal* or variation of it) mentioned on several pages in the *Sharafname*, to imply crucial attributes of independent statehood these rulers had acquired, such as "striking coin, reciting the name of the ruler in the khotbe, the Friday prayer sermon (e.g. pp 401, 495-96) and "not obeying any sultans."(p.486) The efforts made by the rulers of the Baban principality for "ascension and expansion of the territory (oruj va khoruj) were other important undertakings in governmental policy".[174]

The unity of the different principalities is another significant issue which preoccupied Sharaf Khan. He was an exponent of the unification of these principalities, with the aim to bring about a centralized Kurdish state

---

[172] Amir Hassanpour, *The Making of Kurdish Identity: Pre-20th Century Historical and Literary* Sources, in Abbas Vali (ed.) (2003), p.111.
[173] Quoted in Ibid., p 112.
[174] Ibid, p 113. The page numbers in the brackets refer to the *Sharafname*. Sharaf khan dedicated the first sahife to the Kurdish governors who hoisted the banners of dynasties and whom the historians have included within dynasties. He divides them in five chapters (fasl) as following: the governors of Dyiarbakir and Jazira, the governor of Hasnawyia, the governors of the greater Lur, the governors of the smaller Lur, and finally the governors of Egypt and Sham , who are known as the Ayyubids. pp. 36-116.

power "stretching from the farthest reaches of the east to the end regions of the west." (p.25) Furthermore, within this vast territory "populated by different ethnic peoples at different times",the *Sharafname* "presents the land as a geoethnic entity belonging to the Kurds, who are defined both positively and negatively. They do have their own characteristics, ways of life, modes of living, morality, and thinking." (pp. 18-35) At the same time, they are opposed to non-Kurds, especially the Ottoman Turks and Iranians. Sharaf Khan delineates the Kurdish territories where four main branches of the Kurds-Kurmanjs, Lurs, Kalhurs and Gorans are settled down. The borders of this "symbolic" homeland is delineated as follows:

... and the beginning of the vilayet of Kurdistan is from the coast of Hermoz sea, which is situated on the shores of the Indian Sea, and from there continues on a straight line until it ends in the vilayet of Malatiyeh and Marash, and in the north of this line there is the vilayet of Fars, Iraq-e Ajam and Azerbaijan and Lesser and Greater Armenia, and its south side lies Iraq-e Arab and Mosul and Diarbakir (pp. 24-25).[175]

Hassanpous contends that his approach to the question of Kurdish nationalist development is based on Marxist analysis considering the mode of production as the driving force behind the emergence and development of social classes and their national identities. Accordingly, he employs terms such as "feudal" and "bourgeois nationalism" in his periodization of the Kurdish nationalism beginning from the time of the publication of the *Sharafname* in the late seventeenth century. This approach to the question of the origins of the Kurdish nationalism has been opposed by other scholars on the grounds that "his discourse signifies not only the predominance of the uniform national origin, but also a class conception of history, politics and culture entailed in the Marxist theory of the modes of production. Consequently, his concept of national origin has invariably a class identity."[176]

Another prominent literary work, also significant for the determination

---

[175] Ibid., pp. 113-115.The page numbers in the brackets refer to *Sharafname*.
[176] Abbas Vali, *Nationalism and the Question of Origins*, in Abbas Vali (ed.), (2003), pp. 9-10

of Kurdish nationalism, is Ahmad Khani's major epic *Mam u Zin* (Mem and Zin), [177]written in 1695, a century after the appearance of Bitlisi's *Sharafname*. In the introductory part of Mam and Zin we can read:

> Look, from the Arabs to the Georgians, The
> Kurds have become the towers.
> The Turks and Persians are surrounded by them The
> Kurds are on all four corners,
> Both sides have made the Kurdish people, Tar-
> gets for arrows of fate.
> They are said to be keys to the borders,
> Each clan (tayife) forming a formidable bulwark.
> Whether the Ottoman Sea (Ottomans) and the Tajik Sea (Persians) Flow out
> and agitate,
> The Kurds get soaked in blood
> Separating them (the Ottomans and the Persians) isthmus (cc 220-25).

In his work Khani expresses lamentation on the cruel behavior of the Ottoman and Persian rulers toward the Kurds and their devastation of the Kurdish land describing the two powers as "mean" (le im, c. 205). Although he defends the rights of the Kurds against the non-Kurdish rulers and stresses their good qualities and capability to govern themselves, he pays special homage to the Kurdish rulers (mirs) ascribing them attributes such as Rostam-like combat (rezme Rostam), chivalry (cwameri), zeal (himmet), generosity (sexawet), regnancy (mirini) and firmness (celadat, cc 219, 225). Nevertheless, Khani like Bitlisi complained about the prevailing disunity and discordance among the Kurdish mirs. He advocated union and organization under a Kurdish king. Governing and statehood were tasks to be undertaken by the rulers (hakim u emiran) not by common people such as "the poets and the poor" (sari u feqiran) who were "orphans" (yetim) and in need of protection by a patron; "if we had a king, if God had found

---

[177] Mam and Zin is a tragic love story between two lovers Mam and Zin. Their efforts to unite fails due to Bakir's intrigue, Mam dies during the conspiracy of the latter. While mourning the death of Mam, Zin dies too at his grave. When Bakir realizes that his role in the death of Mam and Zin is revealed he fears for his live and hides between the two graves. He is killed there and out of his blood grows thorn bush the roots of which penetrate deep into the earth, separating Mam and Zin even after their death.

him worthy of a headgear, if a throne had been assigned for him, our fortune would be realized." (cc. 201-203)

Khani's zeal for a united and centralized Kurdish political power could only be realized with the help of cultural power. He underscored the importance of the Kurdish language for the Kurds in the struggle against the two dominant languages, the Persian and the Arabic, even if the spoken language of the Safavid court was Turkish. A Kurdish language with high prestige was also significant for the revival of previous poets such as Ali Hariri, Mele Jaziri and Feqe Teyran (cc. 247-52).

Thus, for Khani, political achievement, like the establishment of a Kurdish state, was as crucial as literary achievement such as reading and writing in Kurdish language.[178]

Like Bitlisi's *Sharafname,* Khani's Mem and Zin is regarded by most Kurdish nationalists as an indisputable historical document in which the author emphasizes significant Kurdish particularities such as their ethnicities, language, territory and rulers.[179] The nationalist reading of the *Mam u Zin* is, however, criticized by scholars such as Martin van Bruinessen who takes a constructivist or modernist approach to the question of Kurdish nationalism. Although he acknowledges that Khani was proud and cognizant of his Kurdish origin and regarded his cultural activity to serve the Kurds, he questions whether Khani really was a nationalist who envisaged establishing a Kurdish state. He holds the view that a nationalist reading of Khani is misleading and is based on a misconception of the historical and socio-economic conditions of the period during which Mam and Zin appeared. Similar to Anderson he underlines the role that the printing technique played in dissemination of books which, until then, were accessible to only a few who could read and write.

As has been noted in chapter one, the mass-production of literary works

---

[178] Hassanpour, (2003), pp- 118-123. All Pages in brackets refer to *Sharafname.*

[179] A nationalistic interpretation of Mem and Zin is also made by Ferhad Shakely, *Kurdish Nationalism in Mam u Zin of Ahmad-I Khani* (Brussels: Kurdish institute of Brussels, 1992).

which occurred during the era of industrialization facilitated the communication between villages and regions and thereby contributed to the dissemination of nationalist ideas. Some centuries earlier, at the time of publishing Mam and Zin, no similar condition existed in the Kurdish territories. As long as ethnic distinctiveness and national awareness is not rooted among all groups in a society, emergence of some form of nationalism is unthinkable. Van Bruinessen rightly does not believe that Khani indeed regarded the Kurds and Kurmanc as a nation and that he in his definition of these words excludes the non-tribal peasants from the Kurds. At that time the term "Kurd" did not include all Kurds, it referred solely to the Kurdish tribes and a section of the urban aristocratic elite, excluding the non-tribal peasantry. This is also true about Qadri Cemil Pasha a Kurdish nationalist from a Kurdish aristocrat family, who at the beginning of this century sought support among the tribal chieftains (*aghas*) for his nationalist activities. For the *aghas,* the Kurdish nation did not make any sense and even less so for the common tribesmen and peasantry. Van Bruinessen doubts whether Cemil Pasha and his friends viewed the peasants as Kurds. He is of the opinion that the inclusion of the peasantry contributed to the development of the Kurds as a nation in the modern sense.[180]

The Decline of the Kurdish Emirates and the Rise of the Shaikhs: The Tanzimat Reforms

It will be remembered that one of the aims behind the Tanzimat reform program was the creation of a centralized system of administration. One consequence of this policy was that the collection of taxes, which before was carried out by the emirs, was taken over by the state administration in order to increase the state revenues. The Emirs disapproved of the idea of the new reforms since it enervated their authorities and consequently

---

[180] Martin van Bruinessen, *Ehmdi Xanis Men u Zin and Its Role in the Emergence of Kurdish* National *Awareness.* In Vali (ed.), (2003), pp.40-57, See also Martin van Bruinessen "Kurdish Society, Ethnicity, Nationalism and Refugee Problem" , in Philip G. Kreyenbroek and Stefan Sprel (eds.) *The Kurds: A Contemporary Overview*, (London: Routledge 1992), pp 37-43;

threatened their *de facto* semi-autonomous *emirates* (principalities).

Concerning the semi-autonomous Kurdish *emirates* that existed before the reforms of the Tanzimat Haka Özoglo writes:

> Although the Ottoman state oversaw the function of the Kurdish Emirates, organized as districts or *sancaks,* Kurdish rulers enjoyed *de facto* autonomy, particularly in the late eighteenth and early nineteenth centuries; the strongest emirates were almost in complete control of their own internal affairs, paying only lip service to Istanbul.[181]

The destruction of the structure of the Kurdish *emirates* formed a new social structure that produced a new class of bureaucrats, the memurs, who replaced the old ruling class of the Ottomans. This in turn necessitated the introduction of a new school system. The number of schools, especially the technical and millet ones, increased dramatically in 1895. The emergence of the new middle class:

> took place just when the men of the Tanzimat were trying to extend the central government's power to the older notables, the remnant of the Janissaries, the nomadic tribes, and the ulema, who resented the Tanzimat's encroachment into their operation of justice and education within Muslim community. Using the newly developed 'people'against the element of the old authority, theTanzimat incorporated the former into the administrative councils, thus giving them the political power that they had sought. [182]

The new "modern middle class" gave birth to a cultural revival accompanied by a new Ottoman intelligentsia, which deprived the *ulema* from their traditional authority of cultural life in the Muslim community. Consequently, a new cultural life emerged, which was displayed by an upswing in the press that contributed to the dissemination of the ideas of this group.

---

[181] Hakan Özoglu, *Kurdish Notables and the Ottoman State: Evolving Identities, Competing Loyalties and Shifting Boundaries* (New York, 2004), p.59.
[182] Quoted in Ferhad Ibrahim, *Die kurdische Nationalbewegung im Irak, Eine Fallstudie zur Problematic ethnischer konflikte in der Dritte Welt.* (Berlin: Klaus Schwarz forlag, 1983), p.126.

The Tanzimat reforms were carried out in Iraq with some delays compared to other parts of the Ottoman Empire. The reforms started first in the Baghdad province in 1844 and in the Mosul province in 1849. However, they were not fully implemented due to financial obstacles, coupled with a refusal of the Iraqi tribes to pay taxes. Then, a considerable change happened, when Midhat Pasha was appointed as Governor of Baghdad between 1869 and 1872. During this period, the Iraqi provinces were further put under Ottoman dominance. At the same time, the development of communication throughout the nineteenth century facilitated the involvement of the Ottoman government more into the affairs of the Iraqi provinces. By the arrival of the telegraph and the steamships on the Tigris as well as the opening of the Suez Canal in 1869 the connection between Iraq and the Central Power in Istanbul became more tightened than ever. As a result of these new communication possibilities, the trade market flourished remarkably, which was indicated by the development of the region's transport system and its reformed land system. Midhat Pasha's policy generated significant socio-economic changes such as: centralization of the provincial administration under the 1864 Vilayet Law; road construction; publishing regional newspapers and building governmental schools with standardized curriculum enabling the Iraqis to attend military and law school in Istanbul. [184]

Following the centralization policy during the Tanzimat the Kurdish semi-autonomous *emirates* declined and a new Kurdish intelligentsia group emerged consisting of army officers, bureaucrats and intellectuals,

---

[183] Until 1840 only one official newspaper "*Tekvim-I Vekayi*" (The calendar of the Occurrence) was issued. At the beginning of the Tanzimat reform some private newspapers such as "*ceride-I Havadis*" (Chronicle of the Events), "tefsir-I Efkar" (Description of the ideas), "*Muhbir*" (informer), "*Basiret*" (Perception) were published. Ibid., p. 126.

[184] Zoe Preston, *The Crystallization of the Iraqi State, Geopolitical Function and Form* (Bern: Peter Lang, 2006), pp.112-15

some of whom later embarked on political careers in the Ottoman Em-pire.[185]

The Rise of the Shaikhs

The decline of the semi-autonomous Kurdish principalities during the first half of the 19th century partly occurred as a consequence of the "modernization" of the Ottoman administration mentioned above, and partly because the great powers pressed the Ottoman government to punish the *emirates* for their mistreatment of the Christians.[186] The suppression of the Kurdish *emirates* did not occur solely for the act of punishment or to force the Emirs to obey Ottoman authority. The main intention of Sultan Mahmud II was to reconquer and ultimately incorporate these territories into the Ottoman Empire.[187] Nevertheless, the Ottoman proved incapable of imposing its authority to restore law and order and to fill the vacuum created by the disappearance of the Emirs' authority. This paved the way for the religious shaikhs who emerged as new political leaders. [188]

As far as South Kurdistan was concerned, the Tanzimat reforms elimi-nated the power of the native princes. During the Ottoman dominance, South Kurdistan was divided between three principalities that were in con-stant competition amongst themselves and with the central government to extend their authority. These *emirates* consisted of the Banids (which fell in 18439, in Kirkuk and Sulaimanya; the Sorans (1534-1833) in the region between the two Zabs; and the *emirate* of Bahdinan *al-Abbasiyah* (1402-1843) in the Kurdish region of Mosul *liwa*.

Owing to the elimination of the *emirates* the *aghas* became imperative to the Kurds. They assumed the role of mediators between the Kurdish peasants and the foreign Turkish civil servants imposed upon them. However, the rivalry between Kurdish chieftains to consolidate their

---

[185] Ibid., p.127.

[186] Martin van Bruinessen, *Nationalismus und religiöser Konflikt: Der Kurdische Wiederstand im Iran.* In *Kurdish Ethno-Nationalism Versus Nation-Building States* (Istanbul: Isis Press, 2000), p 170

[187] Wadie Jwaideh, *Kurdish National Movement: Its Origins and Development* (Syracuse University Press 2006), p. 54.

[188] Van Bruinessen, (2000), p.170.

positions, combined with the absence of governmental rule, made the religious shaikhs the only *de facto* authority for the Kurdish rank and file. Consequently, the shaikhs of Barzinja took over the authoritative role the Baban princes had enjoyed in the Sulaimanya region, and the shaikhs of Barzan filled the power vacuum which was left after the destruction of the Abbasid *emirate* of Badhinan. The Talabanid Naqshbandi shaikh "became the champion of the land-less peasantry of Kirkuk liwa."[189] The shaikhs, who enjoyed a solid social base among the peasantry, led several significant uprisings against the Ottoman government. These abortive attempts which often were conducted with patriotic and messianic aspects were preludes to the birth of Kurdish nationalist sentiments.[190]

Concerning the messianic characters of Kurdish rebellions, Van Bruinessen believes that many of the earlier Kurdish movements had "messianistic/millenarian "character and were led by shaikhs embodied in messiah, equivalent to Mahdi in Islam. Accordingly, several of the Kurdish movements of the nineteenth and early twentieth centuries which he calls "proto-nationalist" displayed "distinctly millenarian features." The shaikhs' symbolic actions were often instigated by foreign intruders whose values constituted a threat to their traditional mode of life and their values. Revolts with millenarian characters appeared clearly accompanied by nascent nationalist sentiments and were carried out by the shaikhs of Barzan and the peasantry. The village of Barzan became a center of Kurdish nationalism when refugees without shelters or activists, both Muslims and Christians, who were in need of protection took refuge with the family of Barzan.[191]

Another outstanding shaikh who played a messianic role was Shaikh Ubaydallah of Nehri. Ubaydallah attained his prominent position by virtue

---

[189] Othman Ali, (1997) *South Kurdistan during the Last Phase of Ottoman Control: 1839-1914*, Journal of Muslim Minority Affairs, 17:2, 283-291, DOI: 10.1080/13602009708716377. P. 287.

[190] Gerard Chaliand, *Le Malheur Kurde*, (Editions du Seul, 1992), P. 58.

[191] Martin Van Bruinessen, *Agha, Shaikh and the State: The Social and Political Structure of Kurdistan* (London, Zed Books, 1992), pp.249-251.

of the immense religious prestige he possessed among his followers who considered him a holy man. At that time in Kurdish society, obeying shaikhs was a religious duty. Many religious followers (murids) deemed the shaikhs as Mahdi (messiah) and expected them to provide them a better life. The power and prestige of the Shaikh were achieved also "because many tribal chiefs owed him allegiance through marriage, as followers (murids) or for services rendered."[192]

In Addition, the shaikhs, *aghas*, tribal chiefs and leaders, government officials and rich merchants, due to their powerful position in Kurdistan, benefited from the Ottoman Land Code of 1858 by allotting them more land. Yet, the Ottoman government continued to grant the shaikhs and tribal leaders land, even after 1858, as part of its centralization policy in the latter half of the 19th century in eastern Anatolia and Iraq.[193]

The Rebellion of Shaikh Ubaydallah of Nehri

It will be recalled, after the distraction of the semi-autonomous Kurdish *emirates* in the 1830s and the1840s, disorder, tribal dispute and insecurity permeated the Kurdish land. This situation went from bad to worse after the Russo-Turkish war of 1877-1878 as famine became widespread and violence reigned. The state of affairs was uncontrollable for the Ottoman government and people desperately looked for a strong leader who could put an end to their suffering, save them from the miserable conditions, and restore law and order. People saw in Shaikh Ubaydalah the attributes they wanted; he was "God sent" for them, and the Shaikh had the same perception about himself. Ensuing achievements confirmed this belief that he was "a man with a mission and that he was so regarded by the numerous followers and adherents who flocked to his banner." [194]

An important factor that contributed to the making of Shaikh Ubaydallah in becoming such a paramount leader was when the sultan-

---

[192] Robert Olson, *The Emergence of Kurdish Nationalism and The Sheikh Said Rebellion, 1880-1925* (University of Texas press, 1989), p. 3.
[193] Ibid., p.4.
[194] Jwaideh, (2006), pp.76-7.

caliph appointed him to be in charge of the Kurdish forces for the defense of the northern parts of the Empire during the Russo-Turkish war. Subsequent events in Kurdistan were crucial for the Shaikh's rise as an Islamic as well as a Kurdish leader "a role that no other person had assumed since the great Saladin of Crusades fame!"[195]

When in 1880 Shaikh Ubaydallah's forces penetrated deep in Persian territory he claimed that he acted on behalf of the Kurdish nation. He sent the following message to William Abbott, the British Consul-General in Tabriz:[196]

> The Kurdish Nation... is a people apart. Their religion is different [from that of others], and their laws and customs are distinct .. the Chiefs and Rulers of Kurdistan, whether Turkish or Persian subjects, and the inhabitants of Kurdistan, one and all are united and agreed that matters cannot be carried on in this way with that two governments [Ottoman and Qajar], and that necessarily something must be done, so that European Governments having understood the matter, shall inquire into our state. We also are a nation apart, We want our affairs to be in our hands.[197]

The revolt broke out due to an extensive tribal dispute in a region that already was plagued by such kinds of conflicts. Despite its devastating effect the dispute gave impetus to the subsequent Kurdish nationalist

---

[195] Ibid., p. 77.

[196] There are different views about to whom this letter was sent. According to Robert Olson, Shaikh Ubaydallah sent his letter in July 1880 to British Vice-Consul Clayton in Baskale, while van Bruinessen writes that the letter was sent on October 5, 1880 to the American missionary Cochran in Urumiyah.

[197] Quoted in David MacDowall, *A Modern History of the Kurds* (London: I.B.Tauris & Co Ltd, 2000), p. 53 Martin Strohmeier points out that despite the fact that the letter expresses a distinct Kurdish national feeling, it is important to observe that it was addressed to a foreigner and apparently was not meant for local consumption. In order to counteract the Armenian strategies Kurdish leaders believed that they would receive foreign support if they were recognized as a "nation". He doubts that Ubaydullah's "nationalist" statement was an indication of "new concept of goals or self-definition or motivated the sheykh's followers." See Martin Strohmeier, *Crucial Images in the Representation of a Kurdish National Identity: Heroes and Patriots, Traitors and Foes* (Berlin, 2003), p.15.

movements. The revolt was triggered in 1880 by Abd al Qadir, Shaikh Ubaydallah's second son in the border villages whose population were faithful to Nehri saiyeds. He was appointed by the governor of Urumiya as their intermediary to secure the tranquility of the local tribes. The rebellion seemed to have been generated by the local authority's cruel treatment of some tribal chiefs without consulting Abd al Qadir. Abd al Qadir, observing his authority undermined by this act, undertook to lead these discontented chiefs. According to Ubaydallah, the revolt had its origins in his dissatisfaction with the prevailing situation characterized by lawlessness and the inability of the Iranian authorities. [198]

William Abbott, who was well acquainted with the Shaikh through his deeds and utterances, maintained that Ubaydallah's goal was "to place himself at the head of a Kurdish principality, and to annex the whole of Kurdistan, both in Turkey and Persia."[199]

In Jwaideh's opinion Ubaydalla's chief intention "was to unite the Kurds and to set up an independent Kurdish state", and that the events during the war of 1877-1878 as well as the subsequent events had great impact on the Shaikh's political-religious thoughts and orientation. As a holy leader with a prominent position in Kurdistan, he acquired extraordinary power, which he used to dominate the situation in the aftermath of the war. This caused a shift in his zeal and ambitions, thus abandoning local preoccupations and interests and aiming at a higher goal: to unite the Kurds and establish an independent Kurdish state.[200]

The establishment of an Armenian state is considered to be the chief reason behind the Shaikh's ambition to create a Kurdish state. The Russo-Turkish war was ended by the signing of the Treaty of Berlin on July 13, 1878. Article 61 of this treaty stipulated that the Ottoman government was

---

[198] Ibid., pp.53-54.
[199] Quoted in McDowall, (2000), p.55.
[200] Jwaideh, (2006), p. 80. On the question whether the revolt of Shaikh Ubaydallah had a nationalistic character van Bruinessen believes that such revolts cannot be considered as expression of nationalist feelings but rather as typical peasantry solidarity "bauerlischen Gemeinschaften." Van Bruinessen, (2000), P. 171.

imposed upon for "improvement and reforms demanded by local requirements in the provinces and inhabited by the Armenians, and to guarantee their security against the Circassians and Kurds."[201]

The implementation of Article 61 would imply that an Armenian state was to be established on the Kurdish territory or partly overlapping the area where Ubaydallah had his influence. The reaction of the Shaikh upon hearing this article is said to have been, "What is this I hear, that the Armenians are going to have an independent state in Van, and that the Nestorians are going to hoist the British flag and declare themselves British subjects." [202]

From that time on Shaikh Ubaydallah mobilized his power and efforts to counteract the Armenians' attempts for realization of the establishment of an Armenian state. In so doing, the Shaikh initiated diplomatic activities in order to coordinate all Kurdish movements that existed for the creation of a Kurdish League, which was unique in its kind. The main aim of the League was to prevent the implementation of the Treaty of Berlin, which would constitute a serious threat to the Kurds and their national ambitions. The Kurdish League's activity, although it was short-lived, was successful, above all else, thanks to the Ottoman government's support and cooperation with the Kurdish forces. That the Kurdish League was reinforced by the Ottoman government was understandable on the grounds that the League's policy coincided with that of the Turks; to prevent the great powers' plan to carve more territory from the Ottoman Empire which had already lost vast territories in the Balkan and in Egypt throughout the 19th century. The Port was well aware of the importance of the Kurdish help to them, especially when Ubaydallah called for (Jihad) against the Russians during the war. [203]

However, the alliance between Shaikh Ubaydallah and the Sublime

---

[201] Quoted in Robert Olson, (1989), p. 5.

[202] Quoted in McDowall, (2000), p. 57.

[203] Robert Olson, (1989), p 6. McDowall doubts that the Kurdish League was created by Shaikh Ubaydallah and supports the Armenian patriarchate's claim that the League was created by the port in order to "stifle the Armenian's question" He also doubts that such a League existed and even if it did "apparently never made any statement nor took any action in that name." McDowall, (2000), p. 58.

Porte did not last long. It took an abrupt turn as soon as he exerted his growing power that he acquired in connection with the invasion of Iran in 1880 to establish a Kurdish state. [204]

Prelude to Kurdish Nationalism

As mentioned previously, the driving force behind the Young Turk Revolution of 1908 was to compel the sultan-caliph Abdul Hammid II to restore the constitution and inaugurate parliamentary election. Those who constituted the nucleus of the Committee of Union and Progress (CUP), were students who had fled the country and settled down in Europe, where they were "particularly influenced by egalitarian and libertarian ideas of the French Revolution and doctrinaire nationalism." [205]The CUP, as a secret society was modeled upon European secret societies like the Carbonari, the International Macedonian Revolutionary Organization (IMRO), and the Freemasons. Two of the organizers of the CUP Ishak Sukuti and Abd Allah Jawdat, were sons of outstanding Kurdish families who played a prominent role in the activity of the Committee. These two opposed Abd al Hamid's Islamic policy and were influenced by the modernization ideas of Europe which they advocated. Jawdat remained faithful to the political, social, intellectual and religious liberties expressed in the articles entitled 'A very Wakeful Sleep' and issued in his journal *Ijtihad* in 1902.

In addition, he translated numerous items of European literature (English, German, French and Italian) into Turkish (not Kurdish) which "was in its way a testimony to the consistency of his modernizing belief "that "civilization means European civilization." [206]The Committee comprised other members from outstanding Kurdish families such as Bedir Khan, who was still engaged with the Young Turks movement, but inclined toward the "decentralist and liberal" wing of the party rather than the "Turkish nationalist" nucleus. The objective of these patriotic Kurds, who were less assimilated within the Ottoman intelligentsia was a

---

[204] Olson, (1989), p. 7.

[205] Jwaideh, (2006), p.102.

[206] McDowall, (2000), p. 91.

decentralized Ottoman confederacy with an autonomous Kurdistan. Kurdish intellectuals, who were successfully assimilated such as Ziya Gökapl and Abdulla Jawdat became prominent figures in the foundation of Turkish nationalism.[207]

Kurdish Cultural and Ethnic Distinctiveness

It will be recalled that earlier expression of affinity for Kurdish language and history as well as knowledge of their own ethnicity and concern for the Kurds' destiny can be traced back to Kurdish classical works such as *MeM u Zin* and *Sharafname*. Likewise, at the turn of the century, a feeling of national belonging was reflected in oral literature i. e. *beyts* (popular Ballads). For instance, the Ballad *Dimdin* portrayed the resistance of Khan of Bradost against the Safavid (in 1608) and the Ballad of *Qer u Gulzer* depicts the consequence of the division of Kurdistan. In the Ballad of Abdulrahman Pashay Baba (Mann 1906) the Khan of Baban principality is called "the king of Kurdistan."[208] Haji Qadir Koyi (1817-1897) inaugurated a new era of the Kurdish national development; he broke with feudal "nationalism" and promoted the Kurdish cause from a middle class point of view. Challenging the traditional aristocratic leaders and clergy, he urged for the creation of a Kurdish state and demanded the employment of the Kurdish language and literature as well as endorsement of modern secular education. Living in Istanbul during his last years, Haji became cognizant to the use of language in the scientific realm of the modern world. He bemoans:

> Only the Kurds, among all nations, are De-
> prived of reading and writing
> By translating into their own languages, the foreigners Became
> familiar with the secrets of other peoples´books None of our
> scholars (Ulema), great or small,
> Has ever read two letters in Kurdish...

---

[207] Omer Taspinar, *Kurdish Nationalism and Political Islam in Turkey: Kemalist Identity in Transition* (New York: Routledge 2005), p. 72.
[208] Amir Hassanpour, *Nationalism and language in Kurdistan 1918-1985* (San francisco: Mellen Research University Press, 1992), p.5.

Her Kurde le beynî kullî millet
Bê behre le xöndin û kitabet
Bêgane le tercumey zubanî
Esrarî kitêb xelkî zanî
Yekser 'ulema dirist û wirdî
Ney xönduwe hîc dû herfi Kurdî...

Haji was not only preoccupied with the Kurdish language, but also with important political matters such as independence for the Kurds. He referred to the East European nations such as the Bulgars, the Serbians, and the Greeks as well as to the Armenians, who he considered to be smaller than the Kurds, but had achieved sovereignty, and called for armed struggle in order to attain the same goal.[209]

A prominent Kurdish figure who in the mid-19th century contributed to the development of Kurdish language was Mala Mahmud Bayazidi. Most of his efforts concerned Kurdish language textbooks and grammar. During the 1850's, he collected and translated many works on Kurdish grammar, manners and customs of the Kurds as well as the history of Kurdistan in Bitlisi's *Sharafname*. [210]

Thus, broadly speaking, the Kurdish cultural activities and ethnic awareness outlined above correspond to Hroch's first stage of development of small non-dominant nations. Affection for Kurdish language, and patriotic utterance was individual and remained at the personal level. These kinds of activities for the national revival were, for the most part, limited to the intellectuals, poets, mullas, members of princes' families, etc. Any engagements on the part of the population in cultural activities, let alone political ones, were conspicuous by their absence. The endeavor for the Kurdish national and cultural revival did not cease at this stage, however. It continued until the rise of the first Kurdish political organizations and developed alongside them.

---

[209] Ibid., p. 93.
[210] Ibid., p. 81.

Foundation of Kurdish Cultural and Political Organizations

In the wake of the revolution of the Young Turks in 1908, the Kurds were given the opportunity to express their cultural distinctiveness, thereby enhancing their ethnic particularity considerably. A few Kurdish notables, who were affected by European nationalist ideas, established Kurdish organizations with nationalistic characters in Istanbul. They formed the first Kurdish organization in 1908, the *Kurd teavun ve Teraqqi Jamiyati* (Kurdish Society for Mutual Aid and Progress). Some of its founders were from high-ranking Kurdish families. The offspring of the *emirs* and *agahas*, such as Muhammad Sharif Pasha of the Baban Family, previously served as Ottoman envoy to Stockholm, an ardent loyal of Sultan Abd al Hamid and an opponent to the Young Turk), Emin Ali Bedirkhan (leader of the Bedirkhan clan in Istanbul), and Sheikh Said Abdulqadir (son of Shaikh Ubaydallah, later was appointed as president of the Council of State).[211] The organisation published a journal in Turkish, *Kurt Teavun we Terekki Gazetesi* (Kurdish Mutual Aid and Progress Gazette) which was the first Kurdish journal to be published. The Gazette became a focal point in an immense discussion pertaining to the problems of the Kurdish culture, language, and national unity, and soon gained enormous popularity among all of Istanbul's émigres.[212] The following year marked a shift in the policy of the Young Turks as they carried out a Turkification policy and closed the Kurdish organizations.

The reason behind the Young Turks' act (which was facilitated by the dispute between the Bedirkhans and saiyed Abd al Qadir) was, according to van Bruinessen, the organization's ethnic belonging and its opposition

---

[211] Van Bruinessen, (1992), p. 276.

[212] Kendal Nezan, *The Kurds under the Ottoman Empire*. In Gerard Chaliand (ed.), *A People Without A Country, The Kurds and Kurdistan* (London, 1980), p.27.

to the CUP's ideas. [213]Other Kurdish groups were active in other parts of the Ottoman Empire such as Diyarbakir, Bitlis, Mosul and Baghdad. In Istanbul, the society established a cultural affiliate *Kurt Neshri Maaref Cemiyeti* (society for the propagation of Kurdish Education), that published a magazine, *Kurdistan*, which was earlier issued by Sureya Beg Bedir khan in Cairo.[214]

C.J Edmonds notes that the first newspaper, *Kurdistan,* was founded by the Bedirkhan family in 1897, and was issued until 1902 in Cairo, Geneva, London, and of all unlikely places, Folkestone. In 1908, following the restoration of the Turkish Constitution, the first literary society was formed by General Sharif Pasha of Sulaimanya and the Bedikhans, and several periodicals (including a revived *Kurdistan*), volumes of verse, anthologies and the like were printed in Constantinople. However, these kinds of activities were short lived.[215] The Kurdish society also opened a school for children of about 30,000 Kurds or so in Istanbul. The school was directed by Saiyed Kurdi or Nusri who later became a leading religious figure, an advocate for *Nuruculuk* (Islamic revivalism) with emphasis on Kurdish cultural identity.[216]

After the closing of the *Kurd teavun ve teraqqi jamiyati*, the Kurdish students' union (*Hevi,* hope) was established in 1912. The social base for most of the members of the union was the upper class of the Ottoman society. They were "sons of urban, ottomanized notables. They belonged to the same social stratum as most Young Turks; their romantic nationalism

---

[213] Van Bruinessen, (1992), p. 276. The abandonment of the young Turks' liberal ideas can be explained by, among other things, the lost of territories; Austria's seizure of Bosnia and Herzegovina and Bulgarian declaration of independence, as well as the counter -coup of 1909, prompted the Young Turks to take severe measures against their opponents. As mentioned previously, the Arab clubs and associations were banned due to the same circumstances.

[214] Olson, (1989), p.15.

[215] C.J. Edmonds, *Kurdish Nationalism,* Journal of Contemporary History. Vol. 6. 1, Nationalism and Separatism, (1971), p. 89.

[216] Olson, (1989), p.15. For more information about the Nuruculuk movement see Van Bruinessen, (1992), p. 257.

paralleled that of the Turkish nationalists of their time."[217]

By establishing political organizations and parties and initiating political agitation, the Kurdish national movement marked a transition from Phase A into Phase B. Still, as was the case in Phase A, the social composition of those who were engaged in defusing patriotic attitudes consisted of notables and their sons, intellectuals, the shaikhs, etc. The latter group was the most prominent representative of the nationalist agitation and had a decisive influence on the population. Yet, due to the tribal nature of the Kurdish society, and hence, the sectarian and tribal affiliation to the Kurdish national movement, the shaikhs' revolts and uprisings proved insufficient for a transformation to Phase C. However, there are also other important factors for successful national movements. Hroch maintains that in order for the agitation of the activists engenders a mass movement and attain its ultimate goal, i.e. the formation of modern nations, the existence of the following favorable conditions were necessary:

1. An effective Phase A.
2. Basic volume of vertical social mobility, open to members of the non-dominant ethnic group.
3. A fairly high level of social communication, including literacy, market relations etc.
4. Nationally relevant conflicts of interests.
5. External conditions[218], favorable to the success of national movements.[219]

It is worth noting that Hroch assigns a great importance to the second and third conditions in the process of nation-building. Adopting Karl Deutsch's vocabulary in his work *Nationalism and Social Communication*, he states that a high level of social mobility seems to have been

---

[217] Van Bruinessen, (1992), p. 276.

[218] Hroch refers to the position of the European powers toward the Habsburg and the Ottoman Empires. While these powers acted rather suppresively in the former, national movements in the letter were supported by at least one of the European powers, (in Greece case, there were three powers involved-Great Britain, France and Russia). See Miroslav Hroch, *Cultural Crossroads in Europe*, inTuuli Forsgren and Martin Peterson (eds.) (Uppsala:Ord och Form AB, 1997).

[219] Ibid., p. 49.

favorable for the acceptance of patriotic programs in Phase B. On the other hand, these factors also contributed to "successful upward assimilation" of the members of the non-dominant nation into the ranks of the dominant nation. Hence, it might be appropriate to suggest that Ziya Gökapl and Abdulla Jawdat (two main founders of the CUP mentioned earlier) were good examples of this kind of assimilation. Similarly, Hroch points out that social communication as transmission of information about reality, and of the peoples' opinion toward this reality, was very important in the advent of a modern capitalist society. He concludes that the activists' national agitations appealed effortlessly to those within the non-dominant ethnic group who had at its disposal the best channels of such communications. Furthermore, regions with the densest networks of communication were most receptive to such agitations. Deutsch's view[220], Hroch claims, seems to corroborate that the growth of national movements (or nationalism in Deutsch's words) developed conjointly with the advance of communication and mobility, themselves processes within a general structural change in society.[221] Not all of these conditions existed with regards to the Kurdish national movement, and if some of them did exist, they were not sufficiently decisive to facilitate a transition to Phase C as so far has been observed and as it will be examined later in this book.

Kurdish Nationalist Activities, 1908-1918

If the Young Turks, through their Turkification policy, succeeded in curtailing the activities of the Kurdish cultural and political associations and parties, they had less success in silencing the shaikhs in their *takiyas* (a place where Muslims of specific religious order gather). The shaikhs:

> were closely associated with the Kurdish masses and identified themselves with them. Furthermore, by both training and conviction they stood for the

---

[220] A leading exponent of the so-called "Communications approach" is Karl.W. Deutsch. On his views about the important of the communication Mechanism in the process of modern nation building see his work (1966).
[221] Hroch, (1/198, 1993), pp. 5-6.

traditional Islamic state as opposed to the modern secular state envisaged by the Young Turks... in the eyes of the sheikhs, Abdul Hamid's pro-Kurdish and pan-Islamic policies had made him the ideal sultan caliph.[222]

The shaikhs opposed the secularization idea of the CUP at the initial stage of the Tanzimat reforms which intended to replace Islamic terms like *umma* with secular ones such as 'nation' and 'society' that they considered abstract and lacking any appeal to the sultan and the caliph. Religious shaikhs who were opponents to the constitutional government had, according to Ashrak Safrastian, the British vice-consul in Bitlis:

taking oath upon the Koran and their religion to be faithful to their vow and the cause of the Sheriat ... to carry on a restlessness campaign against everything undertaken by the Young Turks ... The Young Turks are represented as entirely irreligious and violators of Mohammadan traditions, as laughing at prayers, *namaz*, and all such religious duties. [223]

These shaikhs, together with some Kurdish notables, dispatching a petition by telegram to the Porte and the Ottoman Parliament in Istanbul, demonstrated obviously that religious faith overlapped with nationalist sentiments. The petition which was inspired by Shaikh Abd al-Salam of Barzan and Shaikh Nur Muhammad of Dohok, resident in North East of Mosul demanded following reforms:

1-the adoption of Kurdish as the official language in the five Kurdish *qadas* (administrative districts); (2) the adoption of Kurdish as the language of instruction in the Kurdish areas;(3) the appointment of Kurdish-speaking *qaim-maqam* (district deputy commissioners) *mudirs nahiyas* (subdistrict officers), and other officials; (4) the administration of law and justice in accordance with Shari'a (Muslim canon law) in view of the fact that Islam was the state religion; (5) the position of *qadi* (religious judge) and *mufti* (canon lawyer responsible for delivering formal legal opinions) to be filled by adherents of

---

[222] Jwaideh, (2006), p.106.
[223] FO371/1009 Safrastian to McGregor, Bitlis, 22 June 1911, Quoted in McDowall, (2000), p. 96.

the Shafi'i school of law; (6) taxes to be levied in accordance with the provisions of the Shariá, and the abolition of all taxes in excess of or incompatible with the amount established by the Shariá; (7) taxes collected for exemption from labour service remain in effect, provided they were set aside for the repair and maintenance of road in the five Kurdish *qadas*. [224]

In August 1910 Abd al-Razzaq Bedirkhan, from the Badir khans, rival to shaikh Abd al Qadir, returned from his Parisian exile and began developing his idea about a Kurdish autonomous state under Russian protection. He cooperated with Simko of the Shikak, who also was on good terms with the Russians, which increased Istanbul's fear about a Russian-Kurdish plan for creating an autonomous Kurdish state. Shaikh Taha, who after his father's death became a new religious leader for the Saiyeds of Nihri, was also in contact with the Russians, but his endeavor proved less successful than that of his father. However, he, together with other prominent shaikhs like Shaikh Abd al-Salam, was engaged in nationalist activities in 1913. They worked with the head of Badir Khans in Butan, Hussein and his cousin Abd al-Razzaq who were already instigating resistance to the CUP, spurring up Kurdish nationalist feelings for an autonomous Kurdish enclave supported by Russia.[225]

Kurdish Wartime Nationalist Activities

The outbreak of the war implied a further setback for the Kurdish political organizations. By drafting the members of the *Hevi* organization into the army during the war, the Ottoman government practically dissolved this organization. At the same time, Kurdish nationalists living in exile were active in bringing about alliances with anti-Ottoman powers through which they could obtain guarantees for Kurdish independence in future settlements of the Ottoman territories. General Muhammad Sharif Pasha was

---

[224] Quoted in Jwaideh, (2006), p. 107.

[225] McDowall, (2000), p 98-99. Van Bruinessen notes about the Badir Khan's family that they "did not put all their eggs into one basket." Another member of this family, Khalid, has, on the other hand, been appointed as the (Ottoman) governor in Malatya in 1919.

one of those Kurds who tried to realize this idea. He offered his services to the British expeditionary forces in Mesopotamia, but was rejected. Members of the Bedir Khan family, especially Abd al-Razzaq Beg and Kamil Beg Bedir Khan, maintained their good contact with the Russians. They were appointed governor of Erzerum and Betlis respectively while Russian forces occupied eastern Turkey in 1917. Another member of the same family, Sureya Beg, as mentioned above, issued a newspaper, *Kurdistan*, with the aid and approval of Britain, in Cairo, where he was politically active for the Kurdish question. [226]

Still another Shaikh, Saiyed Taha, was as well in connection with the Russians, learned Russian fluently, and returned to the village of Rajan, across the Turco-Persian frontier, as a Russian protégé. Thanks to his cordial relations with the Russians, an official British report informed that he could have been "used as a figurehead of a nominally independent Kurdistan under Russian auspices." [227]However, during the war, he was conceived of as unreliable and was imprisoned by both the Turks and the Russians as he tried to cajole with both sides.[228]

In Istanbul, Kurdish nationalists pursued their activities within the opposition parties like *Hurriyet ve Itilaf* (Freedom and Accord party). Mevlanzadeh Rifat, one of the leaders of this party, issued a newspaper, *Serbesti* (Freedom) in which articles by Kurdish nationalists, such as Kamuran Bedirkhan and Celadet Bedirkhan were printed. Another party, the *Osmanli Demokrat Firkasi* (Ottoman Democratic Party) was built by Abdullah Cevdet and Ibrahim Temo which acted as opposition in the Ottoman parliament. However, as war broke out in 1914, Kurdish nationalists, both those who were against the government and the CUP, and those in favor of them, were obliged to pursue their activities instead of defending the homeland.[229] The war had transformed great parts of Kurdistan into battlefields.The Kurds contributed to the Ottoman army

---

[226] Ibid., p 99.

[227] Jwaideh, (2006), p. 129.

[228] Ibid., p. 129.

[229] Olson, (1989), p. 18.

with considerable manpower. There is no reliable number on how many Kurdish soldiers were drafted into the war. According to Muhammad Amin Zaki, the Eleventh Army based at al-Aziz, the Twelfth Army in Mosul, the Ninth at Arezrum and the Tenth at Siwas, were composed entirely of the Kurds. Zaki estimates Kurdish casualties in the war at more than 300.000. The majority of them died in the war while others died in captivity, of hunger, or of cold. In their battles against the Russian forces in 1916, the Kurds endured enormous losses and casualties. In the wake of the war, a great number of the Kurds died as well due to other causes than the war with Russia and the civil war with the Armenians. According to the immigration bureau as a consequence of the war, about 70,000 Kurds were forced to leave their regions and migrate to other parts of Anatolia. A great number of them died of exhaustion, hunger, or diseases. [230]

Kurdish Activities During the Peace Conference of Paris

The idea of creating an autonomous Kurdish enclave had been in circulation among some Kurdish notables since the ending of World War 1. A leading chief of the Mukri tribe in the Sanju Bulaq district of Persia had presented his scheme of an independent Kurdistan under British protection to Lt.Col. Kennion in July 1918. The Kurds, this chief had maintained, would not oppose the creation of a free Armenian state in the northern part of Turkey, provided that an independent Kurdish state also was established between the Armenian state and the Arab state.[231] A similar idea was proposed by Sharif Pasha, a Kurdish notable, who had resided in Paris since his childhood. He devoted his political activities to the Kurdish cause. Sharif Pasha urged the British to initiate a policy in order to enable the Kurds to realize their nationalist ideas. His suggestion was that the British should guarantee autonomy, under their aegis to the inhabitants of southern Kurdistan, and give them the necessary aid in administrative and financial matters just as they had promised to do for the Arabs. Sharif Pasha was eager

---

[230] Muhammah Amin Zaki, *Kholaseh Tarikh-i-Kurd U Kurdistan*, Barg-i-yakem u Duwam (Slemani, 2000), pp. 178-179.
[231] Wilson, A.T. *Mesopotamia 1917-1920:A Clash of Loyalty* (London,1931), p.130.

to reach an understanding with the British before any formal decision was made by the Peace Conference. He proposed, "Let us make no annexations, but set up autonomous States and control them". According to A.T. Wilson, the British Civil Commissioner in Iraq, "His scheme in fact, was an intelligent anticipation of the Mandatory system." [232]

It was believed that his proposal would gain the approval of the Allies with respect to the Armenian massacres and be embraced by the peacemakers because it was in line with one of President Wilson's fourteen points, according to which the inhabitants under the Turkish dominance were assured "an unmolested opportunity of autonomous development."[233] Acting on behalf of the Kurds Sharif Pasha handed in a memorandum to the Peace Conference in which he demanded the setting up of a Kurdish state:

In virtue of Wilsonian principal everything pleads in favor of the Kurds for creation of a Kurdish state, entirely free and independent. Since Ottoman Government has accepted Mr. Wilson's fourteenth points without reservation, the Kurds believes that they have a right to demand their independence, and that without in any way failing in loyalty towards the Empire under whose sovereignty they have lived for many centuries, keeping intact their customs and traditions...

... we demand, that independence which is our birthright, and which alone will permit us to fight our way along the road of progress and civilization, to turn to account the resources of our country and to live in peace with our neighbours ...[234]

Then the Kurdish and Armenian delegates discussed border issues between their territories as well as the relationship between their peoples in case, in the future, the creation of the promised states was realized, and an agreement between Boghos Nubar and Pasha was signed to that effect.[235] At the

---

[232] Ibid., p. 13.
[233] Ibid., pp.10-131.
[234] Hannelore Kuchler, *Öffentliche Meinung: Eine theoretisch-methodologische Betrachtung und eine exemplarische Undesuchung zum Selbstverständnis der Kurden* (Berlin, 1978), p.168.
[235] Ibid.

same time, and to counteract the Kurdo-Armenian accord, the Turks arranged for building a special council consisting of Turkish and Kurdish representatives in order to deal with the Kurdish question. A decision was reached granting the Kurds considerable autonomy, provided that they "undertake to continue being a part of the Ottoman Empire and to continue to recognize the suzerainty of the sultan-caliph."[236]

According to Rifat Beg, a spokesman for Shaikh Abd- al Qadir, the Kurds cooperated with the British owing to their confidence in them and acted in accordance with Wilson's idea of self-determination.[237]

However, as the negotiations at the Peace Conference were in progress British policy with regards to Kurdistan was discussed in a telegram sent on March 26, 1920, from Lord Curzon to Admiral Sir J. De Robeck, the British High Commissioner to Turkey, in which he made clear that the proposed form of government for the Kurds was "neither a single protectorate for England or France, nor a divided protectorate, nor a group of States under European protection, but an autonomous Kurdistan, severed from Turkey, and not even under Turkish suzerainty."[238] In order to ascertain whether that solution was practicable or if it was feasible to reconcile the interests of the Armenian and the Christian minorities, living in the Kurdish areas, with those of the Kurds, it was desirable to know the opinions of the responsible Kurdish leaders on the matter. These leaders, according to Curzon's thought, were Said Abdul Kadir, President of the Kurdish club formed in Constantinople soon after the armistice, and Sharif Pasha, who was chairman of the Kurdish delegation in Paris. Similar enquiries were addressed to Baghdad concerning eastern and southern Kurdistan.[239]

In his answer to Curzon, De Robeck doubted whether independence or autonomy of Kurdistan was a proposition at all and he believed that there

---

[236] Jwaideh, (2006), pp. 130-131.

[237] Ibid., P. 131.

[238] Documents on British Foreign Policy 1919-1939, In Rohan Butler, M.A. and J.P.T. Bury, M.A.(eds.) First Series, Vol. X111 (London, 1963), p. 49.

[239] Ibid.

was no "Kurdish opinion" in the sense of coherent public opinion. He maintained that the majority of the Kurds were more inclined to be put under the authorities of other powers:

> Few looking higher that tribal Agahs or religious Sheikhs amongst whom there is little common ground, but whose opposition it is desirable to avoid challenging if we wish to evolve a system ensuring reasonable good Government for ... people including non-Kurdish minorities." [240]

Kurdish leaders with separatist ideas outside of Kurdistan rather exaggerated their influence and importance. Sharif Pasha for example, "carried practically no weight and in view of his recent gravitation back toward Turks ... he merits little or no attention." However, when the last Eastern Committee, i.e. Inter-departmental Conference on Middle Eastern Affairs, was held at the Foreign Office on April 13, 1920, discussing the Kurdish question, it was taken as settled that the Kurds had no responsible leaders.[241] This fact was reflected in Britain's change in attitude toward the Kurdish question, after the settlement of San Remo, which took the position that the British should not directly be involved in Kurdish affairs. The rebellious attitudes of the Kurdish tribes and their hostility to any foreign authority induced Lloyd George to state that:

> He himself had tried to find out what the feelings of the Kurds were. After inquiries in Constantinople, Baghdad and elsewhere, he had found it impossible to discover any representative Kurd. No Kurd appeared to represent anything more than his own particular clan ...On the other hand, it would seem that the Kurds felt that they could not maintain their existence without the backing of a great Power ...[242]

The Turks, however, exploited the disunity and rivalry between different Kurdish factions. Mustafa Kemal had initiated contact with the Kurdish chiefs between 1919 and 1921 in whom the latter found more confidence than in the nationalist organizations which had pinned their faith on

---

[240] Ibid., p. 49-50.
[241] Ibid., p.50.
[242] Helmriech, (1979), p. 301.

the Allied assistance. According to certain chiefs, the Allies were protectors of the Armenians not the Kurds, a belief that they conveyed by a series of telegrams to the Peace Conference, rejecting any separation from the Turks. Thus, the Kurdish delegation's demand for independence at the Peace Conference was undermined. [243]

It is worth noting that during the Peace Conference in Paris, the announcement of Wilson's principle of self-determination had influenced the members of the Kurdish club in that they radicalized their nationalist demands and attitudes. The chief objective of the club was originally to cooperate with the Turkish forces against the British and the Armenians, but owing to the international development and their embracement of Wilson's ideas they sharpened their tone toward the Turks. Major Noel describes with "sarcasm and evident distaste" the impact of Wilson's idea on the Kurds:

> The tantalizing version of President Wilson's doctrine that everybody should do as he liked, has slowly dawned on their horizon with all its alluring possibilities, and erstwhile Turco-Kurds are convinced that if they should loud enough, President Wilson will hear them and allow them to mismanage Diyarbakir themselves....[244]

---

[243] Van Bruinessen (1992), p. 279.
[244] Quoted in Jwaideh, (2006), p. 137.

7

Great Powers' Interests in the Region: From Preservation to Partition of the Ottoman Empire

The objective of the European great powers of the nineteenth century such as Britain, France, Russia and the Austrian Empire was the preservation of the Ottoman Empire. It was significant particularly for Britain and France, who regarded the Ottoman Empire as a buffer against the advance of Russia in the Near Middle East. In the Crimean War (1853-1856), Britain and France fought against Russia to prevent it from gaining power and territories at the expense of the Ottoman Empire. According to the Treaty of Paris, the great powers concluded the war and agreed that henceforth the Sublime Porte would be "admitted to participate in the advantages of the public law and system (concert) of Europe." [245]Likewise, the objective of the Mediterranean Agreement of 1887, signed by Britain, Austria and Italy and backed by Germany, was to halt the expansion of Russia in the Balkans and thwart its attempt to control the straits. However, due to the formation of the Franco-Russian Entente, through which Russia's fleet could receive assistance from France, Britain diminished its naval strength in the eastern

---

[245]A.L. Macfie, *The End of the Ottoman Empire* (1908-1923) (London: Longman, 1989), p. 98.
Britain and France intervened in other occasions to protect the integrity of the Ottoman Empire, such as during the Eastern Crises of 1876-8, when Russian according to the Treaty of San Stefano (1878) envisaged creation of greater Bulgaria, and again in the Treaty of Berlin 1878, Britain and France compelled the Russians to abandon their idea to create a greater Bulgaria. Ibid. P. 98.

Mediteranean. This change in Britain's posision did not imply that Britainhad abandoned the old policy of the preservation of Ottoman's integrity. Rather their attention was now directed toward more significant alternative positions, namely conquering Egypt and controlling the Suez Canal and the valley rivers in Mesopotamia.[246]

Russia's interests in the straits were paramount. Nearly one-third of Russia's trade, one-half of exports and four-fifth of grain passed through the straits in the early twentieth century. Also, one-third of its population and a great part of its economic resources lay around the Black Sea. On several occasions, the importance of the straits induced Russia to reach an understanding with other major European powers to develop the system of the straits to its advantage; either by discussion or by *coup de main,* but it was in vain. However, France, due to its loyalty to the Entente rather than to any support of Russia's policy in the Near East was prepared to meet Russia's aspirations. France was still advocating the old policy of Ottoman integrity, because of financial and political reasons. It held two-thirds of the Ottoman's Public Dept, and also concentrated on the Rhine and the Near East, even if they were rather insignificant. Despite France's financial and cultural interests in Syria and its desire to develop economic opportunities in northern Anatolia, these interests were not a crucial element in producing French policy.[247]

However, Germany's military, political and economic expansion in the Ottoman Empire gave angst to France, as it was concerned about the potential effects that the new Baghdad Railway construction would have on their interests in northern Syria and Anatolia. After failing to prevent the project, or persuading the Germans for an equal participation in the scheme, they sought to cooperate with the Russians and the British for the internationalization of it. Unable to resist the support of French financial interests of the project, the French government was forced to reach an

---

[246] M.E. Yapp, *The Making of the Modern Near East 1792-1923* (London: Longman, 1978), p.88.

[247] Ibid., pp.88-89 See also idem, *The Near East Since the First World War: A History to 1995* (London: Longman, 1997), pp.1947-1967.

agreement with Germany in 1914, accommodating their wishes to control the railway, in return for which Germany would accept a French sphere of interest in Syria and Anatolia.[248]

As for Britain, Germany's entry and influence in the Ottoman Empire constituted a greater threat than Russia to those areas it considered spheres of interest. Although Great Britain did not oppose Germany's early interests in the Ottoman Empire, the concession of building a railroad, which was granted to them by Abdul Hamid in 1899, was perceived as a counteraction against the Russian and French endeavors in those areas. However, for Great Britain:

> The phenomenal expansion of Germany's industries and her overseas comers, the penetration of markets hitherto regarded as British's own, the sudden growth of Germany's mercantile marine, her Navy bills of 1899 and 1900, the colonial demands and aspirations of German diplomatists, the noisy anti-British demonstrations at the time of the Boer War,... , led the English public, stimulated by the Press, to believe that not only Great Britain's markets but also her political prestige in the East and in Africa were being seriously challenged.[249]

In addition, Germany's economic, political and military influence in the Ottoman Empire was bolstered by ideological support and direction. Alois Sprenger's book, *Babylon-The Richest Land in Ancient Times,* proposes a colonization of Asia Minor by the Germans. In 1892, Carl Kaeger published a book entitled *Asia Minor, a Field for German Colonisation,* in which he suggests economic exploration of the area, and the Pan-German League published, *Germany's Claim to the Turkish Inheritance.*

---

[248]Macfie, (1989), pp.110-111 French interests in Iraq was exclusively cultural.The French Consul in Baghdad was fully engaged with the dispute between Catholic and Nestorian in northern Iraq, and with the excavation work that started in 1903. See Longrigg, Stephen Hemseley, *Iraq, 1900 to 1950: A political, Social, and Economical History* (London: Oxford University press, 1953), p. 67.

[249] PhilipWillard Ireland, *Iraq: A Study in Political Development* (London, 1937), p.51. About Germany's economic and political interests in the Middle East see also W.O. Henderson, *German Economic Penetration in the Middle East, 1870-1914,* The Economic History Review, Vol. 18, No. ½ (1948), pp. 54-64.

The chief ambition for Great Britain was to counterbalance the increasing German influence and threat to its vital interests and prevent Germany from further penetration in the areas considered spheres of influence. With this aim in mind, Britain initiated diplomatic activities with other major powers to curb Germany's "Drang Nach Osten."[251] Finally, in June 1914, an Anglo-German Convention was inaugurated and signed in August, according to which the latter could, without Britain's opposition, pursue the construction of the Baghdad Railway with its terminal in Basra, and preserve its own special spheres of influence in Anatolia, North Syria and northern Mesopotamia, in return for which Britain's dominant position in southern Mesopotamia and in the Persian Gulf was recognized. The German government agreed as well that the Turkish oil-field be controlled by a British company and that southern Mesopotamia and southern Persia solely be under the control of the Anglo-Persian Company.[252] Despite this agreement, Britain did not abandon its interest in Mesopotamian navigation and irrigation, and paid special attention to the oilfields of the Mosul and Baghdad *Wilayats*. The Mesopotamian oil became prominent as the Admiralty Commission experts realized the significance of oil for fueling. Thus Britain was regarding any attempt from Germany to expand

---

[250] Macfie, (1989), p. 100.

[251] Ireland, (1937), p. 58.

[252] Longrigg, (1953), p. 60. From 1900, the Germans considered Iraq as part of their area of eastern expansion. They had initiated early archaeological and excavation work there. They established a German school in Baghdad, and in 1905, appointed a regular Consul there with his Vice-Consul at Basra. In the German-dominated quarter of the town they had established a Consulate, a railway station, and a Customs house. Longrigg claims that Iraq "in fact, seemed destined to afford a stage for full German penetration" p. 66. On the
rivalry between Great Britain and Germany in Mesopotamia See also Cohen Stuart, *British policy in Mesopotamia, 1903-1914* (Ithaca Press, 228), and Edward Mead Earle, *Turkey, the Great Powers and the Baghdad Railway: A Study in Imperialism* (New York, 1923), pp.314-336.See also Henry U.Hoepli, *England im Nahen Osten: Das Königreich Iraq und die Mossulfrage* (Erlangen,1931), pp.26-29.

its influence in that region with anxiety. Sir Nicolson O'Connor, British Ambassador at Constantinople, argued that the Germans already controlled the Baghdad Railway, and endeavored to control river navigation too; "if they also get the oil concession in Mesopotamia and Persia they cannot fail to acquire enormous political influence to India."[253]

On the eve of the First World War Great Britain's strategic interests had to be safeguarded by the preservation of its supremacy in the area of the Persian Gulf to defend India and in the Nile Valley to defend Egypt and the Suez Canal, which was the main route to its Empire in the east. The defense of its interests in Europe, the Near East and the Middle East as well as in the world necessitated the protection of the straits, which were threatened by the presence of Germany and Russia. [254] In addition, Great Britain had significant financial and commercial interests in the Ottoman Empire. It possessed about 15 percent of the Ottoman Public Debt, and 14 percent of the investment in private enterprise. In Mesopotamia and in the Persian Gulf, Great Britain also was allotted worthwhile oil concessions; two thirds of the import-export trade was under its control. Britain also controlled several important industries and institutions such as the Izmir-Aydin railway, the National Bank of Turkey, the Euphrates and Tigris Steam Navigation Company and the Constantinople Telephone Company, were controlled by Great Britain.[255]

Consequently, during the years leading up to the First World War, the preservation of the Ottoman Empire on the whole continued to be a leading foreign policy objective for the British as well as for the French. Simultaneously, Great Britain's concern was that the Ottoman Empire, in case of an outbreak of a war between the great powers in Europe, would enter the war on the side of the Central Powers. Britain feared that the Ottoman Empire, which was supported and equipped by Germany and led by German officers, would strike Britain's position in Egypt and the

---

[253] Joseph Heller, *British Policy Towards the Ottoman Empire, 1908-1914* (London: Cass,1983), pp.90-91.

[254] Macfie, (1989), p.

[255] Ibid., pp-12-113.

Persian Gulf. Britain was also anxious about possible insurrections among the Muslim peoples of Egypt, Afghanistan and the Indian sub-continent instigated by secret agents and backed by a pan-Islamic propaganda campaign. This would enable the Central Powers to control the straits, and hamper the main supply line between the western Entente Powers, Britain and France, with Russia.[256] In conjunction with other powers of the Entente, Britain attempted to persuade the Ottomans to remain neutral in the war. Whilst the negotiation with the Turks went on, Sir Edward Grey, the British Foreign Secretary, dispatched a letter on August 15 to Sir Francis Bertie, the British ambassador in Paris:

> If she [Turkey] decided to side with Germany, of course there was no help for it; but we out no to anticipate this…. The proper course was to make Turkey feel that, should be remained neutral, and should Germany and Austria be defeated, we would take care that the integrity of Turkish possessions as they now were would be preserved in any terms of peace affecting the Near East; but that, on the other hand, if Turkey sided with Germany and Austria and they were defeated, of course we could not answer for what might be taken from Turkey in Asia Minor. [257]

The efforts of Great Britain and France to prevent the Turks from participating in the war on the side of the Central Powers were in vain. The Ottomans feared that if the Entente won the war, Russia would occupy Ottoman territory, with the opportunity offered by the Allies in view, and possibly the straits.[258]

---

[256] bid., p. 113

[257] Ibid., p. 123

[258] Ibid., pp.123-124. For centuries, Britain had maintained the 'Ancient Rule of the Strait' which prevented any ships of war from foreign powers from entering the straits of the Dardanelles and the Bosporus. However, in 1914, Turkey broke this rule by permitting the German battle-cruisers *Goober* and *Breslau* to enter the Dardanelles. The closure of the Straits to Allied shipping during the war, according to Lloyd George's estimation, contributed to the extension of the war for two additional years and to the collapse of Russia. Thus, to the British the opening of the Straits after the war was the most important achievement against the Ottoman Empire. See, A.E.Motgomery, *The Making of the Treaty of Secret of 10 August 1920*, The historical Journal, Vol. 15, No. 4. (1972), p.780.

However, the entry of the Ottoman Empire into the war in alliance with the Central Powers was believed to be forced by Germany, who due to its supreme position in the Ottoman Empire could persuade the leaders of the Ottoman Empire to embrace a policy that was not in its favor in the long term. At the same time, within the context of great power adversaries, Britain was compelled to revaluate the nature and direction of its traditional policy toward the Ottomans owing to advancing Russia in Asia, which threatened to close the straits, in case Britain declared war against it, and to the emergence of Germany as a major power in Europe. [259]

Decades before the outbreak of the First World War, Great Britain's foreign policy toward the Ottoman Empire convinced many historians to derive the conclusion that Great Britain did not fully support the principle of the integrity of the Ottoman Empire. It has been claimed that during the Crimean War, Great Britain, according to Lord Salisbury, simply "backed the wrong horse", when they continued resolutely to give their support for the principle. In addition, the unsuccessful implementation of the reform program connected with the Tanzimat, and the insolvency of the Ottoman state coupled with the terrible massacres of the Bulgarians and the Armenians, seriously impaired the support for the empire. Consequently, British public opinion was inclined to accept a policy of ignorance, or as William Gladstone, the Liberal Prime Minister had labeled, "a bag and baggage" policy vis-à-vis the Ottomans.[260]

The yearning for independence among the nationalities of the Ottoman Empire made the preservation of the integrity of the empire impossible. Greece was the first country that seceded from the Ottoman Empire and obtained its independence. Then, in 1878, a major breach occurred when Serbia, Montenegro and Romania became independent, followed by the independence of Bulgaria in 1908.

Thereafter, as Yapp states:

the integrity of the Ottoman Empire was no longer a question; the Ottoman

---

[259] Macfie, (1989), p. 118.
[260] Ibid., p. 114.

Empire was merely a convenience for delaying a solution to the intractable problem of Macedonia, an almost indispensable device for preventing a major conflict over control of the Strait, and a still valuable element for the disposition of the territories of western Asia, an empire whose existence yet prevented a struggle for preponderance within those Asian territories which could threaten a European war.[261]

The idea of any dismantling of the Ottoman territories in the near future led the leadership of Great Britain's foreign policy to envisage a plan for protecting their predominant interests and prestige in the Empire, particularly in Mesopotamia where they had a greater claim in regards to spheres of influence. The telegram that the Resident of Baghdad dispatched, on Jun 23rd 1913, to the Government of India and H.M Ambassador at Constantinople demonstrates this preoccupation:

> In view of the possible break-up of Turkey and in the meantime the development of preparatory foreign sphere of interest, it seemed incumbent on the British Government to preserve every kind of priority which they already possessed in Mesopotamia, their natural sphere in the Ottoman dominions. Hence, the abolition of the British Post Offices in Turkey should not extend to those at Baghdad and Basra...[262]

The following month, the Acting Resident in Baghdad presented an elaborate plan for developing Great Britain's position according to which the extension of the irrigation system had to be put under British aegis and with this end goal "to gain control of this system and create an *imperium imperio*...[263] The importance of controlling the water was not confined to control of revenue assessment or collection; for the British it had geopolitical significance. As early as 1860, the brothers Lynch established "The Euphrates and Tigris Steam Navigation Company", and from this time on the Lynch Company possessed, besides the Turkish National Society,

---

[261] M.E.Yapp, (1978), p. 91.

[262] *Reports on Events in Turkish 'Iraq*, June, 1913. Quoted in Ireland, (1937), p. 57.

[263] Ibid., p. 57.

which was established in 1867, the monopoly rights for navigation in Mesopotamia. [264] In 1909, another monopoly term for the navigation in the Mesopotamian water route was concluded. A year earlier, Lloyd George had, in a letter dispatched to Lynch Brothers Shipping Line, underscored the importance of navigation for Britain's imperial enterprise:

> I venture to submit that any weakening of our present position on the Tigris means not only a weakening our whole position in Mesopotamia, but a corresponding increase of German trade and activity... I suggest also that, in view of the river being one of the important lines of communication to Persian Gulf and India, it was wise to be careful that it should in no way fall from our grasp, and our privileged position on the river was now becoming daily more valuable, in view of the approach of the Baghdad Railway, and in view of the fact that navigation may probably be at Baghdad to Bussorah. [265]

The river valleys were strategically placed, and therefore vital to secure external trade as British monopoly and influence. The British politicians regarded them as a commercial, political and geographical extension of the Persian Gulf, and according to Lord Curzon their significance "involved the security, integrity and safety of India itself." [266] In 1892, he had also confirmed, "Baghdad, in fine, falls under the category of the Gulf Port, and must be included in the zone of indisputable British supremacy." [267] This argument was deepened as he stated in 1911, in the House of Lords:

> It would be a mistake to suppose that our political interests are confined to the Gulf. They are not confined to the Gulf; they are not confined to the region between Basra and Baghdad; they extend right away up to Baghdad. [268]

From Great Britain's view, Mesopotamia had the same strategic importance as the Gulf and any change in its *status quo* was regarded as a

---

[264] Ibrahim, (1983), p. 250.
[265] Quoted in ibid., p. 252.
[266] Ireland, (1937), p. 49.
[267] Ibid.
[268] Quoted in ibid., p. 49.

change in the Persian Gulf itself. This inspired H.M. Government for realization of early trans-Mesopotamian schemes of communication.[269]

Safeguarding the supremacy of Great Britain in Mesopotamia and the Persian Gulf was central to deter the German threat to its interests and prestige as its rival in the region and also to protect the route to India.

The Significance of Iraq and its Oil in Great Britain's Middle Eastern Policy

Another factor of great importance which appeared prior to 1914 was the oilfield of South West Persia and the abundance of oil resource found in the Ottoman Empire. This included the Transferred Territories. The enormous oil bulk in South West of Persia had been established since 1907, and the British started a process to increase their shareholding in the Anglo-Persian Oil Company in 1914, to secure a constant supply for the Royal Navy. When the Ottoman Empire participated in the war as an ally with the Central Powers, Britain feared that the Ottomans, who were backed by the Germans, would prevent trade and communication with India, and would threaten the Persian oilfield as well.[270]

By the autumn of 1914, the Anglo-Persian Oil Company produced and exported 25,000 tons of petroleum products per month from Abadan, which was an essential military and imperial asset.[271] On October 2 , the Foreign secretary in India, who had served 12 years in the Gulf, Sir Percy

---

[269] Ibid, Great Britain's early interests in communication with India, was profitable. The expedition sent out from 1834, combined with the presence of armed steamers on the Tigris, facilitated in the establishment of British mercantile lines on the Tigris.This considerably contributed to the predominant position and influence that Great Britain exerted in Turkish Arabia. Between 1911 to 1912, the average imports through Basra and Baghdad, for each of the two years, was 3,100,000, pounds, of which the greater bulk were British and Indian goods intended for re-export to Persia through Kermanshah. The average export by the sea for the same year was 3, 247, 500 pounds. Ireland, Ibid., pp.47-48.

[270] Peter, Sluglett, *Britain in Iraq: Contriving King and Country*,(London, 2007), pp.3-4.

[271] Stephen Hemsley Longrigg, *Oil in the Middle East, its Discovery and Development* (London, New York: Oxford University Press, 1968), p. 34.

Cox, the chief political officer in Mesopotamia, decided to dispatch an Expeditionary Force, whose "mission would be to protect the Abadan oil installations, cover the potential landing of reinforcements, and reassure the Arab potentates."[272] When the Indian Expeditionary Force "D" entered Basra, on November 22, 1914, it marked the beginning of the occupation of Iraq.[273]

During the years immediately before the outbreak of the First World War, Great Britain's chief objective was, thus, to consolidate its position as a prevailing European power in the region and enter into a new phase of its colonial enterprise in the Middle East and particularly in Iraq, which was now realized by the conquest of Basra.

Despite the conclusion of the Sykes-Picot agreement in 1916, access to the potential oil wealth of Mesopotamia was of great importance for the British government, and remained so during the course of the war. Soon after the agreement had been signed, the War Committee discussed Britain's interests in the Middle East. At a meeting of the committee on July 6, 1916, Sykes emphasized the great strategic importance of the Middle East for Britain, and stressed "The great value of the immense oil areas to whoever should possess them."[274]Such an opinion was expressed in strong terms by Rear-Admiral Sir Edmond J.W. Slade who headed the Admiralty. In a Cabinet memorandum of October 31, 1916, he eagerly advocated se-

---

[272] Longrigg, (1953), pp.77- 78. However, S.A. Cohen argues that the motives which incited the despatch of the Indian Expeditionary Force (IEFD) were less strategic; to safeguard Great Britain's oil supply of the Abadan stores and Persian oil fields at the Gulf. The primary objective of the Force was to "conciliate the Arbs". The British wanted to create a friendly impression among the Arabs, hoping that in case of outbreak of war, the latter be used as a means against their Ottomans masters. British consular and diplomatic
officials had, over a long time, observed the scope of the anti-Turkish feelings of the Arabs of Mesopotamia. See S.A.Cohen,*The Genesis of the British Campaign in Mesopotamia,* Middle East Studies. Vol. 12, No. 2, (May, 1976) 1914. pp. 119-132.

[273] Ibid.

[274] Maria Kent, *Oil and Empire: British Policy and Mesopotamian Oil 1900-1920* (The Macmillan Press LTD,1976), p. 124.

curing control of all oil rights in Mesopotamia, Kuwait, Bahrain and Arabia. As the question of defining war aims was under consideration near the end of the war, Slade evolved his ideas in a lengthy paper, entitled "The Petroleum Situation in the British Empire," which he dispatched to the Admiralty on July 29, 1918. His conclusion of the British oil situation was that "It is evident that the power that controls the oil lands of Persia and Mesopotamia will control the course of supply of the majority of the liquid fuel of the future..." Britain must therefore "at all cost retain [her] hold on the Persian and Mesopotamian oilfields." [275]

Against this background the control of the Mosul *Wilayat* became a priority in British policy in Mesopotamia. Although the meeting of the war cabinet was held to consider the question of war aims and the reorganization of the Sykes-Picot agreement with France, it did not specifically discuss the subject of oil, but subsequent negotiations with France left no doubt that the possession of Mosul was a core objective in Britain's imperial calculations.[276]

Oil factors were introduced into top level discussions of war aims by Maurice Henkey, the British Cabinet Secretary. In August 1918, he wrote to Balfour, on the subject of oil in Mesopotamia, before the meeting of the second Imperial War Cabinet at which British ministers were to discuss war aims with their colleagues from the Dominions:

> As I understand the matter, oil in the next war will occupy the place of coal in the present war, or at least a parallel place to coal. The only big potential supply that we can get under British control is the control is the Persian and Mesopotamian supply. The point where you come in is that the control over these oil supplies becomes a first-class war aims. I write to urge that in your statement to the Imperial War Cabinet you should rub this in. You will do it much better than the Admiral will and as an ex-First Lord you have a greater interest in it that most. Admiral Slade tells me that there are important oil deposits in Mesopotamia north of our present line. I have asked him to let the War Cabinet have any evidenced as to the real importance of these deposits as they

---

[275] Ibid., p.125.
[276] Ibid., p.127.

might have an important influence on our military operations...[277]

Balfour shared Henley's view in principle that Mesopotamia could supply the British Empire with oil, a natural resource that it had a shortage of. [278] Balfour asserted "I do not care under what system we keep the oil, whether it is by a perpetual lease or whatever it may be, but I am quite clear it is all-important for us that this oil should be available." Lloyd George for his part favored a military occupation of Mosul *Wilayat* before the end of the war.[279]

Even after the war, securing future oil supplies was an economic objective that Great Britain desired in its post-war negotiations with France over the Middle East. Britain's negotiators, Kent points out, "Were determined to gain for their country *de jure* sanction for their *de facto* military occupation of Mosul as an integral part of the new Iraqi state."[280]

---

[277] Quoted in V. H. Rothwell, *Mesopotamia in British War Aims, 1914-1918,* (1970), The Historical Journal. Vol.13, No.2, p, 289.

[278] During the war, the British policy-makers realized that Britain was almost entirely dependent on foreign oil. The rate of consumption for oil increased from 2.5 to 6.5 million tons as petroleum became important in ammunition production, the army motorized faster, and the navy converted increasing amount of ships to diesel. Britain's dependence on supplies from the United States also increased considerably, from 62.3 percent imported before the war to 77 percent in September 1918. The imports from APOC's Persian oilfield were only 7 percent. Thus, the British officials were profoundly anxious in case these supplies were suspended, particularly after May 1917 as it appeared that the Royal Navy might be out of oil. Similarly, during the war, the shortage of oil caused the French policy-makers to very much appreciate the strategic importance of oil. By July 1917 French oil consumption increased to 50,000 tons a month, whereas imports only totaled 30,000 tons. This critical situation reached a peak in December, when Clemenceau in a note to President Wilson asked for more supplies. As a matter of fact, by September 1918, France's import of oil from the United States was more than 90 percent. See Luigi Scazzieri (2015) *Britain, France, and Mesopotamian oil, 1916-1920*, Diplomacy and Statecraft, 26:1, 25-45, DOI: 10.1080/09592296.2015.999623. p. 26.

[279] Ibid., p. 290.

[280] Maria Kent, *Great Britain and the End of the Ottoman Empire 1900-1923*. In Maria Kent (ed.) *The Great Powers and the End of the Ottoman Empire*, (London: George Allen and Unwin, 1984), p. 191.

Great Britain's Occupation of Iraq: Direct or Indirect Rule

After the occupation of Baghdad in March 1917, Britain had no clear-cut policy regarding the future of Iraq. Serious contradictory standpoints and uncertainty existed between various British offices of states such as the Indian Office and Foreign Office, and the key politicians on the spot, London and Delhi, which hindered taking any decision concerning the administration of Mesopotamia. The fundamental questions that were pondered were: should they annex Mesopotamia, and if so, parts or the whole of it? Also, should they deal with the three *Wilayats* of Baghdad, Mosul and Basra separately or be regarded as a single unit under British control? should it be ruled directly or indirectly? and should Mesopotamia be ruled by the indigenous or by foreign rulers? The Foreign Office continued to regard all proposals that pertained to the future administration of Iraq with "*non possumus* attitudes."[281]

When the first instruction came in March 1917, it indicated a continuation of *ad-hoc* practices of Britain's administration on the spot. The British government decided that Basra *Wilayat* would be permanently put under British auspices and Baghdad should be an Arab state with a local ruler or government under British protection. In May 1917, a committee of the Imperial War Cabinet issued a report formulated by George Curzon on the British war aims, which further determined this policy when it declared to retain both Palestine and Mesopotamia after the war. [282]

However, during 1918, British imperial policy was compelled to change owing to the emergence of new international diplomacy that sought to contrive a contrast to traditional European diplomacy of annexation and balance of power and also to provide the peoples of the previous Ottoman Empire some form of self-determination. Events of great importance that made themselves felt in the Middle East and Iraq were; the British Prime Minister's Declaration of January 5th, regarding the non-annexation of the Turkish areas of the Ottoman Empire, and the publication of Wilson's

---

[281] Charles Townshend, *When God Made Hell: The British Invasion of Mesopotamia and the Creation of Iraq 1914*-1921, (London, 2010), p. 445.
[282] Toby Dodge, (2003), p. 10.

fourteen points on October 11th, in Iraq, [283]followed by the Anglo-French Declaration, which was simultaneously released in London, Paris, Washington and Cairo on November 7th and published in Iraq on November 8th. It stipulated that the victorious powers would refrain from provoking non-Turkish nationalities into hostile actions against the Ottomans and that France and Great Britain were "at one in encouraging and assisting the establishment of indigenous Governments and administrations in Syria and Mesopotamia ... and recognizing these as soon as they are established."[284]

For the British colonial administration, Wilson's fourteen points were to be under particular considerations since the:

> Long established and hitherto almost unchallenged assumptions of British imperial policy had to be reconciled with a whole set of new requirements. In Iraq, it was necessary to adapt the existing machinery, derived from Indian administration models, to a new and less direct form of control, which was both unfamiliar and unpalatable to many of those called upon to operate it.[285]

For those on the ground, in India and Mesopotamia, adjustment to new political premises was perceived as inconsistent with the traditional aims of Great Britain's policy in the Middle East.

One of the leading decision makers in Iraq was A.T. Wilson, who served in India, Persia and the Persian Gulf. He became Acting Civil Commissioner in Mesopotamia between September 1918 and June 1920, replacing Sir Percy Cox when he was appointed Acting Minister in Teheran. Wilson withheld the publication of President Wilson's fourteen points until October 11 because he and local official circles perceived it to be too idealistic to constitute the basis of official policy. However, its publication had "thrown the whole of town (of Baghdad) into ferment."

---

[283] The announcement of President Wilson's fourteen points which he in a speech delivered to congress on January 8 1918, was withheld in Iraq by authorities until October 11 the same year.

[284] Bruce Westrate, *The Arab Bureau: British Policy in the Middle East*, 1916-1920 (Pennsylvania, 1992), p. 167.

[285] Sluglett, (2007), p. 13.

[286]In his opinion, Great Britain's interests in the Middle East were paramount and he thought that relinquishing Iraq to an indigenous administration would undermine these interests. He dispatched a telegram, on December 10th, 1918, as a reaction to the Anglo-French Declaration. In it he underlines the importance of Iraq in the British Middle Eastern policy:

> My view is that the strategical canters of the Middle East lie in Baghdad and the Caucasus, in both of which the Muhammadan population greatly predominates. ... By occupying Mesopotamia during the war we drove a wedge into Muhammadan World, thereby preventing the possibility of a combination of Muhammadans against us in the Middle East. I submit that it should be our policy under peace condition to keep Mesopotamia as a wedge of British Controlled Territory.[287]

The telegram also indicates what kind of administration he intended to set up for Iraq. One, which he believed to serve the interests of Great Britain and the Iraqis. He also sought to treat Mesopotamia independently from the rest of the Arabs. In his opinion the Arabs of Mesopotamia would reject any involvement of foreign Arabs in their state of affairs, whether it was the Arabs of Syria or of Hijaz. Wilson believed national unity for them was "unity of Mesopotamia, and not unity with either Syria or Hijaz. So, too, they resent the importation of social or administrative institutions or methods that savor of India."[288]

He considered that the Arabs of Iraq realized it was in their best interest and would cultivate their national unity if they were governed by the British because:

> The average Arab, as opposed to the handful of amateur politicians of Baghdad, sees the future as one of the faire dealing and material and moral progress under the aegis of Great Britain, and is clear-sighted enough to realize that he would lose rather than gain national unity if we were to relinquish effective

---

[286] Ireland, (1937), p. 156.
[287] Wilson, (1931), p. 104
[288] Ibid.

control.

In compliance with Cox wishes, he concluded "I submit, therefore, that our best course is to declare Mesopotamia to be a British Protectorate....[289]

In November 1918, London sough the assistance of Wilson to find a fitting candidate to rule Mesopotamia. He suggested public opinion should be consulted for electing a candidate. Among the candidates, he suggested the son of the Sharif who he believed to be accommodated with "widespread acceptance." Wilson personally preferred Cox as a suitable head of an Arab state with no Arab Emir, an idea which was embraced by Gertrude Bell, his oriental secretary. In a letter to London she claimed that "on two points they (the Iraqis) are practically all agreed; they want us to control their affaires and they want Sir Percy as Commissioner." [290]

The convenient solution for London was election by a "plebiscite", and in an instruction sent to Baghdad some days later opposing Wilson's standpoint in that they restated the policy inherent in the Anglo-French Declaration, it was emphasized as a matter of fact that there would be a more elaborate settlement to wait from the Peace Conference:[291]

> ...It will be understood by all that the Peace Conference will settle the ultimate status of all Arab provinces... It is laid down meanwhile in the Declaration that His Majesty's Government will as part of their policy assist in the establishment of native government in the liberate areas, and do not intend to impose on the population any governments which are distasteful to them. We desire to see the strongest and most settled government in Mesopotamia which is compatible with those two conditions, and to further this end we are prepared to render all British assistance that is necessary, including an army of occupation. [292]

Wilson became isolated as Gertrude Bell distanced herself from his attitudes and approached the policy of London. She was initially in favor of direct rule and her cooperation with Wilson was harmonious. As Wilson's

---

[289] Ibid., p. 105.
[290] Quoted in Sluglett, (2007), p. 24.
[291] Ibid.
[292] Wilson, (1931), p. 111.

representative she attended the Paris Peace Conference to present a *Memorandum* on *self-Determination in Mesopotamia*, approved by Wilson who also later arrived at the Conference. The Memorandum was of great importance; it was the result of referendum that took place in different parts of Iraq, according to which the majority of the Iraqis desired the continuation of British rule and in case an Arab Emir was designated to the throne of Iraq he should be under British protection. [293] During this time, Arab nationalists were strongly inspired by the Wilsonian idea of self-determination and were engaged in anti-British activities for Iraq's independence. [294] Contrary to Wilson, Gertrude Bill was more realistic and saw the growing national sentiments among the Arabs and paid considerable attention to them. She enthusiastically supported self-government for Iraq under British tutelage. Consequently, she persisted that the British government should cooperate largely with the urban and Sunni nationalists to modernize the country and counteract, "the reactionary and obscurantist influence of the shi'i clerics and their tribal followers." [295]

The Plebiscite of 1919: Preparation for the Making of Iraq

As has been noted, one of the supreme principles that dominated the post World War 1 period was the principle of self-determination. In Iraq, the British seemed inclined to adapt this principle, albeit not in the true sense of it. In the plebiscite conducted in 1919, the British government sought to utilize this principle as an instrument to manipulate the public opinion in order to reach its foremost objective- to unite the three provinces of Baghdad, Basra and Mosul to a single unity.

As Acting Civil Commissioner, Wilson was the man who with the approval of the foreign office, was in charge to carry out the plebiscite. He

---

[293] Sluglett, (2007), p. 27.

[294] Ahmad Rafiq al-Barghawi, *Al-Ilaqat al-Syiasyiah Bain al-Iraq wa Baritania 1922-1932*, (The political Relations between Iraq and Britain,1922-1932), (Dar al-Rashid, 1980), p.18.

[295] Tripp, (2000), p. 39.

spelt out his idea in a telegraph that an Arab state, including Basra, Baghdad and Mosul under an Arab Emir was considered as ideal by all. [296] The position of Mosul in a future Iraqi state was fundamental for Wilson; it constituted a vocal point in his arranged plebiscite. Excluding Iraq from any contemplated Sharifian settlement, he suggested four candidates for the throne of Iraq, of whom Hadi Pasha al-Umari was the most eligible one on the grounds that he "would be especially welcomed in Mosul, from which his family originally came." [297] The fourth candidate put forward was not convincing. Abdul Rahman-al Gilani, a respected religious dignitary and Naqib of Baghdad, was, beside his failing health and great age, not known in Basra and Mosul. His election would hence be detrimental in case Mosul and Kurdistan were included in the Iraqi state.[298]

Wilson received an instruction from the Indian Office on October 30 which coincided generally with his attitudes toward the establishment of an Iraqi state. He was authorized to carry out a plebiscite in order to obtain the expression of the public opinion:

We are in anxious in particularly that you should render us an authoritative statement of the views held by the local population in the various areas affected on the following specific points:

1 Do they favor a single Arab state under British tutelage stretching from the Northern boundary of the Mosul Wilayat to the Persian Gulf?

2 In this event, do they consider that a titular Arab head should be placed over this new State?

3 In this case, whom would they prefer as head?

In our opinion it is of great importance to get a genuine expression of local opinion on these points, and one of such a kind that could be announced to the

---

[296] Ireland, (1937), p. 158.

[297] Ibid. The other candidates were one of the sons of Sharif of Mecca who he believed would be met with widespread acceptance. However, he was "strongly" against him because of politics that connected him with Persian Gulf and Central Arabia. Another one was a member of family of sultan of Egypt. Ibid., p. 159.

[298] Ibid., p. 159.

world as the unbiased pronouncement of the population of Mesopotamia.[299]

According to the British in charge of the plebiscite, "those consulted were unanimous in saying that they wished to belong to State consisting of three Wilayets [provinces],[300] and "the whole country was agreed that, whatever form the government might be set up in Iraq (as to which there was a wide divergence of opinion), Mosul should not be separated from the remainder of Iraq."[301] However the credibility of the plebiscite was highly questioned since the petitions the British collected, numbered twelve and signed by 342 notables from Mosul *Wilayat,* were collected from some districts of Mosul such as Kirkuk, Kifri and Mosul city and excluded the cities Arbil and Sulaimanya. The statistics showed that only two of the 57 signatures of these petitions were Kurds and yazidis who both were against the annexation of Mosul to Iraq. Arabs and Christians who lived in the Mosul city and who wished the annexation of Mosul to Baghdad accounted for the majority of the signatures.[302]

Apparently, the plebiscite was by no means a reflection of an "unbiased pronouncement" of the public opinion in Iraq, but a device through which Wilson obtained the acquiescence of leading local notables and shaikhs in the three provinces. According to the result of the plebiscite, which corresponded with Wilson's opinion, there was a general desire among the population, with the exception of the Kurdish areas, that Mosul should be included in the new state.

---

[299] Wilson, (1931) p. 111. The idea of Plebiscite was not new, it was conducted in 1791-3, whereby Avignon, Savoy, and Nice were annexed to France, and in Italy plebiscite was held several times between 1848 and 1870, and the Schleswig question was settled in 1866 also by plebiscite. The idea was wholly novel to Asia, and the plebiscite which was held in Norway served as a practical guidance to the plebiscite in Mesopotamia. Ibid. p. 111.

[300] "Questionnaire for the British Government with answers" in Air Ministry Files, Public Records Office, 5/389Pts, Quoted in Fuat Dundar, *Statisquo, British Use of Statistics in the Iraq Kurdish Question 1919-1932,* (Brandies University, 2012), p.15.

[301] *The Question of Mosul: Memorandum by the Secretary of State for the Colonies* [Devonshire], Quoted in Dundar, (2012), p. 15.

[302] Ibid.

With regards to the British presence in Iraq, once the plebiscite was held shaikhs and land-owning dignitaries who, according to Wilson were representatives of their illiterate tribesmen and followers for economic benefits expressed their desires for a continuation of British presence through *madhabit* (declarations) submitted to him.[303]

There was no doubt that the British, despite their endorsement of the idea of self-determination, only paid lip service to it; a genuine implementation of the principle would certainly have been incompatible with the policy they wanted to pursue in Iraq, as Dawisha argues:

> The referendum exhibited the contradictions inherent in Britain's policy in Iraq. On the one hand, Britain had expressly committed itself to the notion of self-determination. London had declared more than once, its desire to see Iraqis choose a representative government. Yet the British also well-understood Wilsons's plea for an effective political and security structure in Iraq. And Wilson argued with passion and more than a little justification that such an outcome was possible only under British rule.[304]

However, the discovery of oil in Mosul *Wilayat* to a great extent enhanced its strategic importance and, hence, intensified the struggle for its possession between Turkey and Great Britain, but the province was also considered to be part and parcel of Iraq by King Faisal as he ascended the throne of Iraq 1921, and of course by the Iraqi government and other Arab nationalists as this study in subsequent chapters will show.

According to the above-mentioned plebiscite the attitudes of the Kurds of the Mosul *Wilayat* who at least constituted half of the population, was "strongly" anti-Arab.[305] During late 1918, national awareness had gradually taken firm hold among the Kurds spurring them to act in compliance with the principle of self-determination. By the occupation of the Mosul *Wilayat* by the British troops on October 30, 1918, one week after the

---

[303] Dawisha (2009), p. 45.
[304] Ibid. p. 46.
[305] Wilson, (1931), p. 112.

Mudros Armistice, Kurdish aspiration for self-government proved irreconcilable with the interests and imperial policy of Britain in Iraq. This inevitably sparkled clashes and hostilities between the Kurds on the one hand and the mandatory power, and the Iraqi government on the other hand.

8

The Occupation of Mosul and the Kurdish Question: From Shaikh Mahmud's Revolt to the Lausanne Conference, 1919–1922

During late 1918 there were still no decisions from London about the constitution or the shape and form of the Iraqi state. When the British troops occupied South Kurdistan, these officials sought to introduce a temporary system of government there, which would accommodate the needs and wishes of the Kurds for a Kurdish administration. With this purpose in mind, Wilson dispatched Major Noel to Sulaimanya, after the withdrawal of the Turkish troops from the town, to inform him about the situation there. In the middle of November 1918, Noel, received the following instructions from Wilson:

> You have been appointed Political Officer, Kirkuk Division, with effect from November 1st ... The Kirkuk division extends from the sphere of military occupation and north-east to the Turco-Persian frontier. It forms part of Mosul wilayet, the ultimate disposal of which is under the consideration of H.M.'s Government.

> For the present it must be considered as falling within the sphere of military occupation and administration of the Force, and you should proceed on this assumption in your dealings with local chiefs, bearing in mind that it is improbable that the military authorities will see their way to detach troops permanently to Sulaimani or to other places east of our present line. It should

be your object to arrange with local chiefs for the restoration and maintenance of order in areas outside the limit of our military occupation, for the exclusion and surrender of enemy agents and for the supply of commodities needed by our troops. You are authorized to incur such expenditure as may be necessary to this end, subject to previous authority in case of large sums and on the understanding, which should be made clear to the chiefs, that any arrangements you may make of necessity provisional and subject to reconsideration at any time. You are authorized to appoint Shaikh Mahmud as our representative in Sulaimani, should you consider this expedient, and to make other appointments of this nature at Chanchamal, Halebja, &., at your discretion....

It should be explained to the tribal chiefs with whom you enter into relations that there is no intention of imposing on them an administration foreign to their habits and desires. Tribal leaders will be encouraged to form a confederation for the settlement of their public affairs under the guidance of the British Political Officers. They will be called upon to continue to pay the taxes legally due from them under Turkish law, modified as may be found necessary, for purposes connected with the maintenance of order and the development of their country.[306]

In accordance with this instruction Shaikh Mahmud was appointed *Hukmdar* or Governor of the district, and Kurdish officials were appointed for each of the minor sub-divisions and were guided by British political officers. Native Kurds took over the work of Turkish and Arab officials, whilst Turkish troops and officers were dispatched to Baghdad. Through Shaikh Mahmud, Kurdish chiefs were under the responsibility of the British officials for the government of their own tribes and were recognized and paid as government officials. [307]

Major Noel had thus organized a South Kurdish Confederation headed by Shaikh Mahmud Barzanji. This new system of government was built according to British colonial experience in India. The application of this

---

[306] Ibid.,p. 128.
[307] Ibid.

system implied that local rulers retained their traditional administrative authority and competence to legislate, but they were subjected to British control. Characteristic of this system was, besides being cheap, it required fewer administrators and, in the case of South Kurdistan, less military presence. In other words, the confederation that Noel established in South Kurdistan constituted a local power structure through which the British ruled. This indirect rule system seemed initially to coincide with Kurdish aspirations and with the kind of administration policy the British envisaged in South Kurdistan.

The idea of "Kurdistan for the Kurds" under British protection, Wilson believed, was reaching acceptance, although there existed a divergence of attitudes and expectations among the members of the leading chiefs in Sulaimanya with regards to Britain's position about the Kurdish question and to Shaikh Mahmud. In his visit in Sulaimanya on December 1st, Shaikh Mahmud delivered Wilson an agreed-upon document, signed by some forty chiefs which run as follows:

> His Majesty's Government having announced that their intention to liberate the Eastern peoples from Turkish oppression and to grant assistance to them in the establishment of their independence, the chiefs, as the representatives of the people of Kurdistan, beg Government to accept them also under British protection and to attach them to Iraq so that they may not be deprived of the benefits of that association. They request the Civil Commissioner of Mesopotamia to send them a representative with the necessary assistance to enable the Kurdish people under British auspices to progress peacefully on civilized lines. If Government extends its assistance and protection to them, they undertake to accept its order and advice.[308]

In his meeting with Wilson, Shaikh Mahmud demanded further British officers for all government departments, including officers for Kurdish levies and emphasized that subordinate Arab staffs be replaced by Kurdish ones. In answer to Shaikh Mahmud's document and his demand Wilson handed him a letter stating that:

---

[308] Ibid. P.129.

any Kurdish tribe from the Greater Zab to the Diyala (other than those in Persian Territory), who of their own free will accepted the leadership of Shaikh Mahmud, would be allowed to do so, and that the latter would have our moral support in controlling the above areas on behalf of the British Government, those orders he undertook to obey. [309]

The tribes and townspeople of the Kifri and Kirkuk divisions refused to be under Shaikh Mahmud's authority and preferred instead direct British administration. Shaikh Mahmud did not insist on their inclusion. [310]

Wilson's letter implied his confirmation of Major Noel's previous appointment of Shaikh Mahmud as *Hukmdar* for the South Kurdistan Confederation. This arrangement was confined only to the southern Kurdistan whilst Kurdish tribes in Persia were excluded from this Confederation and British protection; they must remain loyal Persian subjects.[311] An explanation for this exclusion might be that Britain, as noted, had yet no clear administration policy at the time and the Kurdish Confederation was a temporary solution, or in Longrigg's words "a large- scale experiment "[312]in Sulaimanya. The problem of southern Kurdistan in November 1918, Longrigg states, "was that of installing a regime better than anarchy, and harmless to its Persian and Iraqi neighbours, without the use of troops- since none were available."[313]Britain probably also feared that a unification of the Iraqi and Iranian Kurds would strengthen Shaikh Mahmud's power, and thereby lead to undesirable consequences for them. Wilson, in fact, regarded Shaikh Mahmud as his agent who could obtain support from Britain only if his action was in accordance with the provisions embodied in the above letter.

Shaikh Mahmud himself was not satisfied with this arrangement since the Allied declarations had given impetus to his movement and widened his nationalist expectations; "strapped like a talisman to his arm was a

---

[309] Ibid.
[310] Ibid.
[311] Ibid., p. 131.
[312] Longrigg, (1953), p. 103.
[313] Ibid.

Quran on the flyleaves of which was written in Kurdish the text of Wood-row Wilson's twelfth point and the Anglo-French Declaration of 8 Novem-ber."[314] He claimed that he acted in the name of the Kurds and that he had mandate from all the Kurds of Mosul *Wilayat,* and many in Persia and else-where have expressed their aspirations to form a unitary autonomous state led by him under British protection.[315]

Wilson appraised Shaikh Mahmud's idea, which if possible, would greatly simplify the question of forming an Arab State from the rest of the three *Wilayats.* The idea of a scheme for creating an independent Kurdistan under British aegis, as mentioned earlier, was not wholly novel, it had been approached by leading chiefs of the Mukri tribe in the Sauj Bulaq district in Persia and Sharif Pasha, a Kurdish notable resident in Paris. Wilson regarded the latter's scheme as "an intelligent anticipation of the Mandatory system." [316] In October 1918, Sharif Pasha wrote to call attention to the situation that had been more difficult owing to the activity of the Turks in whipping up hatred between Kurds and Armenians, with the aim of eliminating the Armenians and later, depriving the Kurds of any possibility to achieve national autonomy. [317]He maintained, like the Mukri chiefs, that a durable and honorable settlement could only be realized if the Kurds and the Armenians were regarded alike as nationalities with an equal demand to national rights in their respective areas. [318]

Due to the public opinion in the Allied countries and in the United States concerning the horrible massacre of the Armenians by the Turks,

---

[314] Wilson. (1931), p. 139.

[315] Ibid., p. 131.

[316] Ibid., p.130.

[317] Ibid p 131. Wilson points out that in the towns, where the presence of the Chris-tian communities was large, and in numerous Christian villages on and across the Kurdish border, the Turkish influence was still strong and the Armenian question still acute. Beyond the frontier, the Turks were fomenting anti-Christian and anti-British opinions by distributing leaflets in those areas with texts such as "Before long, your ears will be deafened by the sound of the bell- the voice of the mu`zzen will no longer be heard. Christian officials will treat you as did the Russians, and you will have to kiss the feat of Arabs and Chaldeans." Ibid.
[318] Ibid.

Sharif Pasha's suggestion seemed to have sympathetic hearing at the Peace Conference that a solution on these lines would be possible, bearing in mind that one of President Wilson's fourteen points asserts "The Turkish portion of the present Ottoman Empire should be assured a secure sovereignty, but the other nationalities which are now under Turkish rule should be assured... an unmolested opportunity of autonomous development."[319]

However, at the time, the British who were charged with the foundation of an independent southern Kurdish State realized that it was not feasible due to the "undeveloped state of the country, the lack of communications, and the dissensions of the tribes." [320]Besides, the British administrators believed that for geographical and commercial reasons the prosperity of South Kurdistan could only be guaranteed if it constituted an integral part of Mesopotamia. Mosul and Baghdad were the only possible markets and the only communications ran through Mesopotamia. It seemed that an understanding was reached between the British and some "more enlightened Kurdish leaders" that a Kurdish autonomy could be established within the framework of an Arab state provided that it was under British auspices. However, a permanent subordination to an Arab state was unthinkable for the majority of the tribal chiefs.[321]

Whether the aspiration for creation of an independent southern Kurdistan derived from nationalistic ideas or it was the work of some Kurdish leaders who by provoking nationalistic sentiments envisaged to obtain personal gain and advantages were questions that the British had no clear answers to. For them, however, it was clear that the Kurdish national movement in Sulaimanya was certainly strong and therefore had to be coped with.

As far as the British were concerned the Kurdish leaders could obtain help and advice only as long as they complied with the instruction and policy laid down for the Kurdish areas. According to the new system of government that was introduced to the Kurds:

---

[319] Ibid.
[320] Ibid.,p.133.
[321] Ibid.

The personal administration was to be as possible Kurdish; levies were to be organized under Kurdish officers; while the Kurdish tongue was to be the official language of government. Law would be modified to conform with the custom and usage, and the system of revenue collection and taxation devised to meet the needs of the people. Tribal custom law would be allowed to exercise authority over their clansmen as heretofore.[322]

Shaikh Mahmud's First Rebellion

By the time Shaikh Mahmud was appointed as *Hukmdar* a series of circumstances contributed to the consolidation of his power; during the winter of 1917 until 1919 almost famine-like conditions prevailed throughout South Kurdistan; in the North the Penjwin district was demolished by the Russian army, in particular by the act of vengeance of the Christian tribesmen. In addition, Turkish grain requisitions had been on such a scale that seed grain for the 1919 sowing was almost inaccessible. The conditions were so desperate that "the tribesmen were prepared to swear allegiance to anyone in return for substantial subsidies." [323]

The Shaikh was the only predominant religious leader in Sulaimanya with a great influence, which he attempted to expand beyond the region of his authority. The British were aware that he had many followers in South Kurdistan; for one who disagreed with his authority there were four others who desired it. The British, however, soon understood that Shaikh Mahmud's influence could only be usefully exerted in Sulaimanya. The British, then, approached the Shaikh for his support despite the fact that he, in the absence of Captain Noel and of any military garrison in Sulaimanya, had abused his authority and set out to plan a *"coup de'état "* there. [324] Wilson points out:

> Without the full measure of co-operation and assistance which he was giving us, it would have been necessary to bring in a strong garrison, which was held by the military authorities to be out of the question. From the political point of

---

[322]Ibid., P. 134.

[323] G.M. Lees, *Two Years in South Kurdistan*, Journal of the Royal Central Asia Society, Vol. 15, Issue 31, 1928, p. 254.

[324] Wilson, (1931), pp. 132-33

view, too, it was of great importance that we should maintain order in the area and at the same time should avoid the appearance of using force for this purpose.[325]

By the end of December, Noel traveled to districts beyond Sulaimanya as far as Rowanduz in order to introduce the new system of government. He dispatched political officers to Koi, Rania and Rowanduz where order was soon restored.[326] Having delineated the scheme for the future Kurdistan for the tribal chiefs, they expressed their willingness to accept Shaikh Mahmud as the British representative in Kurdistan and their readiness to join the Kurdish confederacy. But by no means was everyone satisfied by this appointment and some tribes had at least four candidates, none of whom were accepted. Cultivators and villagers expected the British to restrain the cruelty of the chiefs and bring back "bureaucratic administration on Turkish lines. However, for the moment, they welcome any measure from us provided that it would bring about peace, trade and prosperity."[327]

In this respect major Soane wrote:

> Thus tribe after tribe which hitherto had been barely cognizant of Shaikh Mahmud, or at best had known him as an unworthy descendant of a good man, signed the stereotyped memorial praying for inclusion in the new State under Shaikh Mahmud, a condition which they imagined the British government to have made essential, for reason of its own.[328]

Shaikh Mahmud was by this time the unchallenged Kurdish leader who strove to accumulate all the power into his hands and to become the master of the situation in South Kurdistan. The loyalty of the tribal chieftains and their obedience to his authority were crucial factors for consolidation and exercising of his power. With this aim in mind, he used the subsidies he had received from the British for salaries and for the reconstruction of areas

---

[325] Ibid.,p.133.
[326] Jwaideh, (2006), p. 168.
[327] Wilson, (1931), P. 133.
[328] Quoted in Mcdowall, (200),p.156.

damaged by the war, to strengthen his position among the tribes. According to a report written in 1919:

> Also, allegiance to Shaikh Mahmud as *hukmdar* of the state had a condition which made him- thanks to the funds of H.B.M.'s government-at once a popular figure and a royal road to prosperity. Following allegiance came allowances in ready cash-rare sight in those days- and the system whereby the tribal chief assessed his own goods and those of his tribe without the critical eye of a government official.[329]

With great amounts of governmental funds [330]in his possession and constantly acquiring adherents Shaikh Mahmud aimed to dominate the administration system. He was eager in Soane's word:

> To fill every post with did own relation regardless of their character of capability, and to exclude all whom he did not consider personal adherence ... Every important post from that of outside petty governor to that of judge of Sulaimaniyah Religious Court was held by his relatives and sycophants.[331]

Civil Administrators and Kurdish levies that were under creation in South Kurdistan were forced to swear personal allegiance to Shaikh Mahmud.[332] According to Bell "The Kurdish levies led by Kurdish officers were ready to support Shaikh Mahmud, to whose influence they owed their appointment."[333] After the appointment of Soane, public order and trade flourished and the population changed their attitudes toward Shaikh Mahmud. Many expressed their dislike toward the Shaikh suggesting that they did not accept his rule willingly, but out of fear of his power and

---

[329] Iraq (British Administration), Office of the Civil Commissioner, Administration Report of Sulaimanyah Division for the Year 1919, (Bagdad Government Press, 1920) 1. Quoted in Jwaideh p. 169

[330] The British allotted Shaikh Mahmud a monthly allowance of 15,000 rupees and appointed Noel as his advisor. See Aziz al- Haj, *Al-Qadiyah al-Kurdiya fi-al-Ishriniyat*, (Beirut, 1984), p.32.

[331] Quoted in McDowall, (2000), p. 156.

[332] Jwaideh, (2006), p. 169.

[333] Wilson, (1931), p.135.

because he gave the impression that the British "were ready to establish his Governorship, if necessary, by force." [334]

The war had made a detrimental impact on the Kurds. They were not in a position to resist Shaikh Mahmud's personal ambitions nor had the British any intention of curbing his power, and instead they pursued their policy of the tribal system in South Kurdistan under the leadership of Shaikh Mahmud, which was implemented without any objection.

Major Soane, who had replaced Noel, the founder of the tribal system, was a strong opponent of this system. He had demonstrated in detail, in many reports, its devastating impact for the Kurdish society. In a section of one report entitled "Note on the Tribal System of Administration" he attacked the adaptation of the new administration system:

> [A] system of administration which one may call the Tribal System, was adopted. It was considered by the Political Officer in charge that this best meet the national aspirations and preserve the characteristic feature of Kurdistan. It was considered by Sheikh Mahmud equally desirable to institute the tribal system as by that means he could more easily bribe or threaten the chiefs, could more readily centralize the control in himself and more rapidly attain the position of absolute power which was his aim. A system of direct government by officials, which naturally tends to disintegrate tribes and create democratic and industrious homogeneous population, was by no means to his taste. As the principal adviser of the Political Officer, he therefore encouraged the revival of the tribal system which was-in Sulaimaniyah-Moribund. [335]

Soane did not conceal his reluctance toward Shaikh Mahmud. The question in this connection, however, was whether his aversion toward the Shaikh stemmed solely from the fact that the latter was abusing the tribal system for his own personal benefit or that he was against a policy that the colonial power envisioned putting into effect in South Kurdistan as well as in the rest of Iraq. Soane was part and parcel of the colonial power which he

---

[334] Ibid., p. 135.

[335] Iraq (Biritish Administration), Office of the Civil Commissioner, *Administration Report of Sulaimaniyah Division for* 1919, Quoted in Jwaideh, (2006), p. 171.

served and undertook to implement its policy in Iraq and elsewhere. His defiance of the tribal system as such might confirm the assumption that he, like some other British politicians in Iraq, belonged to the school of thought that favored a system of direct rule there.

Sluglett argues that the advantages of the tribal system that was implemented in Iraq were that such a system was cheap to administer for the British authorities, and that the tribal leaders who were appointed as head of their tribes owed their authority entirely to the central administration. However, what mattered for the proponents of such a system was its effectiveness, overlooking the fact that it was extremely easy to abuse.[336]

For the British administration, Shaikh Mahmud became a problem that they had to deal with as he attempted to extend his sphere of influence to the regions lying beyond his authority as *Hukmdar* and that he, on several occasions, had clearly expressed his disdain to be subordinate to the British authority in accordance with the arrangement that was decided upon.

The British had now excluded some regions from the Shaikh's orbit so that his authority was eventually confined to the *liwa* of Sulaimanya and certain adjacent districts of the *liwa* of Kirkuk. In fact Shaikh Mahmud had overestimated his popularity when it turned out that not all of the Kurdish communities and tribes, between the Sirwan and the Great Zab rivers, who had the freedom to accept him as their leader made this choice. C.J. Edmonds, the British political Officer, underlines the point that:

> He resented the restriction of his authority to the district just described. Even in Turkish time, as an unofficial citizen, he terrorized the town through his gangs of roughs and, now that he was officially the Ruler, he was quite incapable of understanding the restrain put upon him even by Noel's mild adversary regime.[337]

Indeed, Shaikh Mahmud's ambition to consolidate his power was initiated shortly after he was appointed by the Acting Civil Commissioner as

---

[336] Sluglett, (2007), p. 171.

[337] C J.Edmonds. *Kurds, Turks and Arabs: Politic, Travel and Research in North-Eastern Iraq, 1918-1925,* (London, Oxford,U.P. 1957), P.30.

Hukmdar for South Kurdistan. The British authorities realized that they had to reconsider their decisions about the Shaikh and the whole situation in South Kurdistan. By the end of December 1918, two official reports with identical texts warned that "doubts were beginning to arise as to the wisdom of allowing the power of Shaikh Mahmud to increase to too great an extent."[338]

Aware of the deteriorated situation in the Kurdish region the British attempted to reach a solution which could enable them to implement their desirable policies. With this aim in mind, they decided to curb Shaikh Mahmud's authority and restrain his activities. Wilson stresses the fact that:

> It was by this time clear that we could not prudently lend our active support to Shaikh Mahmud's pretensions to the hegemony of considerable group or tribes, and, this being the case, it was generally agreed that it was necessary to modify our policy in South Kurdistan by the introduction of some sort of administration on line similar to those in force elsewhere in Iraq. [339]

Early in March 1919, Acting Civil Commissioner Wilson arranged for a conference in Bagdad in order to remedy the delicate situation in South Kurdistan. The conference was attended by Noel, Leachman, Soane, Gordon-Walker, and several others with valuable knowledge of the situation. Having thoroughly discussed the position of Shaikh Mahmud and that of South Kurdistan the participants in the conference came to the conclusion "that Shaikh Mahmud's power should be gradually curtailed, but, if possible, in such a way as to avoid an open breach"[340], and that Noel's place at Sulaimanya should be taken by major Soane "who had hitherto no personal relations with Shaikh Mahmud, but had exceptional

---

[338] E.J.R., p.12. See also Bell: review of the Civil Administration, 63. Quoted in Jwaideh, (2006), p. 174.
[339] Wilson, (1931), p. 134
[340] Lees, (1928), p. 255.

qualifications and an intimate knowledge of the whole area."[341] Noel was sent under the guidance of His Majesty's Government, in a lengthy tour throughout Kurdistan, to gauge the opinion of the inhabitants with regards to the implementation of the principle of self-determination.[342]

Wilson, who was informed that the state of affairs in Sulaimanya was critical, decided to fly there toward the end of May 1919 in order to meet Shaikh Mahmud in person and to attempt to find a solution which would sustain the administrative framework of South Kurdistan. Prior to this meeting, however, Shaikh Mahmud desperately attempted to regain his diminishing prestige.[343] By May 23, 1919, Shaikh Mahmud managed to raise a force of 300 tribal followers from the Persian site of the frontier consisting mainly of Hawramani and Meriwan tribesmen, led by Mahmud Khan Dizli, and acting under his command.[344] With this force the Shaikh attacked Sulaimanya and soon defeated the local levies; he was now master of the situation.[345] The British officer, Major F.S. Greenhouse (who was in charge in the absence of Soane) and others were captured and imprisoned.[346] Shaikh Mahmud seized the treasury and proclaimed himself ruler

---

[341] Wilson, (1931), p. 134. In this connection, Jwaideh notes that Soane's reluctance to Shaikh Mahmud developed during the period when he traveled in disguise throughout Kurdistan twelve years earlier. Soane was influenced by the Jaf Begzada of Halabja, especially by Lady Adela, with whom he was on good terms. See Jwaideh footnote 83, (2006), pp. 348-49.

[342] Wilson (1931), p. 134. Helmreich notes that Noel took on this mission enthusiastically, and that the British political advisor at Constantinople regarded him as "fanatic" and "an out and out Kurd". His opinion on the Kurds confirmed this bias. This mission gave rise to considerable hostility between the Turks and the British since the Turks believed that the Kurdish question was an internal affair and claimed that Noel instigated separatist sentiments among the Kurds. See Helmreich, p. 77.

[343] Ibid., p. 136

[344] Jwaideh, p. 180.

[345] Wilson, (1931), p. 136.

[346] Even in Halabja, had the tribesmen under the control of Hamid Beg, Shaikh Mahmud's nominee, besieged Lees, the assistant political there. He managed to escape with the assistance of Lady of Halabja, Adela Khanum for which she was later rewarded the Indian title of Khan bahadur. See Wilson. P. 136. For detailed description of this event see Lee G.M. Lees, *Two Yearsd in South*

129

of all Kurdistan. He appointed his own administrative staff in each district, issued his own postage stamps and hoisted his own flag.[347] The telegraph line to Kirkuk was cut on the morning of the attack on Sulaimanya and Greenhouse's messengers were intercepted. The first news of these occurrences reached the outside world two days later through Halabja and Khanaqin.[348]

Shaikh Mahmud's Defeat and Capture

Following this victory Shaikh Mahmud planned with a great fervor for more action against the British. He proved to be more worrisome than they had believed. Consequently, they did not waste any time to counterattack him. The officer commanding the small garrison of Imperial troops at Kirkuk was ordered to dispatch a detachment along the road as far as the Chamchamal plain, and the brigade at Baáiji was instructed to push on to Kirkuk. The officer commanding at Kirkuk underestimated the fighting qualities of the Kurds and disregarded his order. He decided to continue toward Sulaimanya. He penetrated the mountains with some mounted troops, Iraqi levies, armored cars and Lewis guns in Ford vans, and reached Tasluja pass, twelve miles from the town where British prisoners were held. There, he was surrounded and attacked from all sides and compelled to retire. The Kurdish forces chased the retreating troops over twenty-five miles, inflicting on them serious casualties. They lost four armored cars and nineteen Ford vans. [349] The defeat of the British forces at these battles was a great achievment for Shaikh Mahmud and thereby nationalist impulses gathered increasing momentum in South Kurdistan as well as in Persian territories.

In Wilson's opinion:

The Regrettable incident confirmed the now general belief of the inhabitants

---

Kurdistan.
[347] Edmonds describes the flag of Shaikh Mahmud as a red crescent on a green ground. Edmonds, (1957), p. 30.
[348] Wilson, (1931), p. 136.
[349] Edmonds, (1957), pp. 30-31.

of South Kurdistan that we are no longer able to control events; the rebellion spread across into Persian territory, and several tribes arose against the Persian government, proclaiming themselves partisans of Shaikh Mahmud and his scheme for a united free Kurdistan.[350]

W.R.Hay, a British political officer, who served in the civil administration of Mesopotamia and was at the time of the rebellion in South Kurdistan made the following evaluation of the Shaikh's rebellion:

> The revolt of Shaikh Mahmud in May, 1919, was the beginning of the reaction in Northern Mesopotamia, and though it ended in failure, it showed that it was possible to defy the new government, and sent out waves of unrest over the country.[351]

According to the British, Shaikh Mahmud made a correct analysis of the situation as he announced to his adherents the withdrawal of the British forces from South Kurdistan, but he drew an erroneous conclusion from their disposition. The British had grasped how perilous their position was and accordingly had to act urgently in order to restore law and order; so "The commander-in-chief realized that the impression of British helplessness must be removed forthwith."[352] The task was entrusted to Major-General Sir Theodore Fraser commander of the 18th Division in Mosul. He was instructed to mobilize in Kirkuk a "South Kurdistan Force" composed of two brigades of infantry with cavalry and armored cars, and to push on as soon as possible.[353] By the middle of June, General Fraser's troops were assembled in Chamchamal and prepared to launch operations, and on June 17, he moved forward to attack Shaikh Mahmud, who had in his possession the Darband-i-Baziyan Pass, in the Qara Dagh range, twelve miles east of Chamchamal. By June 18 before daybreak, the force of General Fraser, commenced to scale the almost perpendicular height on

---

[350] Wilson, (1931), p. 137.
[351] W.R. Hay, *Two Years in Kurdistan, Experience of a political Officer 1918-1920* (London, 1921), p. 159.
[352] Ibid.
[353] Ibid.,31.

each side of the Qra Dagh and was nearly in reach of the top as the guns opened on and over the pass. The Kurds, anticipating a face -to- face attack on line with their Turkish foes up the road, were paralyzed as they were attacked from above, and very soon were surrounded and overwhelmed. The British troops inflicted on the Kurdish rebels a heavy defeat, and by dawn they had full control of the pass. Forty-eight of Shaikh Mahmud's force lay dead on the ground; over a hundred were captured, and the rest had dispersed. [354]

In the meantime, General Fraser had to act promptly to rescue the British officers imprisoned in Sulaimanya and in the hands of Kurdish guards. He was worried that they would risk their lives if the news of the defeat of the battle of Biyzan reached the town. He immediately ordered the 23rd Lancers to move hastily to Sulaimanya. The regiment succeeded in overwhelming the guards and released the detainees after ten weeks of incarceration. The main British force arrived at Sulaimanya the next morning.[355] By the early days of August, the situation appeared satisfactory; order had been restored and the control of the country had been reinstated to the Civil Administration. Thus, Wilson states enthusiastically, "ended a brilliant little operation." [356]

Shaikh Mahmud was found severely wounded not far away from the battlefield. Edmonds, who accompanied Fraser's men in the capacity of political officer, maintains that "it was not important that he should not either die before he had been identified by a Kurdish personality, or escape; and any legend of a miraculous disappearance might cause untold trouble later."[357]

Having been transferred to Baghdad, where he recovered from his wounds, Shaikh Mahmud, with his associate Shaikh Gharib, were tried by a military court-martial for rebellion and sentenced to death. The

---

[354] Wilson, (1931), p. 138. Edmonds, (1957), p. 46. The troops involved in this battle, the 85th Burmans, were a battalion consisting mainly of Kachins, a mongoloid race from the *ultuma thule* of Upper Burma. Ibid., p. 138.

[355] Ibid. For further information about the releasing of the prisoners see Edmonds ibid. p. 47. And Lees, (1928), pp. 264-65.

[356] Wilson, (1931), p. 138.

[357] Edmonds, (1957), p. 49

commander-in-chief Sir G. Mac Munn, however "now in the midst of judgment remembering mercy", commuted the sentence to a long-term imprisonment, partly owing to the fact that Shaikh Mahmud had not maltreated the British detainees in his hands and partly that the policy of His Majesty's Government in South Kurdistan barely justified what "the Soviet government would call the supreme measure of social defence."[358]The decision of Sir George Mac Munn was quite comprehensive for Wilson, but he nevertheless was against it on the grounds that his being alive would induce hope in his adherents and fear in his enemies, of his possible return; only with his death would hope and tranquility be regained.[359]

On March 14, 1928, at a lecture given by the Central Asia Society, the commander-in-chief explained the reasons for his forgiveness of the Shaikh:

> Shaikh Mahmud was brought home a prisoner from the Bazian Pass. I had him tried, and he was sentenced to death. I knew he was an infernal scoundrel, and people wanted me to hang him, but I thought there was no fair ground for such action… Shaikh Mahmud owed no temporary allegiance to the British. When he engineered the coup d'état he did not kill the four or five British officers he had in his hands, and I did not think it would be playing the British game fairly to shoot him. I sent him to India with a twenty- year sentence. He was brought back… Shaikh Mahmud would be a suitable thorn in the side of the Turks. [360]

Circumstances Leading up to Reinstallation of Shaikh Mahmud

On January 18, 1920, a new nationalist Turkish Chamber of Deputies passed a manifesto known as the National Pact. Although the first article of this pact granted the right of self-determination for the regions south of the armistice line of 1918 populated by the Arabs, it embodied antagonism toward the seceding of the Mosul *Wilayat* from Turkey.[361]Regardless of the pact,

---

[358] Ibid.
[359] Ibid.
[360] Lees, (1928), p. 277.
[361] Edmonds, (1957), p. 116.

which was issued some months earlier, the Allied powers signed, on August 10, 1920, the Treaty of Sèvres, which marked the beginning of the partition, and the eventual destruction of the Ottoman Empire. The articles 62, 63, and 64 of the treaty provided for setting up a Kurdish national state. Article 62, perhaps the most significant part of the treaty, stipulated:

> A commission sitting at Constantinople and consisted of three members appointed by the British, French, and Italian governments respectively, shall draft within six months from the coming into force of the present Treaty a scheme of local autonomy for the predominately Kurdish areas lying east of the Euphrates, south of the southern boundary of Armenian as it may be hereafter determined, and north of the frontier of Turkey with Syria and Mesopotamia.[362]

Articles 63 and 64 obliged Turkey to accept and execute the recommendation of the commission. If the majority of the population in the areas defined in Article 62 were in favor of independence from Turkey, and if the Kurds were regarded by the Council as capable of such independence, the Turkish government had to agree to execute the recommendation and renounce all rights and titles over those areas. In addition, according to Article 64, in case Turkey abandoned these areas, the Allied powers would not oppose a voluntary union between an independent Kurdish state and the part of Mosul *Wilayat* where the Kurds were a majority.[363] The last clause of Article 64 was remarkable since it concerned a possible reduction of the area under the British mandate for Mesopotamia, although it would not involve the principal Kurdish (and oil bearing) districts included in the mandate, since they fell within the boundary of the ex-Ottoman *Wilayat* of Baghdad. However, no great importance was attached to these clauses, since in March 1921 the Allied governments declared themselves prepared, with respect to Kurdistan, "to consider a modification of the Treaty in a sense in conformity

---

[362] Quoted in Edmund Ghareeb, *The Kurdish Question in Iraq* (New York, 1981), p.6.
[363] Ibid.

with the existing facts of the situation." [364]At the same time, and due to the military achievement and the rise to power of Mustafa Kemal in Anatolia, the articles were never implemented. Thus, the Treaty of Sèvres was still-born, but for the Kurds, the dream of an autonomous Kurdistan stipulated in the treaty still lived, and the destiny of the Mosul *Wilayat* was to be set-tled six years later.[365]

Shortly after the signature of the Sèvres the Turks exerted considerable efforts to give the Kurds of the Mosul *Wilayat* the impression that the treaty was null and void and that it was not "worth the paper it was written on."[366] Edmonds describes the situation as follows:

> There were threats at large-scale invasion, clandestine correspondence with leaders of urban society, secret mission to tribal malcontents, open incitements to rebellion, warning to 'traitors', and, pervading all, their religious appeal for loyalty to the Sultan who was also Caliph. The principal targets of this propaganda, the Kurds, now found themselves torn by every kind of conflicting emotion: loyalty to their religion, respect for and fear of the might of their late master, dreams of an independence obtainable only with a support which the British seemed unwillingly to give, impatience with the restraints imposed by the authority actually governing them, a lively realization that economically they were bound hand and foot to Bagdad, and reluctance to accept subordination, even with a measure of autonomy, to an Arab Kingdom.[367]

The Cairo Conference and the Future of Iraq

In October 1920, The High Commissioner, Sir Percy Cox, returned to Baghdad from London with instructions, based on British acceptance of the mandate, to pursue a policy on liberal line and with regards to the principal of self-determination. This included "the establishment of an Iraqi government, with the due forms of statehood even though possessing

---

[364] H.W.V.Temperley, *A History of the Peace Conference of Paris,* Vol.V1(London,19249), p. 91.
[365] Edmonds, (1957), p. 117.
[366] Ibid., p. 118.
[367] Ibid., p. 118.

at first an independence limited by the advice and control of its Mandatory."[368] Almost at the same time, in England, a separate Middle East Department was established in the colonial office and assumed the responsibility for Iraq instead of the Indian Office, and Winston Churchill was transformed from the war office to the colonial office for this purpose. On March 12, 1921, Winston Churchill convened a conference in Cairo in order to forge united British political strategies for the Middle East. The participants in the conference were high British and Arab officials in the Middle East. The Iraqi delegate composed of High Commissioner Cox, the Minister of Defense Jafar al-Askary, the Finance Minister Sassun Hisqail and the Secretary Oriental of the British Mandate, Miss Bell.[369] The main issues on the agenda of the conference were to debate impending political, financial, and military deals for the mandate territories. Churchill's top priority was to keep a solid British control as cheaply as possible. As Colonial Secretary, Churchill announced "everything else that happens in the Middle East is secondary to the reduction in expense." This became a principle against which all proposals and programs were tested.[370] Accordingly, military cost-cutting and supporting for the candidature for the throne of Iraq of the Emir Faisal [371] were objectives to be achieved. Furthermore, from 1922 onward Royal Air Forces took over the Army's responsibility for the defense and for the preservation of Iraqi internal affairs.

The British had also planned to save from the reduction of their troops in the Kurdish region. In a P.M. to the Prime Minister Churchill had arrived at the conclusion that at that stage, March 1921, if there would be any effort

---

[368] Longrigg and Stoakes,(1958), p. 82.
[369] Abdul Razzaq Al-Hasani, *Tarikh al-Wizarat al Iraqiya,* Vol.1, (Sidon, 1933), (History of Iraqi Cabinets, Vol.1, Sidon, 1933), p. 24.
[370] David Fromkin, *A Peace to end all Peace: The Fall of the Ottoman Empire and the Creation of the Modern Middle East* (New York, 1989), p. 499.
[371] By the time of the Cairo Conference in March, the most principal points between the High Commissioner and Emir Faisal were resolved. The Conference would only ratify Faisal's candidature and determine measures for his installation. Ireland.p. 311.

to force the Kurds under an Arab government, they would certainly resist, and that would complicate the withdrawal of British troops from Mesopotamia. The suggestion was therefore to make clear for both the Kurds and the Iraqi government that the British goal under the mandate period was preserving the *status quo* until such a time as a representative group of Kurdistan territories possibly would opt for incorporation into Iraq. The British would benefit from this solution since it would facilitate the recruitment of Kurdish units under their officers, and precipitate the reduction of Imperial forces in many areas controlled by them. Besides, this policy would as well contribute to discount Turkish efforts to lure the Kurds of South Kurdistan into cooperation with their brethren in North Kurdistan with the purpose of incorporating them into Anatolian State.[372] Thus, as Sluglett concludes:

> Cairo was an expression by Britain of its future military and financial commitments in the Middle East, of the extent to which the 'imperial burden' would be lightened. It marked the beginning of a new kind of colonial policy, and formalized the end of direct British rule in Iraq. The immediate reason for the decision taken is not hard to find: massive expenditure in Mesopotamia could not be continued in the face of so many other more pressing demands on the British Treasury.[373]

Following a decision by the Cairo Conference with regards to the Kurdish districts, Cox took measures to accommodate Kurdish wishes, which finally resulted in a "compromise solution." Kurdish concerns were growing when on November 11, 1920, the Provisional National Government, was formed under the presidency of Saiyed Abul Rahman al-Gilani, Nagib of Baghdad, since they believed that an Arab government would only neglect

---

[372]Mr.Churchill to the Prime Minister. (Received Colonial Office 11.15 pm. March 16,1921), British Documents on Foreign Affairs. Series B. Turkey, Iran, And The Middle East. 1918-1939. Volume 2. *The Allies Take Control*, 1920-1921.p. 313. Henceforth BDFA.

[373] Sluglett. (2007), P. 41.

their rights. [374]The administrative power, which was transferred from Cox to Provisional Government, substantially actualized the determination of the question of South Kurdistan. Accordingly, the solution concerning the administration of the Kurdish districts suggested by Cox was announced in a communiqué on May 6 summarized as follows: [375]

A) As regards the Kurdish districts of the Mosul Division which fall within the sphere of the British Mandate, a sub-liwa should be formed comprising the districts of Zakho, Aqra, Dohok and Amadiya, with headquarters at Dohok, that sub-liwa be under a British assistant Mutasariff. Qaimmaqam for the time being should be British but will be replaced by Kurds or Kurdish speaking Arabs acceptable to the Kurds as soon as competent men are forthcoming. This sub-liwa would be generally subject, for all financial and judicial purposes, to the National Government in Baghdad...

b) British officers should be associated with the administration of Arbil together with Keui Sanjaq and Ruwandiz, and will secure that in the appointment of Government officials regard would be had to the wishes of the people.

c)Sulaimani will be treated as a Mutasarrif (subprovince.add.mine) governed by a Mutasarrif-in Council, the Mutasarrif to be appointed by the High Commissioner and to have British Advisers attached to him; pending the appointment of a Mutasarrif the British political Officer will act in this capacity. To the Mutasarrif-in Council will be delegated such power, including right of appeal to the High Commissioner, as may be approved by High Commissioner, after consultation with the Mutasarrif-in-Council on the one hand and the Council of the State of Iraq on the other. Qaimmaqams for the time being should be British, to be replaced by Kurds as soon as competent men are forthcoming.[376]

---

[374] The withdrawal of British troops from Iraq was only possible if the relationship between the Iraqi and the mandatory power was friendly, in which the creation of the provisional government contributed to it. However, the strong Arab national agitation aimed against the mandate necessitated prolongation of British military occupation to impose a mandatory regime, on a scale which was rejected by the British public opinion. Ireland. p.313.

[375] The communiqué was published about 6 weeks before Faisal's arrival in Basra that is in June 1921, embarked on a British ship. Ibid., p.118.

[376] Special Report by His Majesty's Government in the United Kingdom of Great Britain and Northern Ireland to the Council of the League of Nations on the

However, the administrative program for Mosul, where the sense of Kurdish particularity for the greatest part was indistinct, never materialized. As for the Arbil *liwa* the conflicting attitudes between the provisional government and the British authority hindered the implementation of the provisional administration there. Arbil had been an independent division under British military administration, but the provisional government of al-Naqib suggested the re-establishment of the Turkish organization so that Arbil, Koi and Rawanduz would form separate *qazas* (districts) subordinated to Kirkuk. The government emphasized as well a need to attach the Sulaimanya *liwa* to Iraq, contending that it was bound to it politically and economically and would in that case thwart a threat from the northern part of the country.[377] The High Commissioner, however, implemented his own administrative scheme by letting the division form a sub-*liwa* with a Kurdish assistant *Mutasarrif* who soon became independent of the *Mutasarrif* of Kirkuk in all but name. Even if this administrative proposal for the Kurdish districts was not fully put into effect it was indeed the High Commissioner who practically continued in nearly all matters to be involved in the affairs of South Kurdistan, until after the Treaty of 1926, and actually almost up to the end of the Mandate in 1932.[378] The same can also be said about the *liwa* of Sulaimanya which rejected participation altogether in the referendum of electing Emir Faisal for the throne of Iraq, but continued to be administered even after the referendum by the political officers, with a council but subordinate to the Residency.[379]

In August 1920, almost a year after the defeat of Shaikh Mahmud at

---

Progress of Iraq during the Period 1920-1931 (London, 1931), p. 254. Henceforth Special Report. See also Edmonds , (1957), p. 118.

[377] Kadhim, (2012), p. 141.

[378] Edmonds, (1957), pp. 119-120.

[379] Ibid. According to the result of this referendum 96 percent supported Emir Faisal's election, while Kirkuk accounted for the dissentient four percent. No representatives from either liwa were present at the accession ceremonies held in Bagdad in 1921.

the battle of Bazan Pass, the Arbil division was prone to disarray and trouble. A section of the Surchi confederation stationed in the Mosul division had first attacked a military convoy, and then Aqra district. Before long, their relatives in the Arbil division made joint efforts with dissident Rawanduzi Kurds to fend off the political officers in Rawanduz and Koi-Sanjaq. The rebellion became widespread now and comprised other Kurdish groups such as the Khushnaw, who were previously on good terms with the British. Even Arbil ran the risk of being attacked by the Surchi but was defended by the Dizai tribe with the assistance of the government.

Nationalist- Religious Propaganda and Counter Propaganda:
Turkish Menace and Propaganda in South Kurdistan

Turkish nationalists and members of the Committee of Union and Progress realized the devastating impact of war, both in terms of troops and resources. Among the efforts to find a solution to this situation, was to develop and direct Islamic sentiment in Muslim countries, especially in Mesopotamia. Accordingly, they proposed an assembly of a Pan-Islamic Congress at Sivas, the aim of which was to instigate anti-British and Pan-Islamic sentiments among the Mohammadans of the Muslim world. The British Colonial Power was aware that these kinds of Turkish activities deserved serious investigation and consideration.

In a dispatch written on December 26, 1919, and received on January 15, 1920, Vise-Admiral Sir J. De Robeck summarized this situation:

Generally speaking, there would appear to be in varying degree throughout all the Moslem countries of the Near East and Middle East a growing tendency to react against European domination and control. This is perhaps a natural development, consequent on the growth of a political sentiment among the dominant classes, which becomes more active as the power of absolutism diminished and is replaced by that of the political organizations which exercise control under the cloak of democratic institutions. Pan-Islamism may well be the framework upon which will be built up, on the ground of community of religious and political interests and ideas, and with the object of making a stand against European intervention and exploitation, a general movement in these countries to get rid of foreign control and develop along their own lines. The expression 'self-determination' has echoed throughout the Near East, and though perhaps naturally imperfect understood, it yet forms the theme of every political scribbler and leader of public opinion. All measures tending to co-ordinate Islamic activities must therefore be of first importance to Great Britain during the next ten or twenty years, and require to be carefully followed up.[380]

Indeed, one of Britain's preoccupations in making peace in the Middle East was to be able to influence the large Muslim population in its Empire. When Lloyd George stated at the Paris Peace Conference that he sat there as the representative of "the greatest Mohammedan power" he must have astonished his colleagues. The Muslim population of the British Empire was at the time estimated to be 80 million, a position that was reinforced by the recent acquisition in the Middle East. After the Kemalist success at Chanak, Sir H. Rumbold, the High Commissioner to Constantinople, sent a note to Curzon in which he expressed his concern that Kemal's victory "will have stimulated Moslems all over the worlds and even have raised the question of Islam versus Christianity."[381]

In South Kurdistan, Koi, and Shaqlawa, the Surchi were fervently spreading Turkish propaganda. In the north of the Zab a prominent Shaikh, Ubayd Allah, was among the Shaikhs who led the Surchi tribes. He explicitly expressed his pro-Muslim inclination and his aversion to the infidel British authority.[382]

The British were satisfied with the state of affairs in the Kurdish districts thanks to the fact that internal administration there was conducted extraordinarily well. The Sulaimanya division, the British believed, profited from the organization of the central administration. It was allotted equal services by the British officials in the technical departments of Iraq's

---

[380] British Documents on Foreign Affairs. Part 2 Series B, *Turkey, Iran, And The Middle East, 1918-1939.* Volume 1, *The End of The War, 1918.1920.* Henceforth BDFA.
[381] Erik Goldstein, (2003), *The British Official mind at the Lausanne Conference, 1922-1923,* Diplomacy and Statecraft, 14:2,185-206, DOI:10.1080/09592290412331308861., p. 195.
[382] McDowall, (1957), p.159.

ministries as for the rest of Iraq.[383]

Kurdish chiefs from across the frontier, nevertheless, did not seem too impressed by what the British had accomplished in Sulaimanya and elsewhere as their cooperation with Turkish agents caused disorder in the winter of 1921-22. The British were obliged to an armed clash with the Auraman chiefs, provoked by Mahmud Khan Dizli, a Persian subject. At the end of May the same year, they managed to put an end to these hostilities. During the same time, one of the minor rebellions from across the frontier was overpowered by a joint attack of Iraqi Levies and Air Force (R.A.F.) on the strongholds of Bani Banok near Halabja. In this fight the levies lost Lieutenant M. Mott.[384]

Turkish activities continued with undiminished intensity with the purpose to abet anti-British sentiment in the Kurdish districts. On March 17, 1922, the Turkish government installed one of their agents, a certain Ramzi Beg, as *qaimmaqam* of Rawanduz and he was sent to that district. Toward the end of May, as soon as he arrived, he started with an intensive campaign among the tribes, assuring them that the arrival of the large Turkish military columns was forthcoming, the aim of which was to wrest Sulaimanya, Kirkuk, and Arbil from the British. He was accompanied in the middle of June by a certain Colonel 'Ali Shafiq Beg' popularly known Özdemir (Iron Shoulder), who as a military adventurer was to be a distinguished figure in Turkish propaganda on this frontier. He made no secret that his mission there was to re-occupy the whole of the Mosul *Wilayat*.[385]

Toward the end of May, Turkish agitation to create chaos and disturbance bore fruit. Due to a personal discord, the chief of the Jabbari Kurds attacked and injured the local *mudir* (subdistrict officer) in the proximity of Chamchamal. Owing to this event, the unruly men of the Hamawands who were among the most important tribe of the Chamchamal

---

[383] Ibid.

[384] Great Britain, Colonial Office, Iraq Administration Reports, April 1922 to March 1932, pp.32-33.

[385] Great Britain, Colonial Office, Iraq Administration Reports, April 1922 to March 1923. p.33.

refused to obey the government. The head of these men was a certain Karim Fattah Beg who had participated in Shaikh Mahmud's revolt in 1919. After sending threatening letters to the assistant political officer, Captain Bond, he changed his mind for some inexplicable reason, made believe that he wished to collaborate, and invited the Captain together with Captain Makant, who was responsible of levies, to see him at a conference at a village in the vicinity of the Bazian Pass on June 18. Although these two officers were warned of betrayal, they considered it was their duty to reach an agreement through this meeting and accepted the offer to attend the conference. As they reached the village, they were lured by the amicable welcome of Karim Fattah Beg while his follower shot the officers in the back. After this incident, the Hamawand chieftain and the Jabbari, Saiyed Mahmud, united to wage armed revolt.[386]

The death of these two talented and experienced British officers was a heavy loss for the administration. For more than a month the levies and the Air Force participated in a search operation throughout Kurdistan attempting to capture Karim Fattah Beg. At the end of July 1922, it was reported that the latter had proceeded northward and had sought safe haven in Turkey. [387]

When the levies passed through Zab and entered the Pizhder district of Rania, while chasing Karim Fattah Beg, they found Babbakr Agha pressed by the hostile sections of his tribe who, on behalf of the Turks intended to attack him. The presence of the levies tilted the balance of power and his position became further secure with the intervention of Ismail Agha, generally known as Simko, a leader of the Shikak tribe. Simko, who had his headquarters in the proximity of Lake Urumiya in Iran, was assisted by Saiyed Taha of Nehri. During these circumstances, these two leaders had, through their agents, warned the Persian Kurdish leaders across the border not to incite insurgency in Sulaimanya. [388] Meanwhile, Karim Fattah Beg had moved on to Rawanduz where the Turks had succeeded to mobilize

---

[386] Ibid.,34.
[387] Ibid.
[388] Ibid.

the most influential Kurdish tribal groups hostile to the British in the region such as the Surchi (under Shaikh Ubaydallah), the Zibari (under Faris Agha) the Barzanis (under Shaikh Ahmad), the Khushnaw, and from Kifri in the south, the Zangana. By August the same year, these Kurdish tribes had been reinforced by other Kurdish forces who had abandoned Simko after his defeat in Iran.

The advent of Karin Fattah Beg encouraged the Turks to push on, in small parties, south toward Rania border where the hostile Pizhdar joined them. On August 21, the Indian troops reached Rania and were strengthened by levies at their disposal, but were still incapable of repulsing the growing tribal influx provoked by reports of coming of Turkish reinforcement. On September 1, the British column was obliged to withdraw from Rania.[389]

At this stage, the British seemed to be powerless to deal with the critical political development in South Kurdistan, where Kurdish unrest combined with Turkish provocation and intervention rendered the region uncontrollable. Edmonds writes that:

> The whole position was of course basically unsound. The High Commissioner had surrendered almost all his physical resources to the Iraqi Government and British G:H.Q. were as averse as ever to the employment of Imperial troops in a remote area having no interest for them; sanction for the employment of the British-paid locally-recruited Levies was almost as difficult to obtain…Most of the British officials in the Bagdad ministries and departments were as fanatical as any nationalist Arab in their refusal to admit that these Kurds, who had deliberately chosen to stay without the pale, had any right whatever to their assistance. … In a country where the ordinary obligations of decent citizenship were regarded by nine-tenths of the population as intolerable impositions the political Officer had a fantastically impossible task.[390]

Faced with this entangled and dangerous situation, Edmonds contemplated

---

[389] Great Britain, Colonial Office, Iraq Administration Reports, April 1922 to March 1923, p. 35.
[390] Edmonds, (1957), p.123.

finding a solution. According to him, there were two alternative policies that might lead to an ideal result. The first was that the British would make a unilateral decision to incorporate Sulaimanya and Kirkuk into the Iraqi State, irrespective of the opinions of their inhabitants (in line with the government of al-Naqib's suggestion). This alternative, however, would have contradicted the British Parliament's assurance given to the Kurds that without their consent they would not be subordinated to an Arab government. The second was the replacement of direct by indirect rule. In this case, the person who was to be entrusted with this responsibility had to be an outstanding Kurdish personality who enjoyed general support and who would not be vulnerable to the Turkish caliphate-propaganda, especially considering that there were credulous villagers and tribesmen who were susceptible to such types of religious propaganda.[391]

The Shaikhs of the Barzanja family, who dominated the central and southern part of the Rania and the neighboring districts of the Kirkuk *liwa* and benefited from the unruly tribesmen, were busy disturbing the tranquility of these districts by the pretension of supporting Kurdish nationalism. Shaikh Abdul Karim, who led this agitation, enjoyed noticeable prestige and respect thanks to his moderation and balanced appearance. Their ultimate objection was, to pave the way for the return and final reinstallation of Shaikh Mahmud as *hukmdar*, who already had returned from India as far as Kuwait,.[392]

Due to the inherent danger of the situation, the question of restatement of Shaikh Mahmud became imperative among the British officials. Goldsmith, who had replaced Soane, held the view that Shaikh Mahmud was a better choice, given his evaluation of the environment at the time. Edmonds, on the other hand, had not a high opinion of the Shaikh, regarding him as incorrigible, and instead preferred a certain Saiyed Taha, son of Shaikh Muhammad Siddiq, and the grandson of the celebrated Shaikh Ubaydullah of Shamdinan in Turkey. Noel shared Edmonds'

---

[391] Ibid.,pp.123-124.
[392] Ibid., p. 123.

attitude concerning Shaikh Mahmud's inappropriateness. [393]

British Nationalist-Religious Counter Propaganda

In the meantime, Turkey continued to appeal to the Kurdish national and religious sentiments against the British using one of its most talented officers for this purpose, namely Özdemir.

In some intercepted letters from the Turkish officer commanding the Jezira Front which were dispatched to an important person in the district, Edmonds was informed that the Mosul *Wilayat* would not constitute a part of Iraq, inviting the receiver to take part in the Holy War. A last paragraph of one of these letters stated:

> It is necessary that all our co-religionists should work to achieve the unity which the Ottoman Government has designed … Let the true believers breath again. Your deficiencies in munitions and other necessaries are receiving consideration. All will be provided shortly. May Allah grant victory to those fighters for the faith who, like you, shed their blood in His way. May the curse of the polytheists fall upon those who have sold their religion to the English and Faisal and upon his followers. Amin. [394]

In order to counteract intensified Turkish propaganda, the British were obliged to apply the same method as their opponents. Although the reduction of imperial spending decided upon in the Cairo Conference was to be carried out, the new situation had created obstacles which were not easy to overcome. This was mainly thanks to the increased Turkish threat and propaganda. The British now contemplated falling back to old colonial strategies and methods in combating the Turks. Accordingly, the British policy makers discussed exploiting Arab nationalism as a political instrument and to promote it and give it all their material support they could.[395]

At the same time, Cox wanted to instigate a Kurdish rebellion outside

---

[393] Ibid., p. 124.
[394] Ibid.,p.46.
[395] Olson, (1989), p. 67.

Mesopotamia, but was opposed by Churchill, who intended rather to encourage it in Kurdistan within the British sphere of Kurdish nationalism. Churchill then recommended Major Noel to act with that aim in view, provided that, "Kemalist policy necessitated our resorting to Kurdish propaganda or other measures".[396]

Kurdish nationalists, however, had been in contact with the Greeks outside Mesopotamia. On May 25, 1921, in a dispatch sent to Curzon, Rumbold informed him that Emin Ali Beg, the head of the Bedir khan family, accompanied by his son Jeladet Beg, one of the prominent supporters of Kurdish Nationalism, had been in touch with Ryan, the political officer in the British Embassy in Istanbul and had told him , owing to the present situation that he, together with his friends, had been in contact with Greek representatives in Istanbul who approved the idea of a Kurdish movement against the Kemalists . They would, without any formal cooperation, promote the interests of Greece as well as the Kurdish nationalists. However, Halil Beg told the Greeks that without the sanction of the movement by His Majesty's Government, they could not go ahead with the subject. Halil Beg asked whether he and his friends were allowed to go to Mosul and whether it was granted to establish a Kurdish organization on territories occupied by the British for the purpose of political activities. Following the instructions of the foreign office since the armistice, Ryan informed Hail Beg that, given the situation, the British could not support efforts to incite a Kurdish national revolt or a Kurdish rising backed by the Greeks against the Turks. As for the travel of Hail Beg to Mosul, Ryan replied that the High Commissioner would not oppose members of the Bedir khan family to go there provided that applications should follow ordinary channels.[397]

Although Rumbold admitted the complication of handling a Kurdish national movement he intended to take in consideration the support of the anti-Kemalist section of the Kurds in case the extremist policy of Angora

---

[396] Quoted in ibid., p. 67.
[397] BDFA.Vol. 2. *The Allies Take Control, 1929-1921*, p. 304.

compelled the British and French into a conflict with the Kemalists. [398]

Toward the end of October the same year, Hail Beg Bedir Khan and five members of the Society of the Rise of Kurdistan showed up in Baghdad while they were preparing a Kurdish revolt. Their plan was for areas such as Dermis, Diyarbakir, Battles, and Van, with about five to six million inhabitants, were to revolt simultaneously. In materializing this revolt Hail Beg asked for Noel's support, British guns, and some other assistance. According to Cox's recommendation British support toward the Kurdish revolt against the Turks in Anatolia, to relieve the Greeks, should occur with the objective to force the Turks into negotiations, and, if the French still resist agreeing with British policies in the Middle East.[399]

Cox believed that despite the fact that Britain was a signatory of The Arm Convention, supplying arms to the Kurds through Iraq in case of war with the Turks was without obstacles just as the government of India had supplied arms to Tibet. Since Great Britain was at war with the Kemalists passing arms to the Kurds would not be regarded as an infringement of international law.[400]

Cox's suggestion to instigate a Kurdish revolt against the Kemalists was opposed by J.L. Hall who maintained that it would fail and create preconceptions toward British efforts to further negotiations with the Kemalists. Since Faisal had already contacted the Kemalists in anticipation of British approval, Hall argued that British support of a Kurdish revolt would discredit Faisal, especially in a case where the arms supply was supposed to reach the rebellion through Iraq. [401]

In a telegram to Cox, Churchill reiterated his objection to instigate a Kurdish revolt outside the mandate territory, especially in cooperation with the Greeks and asserted, "We have not yet been able to liquidate all the promises given or alleged to have been given to the Arabs during the war.

---

[398] Ibid.
[399] Olson, (1089), 73.
[400] Ibid.
[401] Ibid.

I am entirely opposed to creating similar difficulties with the Kurds."[402]

On December 1, 1921, Cox's proposal to encourage a Kurdish revolt against the Kemalists outside Mesopotamia, with or without an alliance with the Greeks, was met with unanimous objection. However, until the settlement of the question of the frontier of Mosul *Wilayat* by the Turkey-Iraq Treaty of June 1926, British policy was "to keep in with the Kurdish revolutionaries as a necessary precaution." [403]

In a telegram dispatched on March 29, 1922 to Marques Curzon, Rumbold alluded to the Kurdish question and the implications of the British getting involved in a Kurdish revolt in Turkey. He wrote he had been informed from a reliable source that the Great National Assembly was busy debating a proposal law concerning the administration of Kurdistan outlined by a special commission. Some members of this commission were sent to inquire about the reasons behind the rebellion of the Kotch Keri Kurds. The telegram indicated that Salih Efendi, the deputy from Erzerum, opened the debate by opposing the proposed law on the grounds that it lacked serious measures to solve the Kurdish question. He argued further that:

> The rising was due to the tyranny of the Administration and to the attitude of the Angora Government towards the caliphate. The use of violence would only aggravate the situation. It was nonsense to say that there was no revolt in Kurdistan, for one had no need of a guide when the village could be plainly seen. The movement is being supported by the Emir Faisal and the British, and in the interests of the country the matter should be dealt with without using violence.[404]

Rumbold's dispatch did not give any further explanation as to the nature or the extent of this support; however it must have been in accordance with a decision taken by the British administration to instigate a Kurdish revolt

---

[402] Quoted in ibid.,p.76.

[403] Ibid.

[404] BDFA. *The Turkish Revival, 1921-1923*, Vol. 3. P. 63. For more information about the Kotch kiri rebellion see Olson pp.26-41 and McDowall. pp.184-190.

outside Mesopotamia, contrary to the Cairo Conference recommendation.

King Faisal's Position: Defending Iraq's Unity

King Faisal, who once was the leader of the Arab revolt against the Ottoman Empire, was conferred this time to assist the British in their campaign against the Turks. At the end of May 1921, Cox "took upon himself to ascertain the wishes of the Kurds" and propounded a solution that they constituted an integral part of Iraq provided they could enjoy a certain degree of local autonomy in domestic affairs and be under direct instruction of the High Commissioner, rather than the government of Iraq. Cox was opposed by both Young and Lawrence, who recalled that the "balance of opinion at Cairo had favoured a separatist policy in Kurdistan." Churchill discussed the issue with Cox, preferring to set up Kurdistan as a buffer zone between the Arabs and the Turks as it was basically envisaged at Cairo. However, Cox's action forestalled any efforts to realize this.[405] On October 24th, Cox and Young, in the presence of Kinahan Cornwallis, Faisal's adviser, had preliminary talks with Faisal on the Kurdish question. Young explained thoroughly that the opinion of His Majesty's Government on following lines "was encouragement of Arab Nationalism not Arab Imperialism", and in this connection emphasizing for Faisal:

> To Iraq friendly Kurdistan was vital as being potential shield against Turkey and ... To Kurdistan friendship of Iraq was vital as containing chief if not only outside markets and being only outlet to see. Without considering outside factors community of interests alone should lead to close co-operation and friendly relations between these two areas each of which was at mercy of the other.[406]

The obstacle to implementing this policy was Turkey, Kurdistan's neighbor, hostile to both the British and Arabs. The objective of Turkish policy was identification of the Kurdish with the Turkish interests and ultimately,

---

[405] Aaron S. Klieaman, *Foundations of British policy in the Arab World: The Cairo Conference of 1921* (Baltimore and London, 1970), p. 168.
[406] Cox to Churchill No. 616, October 25, 1921, received October 26, 1921. CO. 730/6.

to return to the border of Iraq from Mosul to Kirkuk, which was by that time expressed in Turkish propaganda with two bases: the appeal to religion to instigate the Kurds against the British and, the appeal to anti-Arab prejudice to instigate the Kurds against the Arabs. Thus, on that matter, it was for Cox and Faisal recognized:

> Unless a Moslim focus could be found for Kurdish nationalism the policy of treating Kurdistan as purely British dependency while removing second(? basis of) propaganda would encourage first. On the other hand treating it as integral part of Arab Kingdom under Moslim ruler would remove first except in so far as that ruler was under British influence but give added strength to second.[407]

That would imply, in case Kurdistan was subordinated exclusively to British authority, the Turks' anti-Arab provocation would be undermined, and instead they would appeal to anti-British Islamic propaganda. But if Kurdistan were to be incorporated into an Arab kingdom under a Muslim Arab ruler (such as Iraq), Turkish anti-Islamic propaganda would be then ineffective, but it would strengthen their anti-Arab sentiment among the Kurds. The British contemplated now how to find out a compromise between these two extremes.

In reply to these two options, Faisal said before he could pursue any policy he wished to know whether the British expected him to speak as an "Iraqi" regarding Kurdistan as an integral part of Iraq or as King of an Arab country from which Kurdistan was seceded. Faisal was told that for the present purposes they had a discussion with him before his "accession" and he had agreed "that whole question was still open." With respect to this situation presented to him Faisal replied that until he knew to what extent military responsibility rested with him and to what extent with the British, he could not express any definite opinion. He then put forwards these four questions:

1-If Great Britain prepared to undertake defending Kurdistan if attacked from

---

[407] Ibid.

outside and consequently to guarantee Iraq against attacks through Kurdistan-if so for how long?

2-Is she prepared to accept responsibility to prevent internal disorder in Kurdistan which might be a danger to Iraq-If so for how long?

3-Having regard to the fact that some Kurdish communities have expressed preference for inclusion in Iraq is it the intention of Great Britain to compel them to remain separate-if so for how long?

4-In the event of separation what form of Government does Great Britain propose and with what ultimate end in view?[408]

In reply to these questions Faisal was told that Great Britain did not strive to establish a Kurdish state, but intended to incorporate Kurdistan into Iraq within the framework of a confederation. Besides, the British government would not prevent any part of Kurdistan from being integrated with Iraq, and the idea of providing autonomy to the Kurds was to satisfy them thereby discouraging Turkish propaganda.[409]

On September 20, 1921, Cox informed Churchill in a note that the question of the status of Kurdish districts was still uncertain and that it would be specifically brought up in connection with elections for a Constitutional Assembly. He discussed the issue again with Faisal, who was still not very clear about the real intentions and the policy of Britain. Faisal was concerned as to what political line to pursue. From a conversation with Kurdish exiles in Baghdad as far as he had understood:

> There was very strong movement on foot in northern Kurdistan for establishment of independence from Turkey while those Kurdish elements hitherto subject to Persia were said to have combined with Turkish Kurds and were similarly bent on achieving independence from Persia. That being the case it must be assumed that unless it was soon decided what was to be status of Kurdish districts in Iraq some if not all of them would certainly secede and join up with elements above referred to.[410]

---

[408] Ibid.

[409] Ali, (2011), p. 415.

[410] Cox to Churchill, No.503. September 20,1921, received September 23, 1921, CO 730/5.

Faisal wished a frank answer from Cox as to the real aims of Britain vis-à-vis the Kurdish districts. Cox replied at the Cairo Conference "there was strong belief in some quarters" that Kurdish districts of Iraq would, as a whole, oppose being put under a direct control of a "benignant government at Baghdad" and would demand local autonomy and administration by Kurdish officials supervised directly by the High Commissioner. On one hand, Cox explained, the British government seemed to be in favor of a "strong buffer presented by Kurdish districts under effective British influence lying between Iraq proper and Persia." Such a buffer would protect Iraq's frontier from the Persian side and, hence, allay the concerns of the Iraqi government from that side. On the other hand, British officers' access to a strong and well trained force of Kurdish levies would ensure the safety of the Iraqi government in case it was exposed to hostility from tribes inside Iraq. Cox's view was that Kurdish districts be administered by Kurdish officials under British supervision and preferably under the administration of the High Commissioner "in consultation with Iraqi Government." The British government preferred that these districts "remained as integral part of Iraq rather than that they should secede to northern Kurds." [411]

Cox then said that on his return to Iraq and after sounding out Kurdish communities, he realized there was no unanimity among them, regarding secession from Iraq. On the contrary, due to the economic interests with Mosul, some districts pondered the idea of separation with misgiving and preferred to remain connected to the administration's scheme of Baghdad government, as long as they were assured they would be governed by Kurdish officials and their interests supervised by British officers. [412]

Faisal welcomed the policy laid down above by Cox and finally contended that as king of Iraq he thought of further aspects of the question of Kurdistan which had probably not been fully considered by the British. This pertained to the:

---

[411] Ibid.
[412] Ibid.

Question of preponderance of Sunnis or Shiahs with special reference to question of constitutional (Assembly) shortly to be convoked. As we were aware there was already technical and numerical preponderance of Shiahs and excision of a large slice of Sunni districts of Iraq out of state and exclusion of their representatives from National Assembly would place Shiahs in a very strong position.[413]

Under the pretext that the Kurds lacked a leader who could govern them Faisal opposed any arrangement that implied Kurdish separation from Iraq. In a conversation with Faisal in October 1922, Gertrude bell argued that Faisal's:

Point was that it wouldn't suit us or him to burn our fingers in a Kurdish adventure and that the first thing the Kurds had to be asked to produce was an individual whom they could run for the job of King or President- a Kurdish Faisal in fact. I don't for a moment believe they have one.[414]

Gertrude Bell for her part was particularly concerned with the reduction of British expenditure in Mesopotamia stipulated at the Cairo Conference. She maintained:

I am persuaded that with Kurdistan as with Armenia our Armistice declarations go a great deal further than our capacity to carry them out, that we must be careful to make it absolutely clear that we haven't a penny to spend in furthering Kurdish independence, for if we encourage them we shall only have to abandon them in the hour of need, which would be the worst thing possible.[415]

The uncertainty concerning the Kurdish question filled Faisal with a sense of foreboding. He personally would not oppose an arrangement by which the Kurdish districts were governed by Kurdish officials and, if necessary, be in connection with the Iraq government through the High Commissioner. This would be a better alternative than if they resorted to a

---

[413] Ibid.
[414] Elizabeth Burgoyne, *Gertrude Bell: From her Personal Papers, 1914-1926*, (London, 1961), p. 250.
[415] Ibid.

European mandatory power. Faisal believed the Kurds preferred nominally to be ruled by a Muhammadan king. Cox regarded Faisal's suggestion as plausible, particularly with respect to the importance of the participation of the Kurds in the National Assembly.[416]

The Intensification of Turkey's Activities in Kurdish Areas

Then, on June 23, 1922, ÖzDemir arrived in Rawanduz with the title of "Commander of the National Rising." This event undoubtedly marked an increase of Turkish activities aimed at Rania, Koi and the Arbil areas. On July 2, and in light of the impending development, in a memorandum sent to Goldsmith and the High Commissioner, Edmonds warned of the Pizhdar *aghas* who, through their emissaries, had urged the Turks in Rawanduz to assist them in their anti-British activities. In one of the intercepted letters titled "Commandant of the Islamic Nation of Palestine and Syria" and signed "Commandant of the Islamic Nation of Iraq and Kurdistan" underlined that Mustafa Kemal , the leader of Turkey and, Jawdat, one of the prominent figures of the Committee of union and Progress, were well aware of the services of the Pizhdar *aghas* and had promised them, through a certain Ahmad Taqi "Delegate of Kurdistan" to Wazna (in Persian) assistance in the form of fifty soldiers.

It was then obvious to the British that the Turks were in close communication with the dissident Pizhdari tribes who were waiting for the right moment for action. ÖzDemir, whose mission was considered to be organizing a "national rising" of the tribes, had intensified his activities creating an unbearable situation for the British. In order to deal with this growing threat, Edmonds recommended conducting a punitive operation against the enemy forces in Rania. As far as Rawanduz was concerned, Edmonds, supported by his colleagues at Arbil, Captain W.A. Lyon and Goldsmith at Sulaimanya, asserted that it was "high time that we abandoned our present

---

[416] Cox to Churchill , No. 503. September 20, 1921, received September 23, 1921, CO 730/5.

passive policy"; he urged air action strengthened by ground troops. [417]

Meanwhile, on July 23, Colonel E.C.T. Minet, commanding the Sulaimanya levies, was informed that Karim Fattah Beg had crossed the Zab at Dukan and precipitated toward Rawanduz. The implication of the latter in the battles forced a new power relation; that is, on one hand, it might imply strengthening of ÖzDemir's already strong force by adding to it over one hundred fighters in Kurdistan and enhancing his ability to instigate tribal rising; on the other hand, Minet's column provided sufficient reinforcement that might in due time, commence its crucial punitive operation against the Turco-Kurdish forces. [418]

Once at Rawanduz, Karim Fattah Beg with his Hamawandi tribesmen, as was feared, encouraged the Turks, who after two months' preparation were able to attack Nawdasht and were aiming at Rania and Darband while ÖzDemir was busy disseminating letters among headmen, boosting them to join the invading force.[419]

The situation thus prevailing called for immediate and radical action. On August 17, Edmonds was informed by a telegram about the building of a force to be called Ranicol (Ranya Column) in order to keep at bay the Turco-Kurdish troops from Rania districts.[420] Before long, however, it became apparent that the Ranicol could not resist the onslaughts conducted against it. On the morning of August 31, ÖzDemir launched an attack compelling the commander of Ranicol to withdraw his forces from Darband to Koi Sanjaq, while being chased and fired on along the whole retreating route. He and his fellow fighters were finally protected by the R.A.F.

It was in view of such kinds of disasters and perilous developments in South Kurdistan and generally in the whole of Iraq that the British, on October 1, 1922, decided that the ground forces transfer responsibility to the R.A.F:

Had the air control scheme not offered a cheap but effective alternative to

---

[417] Edmonds, (1957), pp.248-249.
[418] Ibid.,p.250.
[419] Ibid.,p.152.
[420] Ibid.,p.158.

military occupation, it is likely that the British presence would have been curbed or ended, the Arab Kingdom would have been stillborn and the reviving power of Turkey would have engulfed the Mosul and possibly the Bagdad and Basra vilayets.[421]

The Reinstallation of Shaikh Mahmud: His Plan and Cooperation with the Turks

Immediately prior to the reinstallation of Shaikh Mahmud the Kurdish region witnessed events of alarming character. Since the retirement of the British troops from Rania district the Sulaimanya *liwa* had been subject to a Turco-Kurdish attack. It was not long before that the British decided to evacuate their officials as well as other non-Muslim employees in Sulaimanya by air on September 5. [422]

The political officer, Major Goldsmith, before leaving the town, had handed over the responsibility of the administration to the elective council. Shaikh Qadir, younger brother of Shaikh Mahmud, who was allowed to return from Bagdad to Sulaimanya some days earlier, was appointed by the council as president. The Shaykhan, members of the Barzinja family, were informed that in case they refrained from participation in the recent anti-governmental activities, they would permit Shaikh Mahmud to return from Kuwait to Bagdad where they would arrange for the future administration of Sulaimanya. [423]

Meanwhile, encouraged by the withdrawal of the British forces to the Arbil-Kikuk-kifri line, a Turkish reconnaissance party turned up at Lower Zab and threatened to disturb the lines of communication by tribal attacks. ÖzDemir then had Koi in his hold too, and had installed Ramzi Beg as *qaimmaqam* there. He, then, ordered Abbas-i-Mahmud of the hostile

---

[421] Quoted in McDowall, (2000), p. 160.

[422] The total of 67 persons among them Assyrian levies in Sulaimanya were convoyed to Kirkuk within the day without any remarkable difficulty. Great Britain, Colonial Office, Iraqi Administration Report April 1922 to March 1923. p. 35.

[423] At the time the administration transferred its responsibility to the elective council it had 200 Kurdish levies and the treasury at its disposal. Ibid.

Pizhdar to even threaten Sulaimanya. Within a month, however, the R.A.F. and the Iraqi levies managed through a coordinated and successful action to promptly restore the situation there. [424]

It was in this sense of disarrangement that the British were obliged to once again appeal to Shaikh Mahmud to compose the situation, and to expel the enemy from South Kurdistan. At his arrival to Bagdad on September 12, 1922, Shaikh Mahmud agreed to fully comply with the policy of His Britannic Majesty's Government. The British, for their part, convinced the Shaikh that, in rallying national sentiment against the Turks, he would obtain full support both from them and the Iraqi government. King Faisal, the Shaikh was assured, had approved certain Iraqi officers from the Iraqi army to be seconded for service with him in Sulaimanya to assist him in organizing his levy forces.[425]

Shaikh Mahmud arrived in Sulaimanya on September 30, 1922, accompanied by Major Noel as his advisor. Although The Shaikh had assured the British before leaving Bagdad that his activities would not extend beyond his jurisdiction and would be confined to Sulaimanya *liwa*, it appeared that he was not sincere since the Talabani Shaikhs and others had complained that on his way the Shaikh had forced them to sign a memorial in order to include them in a Kurdish state under his leadership. Once at Sulaimaniya, he was received as *Hukmdar* of an independent Kurdistan. The local press enthusiastically foresaw a good prospect for the establishment of a Kurdish national government, and thus presented Noel to accompany Shaikh Mahmud in the capacity of a consul to serve on behalf of the British as his advisor. [426]On October 10, Shaikh Mahmud published a decree announcing the formation of a Cabinet of Kurdistan consisting of eight members; Shaikh Qadir, his brother, as prime minister; Salih Zako Saliqiran, a member of a well-known local family, as minister of national defense; Haj Mustafa Pasha, a previous Ottoman general, as

---

[424] Ibid. See also Edmonds, (1957),pp.296-298.
[425] Great Britain, Colonial Office, Iraq Administration Reports, April 1922 to March 23,p. 36.
[426] Edmonds, (1957), p. 301.

minister of national education; and Abul Karim Alaka, a famous Christian from Sulaimanya, as minister of finance. [427]In November the Shaikh assumed the title of King. He also published postage stamps and a newspaper called *Roj-i-Kurdistan* (Sun of Kurdistan). [428]The paper was issued with the cooperation of some of Sulaimanya's prominent intellectuals and poets.[429]

In order to better grasp the attitudes of Kurdish nationalists concerning the idea of Kurdish national aspirations at this stage of its development it is worth to refer to two extracts from the local paper *Rhoj-i-Kurdistan* the first from no.1, issued November 15, and the second from No.6, issued December 27, 1922:

> It (an Arabic newspaper of Bagdad) talks of Kurdistan as if it were part of Iraq and calls it the liwa of Sulaimani, because it has close commercial and economic relation with Bagdad. It calls the cabinet of Kurdistan by the name of 'provincial Administrative Council'. These remarks are most deplorable. It is unbelievable that any enlightened person could be so unjust or inexact. We never expected our great and friendly neighbor to trample underfoot all our thousand-year-old rights and the good relation of these two governments and peoples, or…to violate our frontiers… The formation of a Government of Kurdistan offers a hundred thousand benefits for Iraq; nay, the continued existence of Iraq can only be achieved through the continuance of the Government of Kurdistan. History and geography bear ample witness that the Kurdish people have always had an individuality in the world and have always established their nationhood by practical proofs. If they were not greater, they were certainly not less than their likes in education, craft, comers, human rights, civilization, lands, population, etc… The law and principle of

---

[427] Jwaideh, (2006), p. 192.

[428] Ibid. See also Great Britain, April 1922-March 1923, p. 36.

[429] These were Nuri (Roji Kurdistan's editor), Arif Saib (Second Secretary in the Royal Chancery), Rafiq Hilmi (Schoolmaster), Ali Kemal (formerly employed in the Sulaimanya Municipality), and Shaikh Nuri Baba Ali. See Jordi Tejel Gorgas (2008) *Urban Mobilization in Iraqi Kurdistan during the British Mandate*: *Sulaimanya 1918-30* , Middle Eastern Studies, 44:4, 537-552, DOI:10.1080/0026320080212068.

self-determination are strongly impressed on the mind and soul of every individual of the nation. In the blessings of rights and frontiers, which have been just allotted by the League of Nations, we too have our share. ... We are not slaves but free... Now, to God a hundred thanks, our night has tuned to day, and... a great head and leader like the King of Kurdistan, King Mahmud 1, has, as if by the miracle of the Messiah, been brought to life again for us... The sacred aim of His Excellency the King of Kurdistan has ever been the protection of right and natural frontiers of Kurdistan and the maintenance of brotherly goodwill with our neighbor.

Kurdistan. When an educated person pronounces this word he does not mean only this zone of Sulaimani, but a board, geographically region, and he thinks of a united numerous Kurdish people. The natural frontiers of this country... are clear... As the population of Mosul is Kurdistan, why should the recovery or retention of this Wilyat be demanded by outside peoples. The Turks, Arabs and Assyrians base their claims on the presence of a small number of their people... The demand we make of the Lausanne Conference is not the protection of a minority, it is the vindication of the right to live of a great independent people with a country of its own.[430]

The core idea inherent in these two articles from a local paper is, obviously, the refusal to be ruled by the new Arab elite or foreign powers and the demand for an independent Kurdish state with Shaikh Mahmud as its leader. However, there were other Kurdish leaders in other parts of Kurdistan who, despite the fact that they basically shared the ambitions of the Kurdish nationalists in Slulaimanya, expressed in the papers, as well as of those who were loyal to Shaikh Mahmud elsewhere in the Kurdish areas, they opposed being put under Shaikh Mahmud's dominion. Such were the divisions Kirkuk, Arbil and the Kurdish *qazas* in the Mosul division. They preferred, pending a decision about the Mosul question in Lausanne Conference, a "special administration" under the British auspices, which was neither to be ruled under a centralized control from Bagdad as the rest of the country, nor under an administration modeled on Sulaimanya. However, certain Kurdish

---

[430] Edmonds, (1957), pp-301-302.

tribes round Kifri, in the Kirkuk division, accepted the shaikh's authority on the grounds they, in this case, would acquire unrestricted individual liberty.[431]

Shaikh Mahmud's Cooperation with the Turks

Hardly a month had elapsed since Shaikh Mahmud's arrival to Sulaimanya as he started his cooperation with the Kemalists. The Shaikh's correspondence with the Turks was revealed when the British seized ÖzDemir's dispatches sent to the Turkish headquarters at Jazira ibn Umar. In these dispatches, ÖzDemir, who had addressed the Shaikh in complimentary terms, had avoided any commitment regarding the Kurdish question. As the British officer recorded in his report, ÖzDemir:

> Evaded every request to make a pronouncement in favour of Kurdish autonomy, and writing to a Turkish committee formed in Kirkuk, he gave frequent assurances that his Government had no intention of favoring the pretensions of Shaikh Mahmud. He was in fact, using him merely as a pawn in the game, the object of which was to recapture the Mosul Wilayat with or against the wishes of the inhabitants.[432]

Shaikh Mahmud's strategy in the conflict between the British and the Turks, which he thought would benefit his cause, was to play the two adversaries against each other, and thus on the one hand, he asserted his faithfulness to ÖzDemir, and on the other, he put heavy demands on the British to expand his authority. [433]

For the British, the situation was far from satisfactory. Efforts were made to counteract the activities of the Shaikh and his Turkish allies. With this end in mind, they approached Saiyed Taha and discussed terms and conditions with him. Saiyed Taha was considered as rather different from

---

[431] Ibid., p. 302. See also Great Britain, Colonial Office, Iraq Administration Reports, April 1922 to March 1923. P.36

[432] Ibid., p. 36.

[433] Great Britain, Colonial Office, Iraq Administration Reports, April 1922 to March 1923, p. 36.

the Shaikh; he was an Ottoman subject, and was very opposed to the Kemalists and had tribal as well as land interests in the Rawanduzi districts.
He had been also a possible candidate for the Kurdish region before Shaikh
Mahmud. The Saiyed was ready to cooperate in re-establishing British authority in Rawanduz which he believed was an easy task due to the small
number of the Turks there. He would use his own tribesmen supported by
air strikes. King Faisal had acknowledged that he could utilize his services
and a small column consisting of Kurds drafted in the Iraqi Army were to
be put at his disposal. As reward for his services the Saiyed expected to be
appointed as head of the districts of Rawanduz, Aqra and Amadiya just as
Shaikh Mahmud had been appointed in Sulaimanya.[434]

In order to re-establish their administration up to the frontier of the Mosul *Wilayat* and at the same time cope with the problem in Sulaimanya by
blocking the Shaikh's connection with the Turks, the British contemplated
using the RAF against Rawanduz. [435]

Edmonds endorsed the idea and recommended it to Bagdad, where Saiyed Taha would fly in order to participate in the tripartite conversation between King Faisal, the High Commissioner and a delegation from Sulaimanya about the determination of the future relationship between Sulaimanya and the Iraqi government. [436]

Saiyed Taha, nevertheless, was unable to conduct his military activity
owing to exceptionally heavy rain, but the rumor of his intended operation
had a great impact on the situation. It helped the RAF to force the Turks to
abandon Rania and retire further north.[437]

Later, in April 1923, Saiyed Taha was installed as *qaimmaqam* in Rawanduz as he had desired. However, on the appointment of Saiyed Taha

---

[434] Edmonds, (1957), p. 306

[435] Ibid., p. 306.

[436] Ibid. The negotiation in Bagdad bore no fruit since the Sulaimanya delegation
had just reiterated Shaikh Mahmud's embellished demands.

[437] Great Britain, Colonial Office, Iraq Administration Reports, April 1922 to
March 1923, p. 37.

there were conflicting views among the ruling elite in Bagdad. While the Iraqi government, King Faisal, the prime minister and the Mutassaref of Arbil and some other British officials opposed it, Sir Henry Dobbs, the High Commissioner at the time, insisted on the Saiyed's appointment as "bullet-proof." [438]

By the approach of the Lausanne Conference, the Turkish threat had a major impact on the political events both in Great Britain and Iraq. Following an agreement reached at the Cairo Conference for the determination of the relationship between the mandate power and the Iraqi government, the Anglo-Iraqi Treaty was signed by the government of Great Britain and the Iraqi government headed by al-Nqib on October 10, 1922. The ratification of the treaty occurred in June, 1924. The reason for this delay, besides the complexity attached to the electoral registration and the electoral system, was the question of participation of the Kurdish districts in the election to the Constituent Assembly whose task was to pass the Organic Law or Constitution and ratify the treaty. After the resignation of the al-Naqib government, Abd al-Muhsin al-Saadun was asked to form his first government on November 18, 1922.

At the time, the situation within Iraq was marked by aggravated struggles between the opposition groups, which had opposed the treaty the months before its assignment, and the government. These opposition groups that were composed of Iraqi political parties, the Shiia *ulama* and other Arab nationalist groups, as well as Kurdish districts of Kirkuk and Sulaimanya, continued to oppose the election to the National Assembly.[439] With regards to Mosul *Wilayat,* these nationalist Arab groups demanded the incorporation of the entire *Wilayat* into Iraq.[440]

---

[438] Edmonds, (1957), p. 326. Jwaideh explains that the term "bullet-proof" was employed by the British to refer to persons who due to their tribal affiliation were almost immune against bullet since the assassin would otherwise incur feud. P. 356.

[439] Lutfi Jafar Faraj, Abd Allah, *Abd al-Muhsen al-Saadun: Dawrahu Fi Tarikh al Iraq al Syiasi al Muaaser* (Abd al Musen al Saadun: His Role in the History of Iraq's Contemporary politics).(Bagdad: Al-Khuld,1988), p.73.

[440] Al-Hasani, Vol. 1. p. 59.

As a matter of fact, neither al-Saadun nor the British wanted the election to be held, on the grounds that the result of the election might benefit the Turks who earnestly pressed for the return of Mosul *Wilayat* to Turkey. The British were anxious that the Kurdish districts would refrain from participating in the election, and, hence, reinforce Turkey's vindication to Mosul *Wilayat* in the negotiation of the Lausanne Conference. Therefore, the election to the National Assembly was postponed, pending the settlement on the Mosul question at the Conference.[441]

Meanwhile, the Turkish threat of war against England contributed to the fall of Lloyd George's coalition government on October 23, 1922, which shortly ensued by the Lausanne Conference at which the Mosul question remained unresolved and, by intensified Turkish activities on the northern frontier. [442]

The Turkish menace continued to make itself felt in England. While part of the British press, especially *The Daily Mail* and *The Daily Express*, had urgently required the evacuation of Iraq in a "bag and baggage" campaign, the Parliament continued with its demand for the reduction of British expenditure. After the fall of Lloyd George's Cabinet, the question of withdrawal from Iraq became highly essential. Supported by a vicious newspaper campaign,[443] certain candidates undertook to work for that objective.[444] The former Prime Minister Herbert Asquith joined the advocates of the British evacuation from Iraq. On February 20, 1923, he stated in Parliament that the British had no basic interests in Iraq. His statement was underpinned by the revelation of the heavy expenses of British presence in Iraq.[445] Consequently, as Bonar Law came into power, he was compelled in December 1922 to form a special Cabinet Committee to explore the British policy in Iraq. The Committee reached the conclusion that by the withdrawal of the British the "Arab kingdom in Baghdad"

---

[441] Abd alla, (1988), p. 73.

[442] Slugglett, (2007), p. 53.

[443] A section of British newspaper during this period had started a violent "Quit Mesopotamia" campaign pressing the government to leave Iraq. Ibid.

[444] Ireland, (1937), p. 377.

[445] Ali. A. Allawi, *Faisal 1 of Iraq*, (Yale University Press. 2014), P.418.

would run the risk of collapsing and might be merged into Turkey. Britain's lines of communication with India, thus, would be intimidated by the Turks, who could appeal to the religious belief of the Muslim of India.[446] For the Cabinet Committee deliberations, which were attended by Cox, it was clear that Great Britain could not withdraw from Iraq until the settlement of the Turco-Iraqi frontier conflict. Accordingly, on his return to Bagdad on March 31, the High Commissioner carried with him a draft protocol, reducing the span of the treaty from twenty years to four. [447]

The government in London was skeptical to back Iraq in curbing the Turkish threat. It might, they believed, generate new Anglo-Turkish aggression for which there would be no public support in Britain. Therefore, during November and December 1922, both the governments of Iraq and England pondered returning Mosul to Turkey.[448]

---

[446] Ibid.
[447] Ireland. (1937), P. 378.
[448] Sluglett, (2007), p. 53.

9

From the Lausanne Conference to the Mosul Question

The disastrous defeat of the Greek army in the battle of Sakarya in the late summer of 1921, which marked a turning point in the Turkish war of independence and the occupation of Smyrna on September 8, 1922, drove another nail in the coffin of the Treaty of Sèvres imposed by the Allied forces upon Turkey on August 10, 1920. During the second week of September 1922, the Kemalist attack on the Allies seemed highly possible; the British in particular were worried about the consequences of such an attack. The troops who controlled the Asiatic shores of the straits were for the most part composed of British, hardly adequate to withstand a Turkish onslaught.[449] It seemed for a while that an Anglo-Turkish clash was impending; thus, the British gave way to the Kemalist demands, and on October 11, 1922, an armistice was signed at Mudanya according to which the Allied governments agreed to the restoration of the Turkish sovereignty in Istanbul, the straits, and eastern Thrance, which was occupied immediately by 8,000 Turkish gendarmes. On October 14, Greece finally acceded to the armistice.[450] Thus, circumstances changed since the signing of the Treaty of Sèvres. According to a Memorandum from the British General Staff, dated October 19, 1922:

This change is due to the creation of national spirit in Turkey, and this in turn

---

[449] A.L. Macfie, *The Straits Question 1908-36* (Thessaloniki, 1993), p. 153.
[450] Bernard Lewis, *The Emergence of Modern Turkey* (New York, Oxford, 2002), p. 254.

has resulted in the recent successes of the Turkish army, with the result that we can no longer treat the Turks as a conquered nation to whom it is possible to dictate any terms we wish.[451]

Under the new government of the Grand National Assembly, the Kemalists no longer recognized the Treaty of Sèvres and decided to replace it with a new one.

The Lausanne Conference that yielded a treaty and contributed to the consolidation of modern Turkish republic was convened on November 20, 1922 in Lausanne, Switzerland with the representatives from Great Britain, France, Italy, Japan, Greece, Bulgaria, Romania and Turkey.[452] The Lausanne conference was unique in the sense that it was the only post-war conference wherein the Allies and the defeated enemy sat at the negotiation table on a completely equal footing.[453] It also demonstrated that the Allies approved the negotiating position of the Turkish nationalists, who were no longer considered as the signatories of the Treaty of Sèvres, representing the defeated Ottoman Empire. Accordingly, the Allies were to deal with a country that struggled for its independence and was at the conference as a victor not as a supplicant. Having accomplished military achievement, the Turks endeavored at the conference to gain diplomatic advantages too. They based their arguments on terms embodied in the Mudanya Convention, whereas the Allies relied on the Armistice of Mudros, which was signed by the defeated Ottoman Empire on October 30, 1918.[454] Furthermore, the main objective for the Turkish nationalists in the

---

[451] Ibid, p. 181.

[452] The city of Lausanne was chosen as a neutral place by Britain, France and Italy to debate the new political development in the Near East. The representatives of the Soviet Union participated solely to renegotiate the straits convention and from the United States observers took part in the conference inasmuch as it concerned its interests .

[453] Briton Cooper Busch, *Mudros to Lausanne: Britain's Frontier in West Asia, 1918-1923* (New York: State University of New York Press, 1976), p.365.

[454] Nevin Coshar and Sevtap Demirci, *The Mosul Question and the Turkish Republic: Before and After the Frontier Treaty, 1926.* Middle East Studies, Vol, 42, No. 1, pp.123-132 January 2006.

conference was to safeguard the National Pact, which the Turkish nationalists attempted to materialize, and based their negotiations with the Allies upon it. The most important points on the nationalists´ agenda at the conference were: declaring the Treaty of Sèvres null and void, arrangement of a plebiscite for demarcation of the territorial affiliation of Western Thrance, the return of Mosul *Wilayat* to Turkey, the freedom of the straits (the security of Turkey's independence and the safety of Istanbul should be provided for), removal of military restrictions, removal of minority provisions (except for those in European treaties), removal of financial and economic control, removal of Capitulations and the recognition of Turkey as an independent sovereign state; in other words, the National Pact altogether.[455]

Given the crucial importance of the Mosul *Wilayat* for the Turks and the British, it was anticipated that it would seriously impede the progress of the negotiation to create peace in the Near East. On November 6, 1922, two weeks before the opening of the Conference, Rumbold informed Curzon that the "Question of Mosul will be [a]test of [the] Turkish attitude in [the] future… Unless I am much mistaken, [the] Kemalists will press strongly for its retrocession."[456] However, on December 4, Turkey showed a new strategy when Ismet Inonu, the chief negotiator of the Turkish delegation, sent his delegate to inform Curzon in private that Turkey would agree with the British on all points and even abandon Russia "… if only we would give them Wilayat of Mosul." [457] The Mosul question was the most complicated issue of the Anglo-Turkish negotiation at the Lausanne Conference and Curzon could not of course agree with Inonu's proposal.

The implacable attitudes of Curzon and Ismet Pasha, the British and the Turkish delegates respectively, to win the Mosul *Wilayat* were clearly expressed in a portion of correspondence between them. On December 14,

---

[455] Sevtap Demirci (2010) *Turco-British Diplomactic Manoeuvres on the Mosul Question in the Lausanne Conference, 1922-1923*. British Journal of Middle Eastern Studies, 37:1, 57-71, DOI: 10. 1080/13530191003661138 P.58.
[456] FO800/157,6 November 1922, Rumbold to Curzon, Curzon Papers. Quoted in Sevtap, p. 59.
[457] Busch, (1976), p. 370.

Curzon submitted a memorandum to Ismet Pasha in which he replied to Ismet's claim to Mosul on racial, political, strategic, and historical grounds that he contested each one of those claims and that Britain could not return a country which was entrusted to it under the League of Nations. [458]

The memorandum contradicted each of the reasons the Turkish delegates referred to for the restoration of Mosul *Wilayat* as following:

Racial- the inhabitants of the Mosul *Wilayat* consisted of Kurds, Arabs "Turks" (Turkomans) and Christians, with some thousands of Yazidis. A table of statistics which was compiled by British officers working in Mosul in 1921 indicated a total population of 785,468 in the divisions of Mosul, Arbil, Kirkuk and Sulaimanya which were composed of Arabs, Kurds, Turks, and Christians. The proportion of the Arabs only in the town of Mosul numbered 170, 663, were considerably more than the "Turks" numbered 14,895. Kurds numbered 454,720 were twice as much as the Arabs numbered 185,763 in the whole of Mosul *Wilayat* and almost seven times more than the Turkomans.

Political- the claim of the Turkish delegation that the inhabitants of the Mosul *Wilayat* wished to be included in Turkey, owing to its political or historical affinities with the country was rejected as groundless. The memorandum asserted that the plebiscite held in 1919 proved that the Arabs of Mosul ardently supported the unity of the three *Wilayats* of Basra, Baghdad and Mosul for the formation of the Iraqi state and, since the arrival of Emir Faisal, wished to be linked to the government of Bagdad and ruled by the latter as King. Concerning the plebiscite, it comprised the whole of *Wilayat* other than the Kurds in Sulaimanya, Rania and Rawanduz districts. The Arab areas with the Kurdish districts in the neighborhood, as well as the Turkoman towns, all participated in the plebiscite, and with the exception of Kirkuk, all voted for the incorporation into the Iraqi state and for the ascendancy of Faisal to the throne of Iraq.

---

[458] BDFA. p.Vol.3, p.214.

As for the Kurds' participation, alongside the Turks in WW 1 as the Turkish delegate had claimed, the memorandum replied that the Kurds of the Mosul *Wilayat* had by no means any common cause with the Turks, nor did they assist them in their war against the entente powers. The Turkish delegate was challenged to present any information which confirmed that the Kurds had supported the Turks against the British forces, barring a small Kurdish troop who joined the Turkish force at Shu'aiba, close to Basra in the spring of 1915.

Historical- Turkish contention that Mosul had been submitted to the rule of the Ottoman Empire for centuries would not justify its restoration to Turkey, because even Baghdad was as long as Mosul under the Turkish dominance. Both towns were inhabited by Arabs and built by Arabs; Mosul had been, as late as the end of the nineteenth century, administered from Baghdad during the period Midhat Pasha governed as *Wali* (governor) there. By virtue of historical reasons the Turks could correspondingly even demand the return of those areas and states they had lost in the war; furthermore, all countries that lost territories in the war could justify their demand based on historical grounds.

Economic- the economic reason was considered by Curzon as the weakest of all. According to him the Mosul *Wilayat* had established its economic relations exclusively with Baghdad and with the Arab town of Aleppo. These two towns were not included within the boundaries of the National Pact. In addition, the three largest cities in the *Wilayat* namely Sulaimanya, Kirkuk and Mosul were economically interdependent and their prosperity relied upon the maintenance of their contact with each other. Despite the proximity of Mosul to Turkey, it was well-known that the greatest part of the trade of Mosul was down-river with Baghdad and across the desert with Syria. Besides, Baghdad was reliant on the grain supplies from the Mosul-*Wilayat*.

Strategic-the request of the Turkish delegation, to make the southern boundary of the *Wilayat* of Mosul the strategic frontier between Turkey and Iraq, was turned down categorically since it would hamper the economic relations between Iraqi cities and with adjacent countries; moreover, it would jeopardize its security.[459]

Finally, Ismet Pasha supported his main argument for the restoration of Mosul to Turkey by the first article of the National Pact which read as follows:

> Inasmuch as it is necessary that the destinies of the portion of the Turkish Empire which are populated exclusively by an Arab majority, and which on the conclusion of the armistice to the 30th October, 1918, were in the occupation of enemy forces should be determined in accordance with the vote which shall be freely given by the inhabitants, the whole of those parts, whether within or outside the said armistice line, which are inhabited by an Ottoman Moslem majority, united in religion, in race and in aim, imbued with sentiments of mutual respect for each other and of sacrifice, and wholly respectful of each other's racial and social rights and surrounding condition, form a whole which does not admit of division for any reason in truth or in ordinance.[460]

Concerning the first proposition of the article, where it proposed holding of a plebiscite in the areas " populated exclusively by an Arab majority" Curzon, who already had, in connection with the racial and political arguments, illustrated the compound of the population in the Mosul *Wilayat* and their position toward the Iraqi government and the king, referred once again to those figures and replied that this was not the case since the Arabs did not constitute a majority of the population in Mosul and were outnumbered by other minorities such as the Kurds. He concluded that a plebiscite would not be applicable in the Mosul *Wilayat*.

The second part of the article refers to the unity of the Ottoman Muslim majority within and outside the armistice, which evidently could be deemed as an appeal to pan Islamism. As it is known, pan-Islamism appeared during the second half of the 19th century as a response to the growing European domination and influence in the Muslim world, to which the

---

[459] DBFA.Vol.3, pp-214-219.

[460] Quoted in Spencer William, *The Mosul Question in International Relations* (Ann Arbor Michigan, 1988), p. 46.

Ottoman Empire contributed a great deal through their aspiration to reform. During this period, the Ottoman Empire had used pan-Islamism as a viable instrument to maintain its sway over the Muslim population, to undermine the increased European impact upon them. It also proved to be a practicable state policy to expand its political authority beyond the Empire. Given the secular nature of the Kemalists, their appeal to the religious sentiment of the Muslims in line with the Ottomans indicated that the idea was still a current political coin which served their intentions. So the Turks´ attempt to utilize religion and pan-Islamic propaganda amongst the anti-British section of the Kurds against the British could be seen in this light.

Curzon, however, focused on another aspect in the article, namely the recognition of religion as a common denominator of the Muslims, and noted that it was difficult to maintain the unity of the different nationalities like the Arabs, the Kurds and the Turks; additionally outlining that their unity had been once imposed upon them by the Ottoman Empire, from which they had the right to be detached.[461]

The question of nationality and ethnic belonging was a matter that the Turkish delegate attached great importance to. In his reply to Curzon, Ismet Inonu countered the statement of the British delegate concerning the ethnic origin of the Kurds, by claiming that the Encyclopedia Britannica stated that the Kurdish people were not from Iranian origin but from Turanian origin. This was an opinion shared by almost all historians who specialized on that subject; therefore, according to Inonu, the ethnic considerations that he had presented sufficed to justify the return of the *Wilayat* of Mosul to Turkey.[462]

The attitudes of the Turkish nationalists vis-à-vis the Kurds, prior to the Lausanne Conference were being altered depending on the political development in Turkey. During the time Mustafa Kemal led his battle against the Allies, especially against the British, he accentuated the Turco-Kurdish unity, a unity that was intended to be permeated with Islam to constitute a pillar in their fight against the Christian occupants. The existence of two

---

[461] DBFA. Vol.3, p. 220.
[462] Ibid., p. 222.

distinctive ethnic nationalities within the homeland Turkey was expressed unambiguously by Mustafa Kemal on May1, 1920, in the Grand National Assembly:

> ... There are Turks and Kurds. We do not separate them. But while we are busy to defend and protect, of course, the nation is not one element. There are various bonded Muslim elements.... They respect each other, they have every kind of right, racial, social and geographical... The unity we are trying to create is not only Turkish or Christian. It is a mixture of one Muslim element.[463]

Whereas at this stage, the Kurds were regarded by Mustafa Kemal as unique ethnic elements and as a substantial part of Turkey, Article 15 of the proposed draft law from March 1922 for the administration of Kurdish areas in the eastern provinces stated that the Turkish language was only allowed to be employed by the suggested Kurdish National Assembly, in the service of provinces and in the administration of government. However, the Kurdish language might be taught in schools and the governor could encourage the use of the language if it could not be referred to in the future for the recognition of the Kurdish as the official language of the government.The draft law was rejected by the Kurdish deputies firmly as was anticipated.[464]

Among the reasons mentioned above, despite their importance, the strategic location of Mosul *Wilayat* and its economic significance in terms of the existence of great quantities of oil reserves were most valuable. Essentially, Turkey's attitudes toward the *Wilayat* derived from the perception that the *Wilayat* constituted a natural part of Turkey, a territory which was inseparable from the fatherland. As expressed in the resolution of the Sivas Congress held in 1919, "The fatherland within its natural frontiers, comprises a unified whole, whose parts cannot be separated from each other."[465]Turkish unyielding standpoint for retention of the Mosul *Wilayat* at the Conference, hence, coincided with the tenets embodied in the Sivas

---

[463] Quoted in McDowall. (2000), P. 188.
[464] From Sir H. Rumbold to the Marques Curzon of Kedleston-Constantinople, March 29, 1922, (Received April 3) British Documents, Vol.3, p. 64.
[465] Spencer, (1988), p 46.

resolution, and was reiterated in the second article of the National Pact:

> We are willing that in the case of the three sanjaqs, [Wilayats] which united
> themselves by a general vote to the mother country when they were first free,
> recourse should again be had, if necessary, to free popular vote.[466]

At the initial phase of the Lausanne conference, the negotiation on the
question of Mosul shifted from public discussion to corresponding between Curzon and Inonu, which started from November 26th i.e. a day
before the Mosul's question was expected to be debated in the Territorial
and Military Commission. Curzon however, accommodated Inonu's wish
to uphold a public discussion, and discussed the matter with him outside
the Conference with the ambition to reach a private compromise.[467]

The private conversation, however, was to no avail. The stubborn positions of both representatives in the course of the negotiation rendered an
understanding on the Mosul dispute unattainable. Yet, Inonu, being aware
of Great Britain's urgent need for oil, a matter that the Britain denied and
dissociated from the Mosul question, made a last effort to regain Mosul to
Turkey. He instructed two private Turkish representatives to arrange for an
oil agreement in London with the British government or with private persons. The British was also informed that:

> The sole point of disagreement which prevented signature of treaty of Lau-
> sanne was Mosul and that Ismet Pasha would confirm that if [the] question of
> Mosul was settled in favor of Turkey, [the] treaty would be agreed [to] to-
> morrow. [468]

Ismet Pasha's efforts to determine the Mosul question in London and not
in Lausanne, was met by Curzon's indignance. On January 11, 1923, he
wrote to Crowe that:

> Ismet Pasha is endeavoring without success to persuade, threaten or force me

---

[466] Quoted in ibid.

[467] Demirci, (2010), p. 60. See also Spencer, (1988), p. 48.

[468] FO839/16,8 January 1923, Crowe to Curzon, Mss Eur F112/285, No. 121, Curzon Papers. Quoted in Demirci, p.62.

to surrender to Turkey the Mosul Vilayat including of course the oil-bearing region... Recognizing his failure here, he sends behind my back... agents to London... so that I may, ... be confronted with an agreement or understanding of which I knew nothing, and which is in direct opposition to the policy which I am pursuing here. [469]

However, the Conference displayed a conspicuous controversy between the United States and Britain in terms of the Middle East oil. Oil companies in both countries, were supporting their respective governments in search of concession for foreign oilfield, especially those in the Middle East.

One of the main reasons for the British occupation of Iraq, it will be recalled, was the controlling of the oilfields in the country. British oil companies in Iraq, however, were challenged by American ones, supported diplomatically by their government. The rivalry between the two countries was, accordingly, reflected in the events of the Conference. During the Lausanne Conference:

> The tension between Great Britain and the United States over Iraq oil helped to shape both Britain and American policies and actions... a closer examination of events, not only at Lausanne but also in London and in Washington, demonstrates ... the Anglo-American oil war, rather than a mutual desire[470]for an Anglo American world order that most influenced development .[471]

---

[469] FO371/9059/E589/1/44,11 January 1923, Curzon to Crow; DBFP, XV111 (325); Shimshir, Lzan Telgraflan 1, No, 339. 13 January 1923, Ismet Pasha to Rauf Bey; FO839/16, 963; F112/295 f.12.Quoted in Demirci , p. 62.

[470] Refers to William Stivers, a historian, who is of the opinion that British policy in Iraq was backed by the United States government on the grounds that it believed to have common interests with Great Britain, both in Iraq and in the rest of the world.

[471] Fiona Venn (2009) , *Oleaginous Diplomacy: Oil, Anglo-American Relations and the Lausanne Conference, 1922-1923*, Diplomacy and Statecraft, 20:3, 414-433.

The United States' Open Door Policy

Toward the 22nd session of the Territorial and Military Commission at the Lausanne Conference, in January 1923, American observers by a statement reminded the delegates that:

> ... without seeking special privilege or favor, the government of the United States has not assented to the principle that it may be dissociated in the right of peace from the usual consequence of association in war, nor other cases where another principle is involved will it abandon the policy of open door.[472]

The United States' interest in the Middle East oil came into being as a direct consequence of the accelerating depletion of the national oil reserves following WW1. Due to the extremely high oil consumption during the war, the attention of the American government drew toward regions where oil reserves were accessible for future exploitation. The investigations initiated there predicted a cessation of oil supply within somewhat more than two decades, which evoked anxiety and, hence, increased activities for future accession of oil from overseas sources. Consequently, on May 31, 1919, all American consulars in regions where oil could be found were instructed to report on the prospect of oil and the possibility for the participation of the United States in the exploitation of oil in their districts.[473]

In the meantime, the Senate debated the so-called "Aliens Clause" which forbade foreigners the right to ownership of oil leases because of the anticipated deficiency of oil in the country. It also discussed the alleged policy of Great Britain with regards to the domination of oil in the world, particularly in the Middle East, which caused sharp controversy between the United States and Britain, accusing each other of controlling vast oil resources. In the subsequent two or three years a considerable portion of the open public meeting in the United States dealt with British endeavors

---

[472] Foreign Office.Turkey No.1,1923. Lausanne Conference on Near Eastern Affairs, 1922-1923. London, HMSO, 1923 (1814). Quoted in Spencer, (1988), p. 51.

[473] Laurence Evans, *United States policy and the Partition of Turkey, 1914-1924* (Baltimore: The John Hopkins Press, 1965), p. 294.

to block American interests to take part in the development of foreign oil deposits, which induced the British Embassy to protest against these allegations.[474]

American rights in the oil resource of the former Ottoman Empire were based on two distinctive grounds: current rights demanded by the American oil companies and the rights demanded by the American government under the open door principle. In both cases, the policy pursued by the United States "was governed by- and to a great extent influenced in its turn- American policy on mandates, the oil lands in question being located in mandate territory. The oil question arose while the United States was still an active partner with the Allies in determining the future of the Middle East." [475]

At the Conference of San Remo 1920, the Mosul *Wilayat* allocated to France, according to the secret wartime agreement, was returned to Iraq to form part of the British mandate there. Following the signing of the Anglo-French agreement at the same conference on April, 24, 1920, the French company, *Compagnie francaise des Pe'troles*, was given 25% shares in TPC [476] which was previously held by the Deutsche Bank, as spoils of the war much to the exasperation of the Americans, who believed they had been excluded from the oil in the Middle East, and regarded the agreement as a clear breach with the principle of the open door. Thus, during the years 1920 and 1921, the United States, would only approve the League of Nation's attempt to entrust Great Britain the mandate for Palestine and Mesopotamia on the condition that the latter would approve the open door principle.[477]

Once the San Remo Petroleum Agreement was announced the United

---

[474] Ibid.,pp- 294-295.

[475] Ibid., p. 295.

[476] Turkish Petroleum Company (TPC), a British registered company, was formed in 1912 by a group composing of British, German, Dutch interests. in order to acquire concession from the Ottoman Empire to prospect for oil in the Baghdad and in the Mosul *Wilayats*.The largest shareholder in the company was the British-controlled Anglo-British Oil Company (APOC) with 50% shares by 1914. It was the precursor of the Iraqi Petroleum company. (IPC).

[477] Spencer, (1988), p. 53.

States Government:

> Queried the validity of the TPC claim, and a long and acrimonious diplo-
> matic correspondence between the American and the British governments
> ensued, which exacerbated Anglo-American tension in the period from
> 1919-21, obstructed the exploitation of Iraqi oil, and also delayed the ratifi-
> cation by the League of Nations of the mandate for Iraq.[478]

However, following a decision from the British government in November 1921, American companies were basically allowed entry into Iraq, hoping that it would coincide with American open door policy.[479]

Yet, despite a satisfactory agreement between the British and the Americans concerning the commercial negotiations, the Americans were reluctant to act in line with the British policy at Lausanne. Whilst British officials in London were more focused on protecting commercial inter-ests, the negotiations in Lausanne were ongoing to determine the fate of the Mosul *Wilayat*. Rumors of an agreement between Britain and Turkey, to the effect that the Mosul *Wilayat* would be reverted to Turkey in return for significant oil and railway concessions, rendered the State Department more adamant in asserting the open door. Although on January 23, 1923, Curzon reiterated the insistence on the validity of the TPC claim in full session; he disconnected the importance of Mosul oil from the British ne-gotiation at the conference. The State Department replied by instructing its observers in Lausanne to bring to Curzon's attention the American note of November 1921, suggesting that the TPC claim to hold a pre-war commitment to a concession should be determined by arbitration.[480]

However, the support of some Americans at Constantinople of Turkey's intention to defer the settlement of the economic clause until the signing of the Peace Treaty was complete, made the already complex situation more complex. In the meantime, on April 10, 1923, just prior to the reopening of the negotiations in Lausanne, the Turkish Grand Assembly

---

[478] Venn. (2009), p. 415
[479] Ibid.,p. 416.
[480] Ibid.,p. 225.

approved a new concession to the Ottoman-American Development Company, the former Chester Group, for an area three times as large as the original concession. Several observers and diplomats in Lausanne believed that the secret moral back up of the American politicians and businessmen for Ismet Inonu finally prevented the determination of the Mosul question in accordance with the British policy, thereby referring the matter to be settled by the League of Nations. In a statement, the American secretary of State Hughes made clear that:

> We maintain the policy of the open door... we demand a square deal for our nationals ... We objected to the Turkish Petroleum concession... because it had never been validity granted and in so doing we stood for American rights generally and not for any American interests.[481]

Several American newspapers supported Hughes' political statement and claimed that the cause of the dispute on Mosul stemmed from economic interests rather than human rights consideration. *The Detroit News*, therefore, estimated the Mosul fields to "comprise one of the richest oil territories in the world"; *The Dayton News* wrote "If there wasn't a lot of oil in Mosul, there wouldn't be so much diplomatic interests in the land." Furthermore, the opinion of *New York Journal of Commerce* on Mosul was that "No good can come of its return to Turkey, and it is not yet in a condition for self-government. The only alternative is a continuation of supervision by a western power."[482]

The influence of the United States during the Lausanne Conference "frustrated" Foreign Office officials who were concerned about a possible American support of Turkey in the approaching negotiations on Mosul. However, they proceeded to work on commercial cooperation between their

---

[481] The New York Time, January 24, 1924, p.10. Quoted in Spencer, p. 54.

[482] These comments are quoted in *The Literary Digest*, February 17, 1923, "Mosul the Desired" pp.12-13. Quoted in Spencer. p. 55. For a detailed study of Anglo -American diplomatic and economic cooperation in terms of oil and the open door policy in Iraq see William Stivers *International Politics and Iraqi oil, 1918-1928: A Study in Anglo -American Diplomacy*, The Business History Review, Vol. 55, No. 4, (1981), pp. 517-540.

companies hoping that by accepting American demands in TPC shares, the State Department would finally comply.[483]

Although the American role in the Lausanne Conference was to secure its economic interests as a country that participated in the war on the side of the Western Powers, the territorial issue was central for the Turks and the British. The dispute over the Mosul *Wilayat* at the conference, however, proved tedious and protracted; both adversaries refused to budge from their attitudes and positions. While Inonu asserted that the government of Turkey could not "for a moment "disregard their legitimate claim to the disputed territory, Curzon maintained that his government could not ponder the restoration of the *Wilayat* to Turkey. [484]Consequently, the negotiations reached a deadlock and on February 4th, 1923, it was agreed to exclude the Mosul question from the program of the conference, in order to give the British and the Turkish governments a year during which they would attempt to arrive at a friendly settlement by direct negotiations. Accordingly, the conference resumed discussions on April 23rd, (the day the British reoccupied Rawanduz) and concluded following the signing of the treaty of Lausanne on July 24th, (five weeks after the British evacuation of Sulaimanya).[485]

Following the interruption of the Conference, the deputies of the Grand National Assembly (GNA) directed pungent criticism against Ismet Inonu's handling of the Mosul question. His consent to a suggestion for direct negotiation and referring the question of Mosul to the League of Nations was regarded by these deputies as a surrender of Turkey's rights to the *Wilayat*. Consequently, by criticizing the government, the Bursa MP Emin Bey, noted "if we lose Mosul we lose all territories up to Erzurum" [486] and Siirt MP, Necmettin Bey explained "To refer the Mosul issue to the League of Nations would be the same to giving Mosul to British."[487]The MPs in the Assembly were to some degree skeptical toward the League of Nations and

---

[483] Venn, (2009), P. 429.

[484] Ottoman Ali, (1997), p. 522.

[485] Edmonds, (1957), p. 348.

[486] Quoted in Demirci, (2010), p. 64.

[487] Ibid.

they equated it with Britain, as it was expressed by an Erzurum MP, "I was shocked to learn that our delegation in Lausanne mentioned the League of Nations, Gentlemen, the League of Nations is British. We must recognize this institution which was set up by the British to deceive the world." [488]

In fact, on January 23, Curzon threatened to leave Lausanne in the event that no rapid settlement of the Mosul question and other disputed matters was reached, but that did not influence Inonu, who by referring to his government's position, opposed the intervention of the League, which was regarded as an instrument under the control of great powers. The implication of the league, Curzon thought, also provided an opportunity through which the Allied powers (divided over the Ruhr problem) could reunite and thus support him against Turkey at the conference. Curzon contended that the lack of unity among the Allied powers left him to fight "a forlorn and solitary battle" on the Mosul *Wilayat.*[489]

The Turks, then, suggested holding a plebiscite on January 23 at the Territorial and Military Commission as the only reliable means for arbitration to determine the fate of Mosul, but were met by the reluctance of the British. Curzon, not particularly delighted by the European plebiscite, did not conceive it as an appropriate method to be applied in the Middle East and still less in the Mosul issue. The reasons for his objection in utilizing plebiscites were, inter alia; that by applying the principle of national self-determination, the strategic, economic and geographical aspects, which in his opinion were equally significant, could be ignored. In addition, it could not provide a precise demarcation of the frontier or territories, nor was it possible to agree upon the extent of the areas to be submitted to a plebiscite. Moreover, a plebiscite would evoke the problem of deciding who was eligible to vote and the type of questions to be posed, and then the illiteracy among the nomadic population of Mosul would only

---

[488] Ibid.

[489] Peter J. Beck, *A Tedious and Perilous Controversy: Britain and the Settlement of the Mosul Dispute. 1918-1926.* Middle Eastern Studies, Vol. 17, No. 2. (Taylor and Francis, April, 1981), pp.156-276.

make the matter worse. The security and orders, during the plebiscite was another problem, which preoccupied Curzon on the grounds that it necessitated the withdrawal of British and Turkish troops from the area in order to enable the voters to participate in a free vote without undue pressure be imposed upon them.[490]

As the negotiation in Lausanne was ongoing the British forces had succeeded to re-occupy Rawanduz and repel Shaikh Mahmud from that region. The Turks believed that the British by this action had upset the *status quo*. In a note on May 2, 1923, at Lausanne, Rumbold informed Curzon about Inuno's allegation on that matter and justified British operation in Rawanduz by saying:

> ... I presume that charge put forward by the Turks as to our modifying *status quo* by occupation of Rawanduz can also be answered on following lines: I understand that Rawanduz was occupied by our authorities, like all the rest of the Mosul Vilayat, soon after the armistice and remained in our occupation until about a year ago. It can be argued that Turkish action in then occupying it was in violation of armistice and that district has since been used as a centre of intrigue against our authority in Irak and Southern Kurdistan. You Lordship claimed throughout recent conference that the whole of Mosul Vilayat should properly be included in Irak State, and ever since the armistice His Majesty's Government have regarded the northern frontier of the vilayat as the *de facto* administrative frontier of the Iraki State. We cannot therefore admit that the termporary evacuation and reoccupation by British forces of one town within that administrative frontier can be regarded as a change in the *status quo*.[491]

Nevertheless, and as mentioned previously, the two parties could not reach an agreement, therefore the Conference was suspended and the settlement of the Mosul question was referred to the League, but despite this fact, the Turks continued with their propaganda for a plebiscite. In the debates of the National Assembly on the Lausanne Treaty, Mustafa Kemal was

---

[490] Ibid., p.260.
[491] BDFA, Vol. 29. *Turkey, August 1922- July 1923*. p. 283.

more persistent than ever with regards to the Mosul *Wilayat*.[492]

In the Assembly, the deputies were also anxious that the aim of the interruption in the Conference was to terminate the unity between the Turks and the Kurds, which consequently would bring about a Kurdish question in Turkey. It was a firm belief among the deputies that the British endeavor was to set up a Kurdish state, in case it was realized it would introduce one more problem into the Muslim world. The sharp criticism continued to the degree that Mustafa Kemal finally felt obliged to intervene on the side of the government and to give priority to a friendly settlement of the matter:

> If the Allies impose their peace proposal upon us, the government and the GNA is left with no choice but to fight. But before reaching that point, all peaceful solution must be exhausted in order to avert war. As long as the conditions crucial to our existence are secured, there will be no one who is not in favor of peace.[493]

The Lausanne Conference failed to yield an agreement on the disputed Mosul *Wilayat,* and the issue was referred to the League of Nations for arbitration. Article three paragraph two of the treaty of Lausanne stipulated:

> The frontier between Iraq and Turkey shall be laid down in friendly arrangement to be concluded between Turkey and Great Britain within nine months. In the event of no agreement being reached between the two Governments within the time mentioned, the dispute shall be referred to the Council of the League of Nations, The British and the British Governments undertake that, pending a decision to be reached on the subject of the frontier, no military or other movement shall take place which might modify in any way the present state of the territories of which the final fate will depend upon that decision.[494]

Whilst the Conference did not provide a sufficient basis for an agreement between the Turkish nationalists and the British, it nevertheless paved the

---

[492] Ibid., p. 261.
[493] Quoted in Demirci, (2010), p.65.
[494] Edmonds, (1957), pp-348-349.

way for improved relations between the two parties. During the course of the Conference "Conflicting national interests were accommodated through mutual compensations and concessions... In this context, Mosul presented a special case and those deliberations concerning it were agreeably postponed." [495]

However, Lloyd George was discontented with the treaty of Lausanne and at the same time disappointed with the allies when they in September and October 1922 abandoned the "last battle of the Western civilization against the return of savagery" into Europe, leaving the British soldier alone to save Constantinople from "hideous carnage." He maintained that the Pact of Mundanya was not Sèvres, "but it certainly was better than Lausanne. From Sèvres to Mundania was a retreat. From Mundania to Lausanne was a rout... No one claims that this Treaty was peace with honour. It is not even peace."[496]

Political Development in South Kurdistan during the Lausanne Conference

During the ongoing negotiations in Lausanne at the end of 1922, it became apparent for the nationalist Kurds that the whole concept of self-determination had undergone a radical change. While the Treaty of Sèvres provided for an autonomous national state, the Kurds of South Kurdistan were under no delusion that they were now subject to a program of incorporation into the Iraqi state. However, already days before the opening of negotiations of the Lausanne Conference, Edmonds, the political officer in Kirkuk at the time, worked to reach an agreement with the leading citizens of Kirkuk who were dissatisfied with Britain's arrangement for them. He proposed a meeting with the representatives of Kirkuk and Arbil in Bagh-

---

[495] Demirci, (2010), p. 70.

[496] Lloyd George, *The Truth about the Peace Treaties.* Vol. 2 (London, 1938), p. 136

dad at the end of October 1922 to negotiate the viability of creating a federation modeled on an Indian Political Agency.[497] A few days later, a number of nationalists from Sulaimanya had in another meeting with the High Commissioner in Baghdad, introduced a set of demands with respect to Kurdish national rights. These mands consisted of:

> recognition of the independence of Southern Kurdistan; the transfer of all predominantly Kurdish areas to the government of southern Kurdistan; the establishment of a commission to delineate the boundary between southern Kurdistan and Iraq; recognition of Shaykh Mahmud as *hukumdar* of Southern Kurdistan and finally that secondary electors (emerging from the electoral process already taking place elsewhere) should form the nucleus of a Kurdish National Assembly.[498]

In the meantime, as the Lausanne Conference progressed, the Mosul question became dominant for the Iraqi government. The prime minister al-Saadun endeavored to underline the importance of Mosul for Iraq among the Iraqi people. He succeeded in fomenting national sentiments against the Turkish threat and mobilizing public opinions for the defense of the government's position with regards to the question of Mosul.[499]

In a similar vein the British authority and the Iraqi government had to deal with two serious issues; the growing Turkish menace and Shaikh Mahmud's nationalist activities in Sulaimanya in defying the limitation the British had imposed on his sphere of influence. In such circumstances the ideal solution for the British seemed to be to find a kind of *modus vivendi* so that the Arabs and the Kurds of Iraq migt be able to live together in harmony under the same crown. King Faisal "himself too far-seeing a nationalist not to recognize and respect the sentiment in others" contributed to this arrangement and agreed that within the state of Iraq, the Kurdish provinces would exercise a full measure of local autonomy. This being the case, the Kurds themselves would decide upon the manner of conducting their government; however, there was yet to be an understanding regarding

---

[497] Sluglett, (20079, p. 81.
[498] McDowall, (2000), p.168.
[499] Abd alla, (1988), p. 78.

this matter among the Kurds. [500]

At that juncture, according to the British evaluation of the situation, time was now ripe for the Iraqi government and the British to issue a joint declaration with the intention of curtailing Shaikh Mahmud's high aspirations for settlement of a Kurdish autonomy in South Kurdistan. At the same time the moderate elements among the Kurds would be guaranteed some sort of national rights. Thus, toward the end of December 1922, a British declaration sanctioned by King Faisal and his cabinet was issued:

> His Britannic Majesty's Government and the Government of Iraq recognize the rights of the Kurds living within the boundaries of the Iraq to set up a Kurdish Government within these boundaries, and hope that the different Kurdish elements will, as soon as possible, arrive at an agreement between themselves as to the form which they wish that the government should take, and the boundaries within which they wish it to extend, and will send responsible delegates to Bagdad to discuss their economic and political relations with His Britannic Majesty's Government, and the Government of the Iraq. [501]

However, this declaration was considered by Shaikh Mahmud and other Kurdish nationalists as a real step backwards as to the Kurdish question. Despite this fact, King Faisal, who had given his approval to the declaration, felt apprehensive to this arrangement. He had previously expressed his concern about the consequences of excluding South Kurdistan from Iraq, particularly with regards to the question of Shiites and Sunnis for Iraq's policy. In a few occasions Cox told King Faisal that the policy decided on at the Cairo Conference did not mean that the British government would accept Kurdish districts being carved out of Iraq and that he always had believed that they should be governed by Kurdish officials under British guidance and rather be administered by the High Commissioner in dialogue with the Iraq government. Cox held the view that these districts preferably were to constitute part of Iraq rather than be

---

[500] Great Britain, Colonial Office, Iraq administration Reports, April, 1922 to March 1923.P.38.
[501] Ibid.

integrated with northern Kurds.[502]

After the Anglo-Iraqi declaration Cox thought that it was necessary to once again assure Faisal that this declaration "in no way implied separation politically or economically of Kurdistan from Iraq."[503]

Edmonds was authorized to announce the declaration to the tribal chieftains in South Kurdistan. Schooled in the British colonial policy, he seemed to take the declaration with a grain of salt, stating:

> This text, in particular the use of the words 'Kurdish Government' rather than 'Kurdish administration' and the absence of any geographical definition, went far beyond anything which the previous attitude of the Iraqi Government, and indeed of the High Commission, had led me to expect, and I translated orally to Abdul Kerim with some misgiving. In Baghdad, however they had felt no suchqualms and had published it simultaneously in an official communiqué.[504]

Continued Turkish Threat and Islamic Propaganda

In the meantime, the escalation of Turkish troops in early January 1923 at Jazira bin-Umar some miles from Zakho intended to occupy Kurdish areas. On this imminent threat from the Turks, Gertrude Bell wrote anxiously in her diary in late January, that she had a conversation with Faisal dwelt on the necessity of avoiding a war, but in case it came, he would offer his life for the defense of his country:

> Today H.M. summoned me to tea; he was very gallant and courageous, but naturally anxious to know whether at the last resort we were prepared to defend the country, or whether we meant to leave it to him. He told me that if necessary he would accept a plebiscite, on condition that it should extend also to predominantly Arab districts now held by the Turks, such as Nisibin and Mardin, and that on both sides armed forces should be withdrawn while a neutral power presided over the plebiscite. But he would ask us also to

---

[502] CO 730/5 23rd September 1921, Cox to Churchill.

[503] FO 371/9009 Iraq Intelligence Report No, 1,1 January 1923. Quoted in McDowall, (2000), P. 169.

[504] Edmonds, (19579, p. 312.

strengthen his hand by renouncing the mandate, if British troops were in danger in Mosul ... and if we withdrew and left the Arabs to defend them, he would go himself to the frontier and spend his life in the last stand. [505]

At the same time, the Turks were engaged with their propaganda in the entire country, which was based on Islamic principles appealing to the Muslims of Iraqi people, that they should defend their Turkish co-religious and not the "infidel" British. Turkish propaganda had considerable impact on religious classes who were not nationalists, or had not yet accepted the notion of a nation state.[506] In this connection, on April 12, 1923, Gertrude Bell wrote to her father:

This morning a fatwah forbidden the defence of the Iraq against the Turks was posted up in the Kdhimain mosque. A copy was brought in to me early this morning. The question is now what should the Iraqi... [government] do. Mr. Cornwallis thinks they ought to deport the *Mujtahids* who are signatory to the *fatwah* to Persia-they are all Persian subjects; but it's a serious decision. If only the King would have left things alone. With Ramadan close upon us, and the religious excitement it induce, the next few days may be momentous. [507]

The fatwa was regarded as a direct challenge to the Iraqi and the British authorities. The advisor to the Ministry of Interior, Cornwallis, suggested the deportation of these *Mujtahids* since they were Persian subjects. Faisal, on the other hand, was cautious and still hoped to be on good terms with the Mujtahids, especially Ayatollah Mahdi al-Khalesi, the adamant opponent to the mandate in Iraq.[508]

Shaikh Mahmud's Second Rebellion

In order to counter the Turkish threat and propaganda, British troops were redistributed in Kirkuk. These deployments of forces seemed provocative to the Kurds, and were soon coupled with the turmoil caused by the news

---

[505] Quoted in Allawi. (2014), P. 416.
[506] Ibid., p.417.
[507] Burgoyne, (1961), p. 313
[508] Allawi, (2014), p. 417.

of shelving the Mosul question and uncertainty of its future.[509] Matters seemed to take a turn for the worse; after having restocked his depleted treasure by collecting tariff duty on tobacco weeks after his arrival in Sulaimanya, Shaikh Mahmud, who due to pressure from moderate Kurds assumed somewhat agreeable attitudes vis–à–vis the British, harked back to his rebellious position. [510]

He did not turn up at a conference in Kirkuk arranged to discuss the latest development in the Kurdish districts and the two delegates he had sent on January 23 displayed an impractical attitude so they were proposed to return to Sulaimanya, telling them that any negotiation would be based only on the terms and conditions of the recent Anglo-Iraqi Declaration.[511]

Meanwhile Turkish officers visited Shaikh Mahmud in Sulaimanya at the end of January 1923, and devised an attack on Kirkuk and Koi, to be carried out by tribal forces. Besides, the anti-British Persian *ulama* of the holy cities were contacted, and the small, but influential pro-Turkish secret committees in Kirkuk were actively agitating for an uprising.[512]

The Shaikh, who after his return had hoisted his flag in Rania, a district part Sulaimanya at the time, was thus intriguing with the Turks for his forthcoming attack. He was supported by his brother-in-law Fattah Efendi, who had recently arrived from Ankara and had once served the Turkish army as a captain.[513]

Faced with this impending threat the British acted immediately; a large section of the Hamawandi Pizhdar and Jaf beg Zada two of whom had been jailed by Shaikh Mahmud, as well as the prominent members of the Shaikhan family, were rallied by the British to check the conspiracy.[514] The British issued an ultimatum to Shaikh Mahmud, demanding that he be in

---

[509] Edmonds, (1957), p.313

[510] Great Britain, Colonial Office, Iraq Administration Reports, April 1922 to March 1923.p.39.

[511] Ibid.

[512] Ibid. See also Edmonds. (1957), p. 313.

[513] Edmonds, (1957), p. 314.

[514] Great Britain, Colonial Office, Iraq Administration Reports, April 1922-to March 1923. P. 39.

Baghdad personally under guaranty for his life; this warning, however, went unheeded. According to reliable sources the Shaikh was preparing an offensive on the town of Kirkuk.

On February 16, 1923, a conference was convened in Baghdad at which British politicians [515] were attending to make a decision about the situation in Sulaimanya. Accordingly, they created a plan of action:

> (1) On the 21st the High Commissioner would telegraph to Mahmud instructing him to come to Baghdad; (2) Failing his compliance a force of aircraft would demonstrate over Sulaimanya and drop notices announcing his dismissal and giving him five more days within which to report in Baghdad together with all the members of the Administrative Council; (3) Two companies of the 14th Sikhs would be moved by rail to Kingirban and ferried thence by air (a novel operation at that time) to Kirkuk, to reinforce the Levies as a precaution against any impulsive drive in our direction; and (4) The barracks and Mahmud´s headquarters at Sulaimani would be bombed of he refused to leave the town. [516]

On the evening of February 20th, Edmonds telegraphed the High Commissioner's message to Shaikh Mahmud, asserting that he must obey the orders given to him. Edmonds rejected the Shaikh's request for further explanations on that matter on the grounds that he was not authorized in doing so. [517]

On February 22, the transport of the Shaikh to Kirkuk ended and on the following two days, proclamations were dropped by air over Sulaimanya, stating that the Shaikh had not acted in accordance with the terms for his return to Sulaimanya and, hence his government was suspended. [518]

The Shaikh's ploy now was to protract the negotiations with the British

---

[515] The High Commissioner Percy Cox was in Iraq at the time but was busy focusing on other issues such as the constitutional development of the state.

[516] Edmonds, (1957), p. 315.

[517] Ibid.

[518] Great Britain, Colonial Office, Iraq Administration Reports, April 1922 to March 1923. P. 39.

to gain time. He had several hours of intensified telegram exchanges with Edmonds asking for more time. Besides, he gave the impression that he intended to resign while at the same time dispatching column of levies to Chamchamal with the purpose of attacking Kirkuk. Consequently, the British ordered him by March 1st to evacuate Sulaimanya; the inhabitants were warned for action against the town in case he refused to obey. [519]

When Shaikh Mahmud ignored the British request, the government buildings of Sulaimanya were bombed on March 3, 1923. On the same day, a deputation under the Shaikh's brother, Shaikh Qadir, arrived in Kirkuk. Having been informed about the events in Sulaimanya, they urged the Shaikh to leave the town. He left Sulaimanya in the early hours of March 4, taking with him the remaining treasury and accompanied by about 200 levies. The bombing of Sulaimanya, it will be recalled, marked the beginning of the "forward policy" which the RAF strove to adopt as an instrument to assert itself, which provoked huge alarm in Whitehall. Information was conveyed to the local administrative Inspectors that:

> In the course of the operation it is hoped… to extend the influence of the Iraqi government among the Kurds who are at present not subject to it, and any opportunity which present itself… should be seized upon and reported at once.[520]

It was reported that Shaikh Mahmud's followers were being billeted early in March in the proximity of Sardasht, but had been unable to conduct any operation since their activities had been curtailed by aerial raids. The RAF's air operations were very effective in checking the activities of the Shaikh.It was revealed he was retired to the mountain area of Sardash, north of Sulaimanya where he had established his headquarters in a cave at Jasana and was collecting revenue, wielding power in the district as well as in Sarchinar and Shar Bazer. [521]

---

[519] Ibid.

[520] High Commissioner, Baghdad, to Administrative Inspectors, Mosul, Kirkuk and Arbil, Telegram 188/S of 6 April 1923. Delhi, BHCF, ʹEvent in Kurdistanʹ13/14/Vol.111. Quoted in Sluglett. p. 82.

[521] Edmonds, (1957), p. 319.

Shaikh Mahmud did not confine his activity solely to armed struggles, he also understood the effect of religious and political propaganda on the people. He had therefore taken with him the municipal printing press and on March 8 issued the first number of a new organ, *Bang-i-Haqq* (the Call for the Truth or of Right) which replaced *Rhozh-i-Kurdistan*.[522]

There was evidently no hiatus in communications between the Shaikh and the Turks. During these circumstances, he was visited by Özdemir, who encouraged him to recapture Sulaimanya. [523]Without forthcoming military supply from outside, however, the Shaikh's possibility to make any advancement appeared implausible. It was believed, hence, that he was prepared for taking refuge in Persian territory, where he was unlikely to be welcomed. [524]

Having for the moment expelled Shaikh Mahmud from Sulaimanya, the British decided now to thwart ÖzDemir's next move. The intercepted dispatch from ÖzDemir to the Turkish general, Commanding on the Jezira front, approved Shaikh Mahmud's complicity as well as ÖzDemir's projected attack on Kirkuk and Koi. It also disclosed that he had planned an offensive on Arbil; besides that, he had agreed with the Persian military commander over the border as to the crossing of his troops into the Persian territory, as well as recruitment of reinforcement for his irregular troops from Persian tribes. [525]

Accordingly, in March 1923, the air commander, Sir John Salmond, was entrusted to conduct the operation against ÖzDemir. Two columns were formed for this operation; Koinkol under Colonel Commandant B. Vincent, consisted of Imperial troops and Frontiercol, under Colonel Commandant H.T. Dobbin, consisted of levies and police. The operation was carried out successfully according to plan. ÖzDemir's troops who had concentrated at Spilik, a difficult pass, resisted fiercely, but with the assistance

---

[522] Ibid.
[523] Great Britain, Colonial Office, Iraq Administration Reports, April 1922 to March 1923.p. 40.
[524] Ibid.
[525] Edmonds,(1957), p. 318.

of aircraft were finally ousted with relatively few losses. ÖzDemir's defeated troops withdrew from the Spilik position on April 19th-20th, 1923.[526] Rawanduz was occupied subsequently by the British forces on the afternoon of April 22nd, two days before the second conference of Lausanne began its sittings, without any resistance. The district of Rawanduz was put under the Arbil division and Saiyed Taha, the chieftain of Nehri tribes, who was at that time a refugee in Iraq, and appointed as *qaim-maqam*. According to Gertrude Bell Saiyed Taha:

> Was a man of strong character and of great reputation among the Kurds, and his appointment was an earnest of the wish of the British and Iraqi Governments to administer the Kurdish districts through Kurdish officials.

With the assistance of a battalion of Assyrian Levies, he precluded Turkish influence in the important strategic center of Rawanduz. [527]

Joint Anglo- Iraqi Efforts for Incorporation of South Kurdistan into Iraq: The Subjugation of Shaikh Mahmud

Once Rawanduz was reoccupied, a conversation was held in Baghdad to work out a program of action for the reoccupation of Sulaimanya. There was a consensus to the effect that, as long as Shaikh Mahmud's organization established around his headquarters in Sardasht was not destroyed, Kirkuk's possibility to enjoy a peaceful administration would be minimized, even after the eviction of the Turkish troops from Rawanduz.

On May 5, an operation order was proclaimed by the British declaring:

> With the main objective of establishing local government Koikol, re-formed as in the next paragraph, will march to occupy Sulaimni town, leaving Kirkuk as at present arranged on the 14th May. Subsequent to the occupation of Sulaimani minor operation will be undertaken as necessary with the object of effecting the defeat of Shaikh Mahmud and the complete loss of his prestige, and of punishing those tribes which have evinced hostility...[528]

---

[526] Ibid. pp.324-325.
[527] Gertrude Bell, The letters of Gertrude Bell, Vol.2, (London, 1930), p.544.
[528] Ibid., p. 328

This was asserted on May 8, by proclamations dropped by airplane over Sulaimanya and other centers, stating that the government's objective was to reoccupy the town and reassuring the people that they would punish only those who resist the British troops. [529]

At the political level, there still prevailed a substantial divergence of opinion between the High Commissioner and the Iraqi government regarding the form of administration to be created in Sulaimanya. Dobbs was of the firm opinion that as long as Shaikh Mahmud remained, establishment of any kind of autonomous system in Sulaimanya would fail, and, unless he was killed or captured, the ideal solution was to compromise with him. The opinion of the Iraqi cabinet was in sharp contrast to that of Dobbs. They ignored the circumstances, during which the Anglo-Iraqi declaration was issued, and their implication in it, and strove to have a form of Kurdish administration with more submission to their control than the leaders of Kurdish opinion at the time were prone to submit to.[530]

As the political officer on the spot, Edmonds was not convinced by either opinion. Having experienced the years 1919 and 1922, he was assured that dealing with Shaikh Mahmud would only imply the restoration of the *status quo*. His suggestion was a settlement which would rally moderate Kurdish opinion, and the semi-autonomous administration would be given the possibility of maintaining itself with some assistance primarily from mandatory power and eventually from the Iraqi government.[531] Pondering an arrangement to the Kurdish question, Gertrude Bell perhaps had a similar solution. For her, however, creation of a Kurdish state seemed to be definitely out of the question:

We have turned the Turks out of our eastern frontier and I hope we're going to let the Arabs make their own arrangements there with the Kurds. If that happens I really shall for once take some credit to myself. The Cabinet decision is, we hear, going to be for a four years' treaty and it's obviously preposterous to try to set up something which depends on our being there in force to push

---

[529] Edmonds, (1957), p.328.
[530] Ibid., p. 328.
[531] Ibid., pp.328-329

it through, let alone the fact that you haven't anything to build upon with wild Kurdish chiefs. Your material, as Ja'far says, is "so damn." Most of them are holy men, half witted and half starved-wholly barbarous anyhow; and each one hates other like the devil. How are you going to create a Kurdish state?[532]

However, no decision was made and the question of the administration of the Kurdish areas was left in abeyance.

Abd al-Muhsin al-Saadun's Kurdish Policy

Although there was no consensus so far regarding the form of the administration to be established in Sulaimanya between the High Commissioner and the Iraqi government there was at this phase a complete understanding as to the incorporation of the whole of South Kurdistan into Iraq. The question remaining to be agreed upon was the extension of this incorporation with regards to the Kurdish national rights. Similar to the preceding Iraqi governments, al-Saadun, often with consent of British authority, adopted a coercive policy toward the Kurds.

After the resignation of the third government of the al-Naqib, al Saadun built his first government on November 18, 1922, and a month later was implicated in a declaration, which he and King Faisal conceived of with considerable misgiving. Whilst the negotiations of the Lausanne Conference were ongoing, it will be recalled, al-Saadun rallied for anti-Turkish sentiments among Iraqis for incorporation of Mosul *Wilayat* into Iraq. In early months in office as prime minister, it was his ambition with respect to Sulaimanya *liwa* too.

On May 4, 1923, the High Commissioner urged the Iraqi government to present their view regarding the administration of the Kurdish region. The following day a committee was formed, composed of Naji al-Suaidi (justice minister) and Nuri al-Said (vice defense minister) in order to make an inquiry on the subject, the result of which would be introduced as a declaration embodying the best necessary means for the administration

---

[532] Burgoyne, (1961), p. 314.

of Sulaimanya *liwa*. When the committee had terminated its task and the council of ministers had decided on the form of administration, which was regarded as suitable for Sulaimanya, and hence, to be put under the Iraqi government, al Saadun took the result of the inquiry with him to Sulaimanya on the morning of May 29. [533]

Al-Saadun portrayed a satisfactory state of affairs in Sulaimanya. He claimed that he had been greeted by cheerful Kurdish notables and chiefs to whom in a speech he had underscored the yearning of the Iraqi government, in bringing together the Kurds and the Arabs, and that the good intention of his government was amelioration of the Kurds' condition. In a dispatch to King Faisal, he reported on his meeting with Kurdish notables and clan leaders in the government building, where they had expressed their allegiance to King Faisal and their willingness to establish a local administration under the guidance of his government. According to him, he received suggestions from some notables to consider Sulaimanya as one of Iraq's provinces and to appoint a governor there. Furthermore, al-Saadun reported that during his visit to Sulaimanya, he realized that the majority of the people of Sulaimanya opposed Shaikh Mahmud's idea on secession from Iraqi government and expressed their dislike and fear toward him. Moreover, he stated that there were several of the Shaikh's followers who submitted themselves and their weapons. [534]

Nevertheless, the situation altered abruptly when some influential Kurdish leaders, who had endorsed the idea of inclusion in Iraq, in their negotiation with al-Saadun, affirmed that they had entrusted their destiny and interests to the High Commissioner. Al-Saadun did not hesitate to connect these contradicting attitudes with Shaikh Mahmud's propaganda against the Iraqi government, which had caused these leaders to believe in the incompetence of his government in administrating the Kurdish region. However, he held the view that it was as a result of the policy of the High Commissioner who was considering anew the possibility of the

---

[533] Abd alla, (1988), p. 104. Almost exclusively this account is based on documents from Iraqi royal archives.
[534] Ibid., pp.104-105.

reinstallation of Shaikh Mahmud in Sulaimanya. Accordingly, on May 31st al-Saadun, sent the following dispatch to King Faisal, "... owing to the news of the arrival of Majesty High Commissioner to Sulaimanya next Sunday, I ask your Majesty to convince him to abandon the idea of bringing back Shaikh Mahmud which would imply the return of chaos and terror... "[535]

Al-Saadun believed 'that the return of the reign of Shaikh Mahmud' would not only be detrimental to Sulaimanya, but also to the whole of the Kurdish areas under the control of the Iraqi government. He therefore summoned the Kurdish leaders once again to reach an accord with them, and at the same time agreed with Colonel Cornwallis to make some amendments in the program arranged by the Iraqi government [536]for the Kurds. And to appease the anxiety of these leaders, each one was given a translation of these amendments in Kurdish language for better understanding of its contents. [537]

Al-Saadun was one of those politicians in Iraq who vigorously worked for the retaining of British troops in Sulaimanya. The presence of the British troops there, combined with anti-Shaikh Mahmud's section of the population, al-Saadun thought, would constitute a reliable base upon which an effective Kurdish administration could be established and guaranteed the right of all populations. [538]

Given the decisions in London for early reduction of imperial troops in Iraq, al-Saadun's efforts for retaining British troops in Sulaimanya were in vain.[539] In the High Commissioner's opinion army spending in Sulaimanya, as for the rest of Iraq, was a heavy burden for the British government. The conversation in Sulaimanya broke down on the grounds that the High

---

[535] Ibid.,Dispatch from al-Saadun to King Faisal dated 31/5/1923, Al-Sulaimanya no. 2. The Royal Archive, The Kurdistan Archive, No. S/1 (page/47).p. 105. (my translation).

[536] Actually the administrative arrangement they discussed was based on items from Edmond's earlier recommendations, but several points were omitted from it.

[537] Ibid., p. 106.

[538] Ibid.

[539] In London it was decided to reduce the Imperial troops in Iraq to six battalions in all.

Commissioner was unable to give assurance for the remaining of Imperial troops in town until the restoration of the situation. This, despite the fact that the relations between Britain and Turkey deteriorated, which increased the probability of a *coup de main* from Jazira-Ibn-Umar against Iraq. The High Commissioner, however, agreed on postponing the public announcement of the withdrawall of the troops pending one more reference to London. [540]

In light of this, al-Saadun was obliged to reiterate his appeal in a dispatch submitted to King Faisal, to convince the High Commissioner on the necessity of keeping British troops in the region for the duration of no less than two or three months, during which the Iraqi government would be able to set up an administration based on the terms the Kurdish leaders and notables had suggested. Thereafter, according to al-Saadun, the troops could successively withdraw and be replaced by about 500 Iraqi armies. He also proposed to the King that in case these measures proved futile, it was then imperative to include all districts, which by name were part of Sulaimanya to the Iraqi provinces depending on their geographical positions. Al-Saadun's aim with the last suggestion was to entirely isolate Sulaimanya from the remaining Iraqi regions and to deprive it from its important tribes, such as the Jaf, the Hamawand and the Bishdar.[541]

Al-Saadun's mission ended in Sulaimanya and he returned to Baghdad to attend a conference convened on May 4th at the royal palace, to discuss the Kurdish question and the possibility of withdrawal of British troops from Sulaimanya. The conference was also attended by King Faisal, Dobbs and Saldon and others. In the course of the negotiations, King Faisal backed al-Saadun's statement that a rapid departure of the troops from Sulaimanya would bring back Shaikh Mahmud and, thus, disorder and chaos. Al-Saadun for his part emphasized his previous suggestion on keeping the troops for two or three months asserting that it was indispensable for a definite and passable solution.[542]

---

[540] Edmonds, (1957), p. 337.
[541] Abd alla, (1988), pp.106-107.
[542] Ibid., p. 107.

The conference terminated without any pronounced decision made. Nevertheless, the High Commissioner finally pledged to confer with his government on retaining Imperial troops for the period, suggested by al-Saadun and the King. Meanwhile, al-Saadun's cabinet, anticipating complication in the British position, reached a decision on May 6, on reinforcement of the Iraqi Army. The cabinet also demanded that the Ministry of Defense would prepare proposals concerning requirements for an occupation of Sulaimanya in the future by the Iraqi army.[543]

Yet, al-Saadun's cabinet expected that the British decision would coincide with their request to retain the troops in Sulaimanya; otherwise, his cabinet would not be responsible for the consequences of the withdrawal of the troops. When the British decided to reject al-Saadun's request, he determined to implement his plan previously proposed to the king, which he considered as an appropriate measure to curb Shaikh Mahmud's threat. Accordingly, on June 11, the cabinet entrusted the Ministry of Interior in taking urgent measures to detach several districts from Sulaimanya, and attach them to adjacent provinces. The cabinet also authorized the Ministry of Finance to send funds to Edmonds in Kirkuk, to pay the salaries of the police, gendarmeries and the officials there.[544]

It was anticipated that Shaikh Mahmud would return to Sulaimanya on any day after the withdrawal of the British troops. The British were also aware that the administration in Sulaimanya was unable to prevent the Shaikh from returning to the town. Al-saadun's fear of returning Shaikh to Sulaimanya came true. Soon after the British troops' withdrawal from Sulaimanya the Shaikh's followers entered the town, and he himself returned on July 11. This event put an end to al-Saadun's efforts to bring Sulaimanya under the control of the Iraqi government.[545] It was now of particular importance for him to win the loyalties of the remaining Kurdish districts, given the forthcoming election for the Constituent Assembly.

---

[543] Ibid.
[544] Ibid.,p.108.
[545] Ibid.

Shaikh Mahmud himself had currently returned from the Pizhdar region, where his attempt to organize a rebellion in Koikol had been thwarted by Babakr Agha, chief of the Pizhdar tribe.[546] In a letter dated May 14th sent to the column commander at Kirkuk the Shaikh warned him not to advance to Chamchamal. On the same morning, he moved from Jasna toward Sulaimanya in order to mobilize fighters against the column, but upon learning that the troops had already crossed the Tasluja Pass, he ordered a general retreat toward the Persian frontier.

Conditions developed now for the British advantage. During the absence of Shaikh Mahmud, efforts were made to re-establish the administration in Sulaimanya. Edmonds undertook to set up a temporary council until Koikol returned to the town. Ahmad Beg-i-Taufiq Beg was appointed as head of the department of civil administration, and Shaikh Qadir, Shaikh Mahmud's brother, was put in charge of public security. [547]

Shaikh Mahmud himself, according to definite information, had retired to Piran, a village in Mirawan, situated two miles on the Persian side of the frontier. In the meantime, several of Shaikh's followers had made submissions and others were expected to follow suit. [548]

Then, on June 14th, the member of the temporary council resigned as they were informed that the troops would retire and that they within three days should leave the town without accomplishing the reestablishment of the administration or recruitment of gendarme for the local force. Consequently, terrified people were getting ready to quit the town *en masse*. [549]

In a visit to Baghdad, Edmonds introduced the scheme he had previously developed for the administration of Sulaimanya to the effect that Koikol would take over districts adjacent to Kirkuk and Arbil and be administered

---

[546] Edmonds, (1957), p. 330. Shaikh Mahmud's troops consisted of levies and irregular villagers numbered around 600 in all, and were under the command of Salif Zaki Sahib-Qiran.

[547] Ibid.,p. 331. Edmonds used Shaikh Mahmud's office at the secondary school in Sulaimanya, which became political office in 1919, for transaction of business. On the wall behind his chair, hung a photograph of the Shaikh and a Kurdish flag with a tinsel crown. Ibid. 332.

[548] Ibid., p. 336.

[549] Edmonds, (1957), p. 337.

from these centers. His scheme was apparently similar to that of al-Saadun as he envisaged limiting the problem of Sulaimanya to its central district. His idea was backed by Ahmad Beg-i-Taufiq Beg and Shaikh Qadir who even accepted taking responsibility for the central district provided they would be given funds to build a security force of 350 men and a British officer to be with them in town. However, this was rejected categorically by Dobbs. It was arranged that after the departure of the troops the leading citizens would be put in charge of maintaining the town's security, but they were exempt from responsibility for disturbance organized from outside the town.[550]

In Baghdad the prospect of the ratification of the Anglo-Iraqi treaty seemed optimistic. The protocol limiting the duration of the Anglo-Iraqi treaty was signed, and the king and the cabinet undertook properly fulfilling the election to the Constituent Assembly so as to secure the treaty's ratification. [551]

In this respect, it was highly significant to make concession to the national sentiments of those districts which had refused to take part in the election.[552] With this end in view, an agreement was concluded in Kirkuk, provided that a governmental announcement guaranteed that the official language remained Turkish and the officials should be local men; a measure considered as a progress for Kirkuk since the condition of first making peace with Turkey was now omitted. The decision of the notables concerning the election was expressed in a formal resolution approved by the provincial Administrative Council, which was dispatched to Baghdad by the governor of Kirkuk. The Prime Minister al-Saadun acknowledged the resolution on July 11, in a telegram:

> Please inform the Administrative Council that their suggestions have been accepted and that the Government agrees that the appointments be filled by local men only and that the local language be considered official... You May inform the Administrative Council and promise them the fulfillment of these

---

[550] Ibid., p. 338.

[551] Ibid., p. 342.

[552] Even the shi'a clerics most in holy cities had declared the proposal election illegal and were against the ratification of the treaty.

conditions in an official way.[553]

The British also attempted to encourage the participation in the election of those areas where Shaikh Mahmud was blocked from interfering in their internal affairs, according to the scheme called Sanitary Cordon. The council of minister, therefore, adopted and issued simultaneously with the announcement of Kirkuk, one more declaration of the government's attitudes toward the Kurds:

> The Iraqi Government does not intend to appoint any Arab official in the Kurdish districts, except technical officials, nor do they intend to force the inhabitants of the Kurdish districts to use the Arabic language in their official correspondence. The rights of the inhabitants and the religious and civil communities in the said districts will be properly safeguarded.[554]

In respect of that arrangement the Iraqi government aimed to demonstrate its good intention by electing five deputies from Sulaimanya to represent them in the Constituent Assembly following the expulsion of the Shaikh's forces and the restoration of the situation there. Furthermore, the Iraqi government attempted through adopting measures for necessary administrative reforms to secure a foothold there.[555]

With the reappearance of Shaikh Mahmud in Sulaimanya, however, it became urgent that the British defined his position by a new announcement. Edmonds thus formulated a letter addressed to Shaikh Mahmud, which read as follows:

> H.E. The High Commissioner has heard that you have returned to Sulaimani and has ordered me to inform you that he has made arrangements for the administration of the qaza of Ranya, Qala Diza, Chamchamal, Halabja, Qara Dagh with Sangaw, and for the nahiya of Mawat and that you must not interfere in any way with the above mentioned districts, or with the villages appertaining to the Saiyid of Sargelu. If (which God forbid) you act against these

---

[553] Ibid., p. 343.
[554] Ibid., p.344.
[555] Abdul Razzaq Al-Hasani, *Tarikh al-Wizarat al Iraqiya,* Vol.3, (Sidon, 1940), (History of Iraqi Cabinets, Vol.3, Sidon, 1940), p. 157.

instructions and interfere in the said districts or intrigue against the Government in other ways, the most drastic action will be taken against you. For the
present, provided that you do not interfere with the above- specified districts
and provided that you do not commit hostile act, His Excellency does not
intend to take action against you.[556]

Owing to Shaikh Mahmud's disobedience to the British warning letter, and
his interference in the prohibited areas, especially in Mawat district, his
headquarters in Sulaimanya was bombed. In sympathy with the Shaikh's
belligerent stratagem several inctances of "brigandage" ensued in the
vicinity of the highway. [557]

By now, the Shaikh had been delivered serious blows from the British,
thus weakening his forces and his threat was aloof; yet the British could
not underestimate his expected attacks, or according to Edmonds' evaluation of the situation "the pendulum would swing violently the other
way."[558]For this reason, he frequently suggested more air attacks against
the position of the Shaikh and even, in line with al-Saadun's policy, the reoccupation of Sulaimanya by the Iraqi Army. Contrary to the British
troops, the Iraqi Army, Edmonds believed, was unlikely to rapidly abandon
the town once it was there and to give the Shaikh and his followers the
final blow. Nevertheless, even this time, he did not gain the support of the
High Commissioner who instead opted for cautious tactics.[559]

On November 18, 1923, the Turkish government protested to the British
High Commissioner in Constantinople against the August 18 bombing of
Shaikh Mahmud's headquarters, contending that it violated the *status quo*,
which was stipulated in the Treaty of Lausanne. The British answer was
that they regarded the whole of the former Mosul *Wilayat* as still under
their effective occupation and their *de facto* administration until any
changes of its frontier occurred; besides that they did not view the air at-

---

[556] Great Britain, Colonial Office, Iraq Administration Reports, April, 1923 to
December, 1924, p. 31. See also Edmonds, (1957), p. 346.
[557] Edmonds, (1957), p. 350.
[558] Ibid., p. 365.
[559] Ibid.

tacks in question as an infringement of the *status quo,* but as a local administrative measure in order to avert a threat to public security.[560]

In the meantime, the Shaikh, due to his precarious situation, resorted to employing diplomatic and propaganda methods. He addressed a good deal of letters to both Edmonds and the High Commissioner demonstrating his innocence and protesting that he had been misunderstood. In order to maintain control over his followers, he used a line of propaganda indicating that the British declarations and operations against him were only tactics used within the international policy framework, and that he would soon regain his authority.[561]

Nevertheless, a telegram sent from the High Commissioner to Edmonds revealed that the Shaikh continued to act in defiance of the terms dictated upon him, and that they had a considerable amount of evidence disclosing his intention to perform hostile activities in the forbidden areas. Thus, the British decided to bomb his headquarters again. The day of the bombardment was Christmas day 1923 and the operation was conducted from Arbil.

In addition to its punitive purpose the bombing served to uncover the duplicity of Shaikh Mahmud's propaganda that the government intended to restore his authority. Consequently, a number of Shaikh's followers decided to abandon him. [562]

Meanwhile, the frontier commission's visit at the end of February 1924 gave the Shaikh a new hope, but it was dashed since the commission argued that he as an open rebel was not appropriate for corroboration. The body instead interviewed several religious and tribal leaders; among them the Shaikh's brother, Shaikh Qader, who stoutly rejected a return to Turkish rule because the Turks had assassinated his father and one of his brothers.[563]

---

[560] Great Britain, Colonial Office, Iraq Administration Reports, April, 1923 to December, 1924, p. 31.

[561] Ibid.

[562] Ibid.,p.371.

[563] Great Britain, Colonial Office, Iraq Administration Reports, 1914-1932.

In the summer of the same year, the British and Iraqi authorities managed to restore law and order to Sulaimanya. The administration, which the Iraqi Government rebuilt there, had now consolidated and blockhouses manned by police were built alongside the lines of communication. This together with a far-reaching patrol system had considerably restricted the activities of the "brigands". [564]Nevertheless, the unrest in the region of the Qaradagh developed into attacks on the neighboring districts which were checked by the police, assisted by aerial raids, and when necessary, also by a section of the Iraqi Army.[565] Consequently,the whole province witnessed a remarkable amelioration in terms of security; the normal administrative machinery functioned satisfactorily throughout the province except in small areas around Penjwin on the Persian frontier, where administrative officials were not yet appointed. [566]

As for Shaikh Mahmud, the principal figure of disturbance in the area; he had taken refuge to the Persian border with his followers. In June, with a troop consisting of around 800 Persian tribesmen from Auroman and Mariwan districts, led small forces units operating in the neighborhood of Penjwin together with the migration of the nomadic Jaf tribe of Kurds from the north. The Shaikh's operation was repulsed, but near his tribal forces an airplane on reconnaissance work had to land; as a result, the British officer, pilot and his mechanic were imprisoned and taken to the Shaikh's headquarters at the village of Walajir on the other side of the Persian frontier. In August, the Shaikh maximized his effort to recruit and collect sheep tax from the Jaf tribe, who were migrating back into Iraq. However, they were warned by proclamation dropped upon them by airplane, not to participate in aggressive actions. The Shaikh made a further attempt in September when he, with a force of Persian tribesmen moved anew into Iraqi territory, where he coercively collected tribute from the Jaf tribe. Even this time the Shaikh's attack was averted by a military column sent from Sulaimanya to

Vol. 8. 1925-1927.pp. 20-21
[564] Ibid., p. 199.
[565] Ibid.,21.
[566] Ibid.,p. 199.

the Penjwin area. When the Jaf then pushed on southwards, the Iraqi government extorted tribute from them, which occasioned shortage in the Shaikh's treasury so that he was forced to dismiss the rank and file from his troop. [567]

Due to the failure of his tribal attacks, he sought now to discuss his future with the British. Thus, he dispatched a letter to the High Commissioner demonstrating his good intention and asking to see him or a representative for this purpose. The High Commissioner accepted, provided that the two British prisoners would be released before the meeting. The Shaikh agreed and a meeting was organized to be convened on October 9th at the village of Khurmal, in the vicinity of the Persian frontier. It was the intention of the High Commissioner that he himself would meet the Shaikh, but due to a "sudden indisposition" he could not attend the meeting and instead Cornwallis replaced him. The Shaikh kept his word and released the two prisoners whom he had treated with reverence and consideration during their arrest.[568]

During the negotiation at Khurmal, Cornwallis clearly explained the position of the Iraqi government vis-à-vis the Shaikh and, although they could not arrive at a final settlement, it was agreed that the Shaikh should send a trustworthy representative to Baghdad to proceed with the conversation. Toward the end of October, as it was arranged, Shaikh Mahmud's representative came to Baghdad and his discussion with the Minister of the Interior "had reached a point not far from agreement", but nothing more was heard from the upshot of that meeting. [569]

It was reported that at the close of the year 1924, the Sulaimanya town and most part of the province had been brought loosely under the Iraqi government, albeit still under the direct authority of the High Commissioner pending the restoration of tranquility to the town, and the province on a whole experienced a rapid improvement in the aftermath of the

---

[567] Ibid.
[568] Ibid.
[569] Ibid.

Shaikh's mismanagement.[570]

The Shaikh's persisting interference in the affairs of the forbidden districts induced the British to once again occupy Sulaimanya. The town was occupied in the middle of July 1924 by ground troops consisting of a column of Iraqi Army, a force of police, a detachment of Assyrian levies and the RAF. The political officer A.J. Chapman was appointed as head of administration as a *Mutasarrif* under the Iraqi government, but, pro tem, he reported to the High Commissioner and received orders from him. [571]

Despite the presence of the occupation forces, the political situation in Sulaimanya was still unstable.[572] According to Chapman's report, the appointment of "bullet-Proof" *mudirs* of varying competence for the administration of the districts of Sulaimanya valley had not improved the situation there. The operations of the Shaikh's rebel groups from their bases in Shahr Bazher and Penjwin, up to the periphery of Sulaimanya itself, were also contributory factors to this instability.[573]

The British authority, however, seemed to be delighted with the development, with respect to the Kurdish policy during the period 1923-1924. At the close of the year 1924, they summarized the development as follows:

It is with satisfactory to note a general advance in the solution of relations between the Iraqi Government and the Kurdish elements of the State, culminating in the whole-hearted participation of the Kurdish districts in the elections. From the first, Kurds have enlisted readily in the Iraqi army which, indeed, is to a large extent officered by men of Kurdish decent; Kurds are eligible for all offices in the civil service, not in present only, but also in practice. There is no reason to anticipate in the future the occurrence of racial dissension and every ground for hope that further development will follow the lines of closer amalgamation. But Arab nationalists will need to bear in mind that

---

[570] Ibid.,p.20.

[571] Edmonds, (1957), p. 387.

[572] Unlike Kirkuk where King Faisal had paid a visit for the first time since his arrival to Iraq Chapman reported that due to the unstable political situation in Sulaimanya, the King could not visit the town.

[573] Ibid., p. 391.

the end in view will be more speedily and more surely attained if the national aspirations of their Kurdish fellow subjects are treated with as much consideration as the similar sentiments which they themselves cherish[574]

In November two sections of the Pizdhar tribe had reached a settlement, and toward the end of 1925, the hostile one, loyal to the Shaikh, was co-opted; the northern half of the Shahr Bahzer was finally coerced. The Shaikh, who had entrenched himself in the Persian hills and Penjwin, had almost lost his credit among the Jaf tribe.[575] And the consolidation of the administration progressively turned him to the position of a fugitive moving back and forth across the Persian frontier, until he made his submission in June 1927. [576]

---

[574] Special Report, P. 258.
[575] Great Britain, Colonial Office, Iraq Administration Reports, 1914-1932. Vol.8. 1925-1927, p. 22.
[576] Edmonds, (1957), p. 422.

10

The Mosul Question: Territorial Settlement and Consolidation of Iraqi State

The Significance of Territory and Boundary

The dismemberment of the Ottoman Empire after World War 1 by the victorious Allies led to redrawing the map of the Middle East, and particularly that of the Arab territories and Kurdistan into the current form. The radical change of the region's political geography occurred as a result of the ongoing development of the global politics coupled with domestic politics in Great Britain. The mandates system as a compromise between non-annexation policy, promoted vigorously by President Wilson, and colonial rule were superimposed on these countries ignoring the ethnical, cultural or religious diversities among the populations of those territories. A direct consequence of this policy was that states and borders that were arbitrarily created by the Western powers became entangled in ethnic- territorial disputes. The British as the mandatory power delineated the geographical boundaries of the nascent state of Iraq after its creation, through the unification of the three *Wilayats* of Baghdad, Basra and Mosul. However it was not until 1926 that Iraq's boundaries were finally fixed when the Mosul *Wilayat* was awarded to it. The definition of the boundaries of the new state of Iraq was crucial in the process of its formation since it also defined the extent of its territorial jurisdiction and sovereignty.

It was first by virtue of the peace of Westphalia (1648) that states, under the principle of international law, were granted actual territorial sovereignty. According to this treaty, each state could exercise power within a defined territorial entity.[577] A significant feature of the Westphalian sovereignty is the assumption that sovereignty is connected to territory since "territory is a tangible attribute of statehood and within that particular geographical area which it occupies, a state enjoys and exercises sovereignty." [578]The international legal theory is also very important; it stipulates that states are bodies of populated territories under government's control which are able to establish international relations with other states. This definition basically requires that there should be "a definable territorial extent to the state which would, thereby, acquire precise territorial limits." [579]

However, although territory has always been a vital living space for human beings where they have built societies and exercised authority, the significance of territory and its boundaries have been flexible during the course of history. The Roman Empire attached considerable importance to the political-geographical aspects of their frontiers, and had a distinct territorial and frontier consciousness. The Romans were protected by a frontier zone consisting of client territories under the Empire domination; the extent of which was determined by its diplomatic and military influence. The late Roman Empire employed a defense-in-depth defensive strategy using natural featurs such as the Rhine and the Danub. They also used man-made defensive walls, like the limes which functioned as a frontier zone and were built across southwest Germania or Hardian's wall in North Britain. These were to serve as a boundary region separating the Roman from non-Roman societies. Nevertheless, typically penetrable and fluid frontier of the frontier zones did not prevent transition to either side.[580]

---

[577] Jean Gottmann, *The Significance of Territory* (Charlottesville: The University Press of Virginia, 1973), pp-44-52.

[578] George Joffé, *Territory, State and Nation in the Middle East and North Africa.* In Clive H. Schofield and Richard N. Schofield (eds.) *The Middle East and North Africa,* World Boundaries Volume 2, (London and New York, Routledge, 1944), p. 1.

[579] Ibid., p. 2

[580] Roy E.H. Mellor, *Nation, State, and Territory: A Political Geography*

Feudalism as a combination of economic, political and social system was built on a hierarchical structure, and based on personal loyalty to the sovereign rulers. Roy points out that due to the complexity surrounding the legal and moral relations of feudalism, no clear demarcation boundaries developed on the continent. Since "Feudal kingship was a matter of justice and lordship, not of sovereignty, thus, disputes were usually over feudal titles rather than sovereignty", a fact which rendered the drawing of frontier lines difficult. [581]

Earlier Germanic peoples did not perceive frontier as delimited territory, nor had they any word for that. They employed words like *mark* (March) and *forst* (forest) only to distinguish between different political territories[582]. In the Middle Ages, the word march (edge or margin) became institutionalized and served to defend the border against interlopers and regulate trade. As the eighteenth century unfolded, the Habsburg also created an institutionalized border zone, the *militärgrenze* to defend the Empire against Ottoman attacks. [583]

When the monitory economy made people and land subject to taxation, ownership was defined in more accurate legal terms and hence the Absolutist state based its sovereign rule, confirmed in the Treaty of Westphalia (1648), primarily over territory rather than personal loyalty and feudal servitude. This development of the nature of territory and territoriality enhanced the importance of the frontier as a line of division.

(London and New York: Routledge, 1989), pp-74-78. See also Jan Willen Drijvers, *The Limits of Empire in the Res Gestae of Ammianus Marcellinus* in Oliver Hekster and ted Kaizer (eds.) *The Frontier in the Roman World*. Proceedings of the Ninth Workshop of the International Network, Impact of Empire, (Durham , 16-19 April, 2009), (Brill, 2011).

[581] Roy, pp.75-76.

[582] For more detailed discussion on political frontier between state and their replacement by boundaries see J:R:V. Prescott, *The Geography of Frontiers and Boundaries* (London: Hutchinson University Library, 1965), pp.33-87, and *Prescott, Political Frontiers and Boundaries* (London: Allen & Unwin, 1987), pp-43-90.

[583] R.J.W. Evans, *Essay and Reflections: Frontiers and National Identities in Central Europe*, (The International Review Vol 14. No. 3. Agu.1992), pp. .480-482. See also Roy,(1989), pp. 75-76.

The French Revolution with the principle that the primacy of the nation was the focal point of identity and loyalty made accurate territorial limitation more desirable, and in the 19th century, the rising tide of nationalism, which engendered the modern nation-states with sovereign territories, intensified the demand for more precise nation-centered boundaries.[584]Thus, as mentioned above, sovereignty is territorial, and therefore it requires a certain known extent which implies that a territory is submitted to exclusive jurisdiction and is limited by state boundaries. Consequently, the borderlands, and the old marchlands are defined more and more accurately, until there are principally exact border lines.[585]

However, boundaries have been perceived as fixed, stable empirical entities, which separate the global space into bounded units and change primarily due to disputes. Anssi Passi relates this to the fact that "the state-centered system of territories and boundaries largely defines how we understand and represent the world and how knowledge of the geography of the world is produced, organized and used in the reproduction of the nation-state system." This perception stipulates that people should belong to a nation and assume a national identity and state citizenship and that the boundaries of modern sovereign states are fulfillment of a historical destiny. In the production and reproduction of these manifestations of territorialities states play the decisive role. This is realized through education, politics, administration and government; the aim is to marginalize, suppress and eliminate ethnic identity as well as indigenous movements. [586]

Passi dismisses the perception that the boundaries are fixed, and suggests that they should be regarded as social process, since they are not "constants" but their meanings change depending on different contexts and on actions of different actors. However, military leaders and politicians can operate as agents of social action and "produce representations and visions

---

[584] Roy, (1989), pp.76-78.

[585] Ladis, K.D., Kristof, *The Nature of Frontiers and Boundaries*, AAG, (Association of American Geography), Vol.49. No. 3. 1959. pp. 269-282.

[586] Anssi Passi, (1998) *Boundaries as social process: Territoriality in the world of flows*, Geopolitics, 3:1, 69-88, DOI: 10. 1080/14650049808407608, pp. 69-85.

of the meanings of boundaries" which are historically contingent. [587]One of the dilemmas of the nation-states which were superimposed by the colonial powers after World War 1 was how to deal with the question of national self-determination of the peoples living within the boundaries of the former Ottoman Empire. For the Arabs, the partition of the Empire "signaled the consolidation of a regional order composed of self-interested and territorially defined states with a different conception of nationhood-*wataniyya*. This shift meant that the call for an Arab nation was to be gradually replaced by the call for an Iraqi (as well as Syrian, Lebanese, etc.) nation-state." [588]Fred H. Lawson, contends that some nationalist leaderships in the Arab world performed the shift toward territory bounded states based on Westphalian sovereignty comparatively early, for example, in Egypt, while others such as in Iraq made it much later. The reason for this was that different Arab states followed different development trajectories.[589] As far as Iraq was concerned, the application of the western concept of nation-state, based on territoriality, entailed   clashes of loyalties, as well as denial and suppression of minority rights. It also gave rise to borders [590] and territorial disputes. In light of this regional oriented nation-state development, the acquisition of Mosul *Wilayat* assumed a new significance.

The Constantinople Conference

It will be recalled, that in accordance with the Treaty of Lausanne signed July 24th, 1923, the Turkish and the British governments would within nine months settle the Mosul question by "friendly agreement" between themselves. With this end in view, the British conveyed a note to the Turkish government and on October 5th, the Anglo-Turkish negotiations were

---

[587] Passi, pp-80-81.

[588] Mai Taha, *Self-Determination, oil and Islam in the Face of the League of Nations: the Mosul Dispute and the "non-European" Legal Terrain,* in Duncan French (ed.) *Statehood and Self-Determination, Reconciling Tradition and Modernity in International Law.* (Cambridge University Press, 2013). p.335.

[589] Lawson, (2006), p. 50.

[590] For discussions on border settlements during 1920s between Iraq and countries such as Iran, Kuwait and Saudi Arabia see Day, A.J.,*Border and Territorial Disputes* (London: Longman, 1982) , pp. 214-226.

officially initiated. However, due to different reasons, the actual conference was convened on May 19th, 1924 in Constantinople. The British delegation was headed by Sir Percy Cox, [591]and the Turkish delegation consisted of Fethi Bey, Faik Bey and Nusret Bey, as advisers and Colonel
Ishak Avni, as a military adviser. Already from the outset of the discussion, it became apparent that the two parties had not altered their stands in
regards to the disputed territory. The Turks reiterated their claim for the
retrocession of the whole *Wilayat* of Mosul emphasizing that the Turco-
Kurdish brotherhood actually existed and, hence, constituted a Turkish
majority in the region. They were backed by their press, who deemed the
restoration of the *Wilayat* to Turkey as the only fair upshot of the negotiations that would uphold peace and security for Iraq. They also argued that
since the Lausanne Treaty had not been ratified, Turkey had no obligation
to submit to the terms providing for arbitration of the Mosul dispute by
the League. [592]

Cox, on the other hand, maintained that the British attached more
importance to the future of the Assyrians, than it was the case during the
Lausanne Conference and suggested a frontier which would guarantee "the
establishment of the Assyrians as a single compact community ... if not
always in the abodes of their ancestors, at least in the contiguous and
suitable regions." [593]The British also claimed that three additional *qazas*,

---

[591] Edmonds,(1957),p.385,the British delegation included Captain R.F.Jardine,
the Assistant Administrative Inspector of the Mosul *Wilayat*, who had been
working there since 1919 and carried out a special study of the Geography and
the populations of the frontier areas.

[592] Spencer, (1988), p. 97.

[593] The Turkish Red Book (Le Livre Rouge),Turkey, *Haricite Vekali* (Ministry
of Foreign Affairs), *La Question de Mossoul de la Signature du Traité
d'armistice de Moudros, 30 October 1918*- 1 March 1925 (Constantinople,
1925). Quoted in Spencer, (1988), p. 98. The Assyrians composed of Nestorian
and Chaldean Christians settled downed in the Hakkari Mountains of
southeastern Anatolia toward the end of World War 1. While the Chaldeans were
on good terms with the Ottoman Sultan, the Nestorians rebelled against them and
expected support from the Czarist Russia who had invaded Anatolia. The
subsequent Russian retreat and the overthrow of the Czarist government in 1917
left them exposed to the retaliation of the Ottoman Government. Under the

Shamadinan, Beit-es-Shabab, and Ulamerk, be incorporated into the Iraqi territory. The Turks opposed this plan on the grounds that it contradicted the proviso of Lausanne and would carve out more of the Hakkari region. Both sides were intransigent; the Turks put forward a claim for the whole of Kurdistan, which was countered by the Anglo-Iraqi claim to the three *qazas*. Thus, on June 6, the conference dispersed and the British delegation returned home on June 9th leaving the Mosul dispute unsettled. Before long, the Turkish representative was critical of Cox's argument concerning the Assyrian territory north of Mosul stating that the three *qazas* in question were inhabited by Muslims. The Turkish newspapers for their part accused the British of being adamant in their position, blaming them for the breakdown of the conference. The *Vatan* newspaper noted that Cox had devoted his whole existence for the realization of his aim, to forge an English Empire between Basra, Baghdad and Teheran with Kurdistan as its base.[594]

The Constantinople Conference proved once again that the British and the Turks were farther apart than ever in regards with the Mosul question. After the failure to achieve an agreement at the conference, the British were concerned about the Turkish attitudes vis-à-vis the League of Nations. As mentioned previously, the Turks were distrustful toward the League and did not feel the need to be bound by the League's arbitration in any matter. The Turkish delegate asserted that Ankara would oppose bringing the Mosul dispute to the consideration of the League of Nations, unless the British ratified the Treaty. [595]

In the meantime, the British Labour Government of MacDonald, like

---

protection of the British forces they were evacuated in a large refugee camp at Baquba on the Diyala River in 1918. The Assyrians' fighting skills and loyalties were qualities which made the British to recruit a great number of them for services in the Iraqi levies. In 1924, the British High Commissioner for Iraq declared a scheme of local autonomy for the Assyrians in the Hakkari and Dohok areas, but before the plan was realized the Turks extended their administration into the Hakkari area and drove out the Assyrians who had returned there. Spencer. (1988), pp.78- 81.

[594] Ibid., pp. 97-99.

[595] Coshar &Demirci, (2006), p. 126.

the Conservative government of Andrew Bonar, was not very optimistic that the Anglo-Turkish negotiations in accordance with Article 3 paragraph 2 would culminate in an agreement. The lagging in the discussions and the rapid suspension of the conference in early June 1924 reinforced MacDonald's anxiety about the future bilateral relationship, which he intended to improve, following a satisfactory visit to Turkey in 1923. On August 6, 1924, that is, one month after the termination of the nine-month span recommended in the above mentioned Article for direct negotiation, the British Foreign Office in a unilateral action referred the determination of the Anglo-Iraqi frontier dispute to the League.[596]

The Mosul Question Before the League of Nations

According to a decision made in June 1923 by the League's Political Committee, headed by Rumbold, the *status quo* on the frontier would be maintained, pending the Anglo-Turkish agreement. A letter dispatched on August 6, to the league's secretary general Sir Eric Drummond, stated that the withdrawal of the Allied troops from Turkish territory had been accomplished on October 4, 1923, but concerning Mosul "it was found impossible to reach an agreement within the prescribed period, which expired on July 5." [597]The letter also suggested that the Mosul frontier be put on the Council's agenda for its next session, according to the Article 3 of the Treaty, which was honored. Accordingly, Turkey was asked to participate at the forthcoming League session in order to define its position on the Mosul *Wilayat*. The Turkish delegates, somewhat reserved, replied that since they were not officially informed about the coming into effect of the Lausanne Treaty, they would participate in the negotiations twenty days after obtaining a copy of the Lausanne ratification. The Council agreed, and on its third session, August 30, Hjalmar Branting, rapporteur for the Council[598] sent a telegram on that matter to Ismet Pasha, who at the

---

[596] Beck, (1981), p. 261.

[597] Minute on the Thirteenth Session of the Council, Genève, August 29 to October 3, 1924, Annex 667a, p. 1465. Quoted in Spencer, (1988), p. 114.

[598]The Council appointed the Swedish Prime Minister Hjalmar Branting as his rapporteur in August 1924. He was one of the most prominent politicians at the

Council's ninth meeting, on September 20, was replaced by Fethi Bey.[599]

When the session started, Lord Parmoor[600] representing Great Britain as one of the main founders of the League of Nations, had the advantage to address the Council as "my colleagues", as he put forward his remarks to Fethi Bey.

Thus, Britain was placed on equal terms with the Council, contrary to Turkey, which was not a member of the League and had representation on the Council only for this issue. Parmoor and Fethi Bey presented the viewpoints of their respective governments on the question at the session. In broad lines, their arguments were identical to those presented at the Lausanne Conference. While the British confined the issue to solely concern the demarcation of the northern boundary of Iraq, the Turks insisted on discussing the whole province of Mosul. With respect to population statistics and the opinions of the people present, both parties still defended their original attitudes. The Turks once again insisted that there existed a unity between them and the Kurds, therefore, they were in majority in Mosul.[601]

The British and Turkish memoranda submitted to the Council displayed two different compositions of the population in Mosul *Wilayat:*

TABLE 2 Population of the Mosul *Wilayat*
According to Turkish Information

Arabs	43,210
Kurds	263, 830
Turks	146,960
Assyrians	31,00
Jews	16,800
Total	503,000

---

time. See Aryo Makko, *Arbitration in a World of Wars: The League of Nations and the Mosul Dispute 1924-1925*, (2010), Diplomacy and Statecraft, Vol. 21, issue, 4. p.635.

[599] Spencer, (1988), p. 115.

[600] Charles Alfred Cripps

[601] Henry, A. Foster, *The Making of Modern Iraq: A Product of World Forces*, (London, 1936), p. 154.

TABLE 1 Population of the Mosul *Wilayat*
According to British Information

Arabs	185,70
Kurds	454,70
Turks	65,800
Assyrians	77,000
[602]Jews	16, 800
Total	800,000

Besides the fact that the Kurds constituted the majority of the Mosul *Wilayat*'s population, the British rested their argument on three major points: That the interests of more than 90 percent of the population would be best guaranteed if they were under the rule of the Iraqi government than under Ankara, that despite the ongoing hostile dispute between the two parties on the settlement of the Assyrians, the political interests of the local population recommended incorporation into Iraq and, that economically, Mosul had stronger ties with Baghdad and Basra, than with Turkey. Furthermore, the British stated that their proposal of the settlement of the frontier question provided a reliable assurance for the future security and the stability of the region. In fact, British delimitation of the frontier line went beyond the northern frontier of Mosul including Turkish territory. Their purpose was that the three *qazas* in the province of Hakkari would be awarded to them in order to settle the Assyrians there. Therefore, the British memoranda put forward for the Council claimed not only the preservation of the whole of Mosul for Iraq, but also implied an expansion of its northern frontier.

The Turkish reply which was submitted to Drummond maintained that the actual intention of the British policy was to alter the *status quo* of the border and, with this end in view, they utilized the Assyrian problem as a

---

[602] Memorandum on the Frontier between Turkey and Iraq", August 14, 1924, LONA C. 396.1924.V11,1. Quoted in Makko, p. 634.

camouflage to encroach on Turkish territory.[603]

The Turkish delegate also reiterated his demand for holding a plebiscite in the disputed area which was opposed by Parmoor, arguing that the plebiscite was inapplicable due to the problems associated with the delimitation of the frontier line. In addition, the tribal nature of the population rendered a plebiscite for the determination of a complicate matter, like frontier dispute inappropriate. Additionally, it would enhance the threat of military conflicts. Parmoor, then, suggested that the Council appoint a special commission to decide on the contentious issue. Fethi Bey repeated Inonu's old argument that the Turkish claim for the restoration of the whole of the *Wilayat* of Mosul stemmed from geographical, ethnical, economic and military reasons. He asserted once again that holding a plebiscite was essential. [604] He reaffirmed that the entire population of the Mosul *Wilayat* had a fervent desire to be part of Turkey, but he could not comprehend that a commission was capable of determining the wishes of the people.[605]

The will and the desire of the population of Mosul were salient points that both the Turkish and the British delegates referred to. They constituted one of the crucial arguments for the settlement of the disputed question. The basic premise for the idea of the principle of self-determination, being recalled, was that the subjected people had the right to be free from those who governed them, and to choose the kind of rule that complied with their wishes. During the Mosul controversy, the idea of self-determination had gained currency as a slogan. It was generally known and accepted by the population, especially by the nationalists, who referred to it for the vindication of their national rights, such as the Kurds, who aspired to establish a national government of their own, and the Iraqi nationalists who rejected the rule of the mandatory power. For the settlement of the Mosul issue, both parties adhered to the popular rhetoric of self-determination. As Sarah Shields points out, "When the League of Nations agreed to investigate the question posed by Turkey and Great Britain, they assumed

---

[603] Ibid., pp.634-635.

[604] Spencer, (1988), pp.116-117.

[605] Foster, (1936), pp.154-155.

that self-Determination would be a major component of their deliberations. For the League's Commission, then, sorting out the competing claims of the two parties seemed crucial." [606]However, they presupposed that people's ethnicity and cultural affiliation would finally determine their political belonging. So in presenting their memoranda and attitudes, the British attempted to show that the Turkish proportion of the Mosul population was outnumbered by other ethnic groups. The Turks on the other hand endeavored to convince the Council that they were in the majority by referring to the alleged unity between them and the Kurds.

At the next Council session on September 25, 1924, Branting attempted to obtain assurance from the Turkey to abide by the Council's decision; that is, the Council had the final word, and both sides were bound in advance to accept the result. Parmoor had no objection and accepted that the Council enquiry was not confined to the two basic questions, namely " Who shall have Mosul vilayat?" and, "What should be the frontier between Iraq and Turkey?" He agreed that the Council might find any other equitable solution to the issue and that his government was undertaken in advance to accept the Council's decision. Fethi Bey tried to dodge the issue by noting that he agreed that in line with the Article 15 of the League Covenant the Council was authorized to make any equitable solution. Branting, who was still not satisfied with Fethi's commitment, consulted the two representatives privately, and as a result, Fethi Bey agreed that "There was no disagreement between his government and the British government... at the same time adding that he was convinced that the Council would base its decision in the first place on the wishes of the inhabitants." He finally agreed to accept the Council's decision on "any line that it thinks fit to adopt." [607]

On September 30, 1924, the Council adopted a resolution that bound

---

[606] Sarah Shields, *Mosul Questions: Economy, Identity, and Annexation*, in R. Spector Simon and E.H. Tejirian (eds.) *The Creation of Iraq 1914-1922*, (Colombia University Press 2004), P. 54.

[607] Ibid., p.155.

the two parties in advance to accept the Council's decision on matters referred to it and to refrain from military actions, with the intention to change the state of affairs in the disputed territory pending a decision. Furthermore, it decided to create a special commission of three members to explore the situation on the spot and to contribute together with the Council, to resolve the disputed issue.[608]

On October 27-31, at the Council's thirty-first (extraordinary) session in Brussels, the Mosul question was brought up for discussion. The British accused Turkey of repeated intrusions upon the provisional frontier in the vicinity of Amadya in early September, which had been forced out by British airplanes. Parmoor reaffirmed that Turkey had also altered the *status quo* by invasion of a "no-man's land" area, situated between the Anglo-Iraqi administration side, and that of the Turkish administration where the Assyrian Christians had been seeking refuge in 1921 following the outbreak of the war. The Turks had then expelled the Assyrians southwards toward Amadya, demolishing their villages and remained in Iraqi territory.

In his reply, Fethi contended that Turkey's military actions were carried out in response to the British provocations and primarily to curtail the activities of the Assyrian "bandits" in Turkish territory, who had disturbed the internal affairs of their Turkish representative, that is the Vali of Hakkari. He also noted that before July 19, 1924, the day the British occupied Sulaimanya, the town was under the rebellious Shaikh Mahmud, and that the 'no-man's land' the British refers to, did not exist, because it belonged to the *Wilayat* of Hakkari, which had "always been administered by … and… belonged to Turkey." [609]

Although the two parties had committed to respect the provision stipulated in the Lausanne Treaty with respect to *status quo* pending a decision from the Council, yet in the interim, some armed conflicts occurred. The reasons were that the Council's resolution lacked a pronounced definition of the frontier line of the disputed territory. Besides,

---

[608] Edmonds, (1957), p.388.
[609] Spencer, (1988), p. 121

there was no formulated policy to prevent eventual occurrences while waiting for a final decision. Consequently, both the Turks and the British tended to interpret the location of the frontier line according to their interests. The incidents in Hakkari that followed by the Turkish aggressive treatment of the Assyrians, were direct consequences of the frontier line problem. Actually, as the work of the Council was in progress, the British paid more heed to the Assyrian problem. Defending the rights of the Assyrians, it was believed, could put Iraq in a better position with regards to the frontier dispute.[610]

However, although the British had complained to the Council on September 29 and October 5 against Turkish incursion and conducting air raids against Turkish forces, the Turks were still occupying territory that the British alleged belonged to them. The British delegate justified their military action against the Turks by arguing that:

> The British authority, assumed that these forces were composed of irresponsible tribal elements, and were apprehensive that their action, if unchecked, would result in serious troubles amongst the border tribes. Consequently, it took the necessary step to drive some of the invaders back across the frontier by machine-gun fire from the air, which caused some casualties.

Then, Parmoor gave an account of several Turkish hostile activities and added "it was thus clear that the Turkish regular forces... were willfully disregarding the *status quo*." [611] On October 9, the British government conveyed an ultimatum to the Turks, demanding the withdrawal of all Turkish troops within 48 hours and threatening to resume "full liberty of action" in case the Turks refused to comply.[612]

The Turks who opposed the British interpretation of the *status quo* reacted to the latter's ultimatum by appealing to the League of Nations for determining the location of the border and by stressing their national unity. The tension prompted British politicians, among them Sir Ronald Lindsay,

---

[610] Beck, (1981), p. 262.
[611] Foster, (1936), p. 156.
[612] Beck, (1981), P.262.

the British ambassador to Turkey, to suggest that "the issue was worth a war with Turkey in order to teach Kemal a lesson", but the British government was obliged to declare the ultimatum null and void, and by referring to Article X1 of the Covenant, proposed that the frontier dispute be discussed at a special Council session. Accordingly, on October 27, a special session of the Council was convened to handle the basic problem between the two parties, namely a precise demarcation frontier line. A Council sub-committee composed of Branting as the head, and two members, Guano (Uruguay) and Leon (Spain), was formed to study the problem. They suggested to the Council a frontier line, the so called "Brussels Line" as a provisional frontier pending a final settlement of the frontier dispute.[613]

On October 29, the Council, including Turkey and Britain, accepted the demarcation line; the Brussels line laid down by Branting,[614] and it was agreed that the withdrawal of the Turkish and British forces to their respective side of the Brussels line should be completed by November 25, 1924.[615]

In the early days of November, Branting fell sick and was replaced by Östen Undén as the Swedish representative on the Council, and as rapporteur in the Mosul dispute.[616] On October 31, and according to Branting's suggestion, the members of the Special Commission of Enquiry were announced before the end of the Council's session in Brussels.[617] These were comprised of Carl Einar Af Wirsén, Swedish diplomatic

---

[613] Ibid., p. 263.

[614] Branting had proposed that the frontier line be drown between the British and Turkish line which separated the two boundaries by 25 km from each other. He also proposed that the line be drawn according the natural setting of the frontier such as mountain, crest and rivers since the existing line between the two disputants was drawn irrespective of the lie of the land. See Rogers , (2007), p. 361. The Council's decision of accepting the Brussels line was in line with the London's proposal to exclude the three districts of Hakkari which previously the British government intended to incorporate into Iraq. See Makko, (2010), p. 636.

[615] Beck, (1981),p. 263.

[616] Rogers, (2007), p. 361.

[617] Spencer, (1988), p. 122.

representative in Rumania, as Chairman: he was elected because he represented a neutral land, Count Paul Teleki, who had been the Hungarian Prime Minister in 1920-1921, and was involved in the counter-revolution movement of Bela'Kun in 1919,[618] and Colonel A. Paulis with good experience in business and administration in the Congo. The Commission was later assisted by J. H. Kramer, a Dutch orientalist who became an interpreter. His main language was Turkish but he was not fluent in Arabic or Persian. [619]

The Work of the Mosul Commission of Enquiry

Owing to the contentious nature of the Mosul question, the Commission of Enquiry started its work immediately. After visiting London and Angora (Ankara), they arrived in Baghdad on January 16th ,1925. The Turkish delegate who assisted the Commission was headed by Assessor, by General Jewad Pasha, Inspector-General of the Turkish army on the Jezira front, and Commander-in-Chief for the operation against Iraq. He was one of the nationalist leaders who the Allied High Commissioner captured and deported to Malta in 1920. He was accompanied by "experts" such as Major Kamil Bey for Mosul, Nazim Bey Naftchizadeh for Kirkuk and Fattah Efendi for Sulaimanya. [620] Two of these "experts" were well known in Iraq; Nazim had been one of the prominent members of the secret Turkish Committee in Kirkuk and had been involved in a planned scheme for the occupation of Kirkuk and Arbil by Shaikh Mahmud of Sulaimanya in early 1923; he later fled to Angora. The second one was Fattah Beg, Shaikh Mahmud's brother-in-Law who had been his agent in communication with the Turks since 1921. Both had been candidates to represent Mosul *Wilayat* at Angore, but their pretensions had been exposed

---

[618] Edmonds notes that Teleki was basically interested in geographic and ethnic aspects of the Mosul question and that it was rumored that he was a member of some Hungarian "Pilgrims" society based on remote common Turkish-Magyar ethnic origin. The Iraqi felt apprehension on learning this news, especially that his name written in Arabic character, meant "fox" in Turkish.
[619] Edmonds, (1957), pp.395-396.
[620] Ibid.

by Cox at the Constantinople Conference in 1924. The president of the Commission was unaware of their past when he accepted that they could accompany him. Their presence in Iraq provoked anger and misgiving among the Iraqis. The Iraqi Prime Minister Al-Askari lodged a protest with the High Commissioner and at the same time there was apprehension lest they might be attacked by impetuous young Iraqi nationalists. Guaranteeing their security without restricting their free movements was a difficult task.[621]

Nazim and Fattah were scathingly criticized by Arabic press, who were anxious that their prominent position might influence the Commission. Despite the fact that they were under diplomatic immunity, they were lodged outside Baghdad which became tantamount to house arrest. The frontier Commission's *Report* wrote "the Turkish assessor informed the Commission that these experts and aide-de-camp had been placed in an 'entrenched camp' and kept under observation." [622]The High Commissioner, Sir Henry Dobbs, by protesting to the Commission, held the view that the persons, "although nationals of Iraq" were now "availing themselves of the presence of the Commission in order to return to Iraq and possibly, under the cloak of diplomatic immunity, to engage in activities likely to disturb peace and order."

The Commission, "while deploring the fact" that the Turkish government had chosen them as assessors, was "unable to share Sir Henry Dobbs' views" on the grounds that, they "were citizens of the vilayat of Mosul and could not be regarded as Iraqi subjects until the question of the frontier had been finally settled."[623] This induced the Turkish government to complain to the League that this kind of measure undermined the work of their delegates. Another protest note was dispatched from the Turkish Minister of Foreign Affairs, Shukri Kaya, who refuted all allegations against the delegates. They were there, the note maintained, because of their long experience and good

---

[621] Great Britain, Colonial Office, Iraqi Administration Reports, 1914-1932. Vol. 8. 1925-1927. P. 8.
[622] Quotations in Foster, (1936), p. 157.
[623] Quoatations in ibid.

knowledge of Iraq, and they were esteemed by the Mosul's population who shared their desire for the *Wilayat's* return to Turkey. On February 2, 1925, the Newspaper *The Times*, commenting on the Turkish attitudes, wrote that the two "experts" were decent Turkish patriots who worked "in the interest of retaining Mosul for the Mother Country just as the British subjects worked for the retention of Mosul in the British mandate." [624]

Turco-Arab Nationalist Propaganda and Counter Propaganda

By its arrival in Baghdad, the Commission's impartial work, ran the risk of being influenced. The Iraqi Constituent Assembly had attached a rider to the Anglo-Iraqi Treaty, to the effect that the British confirmed to keep Mosul for Iraq. At the same time, the arrival of the Commission evoked clamorous demonstrations in Baghdad's streets organized by Iraqi nationalists; the aim of which was to manifest their firm will to the Commission for the ownership of Mosul, and to remind the British that the Treaty was not binding unless the rider was realized. The Commission stayed in Baghdad until January 26, where they interviewed all leading persons in the town, ministers, government officials and representatives of every class and community. [625]The Commission arrived in Mosul on January 27th, where the excitement among the population of the province was at its highest level. Two days prior to the Commission's arrival, a Committee of National Defence was formed in order to organize a demonstration in Mosul and create branches in all local towns. The organized demonstrations in the town aroused the Commission's suspicions. Consequently, the Ministry of Interior warned that the activities of the Iraqi nationalists could prejudice Iraq position in the Mosul dispute. On February 7, therefore, the High Commissioner reached Mosul to dissipate the miscomprehensions that the recent circumstances had generated. [626]

The visiting of the Commission of Enquiry to Mosul was a good opportunity for the nationalist Iraqi parties and newspapers to give vent to

---

[624] Spencer, (1988), p. 127.

[625] Great Britain, Colonial Affairs, Iraqi Administration Reports, 1914-1932. Vol. 8. 1925-1927. p. 9.

[626] Ibid.

their nationalist feelings. The new organ of the Hizb al-Istiklal party, *Al-Ahd*, exhorted all Iraqis "of Arab blood" to sincerely counteract Turkey's efforts to regain Mosul. In the meantime, between Baghdad and Mosul patriotic telegrams were exchanged incessantly. As the Commission entered Mosul, they were greeted by a delegation of Mosul notables dressed in their traditional colorful silk robes, asserting their loyalty to King Faisal and their desire to be part of Iraq. *Al-Mufid*, enthusiastically addressed the secondary school children, that "we are Arabs and Iraqis and will live and die for the country. Inform the League that even the infant proclaims Mosul as Arab." [627]

Maintaining Mosul for Iraq, the British had evidently realized, was a vital question; it was according to Edmonds a "life-and-death struggle", and the existence of Iraq as a state was dependent upon it, since for economic and strategic reasons, Baghdad and Basra without the *Wilayat* could never create a viable state. This attitude was somewhat eloquent and in unison with the Iraqi nationalists, expressed by King Faisal as he presented his memorandum to the Commission two days after their arrival in Baghdad:

> The bringing into existence and consolidation of a permanent Government in Iraq is dependent on the preservation of the *status quo*, as I consider that it is impossible, both strategically and economically, for a Government in Baghdad to live if Mosul is detached from it and by another government ... that it will be impossible to maintain internal peace except by the creation of a large military force for which recruitment would be impossible if Mosul is separated from Iraq ... I consider that Mosul is to Iraq as the head is to the rest of the body, and ... the happiness or misery of three or four millions of human beings is placed in the hands of your honourable Commission ... [628]

---

[627] *Al-Mufid*, February 2, 1925. The Near East and India for August 17, 1925, however, criticized the Iraqi leaders for being seized by panic to "encourage demonstrations of school children and other rather puerile forms of propaganda" which had made the Commission skeptical to whether Iraq was developing toward independence. Spencer, (1988), p. 128.
[628] Ibid., p. 131.

No doubt due to the investigation of the Commission in Mosul, nationalist sentiments gained momentum among both the Turks and the Arab Iraqis. The latter, however, were in a favorable position since the British, as occupants, had full control of administration, including the police and the latest and most reliable information necessary to gain tactical advantage. It was very practical in manipulating people, in representing a memorandum and setting up a claim for winning the Mosul case, as well as to answer the questionnaires. On the other hand, the Turks relied on old and faulty records provided by Istanbul, and prepared by officers and civil servants with no adequate education or current knowledge of the situation of the disputed areas.

Nevertheless, despite relative stability and administrative amelioration in Mosul, the situation was still precarious in many parts of the country and thus, prone to change. The persisting threat of the Turkish nationalists, underpinned by great victories of Mustafa Kemal, was suitable ground for Turkish propaganda which anticipated the early return of the Turks and the Punishment of all traitors:

> Which had kept the population in a continuous effervescence of hope for some and terror for others. There were many trains of combustible material a spark on which might blow the powder mine sky high, taking with it questionnaires, memoranda, administration and all. Herein lay the best chance for the Turkish Assessors. [629]

The British were aware of the Turkish plan for distribution of thousands of Turkish flags to appear in the windows of Mosul, and other places where the Commissioner intended to visit. The appointment of Nazim and Fattah in this context appeared to be calculated since the Turks had relied on intrigue and propaganda rather than argument founded on facts and

---

[629] Edmonds, (1957), p. 402. Foster observes in this connection that fear of reprisals by the authorities in the country, especially by Turkish authorities in case they seized power there again, was particularly obvious. Several witnesses after expressing their views in privet and in a whisper that they favored Turkey, loudly, declared that they were in favor of the Iraqi government so they might be overheard by those who were waiting outside. (1936), P. 159.

objectivity. The holding of a plebiscite constituted a main idea in the Turk's argument for the settlement of the Mosul question. The fact that the majority of the population was illiterate or had very low education, and would not hesitate to change the authorities who forced them to pay taxes or condemned a relative to them for a crime, made the application of the plebiscite vital, thereby they could alter the situation for their benefit. [630] The memorandum that the Turkish government presented to the Commission was concluded with a considerable emphases on the opinion of the population:

> My Government is convinced… that the expression of the popular will should be regarded as the essential factor in the solution of the problem, and it hopes that the Commission will take into consideration the… free expression of the desire of the population of the Mosul vilayat…[631]

> For the first time since the foundation of the League of Nations, a dispute of considerable importance between a great Western Power and a Near Eastern power regarding the fate of the Oriental people has been brought before the Council of the League … The Government of the Republic is convinced that your Commission sincerely desires to contribute to the creation of mutual confidence between these two parts of the world, which would be so desirable a result, and will wish to ensure the triumph of justice by recommending that the Council should allow the population of the vilayat of Mosul freely to determine its own fate.[632]

The task of the Commission to investigate the wishes of the population, which was crucial for the determination of the Mosul *Wilayat* proved a strenuous one. The members of the Commission were keen not to be influenced by the authorities in control of the *de facto* disputed territory. They were, nevertheless, with no experience in the Middle East, and the British

---

[630] Edmonds, (1957), p.402.

[631] The League of Nations, Question of the Frontier Between Turkey and Iraq, Report of the Commission instituted by the Council Resolution of September 30, 1924 to the Council, p. 6 (the Wirsén Report) Quoted in Spencer, p. 130.

[632] Quoted in Edmonds, (1957), p. 403.

objection to a plebiscite and the government's attempt to maintain law and order, were regarded as confirmed evidence to prevent them from acquiring accurate information and facts about the genuine sympathy of the population. The Commission's suspicions of these kinds of activities were reinforced by the fact that the Iraqi government allowed demonstrations and meetings, organized by the Committees of National Defence in order to foment patriotic feelings and to manifest the "unaltered determination of the nation to defend the sacred patrimony to the last." Consequently, the credibility of the Committee of Defence was undermined to the degree that anything that was done in the name of the Committee was condemned in advance by the Commissioners. [633]

In order to proceed with its work in an impartial manner, the Commission turned down Dobbs' proposal that the Commission could work "in closer touch with the assessors and that public opinion could be consulted through the local authorities." The Commission, Undén stated, welcomed any suggestion from both parties, but they preferred to carry out the inquiry freely according to their instructions. Dobbs had later pointed out that "the inquiries of the Commission had been so secretly conducted that the Iraq government didn't even know how the inhabitants had declared themselves." [634]

The question of impartiality was not the only one that the Commission had to handle in conducting its inquiry. The Commission was faced with other difficulties, especially in the beginning of their mission. Although the Commission had assured the witnesses that their views would be kept secret, many witnesses were unwilling to express their genuine opinions for fear of reprisals. Holding office or a position, as well as rivalries between chiefs in certain districts, also had an impact on how a great number of

---

[633] Ibid., pp. 403-404. According to Edmonds, the allowing of demonstrations together with arrangement of surveillance for the protection of the Commissioners, were two mistakes that the Iraqi government made, which disturbed the work of the Commission as well as the communication between them and the British.pp.403-406.

[634] Before Permanent Mandates Commission, Tenth Session, p. 60, November 8, 1926, Quoted in Foster, (1936), p. 159.

these people voted. Some deputations of Mosul after having overtly expressed their strong desire to be part of Iraq expressed themselves privately as convinced pro-Turks. Some had changed sides as they had been consulted a second time:

Some liked Iraq because of improved conditions and some, because the Iraq government must had been stronger since it won. Certain tribal chiefs were against Iraq, because under Turkey they had been more independent. The educated classes frequently favored Iraq on economic grounds. National sentiment determined the position of the Turks and the Kurds.[635]

However, despite these difficulties, the Commission was able to visit the entire *Wilayat* within two months, investigating not only the wishes of the population for a political settlement of the disputed territory, but also making "a psychological study of the population," and an economic-commercial evaluation. [636]

In order to make a wide-ranging inquiry the Commission broke up in three Sub-Commissions. Wirsén visited Tell Afar, Sinjar, Aqra, and the suburbs of Mosul; Teleki conducted an inquiry in Arbil and its periphery, and Paulis investigated Kirkuk *liwa*. On February 25, 1925, the commissioners met again and traveled together to Kirkuk and Sulaiymanya where they visited authorities, public facilities like hospitals and schools and interviewed tribal leaders, as well as ordinary people at marketplaces.[637] The manner by which the inquiry was carried out was criticized by the British authority, arguing that the work of the League's representatives was "a hidden referendum." The British criticism was based on the assumption that the commissioners were implementing a pro-

---

[635] Foster, (1936), p. 160.

[636] Spencer, (1988), p. 134.

[637] Makko, (2010), pp. 638-639. Spencer observes that the Commission had reunited in Kirkuk to compare notes. They also held audience for the notables of Mosul and provided them with British lists in order to know whether they were pro-Turkish or pro-Arab. The others were composed of *ulama*, landowners, all second degree electors mentioned in old Turkish lists and those who had members of the Mosul municipal council at all since 1905.See Spencer, (1988), p.134.

Turkish agenda which they believed was to their disadvantage.[638]

The British were already at the outset dissatisfied with the delay in forming the Commission and then with their delay in drafting the report which became ready in July 1925. In Britain, the dissatisfaction was expressed particularly by Austen Chamberlain, who became in charge of the Foreign Office in November 1924, but some of his cabinet colleagues and some sections within both the Foreign and the Colonial Offices criticized not only the delay, but also the members of the Commission. Crow and Lindsay from the Foreign Office voiced their aversion toward"small nation mentality of League representatives." They were worried that the commissioners did not act as their duty had dictated, but were under the impression of "matters irrelevant to issues at stake" and, for example, that they gave way to the pressure of the Turkish assessors, or to demonstrate that the League did not always defend the Great Powers against the small ones. Crown, referring to the traditional contradiction between the old and the "new diplomacy", complained that "when important interests of the Great Powers are concerned, decisions are almost inevitably left to subject of minor Powers, who rarely have the courage or experience to handle such questions with real skill, judgment and impartiality." At the same time, Chamberlain attempted to ease the discomfort of Leo Amery, the Colonial Secretary, who was critical of the League as a whole, and to dismiss his idea that the Commission might decide in favor of Turkey to prove that the League was not a means in the hands of the Great Powers.[639]

Turco-British Continued Struggle for Oil

At the same time, and despite the fact that the determination of the fate of the Mosul *Wilayat* was put in the League's hands the hope of reaching an agreement through bilateral negotiations was still alive, particularly for Turkey. In a memorandum dispatched to Foreign Affairs, dated April 2,

---

[638] Ibid., p. 641.
[639] Beck. (1981), pp. 263-264.

1925, Chamberlain noted that Turkey, on several occasions during the protracted negotiations over Mosul, had offered the British economic and commercial advantage as part of a *quid pro quo* arrangement for the retention of the *Wilayat*. The Turks had then believed that if the British need of oil was safeguarded, the latter would abandon the claim for the *Wilayat* since their policy "was dictated by the oil interests." [640]

Actually, Turkey had approached Great Britain for a direct settlement of the Mosul dispute since the Lausanne Conference. At that time, the Turkish minister Zekiai Bey spoke to Austen Chamberlain about the relations between their two countries. He attached significant importance to the economic relations and asked whether there were any obstacles to such collaborations. He personally did not see any insurmountable obstacles on the part of the two countries, and contended, therefore, that the "little affair" of Mosul should not hinder such collaborations. Zekiai Bey also asked:

> Why we could not together settle the question of the Mosul boundary without waiting for the decision of the League of Nations? For Turkey this was a vital matter. She could not acquiesce in the division of the Kurds. If we agreed to cede Mosul to Turkey, arrangements in regard to economic interests could easily be made. We might, he indicated, have the exploitation of the oil-fields and a guarantee from Turkey, as far as she was concerned, of the integrity of Irak as thus delimited. [641]

Chamberlain replied that he regretted that the two governments had not been able to arrive at an understanding on the subject at the Lausanne Conference while he emphasized that the Turkish government was still under the illusion that the policy of the British government was guided by calculations for possession of oilfields which might be found in the region. [642]

Again, at the Constantinople Conference in May and June, due to the

---

[640] BDFA. Vol. 30. *Turkey, July 1923-March 1927*. P. 297.

[641] Ibid., p. 270. The Turks had also proposed to agree on immediate matters, such as the thrancian frontier in line with the British policy in return for winning Mosul *Wilayat*

[642] Ibid.

irreconcilable attitudes of the two parties, when the Mosul issue had been turned over for a decision to the League of Nations in accordance with the terms of the Treaty of Lausanne, Turkey preferred a direct settlement but without presenting any concrete proposals. Turkey had made offers of concessions (inter alia, for exploitation of oil, construction of a port as well as a railway) to different British financial groups with the aim that they bring pressure to bear on the British government on the Mosul question to meet Turkish requests in a direct settlement.

The British, however, firmly rejected all Turkish offers and insisted on referring the issue to the League. As trustee for Iraq, they also refused to abandon the defense of the rights and interests of the Iraqi people in exchange for economic advantages to British financial groups. Chamberlain maintained, acting contrary to Great Britain's commitment toward Iraq would involve:

(1) a complete reversal of policy on our part, (2) a disregard of the provisions of the Treaty of Lausanne, (3) a cynical renunciation of the claim that we have solemnly and consistently urged on behalf of Iraq on racial, economic, geographical and strategic grounds, (4) a highly discreditable desertion, both of the people of Iraq and the Christian inhabitants of the north of the Mosul Vilayet, (5) a substantial risk of getting the worst of a discreditable bargain, and (6) marked discourtesy to the League of Nations, whose Commission of Enquiry have just complete their recommendations.[643]

The Wirsén Report

Leaving Mosul toward the end of March 1925, the Commission arrived in Geneva in April, where they started drafting its report. The Commission's report presented to the Council of the League was formulated by distinguished scholars of Europe, America and elsewhere and it was based on authoritative and trustworthy facts. The report embodied several different points which were understandable given the contradictory nature of the

---

[643] Ibid., p. 298. British reluctance to Turkish offers was primarily, due to the inability of the Turkish market to offer a sufficient security and guaranty for the British companies. The fate of previous investments in Turkey discouraged British companies to seriously undertake further investment there.

disputants, but overall, it was in favor of the British.[644]

The disputed area south of the Brussels line was about 87,890 square kilometers (34,000 sq.mi.) with a population of about 800,000. The size of the area and the number of its people were simply too huge "for it to be said that the question is merely one of delimitation" as the British argued. The Commission also "became convinced of the full force of the British assertion as to the insuperable practical difficulties of holding a plebiscite and the considerable doubt which might still remain as to its trustworthiness." [645] The composition of the population of Mosul *Wilayat* presented by the Commission to the Council was based on the census of the Iraqi government from 1924:

Kurds	494,007
Arabs	166,941
Turks	38,652
Christians	61,336
Jews	11,897
Yezidis	26,257
Total	799,090

For the Mosul town the commission presented the following statistics:

Arabs	119,500
Kurds	88,000
Turks	9, 750
Christians	55,000
Yezidis	26,200
Jews	7,550
[646] Total	306,000

---

[644] Foster, (1936), p.160. Beck points out that when the report was studied in Britain, many previous criticisms about delay and bias that Amery and Crow had leveled against the Commission were forgotten now since their conclusions clearly supported the British's claim. On the other hand, the report confirmed Turkey's suspicions toward the League's impartiality, see beck. P. 264.

[645] beck.P. 264.

[646] Ibid.

According to the Commission's statistics, the Kurds were in a clear majority in the whole of the Mosul *Wilayat*. The Commission also reported, in contrast to the previous Turkish claim that the Kurds were of Turkish origin or that there really existed a Turkish-Kurdish unity, that "The Kurds, though neither Arabs, Turks, nor Persians, were more closely related to the Persians... They differ more from the Arabs than from the Turks" and found that the Turks of Mosul whom Curzon in earlier memoranda described as Turkomans and with no affinity with the Turks were actually Turks. Regarding the opinion of the population, the Commission concluded that there was "no national Iraqi feeling in the disputed territory, "except the educated Arab elite which was rather "an Arab feeling, chauvinistic and anti-alien." Nationalist manifestations were strongest among the Kurds, who showed "a growing national consciousness, which is definitely Kurdish and not Iraqi." Kurdish nationalist sentiments were strongest in the southern part of the *Wilayat* and weakest in its northern part. The attitudes of the Iraqi nationalists toward the British occupants and their antagonism toward the Iraqi government determined to which side they wished to belong. The commissioner observed that the most strongly nationalist Arabs expressed their views in favor of Turkey rather than to an Iraq under British control and that many Arabs, from the poor classes, were pro-Turkish.[647]

However, the situation differed completely in Sulaimanya, where the Commissioner had been inquiring in three days. The leading witnesses expressed themselves as the British expected. They overtly expressed their disdain toward the Ottomans, regarding their government as incompetent and corrupt. The murder of Shaikh Saíd, Shaikh Mahmud's father, in Mosul in 1908 by the Turks was claimed to have been one of the reasons for these negative attitudes toward the Ottomans. Edmonds described the Sulaimanya case as a "victory" the effect of which Wirsén refers to distinctively in this report:

---

[647] Foster, (1936), pp. 160-163.

With the exception of the liwa of Sulaimanya there is scarcely a single district containing several contiguous nahyas where anything approaching unanimity in favor of one of the two parties can be observed.... It was in the liwa of Sulaimanya that the most definite views were expressed ... With very few exceptions the persons we interviewed pronounced in favor of the Iraq Government ... The commission is genuine convinced the wishes of the people were fully expressed ... We found a Kurdish national feeling which, though yet young, was reasonable enough ; for though the people stated their supreme desire was for complete independence they recognized the advantages of an enlightened and intelligent trusteeship. There is no doubt that the ability and good judgment of the British administrators of the province had a large influence on the state of mind of the people.[648]

The statistical sources of data that the Commission examined were Turkish from 1914, British from 1919 and the 1922-24 data which basically was British-Iraqi. Based on these data the Commission reached its final conclusion that "the greater part of the population of the disputed territory is undoubtedly Kurds (about five-eighths). The Kurds are therefore numerically the most important factor ..."[649]

Based on the ethnic argument the Kurdish preponderance in Mosul *Wilayat,* according to the commission, entitled them to an independent state:

If the ethnic argument alone had to be taken into account, the necessary conclusion would be that an independent Kurdish state should be created, since the Kurds constitute five-eighths of the population. Moreover, if such a solution were to be considered, the Yazidis, who racially are very like the Kurds, and the Turks, who could easily be assimilated by the Kurds, should be included in estimating the number of the latter. They would then form seven-tenths of the population.[650]

---

[648] Quoted in Edmonds, (1957), pp. 422-423.
[649] Frontier Commission Report, p. 43. Quoted in Fuat Dundar, (2012), *Statisquo: British Use of Statistics in the Iraq Kurdish Question* (1919-1932) Crown Centre for Middle East Studies, (Brandies University), p. 28.
[650] Zorabê Budi Aloian, *The Image of The Kurds In Hungary: Hungarian Material*

However, the Commission dismissed the idea of creating an independent Kurdistan on the grounds that it was not feasible due to the distribution of the population in the Mosul *wilayat* and poor communications.[651]

The fact that the Kurds constituted the largest ethnic proportion of the Mosul *Wilayat*, thus brought the Kurdish question to the attention of the Commission, which at the same time was also highlighted by Shaikh Said's revolt during the period of February to April, 1925.[652] The Turkish National Assembly in Ankara tried first not to attach any particular attention to the scope of this Kurdish uprising, but soon a Turkish army composed of a 50,000-man troop was sent on a punitive expedition to the south-eastern province, and successfully put down the rebellion.[653] Shortly after this event, British forces attacked local Kurds since they had broken the demonstration ban imposed on Mosul during the visit of the Commission. The British used air raids supported by infantry attacks on a larger scale than previously. This incident was described by the Foreign Office as punishment of rebellious Kurdish tribes who "threatened the region's stability." [654]

Other significant points in the Commission's inquiry were, inter alia, that economic evaluation argued for union between Mosul and the rest of Iraq. Politically, Mosul was still an integral part of Turkey until the country renounced its rights. Iraq had no legal right to the disputed territory by conquest [655] or by law, but morally, it had the right to develop economically

---

on the Kurds from the Ottoman Times until the End of the Twentieth Century, (Spånga, 2008), p.81.

[651] Spencer, (1988), p. 138.

[652] Beck, (1981), p. 265. Beck notes that one observer had described the Kurds as a "turbulent national group with predilection for shooting at moving objects", but that they were rather human and their views should be taken in consideration, despite the Commission's statement on the primitive nature of their nationalism. Ibid.

[653] For a detailed account of Shaikh Said's revolt see Jwaideh, (2006) and Olson (1989).

[654] Makko, (2010), p. 639.

[655] The Commission had accepted the Turkish argument on opposing British view that they by the right of conquest could incorporate Mosul into Iraq.The Commission believed that territories occupied by British were still legally part of

and politically within the frontier, which rendered this development possible. Principally, the Wirsén Commission agreed with the Turks' argument that they were the rightful owner of the Mosul *Wilayat* since they still had it and had never renounced it. The Commission was "of the opinion that from the legal point of view the disputed territory must be regarded as an integral part of Turkey until that power renounce her right," "adding that "it did not feel competent to decide what weight should be given to these legal considerations."[656] However, the legal aspect was left to the Council to determine. Furthermore, the Commission admitted that while Iraq had made considerable progress, particularly in security, public health, and education, the situation in the country was still unstable. Most of the people interviewed preferred Iraq, but "... by economic consideration, rather than by any feeling of solidarity with the Arab kingdom" otherwise probably a great part of them would have preferred the restoration of the territory to Turkey rather than its attachment to Iraq.[657]

With regards to the interests of the population of Mosul *Wilayat*, the commission final conclusion was that it:

would be some advantages that the disputed area should not be partitioned,[658] and on the basis of this consideration the Commission, having assigned a relative value to each of the facts which it has established, is of opinion that important arguments, particularly of an economic and geographical nature ... operate in favor of the union with Iraq of the whole territory south of the

---

Turkey, and that the British conquest argument was open to question. They argued that in light of Kemalist victories, the situation had altered and, hence, the Treaty of Sèvres was dropped, and a new conference was convened to settle this issue. Foster, (1936), p. 164.

[656] Quincy Wright, *The Mosul Dispute*, The American Journal of International Law, Vol. 20, No.3 (Jul.,1926), pp.453-464, (American Society of International Law). 455.

[657] Foster, p. 164.

[658] The Commission rejected the British claim to a frontier north of the Brussels line comprising portion of Hakkari region to settle the remaining of the Assyrians there.

"Brussels line", subject to following conditions; (1) The territory must remain under the effective mandate of the League of Nations for a period which may be put at twenty-five years; (2) Regard must be paid to the desires expressed by the Kurds that officials of Kurdish race should be appointed for the administration of their country, the dispensation of justice, and teaching in the schools, and that Kurdish should be the official language of all these The Commission found otherwise, "it would be more advantageous for the territory to remain under the sovereignty of Turkey, whose internal condition and political situation are incomparably more stable than those of Iraq."[659]

The Wirsén report was presented to the League's Council in July 1925 and its publication in August evoked different reactions from public and official opinions in Britain, Iraq and Turkey. The Iraqi foreign minister, Jafar al-Askari, for instance, reaffirmed in an interview that the people of Mosul expressed themselves in favor of Iraq and rejected returning to Turkey. Similarly, Sassoon al-Haskayl (the former Minister of Finance) argued that Mosul was an Arab area, and their senators and deputies wished to remain in Iraq. The Prime Minister al-Saadun also declared to the Constituent Assembly that the prolongation of the mandate term to 25 years did not constitute any problem given the worthwhile relations between Iraq and Great Britain. [660]Both houses unanimously supported the prolongation of this relation and both chambers conveyed their thanks to Amery for his acceptance of the terms proposed by the Commission, thereby defending the right of Iraq. In Great Britain, it had "alarmed the ultra-nationalist party to find a section of the British press "reluctant to the extension of alliance between Iraq and Britain. Rumors were spread that these British papers received funds from the Turkish government in exchange for their services. [661]The London Observer preferred the return of Mosul to Turkey and criticized British acceptance to stay in Iraq for an additional twenty years, asking when they would quit Iraq.[662]

---

[659] Quoted in Foster,(1936), pp.166-167.
[660] Spencer. (1988), pp. 140-141.
[661] Great Britain, Colonial Office, Iraq Administration Reports, 1914-1932. Vol. 8. 125-1927. P. 15.
[662] Spencer, (1988), p. 141.

When the Council considered the Mosul question again, on September 3 and 4, Roushdy Bey, the new Turkish representative, complained that the British now and then advanced their claim against Turkey, starting with the secret treaty of Sykes-Picot of 1916. He later repudiated Fethi Bey's pledge to abide by the Council decision in advance. He also renounced the Council's disposal of Mosul to Iraq conditioned by an extension of the mandate for twenty-five years explaining that Turkey had refused to recognize the mandatory system. He asserted then, that "Turkey refused categorically to accept article 94-99 of the draft of Treaty of Sèvres relating to the mandate.... The treaty of Lausanne makes no allusion whatever to the mandate." The British representative, Amery, while refuting all Turkish allegations, asked Roushdy about the fate of the Kurds in Mosul in case they were put under Turkish government. Dodging the question, Roushdy maintained that "the only solution was to reinstate Turkish control *de facto* over an area where its *de jure* sovereignty had never ceased." [663] This was followed by his rejection of the idea of establishing a Kurdish local autonomy, claiming that the Kurds in Turkey lived fully on equal terms with the Turks, and that the Anglo-Iraqi authorities had used the Kurdish question as a "smokescreen" since the Commission's enquiry indicated that there "were no Kurds in Iraq." [664]

The Swedish Proposal

Shortly before the Commission's meeting in early September, the Swedish Foreign Office authorized the Swedish delegation to attempt to find a quick and a viable solution, which would take into account the interests of the population of Mosul, as well as to guarantee a sustainable peace in the region. Since the Swedish rapporteur, Undén, was critical of the Commission's report, he suggested an alternative solution to the effect that the border be drawn along the Little Zab River. Based on this proposal, both sides of the Brussels line were to be demilitarized, otherwise imposing regulation of the troops there, furthermore, by an agreement enabling a free

---

[663] Beck, (1981), p. 265.
[664] Spencer, (1988), p. 145.

movement of goods between the regions and ensuring the right of the minority groups as well as exempting the British from extending its mandate period in Iraq. If the proposal materialized, the Swedes believed the Turkish "national honor" would be regained and British expenditure would be reduced, thanks to the creation of a demilitarized zone in the area.

On Undén's suggestion, a three-member-committee, consisting of himself, the Spanish representative and the representative from Uruguay, was formed to express its opinion on the matter. Despite Undén's efforts to convince the other two members of the committee that the Swedish plan was the ideal one they seemed to focus more on the Turks' attitudes toward the mediatory role of the Council. Then, at the Council's meeting on September 17, 1925, it became apparent that a majority of the Council preferred the Council's report (from July 1925). However, after additional attempts to get his plan through, Undén, on December 15, declared that Sweden would support the majority proposal in the Council.[665]

In the meantime, it was reported that military clashes could occur any time in case the league failed to settle the frontier dispute. According to Johannes Kolmodin, a Swedish expert in Constantinople, Mustafa Kemal and his military leadership deployed a military force of 40,000 to the disputed frontier to be used in the event of an adverse decision from the League. [666]Actually, frontier tension had been proceeding since January 1925, when the British lodged a protest with the Turkish government through its representative in Constantinople against violation of the state of affairs at the frontier. In May, a band prompted by Turkey attacked a police patrol south of the Brussels line, and in June, the British government submitted enquiries to the Turkish government since the Turks had mobilized a large military troop north of the Iraqi border despite the fact that the Kurdish revolt was declared defeated.[667] According to the British

---

[665] Roger, (2007), pp. 362-364.

[666] Makko,(2010), p. 642.

[667] Great Britain, Colonial Office, Iraq Administration Reports, 1914-1932. Vol.8. 1925-1927. p. 16. According to Lindsay, the kemalists exploited the revolt of Shaikh Said to crush the growing opposition in the country against the secular regime of Mustafa Kemal and his "de facto autocracy". At the same time, the

the aim of these Turkish military movements were that the Turks intended to reverse the League's decision in case it was in favor of Iraq and for that end, they had contemplated creating powerful "Chetta" (irregular groups) which, would likely be recruited from Turkish forces concentrated at the vicinity of the border. Although the British were of the opinion that there was "No doubt the Turkish political conscience is [was] sufficiently plastic to reconcile an unofficial invasion of Iraq by such bands"; they were uncertain as to whether the Turks actually intended to attack or even threaten Iraq. [668]In addition, the British were informed that the Turks retaliated against the Kurds and the Christians of Goyan who had expressed their wishes to the commission to be included in Iraq and consequently about 500 of them arrived as refugees at Zakho. [669]

Meanwhile, the Kemalists accused the British of whipping up Kurdish national sentiments against them. After the brutal crushing of Shaikh Said's rebellion, Mustafa Kemal hinted about the British involvement in anti-Turkish activities when he stated before the Parliament:

The worst part is that the British are behind the Kurds. You have constantly incited them against the Turks. During World War 1, you sent your brightest

British were anxious that once the revolt was put down, the Kemalists would threat the northern frontier of Iraq or even to conduct a military coup against Mosul, especially in case of an adverse decision from the League. However, that would imply that the Turks defy the arbitrary decision of the League and struggle singlehanded against Great Britain with support from Russia only, a fact not particularly to its benefit. British Documents. Vol. 30. P. 300.

[668] Ibid., p. 323.

[669] Great Britain, Colonial Office, Iraq Administration Report, 1924-1932. Vol. 8. 1925-1927. P. 16. In addition, according to reports received in early September on Turkish ill-treatment of the Chaldaen villages north and also south of the disputed frontier. The villagers who settled in the vicinity of the frontier had never participated in the war against the Turks. Yet, they were systematically evacuated from their places and transported to interior areas. However, many managed to escape and arrived in Zakho, in a miserable state, telling about the massacre and violence. Amery protested in strong terms before the Council in September 1925, but the Turkish delegate refuted the accusation categorically. Consequently, the British asked the Council to send an impartial commission to investigate the matter as well as on charge and counter charge regarding the violation of the disputed frontier. Ibid.

agents... to Kurdistan in order to provoke its inhabitants to attack the Turks.... In the Treaty of Sèvres you promised the Kurds independence. And even now your agents are again at work, rushing across the country and arming and exciting the tribes. England wants Mosul and its oil. The Kurds have the keys to Mosul and Iraq in their hands.[670]

However, Turkey refused to recognize the competence of the Council to render an arbitral decision binding on both sides; therefore, on September 19, the Council asked the Permanent Court of International Justice at The Hague for an advisory opinion on the following questions:

> 1-What is the character of the decision to be taken by the Council in virtue of article 3, paragraph 2, of the Treaty of Lausanne- is it an arbitral award, a recommendation or a simple mediation?
> 2-Must the decision be unanimous or may it be taken by a majority? May the representatives of the interested parties take part in the vote? [671]

The Permanent Court of International Justice

The Permanent Court of Justice opened on October 22, 1925, for an extraordinary session to examine the above- mentioned questions. The High Commissioner for Iraq had already stated that since Turkey refused to accept the League's and the Court's authorities to settle the dispute and admit its violation of *status quo,* the British and Iraq would reconsider their attitudes toward the League and declare their acceptance null and void. The Turks argued that irrespective of the court's position, Curzon's pledge at Lausanne on July 23, 1923, that there would be no decision without Turkey's consent, would remain the same. They pointed out that there was no need for "referring to anything whatever to The Hague Court, as ... the questions put to it are of highly marked political character ... in no manner whatever," they said, "could the consultative opinion of the Court affect the rights of the Turkish Government under the Lausanne

---

[670] Quoted in Erlendur Haraldsson, *Land im aufstand... Kurdistan*, (Hamburg 1966), p.48. (my translation). See also Chris Kutschera, *Le Mouvement National Kurds* (Paris, 1979), p.81.
[671] Foster, (1936), pp. 167-168.

244

Treaty."[672] The opinion of the Court on November 21, 1925, was:

> That the decision to be taken by the Council in virtue of Article 2, paragraph 3 of the Treaty of Lausanne will be binding on the parties and will constitute the definitive frontier between Iraq and Turkey.

The representatives of the two parties (Britain and Turkey) took part in the voting but their votes were not counting toward the requirement of unanimity necessary for the determination of the frontier dispute.[673]

The Enquiry of the Laidoner Commission

The Council acted on Amery's proposal to send an impartial Commission to investigate the allegations regarding Turkey's persecution of the Assyrians along the Brussels line. Accordingly, on September 28, the Council entrusted the task to General Laidoner, an Estonian, to make an on-the-spot enquiry to secure the facts about these accusations and to keep the Council constantly up to date about the development in the disputed area. The Turkish government opposed this decision and refused to allow Laidoner to visit the area north of the Brussels line.[674] The latter reported to the Council complaining:

> My investigation was confined to the area south of the Brussels line; this complicated my work considerably and made it difficult for me to carry it out in the spirit of the first paragraph of the Council resolution.[675]

The Turks justified the deportation of the local Christians by describing it as a Turkish minority question and, hence, with no connection to the development in the disputed border area. Turkey's attempt was to counteract Western press reports about the killing of 300 Assyrians and deportation

---

[672] Quoted in Spencer, (1988), p. 146.

[673] Collection of Advisory Opinions, Permanent Court of International Justice, Series B, No. 12, p.8.Quoted in Spencer, (1988), p. 147.

[674] Beck, (1981), p. 266.

[675] League of Nations, Official Journal, Minutes of the Thirty-Seventh Session of the Council, December 7-16, 1925, Annex 829, "Question of the Frontier between Turkey and Iraq. Situation on the Locality of the Provisional Line Fixed at Brussels on October 29, 1924. Quoted in Spencer, (1988), p. 154.

of 800 more from the frontier under investigations. [676]

Laidoner, who was assisted by a Czechoslovakian, a Spaniard, and two secretaries, arrived in Baghdad on October 26 [677] and Mosul on October 30. Speaking with the local leaders in Mosul, Laidoner made it clear that his mission was confined to investigating the situation around the vicinity of the provisional line and that he was not authorized for mediation or settlement of the dispute. In his report to the Council submitted on December 10, 1925, Laidoner categorized the events along the frontier line as follows:

> Raids by tribal and village chiefs. 2. Occupation of certain villages by Turkish military posts and patrols. 3. Flights over the line by British aircraft. 4. Deportations of Christians. [678]

With regards to the decision of the Council, these incidents, Laidoner believed, were not significant.

The deportation of the Christians, on the other hand, was most serious and detrimental for the Turkish case. During the four-day impartial and detailed investigation among the refugees, Laidoner and his assistants were convinced about the dependability of the refugees' witnesses. They reported that:

> Turkish soldiers, under the command of the officers, occupied the villages, and in the first place obtained delivery off all arms; they then imposed very

---

[676] Makko, (2010), p. 642.

[677] Just before the arrival of the Commission in Baghdad, the refugee camps at Zakho was visited by General Secretary of the Friends of Armenia Society who stated that the Iraqi authorities were assiduous in their work to assist the refugees, but owing their predicament, help from outside was necessary. Accordingly, he dispatched telegrams to different Christian Societies and communities and formed a committee in London to collect funds. The High Commission, then, distributed the received funds through a committee consisting of three British officers who were apprised of the situation in the border area. The British committee sent in December Colonel Fergusson, a member of the King's Bodyguard to take care of the collected funds. Great Britain, Colonial Office, Iraq Administration Reports, 1914-1932, Vol. 8. 1925-1927. P. 16.

[678] Spencer, (1988), p. 156.

heavy fines and demanded women; they then pillaged the houses and subjected the inhabitants to atrocious acts of violence, going as far as massacre. The deportation were deportation *en mass* ... During the deportation several persons fell ill on the way and were abandoned; others died of starvation and cold, for, when leaving their homes, they had to abandon everything and were unable to carry with them either food or clothing.

Laidoner and his group confirmed the authenticity of their report and added that they themselves had witnessed refugees in a miserable state, especially in the Zakho district where about three thousand deported Christians were settled. Since they were unable to investigate in the villages on the northern side of the Brussels line, from where the refugees came, nor could they obtain information from the Turkish authorities, they could not attribute the causes of deportations of the Christians to certain factors. But they argued that the deportation should be given a considerable weight with respect to the situation at the border line. It was believed that Laidoner's report made a great impact on the determination of the final decision of the Council with regard to the frontier dispute.[679]

The Decision of the Council of the League

In December 1925, the British and Turkish representatives presented their views on the adversary's opinion of the Court to the Council. Amery argued that the opinion of the Court confirmed his previous viewpoint that the two countries' commitments toward the Mosul's dispute were not stipulated by "any assurances or declarations that either of the parties have made or may make" but by "the terms of Article 3 of the Treaty of Lausanne." Munir Bey, Turkey's Minister to Switzerland, opposing the opinion of the court, replied that the fact that the Council was obliged to consult lawyers on the matter indicated that there "was a certain doubt in the mind of the members who voted in favor of such a step, and that consequently such an understanding did not result from the text of Article 3 of the Treaty of Lausanne." Turkey opposed asking for the court's opinion, hence, in accordance with Article 15 of the Covenant it should not be considered as

---

[679] Foster, (1936), pp. 170-171.

a unanimous action since it was decided by the court on November 21. Besides, The Grand National Assembly, when ratifying Article 3, realized that it could "not leave the destinies of disputed territory to the luck of arbitration." [680]

Thus, Turkey's representative refused to recognize the arbitral authority of the League Council and did not attend at the Council's seventh meeting on December 10, when Laidoner presented his report, nor did he attend the fifteenth and final meeting on December 16, when the Council discussed the Mosul question. However, a note from the Foreign Minister Roushdy Bey was read to the Council stating:

> ... all the proposals which I have previously made with the object of reaching an agreement ... I find myself obliged to inform you that these proposals are now *ipso facto* null and void... the sovereign rights of a state over a territory can only come to an end with its consent, and that therefore our sovereign rights over the whole of the Mosul vilayat remain intact.[681]

The report represented by Undén to the Council attached a great weight to Article 3 of the Treaty of Lausanne, the report of the Commission of Enquiry, the opinion of the Court, and the Laidoner report. At the Council meeting, Undén noted "The Committee recognized that an equitable solution of the dispute could only be found in following the main lines of the final conclusions of the Commission of the Enquiry." [682] Finally, on December 16, 1925, the Council of the League announced its decision on the Mosul dispute. It was taken by virtue of Article 3 of the Lausanne Treaty, which would be binding by the two parties and would constitute a definite frontier between Iraq and Turkey. The Council decided unanimously, subject to three conditions, that all territories south of the Brussels line be awarded to the new state of Iraq. The two main conditions read:

> The British Government is invited to submit to the Council a new Treaty with Iraq, ensuring the continuance for twenty-five years of the mandatory regime

---

[680] Ibid., p.171.

[681] League of Nations, Official Journal, p. 121. Quoted in Spencer, (1988), P.161.

[682] Foster, (1936), p. 172.

248

defined by the Treaty of Alliance between Great Britain and Iraq and by the British Government's undertaking, approved by the Council on the 27th September, 1924, unless Iraq is, in conformity with Article 1 of the Covenant, admitted as a Member of the League before the expiration of this period.

The British Government, as the Mandatory Power, was invited to lay before the Council the Administrative measures in supervising the guarantees mentioned in the report of The Commission of Inquiry regarding local administration recommended by the Commission in its conclusions.[683] The frontier commission had in its report recommended that:

> Regard must be paid to the desires expressed by the Kurds that officials of Kurdish race should be appointed for the administration of their country, the dispensation of justice, and teaching in the schools, and that Kurdish should be the official language of all these services.[684]

These points were to be carried out within six months and provided the Council's approval the disposition of Mosul to Iraq would be declared definite and the Council would initiate ground demarcation of the frontier.

Reactions in Iraq, Britain and Turkey to the Council's Decision

Public opinion in Iraq had expected the decision of the Council of the League on the Mosul question which was announced on December 17. The possibility of the prolongation of the Treaty of 1922 as a condition for the retention of Mosul had been in circulation since the Frontier Commission visited Iraq.[685] According to British reports, everywhere in Iraq people were deeply satisfied with the acquisition of the Mosul *wilayat* and were optimistic about Iraq's future prosperity in light of the stability that the settlement of the disputed territory engendered.[686] However, a section of

---

[683] Quoted in Ireland, (1937), pp. 406-407. See also Husayn Fadil, *Mushkilat al-Mawsil, dirasah fi-al-diblumasiyah al-Iraqiyah - al-Injiliziyah-al -Turkiyah wa-fi al-ray al-amm*, (Bayrut, 2015), pp. 173-179.

[684] Special Report, p.259.

[685] Ireland, p. 408.

[686] Great Britain, Colonial Office, Iraq Administration Reports, 1914-1932.

the Iraqi vernacular press was prudent in writing about the conditions embodied in the Council's decision. So, *Al-Istiql and Al-Alam al-Arabi* were cautious to the extent that they omitted "over a period of twenty-five years" from the text.

King Faisal [687]expressed his appreciation and thanks in a telegram to King George V. of Great Britain. A similar telegram was sent from the Iraqi Prime Minister to British Prime Minister Stanley Baldwin and to the Secretary-General of the League. Amery, as well received several thankful messages.[688]

Edmonds points out that the general attitudes of the Kurds toward the conditions stipulated by the Commission's decision were gratifying. In order to describe the prevailing positive feelings among the Kurds in Sulaimanya at the time of the visit of the Commission he sent the following letter to Dobbs:

> The visit of the Commission has given a new impetus to the Kurdish nationalism which has swept into the anti-Turkish camp many disgruntled persons whom even the most optimistic among us had at first expected to declare in favour of Turkey. The longer interviews were almost invariably strongly nationalist but not generally separatist in tone ... The Kurds at Sulaimani have struck what may prove to have been the decisive blow in the fight for the preservation of Iraq, and know it. Can the Iraqi Government rise to the occasion and adopt a far-sighted and generous policy towards the Kurds? [689]

Edmonds once again praised the Kurds, in particular those of Sulaimanya,

---

Vol. 8. 1925-1927. P. 18.

[687] According to *current History,* December, 1925, Faisal had stated that "if Iraq is deprived of Mosul, the economic future of the country is blighted ... By the separation of Mosul from Iraq a terrible and possibly fatal blow would be dealt to my country ..." Quoted in Spencer, p. 165. On 21 February 1926, had Faisal declared that "We now know where we are and financial schemes on lines hitherto forbidden by fears as to the future can now be undertaken." *The Times of Mesopotamia.* Quoted in Spencer, p. 165.

[688] Great Britain, Colonial Office, Iraq Administration Reports, 1914-1932. Vol. 8. 1925-1927. P. 18.

[689] Edmonds, (1957), p. 434.

for their position in the determination of the question of the Mosul dispute. Nevertheless, in light of the Kurdish preponderance in the *wilayat* and the manner by which the investigation of the wishes of the population was performed, particularly by absence of Shaikh Mahmud during the visit of the Commission, it was perhaps not unforeseen that the findings of the Commission would be in favor of Iraq. The British politicians, especially those on the spot, were contented since they were now able to achieve two strategic objectives- bringing the Kurds under the control of the Iraqi government, as their national movement had been forcibly pacified, and the consolidation of the Iraqi state following the acquisition of the Mosul *Wilayat.*

On the other hand, the disposition of Mosul to Iraq was met with vexation by the Turkish government as was expected. However, this did not solely stem from the fact that Turkey, by regaining Mosul would as well regain its national prestige and pride. The loss of Mosul would also put the Kemalists in a difficult predicament with regards to Kurdish national aspirations, for in the case that the Iraqi government fulfilled its obligations and the Council's recommendations for the establishment of a Kurdish local administration, it would undoubtedly constitute a source of inspiration for their brother Kurds in Turkey. This was by no means a desirable development for the Turks since it would obstruct their plans of Turkification of the Kurds in Turkey.

Arnold Toynbee, a British diplomat and historian, made a visit to Angora in 1924, where he met several leading personalities, among them was the Turkish Prime Minister, Raúf Bey. Toynbee realized that the Turkish claim for Mosul was not motivated by economic or strategic interests, but mainly by political interests. The Kurdish question was paramount to Turkey's tenacious efforts in regaining Mosul. With respect to this question, he said that "even the Treaty of Sèvres left the northern half of the Kurdistan within the Turkish frontier … ", which conveyed an implicit threat that the Kemalists would strive for more of the Kurdish territory.[690]

---

[690] Foster, (1936), p. 175.

In Britain, however, Amery defended the Iraqi government and the strategic importance of Iraq in Parliamentary debate maintaining that British policy in the Mosul's question had been in accordance with mandatory and Treaty obligations. The opposition, and a great part of public opinion, were critical of Britain's involvement in Iraq, a territory they deemed unproductive and squeezing British taxpayers.[691]

In Turkey, after the defeat of the political struggle over the Mosul Wilayat Turkish leaders used an increasingly aggressive tone in their continued efforts to regain the *Wilayat.* When in October, King Faisal was in London, he necessitated "further expenditure on military preparation" in Iraq in case Mosul was awarded to Turkey. Mustafa Kemal, declared that Mosul was "Turkish and nothing can ever change that fact, even bayonets. We want the whole former wilayat of Mosul on both sides of the Tigris; and mandate or no mandate, we shall never abandon that view." It was reported that Turkey initiated recruitment and concentration of troops and the planting of mines in its harbors.

The belligerent attitude of the Turkish press added fuel to the fire of anti-British sentiments in Turkey. Thus, the Constantinople *Jumhuriat* warned that "Turkey will be obliged to take Mosul not by the mediation of the League but by bayonets."[692] The same paper had said that the League's decision:

> proves once more that the League of Nations is servant of the strongest, namely Great Britain … As the case was during our campaign for nationhood, so now the rights of the Turks are safe under the sharp bayonets of the Turks, and we know perfectly well to take back with our hands "Turkish Mosul" given to Great Britain by the League of Nations-just as we saved Adana, Broussa, Smyrna and Constantinople.[693]

The British, for their part, attempted to prevent the political dispute from escalating to an extensive military conflict with Turkey. At the Committee

---

[691] Spencer, (1988), p. 166.

[692] Ibid. p. 173.

[693] The Literary Digest February 6, 1926. Quoted in Foster, p. 176.

of Imperial Defence, Baldwin reiterated the necessity of refraining from military involvement for defending Iraq. Churchill argued that Iraq alone was responsible for defending itself in case of war; "I am personally opposed to risking a single British unit in defence of Mesopotamia, "since "it would be madness to get entangled there." However, the Cabinet accepted the considerations of the Committee of the Imperial Defence that any British military operation in connection to the Mosul dispute should be limited in nature and conducted in coordination with the League. [694]

The British also sought to bring about some kind of "Triple Entente" with other great powers, such as Italy and France, who had relatively common interests with regards to Turkey. Britain's cooperation with the Great Powers combined with "threat of material and moral sanctions" forced Turkey to agree with the Council's decision on the Turco-Iraqi frontier.[695] In fact, the British were pulling "a few political strings in the Mediterranean." It was rumored that after his visit to Tripoli in April 1926, Mussolini intended to occupy Anatolia in the event of Turkish military activity in Mosul, and Greece would invade Thrace and Smyrna reviving the terms of the Treaty of Sèvres. [696]

At the same time, the British sought to employ the same bargaining strategy that the Turks had employed at Lausanne Conference, namely to offer the latter to relinquish their claim on Mosul for a share of Iraqi oil. Actually, already in Lausanne, Curzon reiterated the proposal of the Colonial Office of November 1922, to the effect that Turkey abandoned its territorial claim in return for being permitted to participate in the development of Iraqi oil, but the talks terminated with no understanding on that matter.

---

[694] Beck, p. 269.

[695] Ibid, p. 270. The British appreciated Italian naval and air support in case of war with Turkey. The Anglo-Italian cooperation was feasible due to the fact that Italian had territorial ambitions in Turkey, and that the two countries envisaged to develop their relations in accordance with the principles agreed on by Chamberlain and Mussolini at Rome in December 1924. In April 1925, for example, Britain agreed on Italian's investment in Iraq to promote its economic development and Italian granted the British similar rights in Ethiopia. Beck, Ibid.

[696] Foster, (1936), p. 17.

However, after the Commission's decision to award Mosul to Iraq, the British, cognizant of the fact that the international prestige of Turkey was linked to the winning of Mosul, pondered offering them some face-saving concessions which might possibly facilitate a rapprochement between the two countries. Thus, In the middle of April, 1926, Lindsay visited Ankara to appease the Turks. He was:

> Authorized to hold out inducement that might, it was feared in London, prove insufficiently attractive; some redrawing of the boundary in Turkey's favour; provision for "good neighbourly" relations between Turkey and Iraq, the application between Turkey and Iraq of certain judicial and commercial conventions signed at Lausanne; and finally, conclusion of a Turco-Iraqi extradition treaty.[697]

Great Britain's appeasement policy vis-à-vis Turkey paved the way for bilateral negotiations in April 1926 and finally the signing of the Tripartite Treaty between Great Britain, Turkey and Iraq at Ankara on June 5, 1926. The treaty, which was ratified on July 18, 1926, stipulated that Turkey accepted the Brussels line as "definite and inviolable" with slight rectification such as to allow it to control the Atamun-Ashunta road. Turkey was also entitled to either 10 percent for Iraqi royalties from Mosul oil for 25 years or a compound of sum of 500,000 pounds.[698] Thus, oil was a crucial element in the settlement of the long protracted and strenuous controversy between the British and the Turks over a territory, which assumed increasing importance. However, oil was also significant in the acquisition of Mosul. Since the occupation of Iraq in 1917, besides protecting its lines of communication to India, Britain's primary objective was also to safeguard its oil interests, which was now realized.

Apart from the supremacy of oil in the Anglo-Iraqi political calculations, two fundamental conclusions could be drawn from the Mosul dispute. First: the winning of the *Wilayat* to Iraq implied that the Kurds were definitely incorporated into the Iraqi state, and their national rights were limited

---

[697] Stivers, pp. 166-171.
[698] Beck, (1981), p. 271.

to pledges made by the Commission of Enquiry in terms of linguistic and cultural rights. This, despite the fact, that the Kurds, given their preponderance in the *Wilayat*, were entitled to a state of their own by the Commission of Enquiry, although it was disregarded. Second: during the Mosul controversy, it became apparent that the principle of national self-determination was not meant to be applied everywhere. Whilst the Turks on several occasions, by referring to the principle, required that the dispute be resolved through a plebiscite thereby the population, based on ethnic belonging, would express their wishes on the subject, the British did not accommodate their request, describing the plebiscite as impractical in those areas. Drawn on the same principle, the British, as has been observed, carried out two plebiscites in Iraq in 1919 for the unification of the Baghdad, Basra and Mosul provinces under the Iraqi State, and in 1921 for the election of King Faisal to the throne of Iraq. According to the British authorities both these elections reflected an "unbiased pronouncement" of the public opinion in Iraq. Their rejection of the Turkish requests (and even of the Kurdish ones, Shaikh Mahmud's demands for plebiscites were turned down), clearly revealed that the British used the principle as an instrument whenever it suited their policy. The principle was interpreted in different ways by all actors for the vindication of their rights, such as the Kurds, the Turks, and the Arab nationalists

11

Anglo-Iraqi Kurdish Policy, 1926- 1931

The new Anglo-Iraqi Treaty, extended to twenty-five years, was negotiated and signed on January 13, 1926, by the Prime Minister Abd al-Muhsin al-Saadun, and was accepted by a large majority of the deputies of the Iraqi Parliament on the 19th of the same month.[699]

The Iraqi government was now obliged to carry out the recommendations of the Commission of Enquiry concerning the administration of the Kurdish areas in Iraq. The implementation of these recommendations was of great significance for the Anglo-Iraqi authorities since it would contribute to Iraq's entry into the League of Nations, especially as the Kurdish question had been highlighted as a result of the Mosul dispute. According to the British annual reports to the League, the Iraqi government had already incurred commitments as to providing the Kurds opportunities for development of their culture and appointment of competent Kurds to official posts. Consequently, the Iraqi government did not have much to do in order to establish the type of administration requested by the League Council. Generally, the report further claimed that in all Kurdish areas, the officials were Kurds and the Kurdish language was

---

[699] Edmonds, (1957), p. 432. Regarding the prolongation of the new Treaty, the Treaty stipulated "Unless before the expiration of that period Iraq shall have become a member of the League of Nations." Iraq became member of the League on October 3, 1932. Ibid.

used as the official language in the courts and schools. In order to underscore this policy and also to dissipate misunderstanding with respect to the Iraqi government's intention for the Kurds, al-Saadun, on January 21, during a debate in the parliament on the decision of the Council on the Mosul dispute declared:

> This country cannot live unless all elements of the Iraq State enjoy their rights. We shall give the Kurds their rights. Their officials shall be from among them, their official language shall be their own tongue, and with their mother tongue their children shall be taught in the schools. All elements of the State shall be treated with justice and granted their rights, whether they be Moslem or non-Moslem.

The prime minister's speech was greeted with keen interest by the all deputies in the Chamber and some days later, the following publications were distributed to all ministers in his Cabinet:

> Your Excellency has no doubt seen the speech made by the Prime Minister in the Chamber of Deputies and published in the Press on the following day. The speech embodies the policy which the Government has pursued and will continue to pursue in the administration of the Kurdish areas, namely, that the officials shall be Kurds and the official language Kurdish. His Excellency has therefore directed me to request you to endeavour to carry out this policy and to adhere thereto in all that appertains to the administration of the areas in question.

The British report stated that the Iraqi government's policy toward the Kurds, declared by the prime minister, had been put into effect by all departments and accepted by all Kurds. It assured also that the new Prime Minister Jaf'ar al-Askari, who assumed office at the end of the year, would pursue the same policy since he was "himself by blood and birth more than half a Kurd" and spoke Kurdish fluently. [700]

Furthermore, the relations between the Iraqi government and the Kurds were described generally to be satisfactory and in accordance with the

---

[700] Iraq Administration Reports, 1914-1932,Vol. 8. 1925-1927, p. 198.

interests of the Kurds. With the exception of Shaikh Mahmud and his "band of outlaws" the Kurds seemed to be active participants in the national life in Iraq. Already in 1924, the Kurds were elected to the Constituent Assembly, and Kurdish notables were also elected in 1925 in Arbil, Kirkuk, Mosul and Sulaimanya and, indeed, except for Mosul, all members from the other three liwas were Kurds. Moreover, the Kurds were represented in the Senate and in the Cabinet. The Iraqi government on its part showed no "tendency to attempt to denationalize the Kurds" and in respecting "Kurdish susceptibility the Iraqi Government has rightly comprehended that a united State can be built up of diverse elements and has set an example among Near Eastern countries." [701]

Apparently, after the disposition of the Mosul *Wilayat* to Iraq, the stage was set for the implementation of the Anglo-Iraqi policy toward the nationalist Kurds, namely to attain their common objective of incorporating South Kurdistan into the Iraqi state. This was feasible when the idea of creating a Kurdish autonomy was abandoned, and Kurdish rights were confined to pledges of establishing a form of administration that would meet Kurdish demands.

In a ceremony, on February 25, celebrating the conclusion of the new Anglo-Iraqi Treaty, the High Commissioner and King Faisal, in their speeches, put particular stress on the importance of the unity between the Iraqi government and the Kurds. The High Commissioner referred to the recommendations of the Commission of Enquiry with regards to the Kurds, he warned the Iraqi government not to commit the same mistake as the Turks made when they attempted to eliminate all national and religious elements instead of treating them as they deserved. The objective of the Iraqi government, hence, should be the unity of all elements that could form good citizens to serve it and to encourage the ethnic and religious characters of these elements. A Kurd was not an Arab and if the idea actually was to make him an Iraqi patriot, that could not be done by forcing

---

[701] Ibid., pp.22-23.

him to quote Arabic or imitate Arab habits; in sum, not by attempting to make him a real Arab, but to give him all opportunities and support to become a real Kurd.The unity of the state which was essential for its progress could not be achieved by eliminating special features of the various elements that constituted the state but to encourage all that was good in those features. At the end of his speech, the High Commissioner, praised King Faisal for following the policy embodied in his speech since it was important to convince the League of Nations that Iraq could be qualified for admittance into the League.

King Faisal for his part told the audience that one of the crucial factors that instigated the Arab revolt against the Turks was their intention of making the Arabs Turks. This idea was undoubtedly one of the factors that caused the dismemberment of the Ottoman Empire. Accordingly, it was impossible to commit the same mistake whose negative consequences were detrimental to a government, which was greater and stronger than the Iraqi one. Faisal said he believed that one of the greatest duties of an Iraqi Arab was to encourage his brother Iraqi Kurd to cling to his nationality and to join him under the Iraqi flag, which was the common emblem of the Iraqis and their source of moral and material happiness; hence, they should be active members for the progress of a common homeland. [702]

In March, 1926, the British Foreign Office submitted a memorandum on the administration of the Kurdish districts in Iraq to the League of Nations in order to present to the League the administrative measures taken by the Iraqi government in supervising the guarantees that the Commission of Enquiry had promised the Kurds on the local administration. The memorandum, which maintained that the present administrative system had helped to apply most of the recommendations of the Commission, was completely based on the following facts related to the measures taken by the Iraqi government for district administrations where the Kurdish elements prevailed: Forty-three out of seventy-five officials employed by the Ministry of Finanand the Ministry of Interior in the Kurdish districts were Kurds, while

---

[702] Ibid., p. 205.

there were nine official Kurds with the same jobs in non-Kurdish areas. The Ministry of Justice had thirteen officials in the Kurdish areas; ten of them were Kurds, the hearings were conducted in Kurdish and the records of the proceeding, which also were in Kurdish, were performed in Sulaiymanya and Coy Sanjaq of Arbil *liwa*. Fourteen out of eighty -eight deputies were Kurds and the Minister of Finance as well as the Minister of Communications and Works were Kurds.

The Kurds comprised about 17 percent [703] of the country's total population and 24 percent of the total police force were Kurds. In the army, they consisted of 14 percent, while 33 percent of the railway workers were Kurds; the total Kurdish employees in the police force, the army and the railways were about 20 percent.

In 16 out of 25 schools in the Kurdish areas the teaching language was Kurdish. Forty-four out of 52 teachers of these schools were Kurds, and the rest were Arabs who could speak Kurdish.

As for the use of the Kurdish language, it must be remembered that, before the war, Kurdish was not used as a medium of communication, either private or official. There had been a considerable amount of poetical works in Kurdish, but the development of the written language as a medium of communication was entirely due to the efforts of British officials, and the languages used previously were Persian, Turkish and Arabic. The use of the written Kurdish had not yet spread to the Mosul *liwa*, where Turkish and Arabic were used. It had gradually spread to Arbil, where it

---

[703] There are no accurate figures on the population of Iraq for that year, but according to statistics for the year 1930, the population in Iraq was estimated to 2, 824,000 and for the year 1932, was estimated to 3,807,077. The Kurds constituted 16-17 percent of the total population. As for the Christians the number was 3-4 percent, and for the Jews was 2,5-2,4. Despite the fact that the Kurdish population was three times more than the two other minority groups together, there were 41 Kurdish schools in the whole of Iraq, while the Christian schools were 47, and the Jewish ones were 19. See Ahmad Muhammad Amin Qadir,*Mawqif-Majlis al-nuwwab al-Iraqi Min al-qadiyah al-Kurdiyah fi al-Iraq, 1925-1945*. The Position of the Iraqi Parliament toward the Kurdish Question in Iraq, 1925-1945, (Al-Sulaimanya: Bnkaizhin, 2007), pp.71-72.

had recently been recognized as the official language for purposes of written communication with government offices. Sulaimanya had for some years possessed a Kurdish newspaper, and for some time had been using the written Kurdish for official and private affairs. The work commenced by the government of occupation was loyally carried out by the Iraqi government. In Baghdad, two newspapers were published and every measure was taken not only to permit, but actively to encourage the use of the Kurdish language.[704]

The Kurdish Question and the Iraqi Parliament

When the Iraqi Parliament opened in 1925,[705] the Kurdish national rights became a Parliamentary concern for the Kurdish deputies. In a meeting held on August 10, 1925, of the first extraordinary session, when hardly a month had passed since the opening of the Parliament, the general issue of education in Iraq and particularly in Kurdistan was brought up for discussion. The Sulaimanya deputy, Muhammad Amin Zaki, presented a report to the Parliament, supported by eleven other deputies, comparing the education system of the country, including Kurdistan, before and after the war and made suggestions to improve it. The report indicated that there were inequalities as to the distribution of schools in the Iraqi provinces. For instance, in one province, there were 72 primary boys' schools, 18 girls' schools and one secondary school, while in Sulaimanya there was only one school, deprived of necessary means and handicapped by

---

[704] Ibid., pp.195-198.

[705] Following the establishment of the Constitutional Monarchy in Iraq in 1925, an elected Parliament was formed. The 1925 Constitution called for a bicameral legislature, consisting of an elected House of Representatives. The Lower House (Majlis an-nuwwab) was elected every four years by manhood suffrage, and the Upper House, the Senate (Majlis- al- ayán) was appointed by the King. The elected chamber worked through seven permanent committees; all bills submitted by the Cabinet were first referred to the appropriate committee, and were returned to the house with necessary amendments. Due to its work, the permanent committees had considerable influence on shaping legislation. The committees were chosen each time at the beginning of a session. Between 1925 and the overthrow of the monarchy in 1958, ten elections were held. See Iraq Administration Reports, 1914-1932. Vol. 8, 1925-1927, p. 14. See also Qadir, (2007)

different kinds of shortcomings, having 105 students and five classes.[706]

The deputies' persistance on the necessity of establishing schools in the Kurdish areas continued even in the session opened on February 25, 1926.The Arbil deputy, Ibrahim Yousef, urged the Ministry of Education to open a girls' school in Arbil, explaining that there were 263 schools in Iraq, hence, in each *liwa* there should be 19 schools, while in the whole of Arbil there were only 6 primary schools. Another Arbil deputy, Ismail Rawaduzi, demanded from the Parliament to open a secondary school in Arbil, which was supported by Mosul deputy, al-Khory Yousef al-Khayat; as he pointed out " if we examine carefully this justified request we will then see that it is of profound benefit and extremely important."[707] The Director of General Education, Sati al-Husri, disagreed with these deputies and argued that the school education in the *liwa* of Arbil still had not reached the required level so that the Ministry of Education could open a high school there, since there were not enough students, consisting only of 8, who hopefully would pass the secondary school. He added that it was." inappropriate to open a high school in Arbil for eight students."Rawanduzi replied that there were two schools in each of Coy Sanjaq and Arbil from where 17 students graduated and that a number of them had quit their studies due to their hard living conditions. Then, he asked al-Husri if there was any scale or legal text according to which a secondary school could be opened. Al-Husri replied that the Iraqi government was concerned about the amount to spend on the opening of a secondary school, which was equivalent to five primary schools. He also asserted that no students from the primary schools had graduated from Arbil yet.[708]

At this session al-Husri's opinion was dismissed by another Mosul deputy, Ali Khayri al-Imam, who attributed the lack of graduates from Arbil schools to the degeneration of teaching caused by the neglect of the

---

[706] Qadir, (2007), pp. 72-74.

[707] Set of memorandum, the first Parliamentary election, the first ordinary meeting, 1925, session 23, at the close of March 1926, p. 9-10, Iraqi Events, nr. 414, 16, 3, 1926. Quoted in Qadir, (2007), p. 74.

[708] Ibid., pp.74-75.

Ministry of Education toward that *liwa* and maintained that al-Husri's explanations with respect to the education in the city of Arbil were false. However, Zaki's report was referred to the government for consideration based on the proposal of Mosul deputy Khayr al-Din Umar. As the session proceeded Rawanduzi and several of his colleagues demanded that the Minister of Education would open a school in his hometown Rawanduz, criticizing al-Husri for what they called "his policy toward the northern liwas." Al-Husri rejected all allegations and held that the Ministry of Education allocated in its budget the amount necessary for building a school in Rawanduz.

However, only a few of the pledges that the Ministry of Education made were fulfilled, and the demand submitted to al-Husri for the opening of a secondary school in Arbil was still not implemented after a year.[709]

In fact, the education policy of al-Husri and the Minister of Education toward the Kurds coincided with that of the British:

... within the last month those Kurds who would have been content with primary education in Kurdish, are now pressing for Kurdish Secondary Schools and Kurdish Training College. This will mean the duplication of instructions already existing in Baghdad, and therefore will involve heavy expenditure. Besides the economic difficulty there is also a serious mechanical difficulty. Kurdish has hitherto been a spoken rather than a written language, and there are practically no Kurdish books. In the early stage of primary education this is not such a serious defect, but something must be done to meet it in the case of secondary schools. And it is not simply the question of translation that is involved. There is before that the question of translation which presents serious difficulties.

Possibly the solution of the problem is to be found in the provision of primary education in Kurdish, at the same time making the study of Arabic as a second language obligatory, and increasing it progressively in the higher primary classes, so that a boy who passes out of a Kurdish primary school would be equipped for an Arabic secondary school.(GB.1925:139).[710]

---

[709] Ibid., pp.74-76.
[710] Quoted in Hassanpour, (1992), pp. 306-307.

It will be recalled that in 16 out of 25 schools in the Kurdish areas the teaching language was Kurdish, but following the recommendations of the Commission of Enquiry on the administration of these areas, the question of teaching in Kurdish language, among other things, was given significant attention by the Kurds. On the other hand, the mandate and the Iraqi authorities showed slight interests in accommodating Kurdish demands on this matter, and instead were deliberately acting in the opposite direction.

Accordingly, in 1925, the Mosul deputy, Hamed Shamdin, raised the question for discussion in the Parliament and underscored the futility of sending teachers not proficient in Kurdish to Kurdish *liwas,* calling on the Ministry of Education to instead send Kurdish teachers to schools in Kurdistan so that children would benefit from them. The General Director, al-Husri, denied sending teachers with no knowledge of Kurdish to those areas, but Shamdin maintained that several teachers in Zakho, Aqra, Dohok and Amadiyah were not proficient in Kurdish and reiterated his demand on sending Kurdish teachers. However, al-Husri admitted that there was an English teacher who was not proficient in Kurdish and promised that as soon as the Ministry of Education acquired an English teacher with proficiency in Kurdish, they would send him to those areas. [711]Al-Husri showed no sign of improving the education system in the Kurdish areas, and his policy was repeatedly criticized by the Kurds both inside and outside the Parliament, but on each occasion, he attempted to circumvent or simply ignore these kinds of criticism.

The British had no intention to alter their principles with regards to the teaching language in the Kurdish areas. In their annual Reports to the League of Nations, for the years 1926 and 1927 respectively, they gave prominence to the fact that:

> The principle has not been abandoned that Arabic should be studied as a second language up to a high standard of proficiency.

And:

> The Iraqi Government quite rightly insisted on the maintenance of Arabic as

---

[711] Qadir, (2007), pp. 103-104.

a second language in the Kurdish schools. This is in the interests of the Kurds themselves. ... As it is, their parochialism has sometimes given openings to their opponents, and embarrassments to their friends.[712]

In fact, education was not the mandatory power's first concern in Iraq. They prioritized other important departments such as Defence, Finance and Interior, which were well financed and closely supervised by British advisors and their deputies, while departments such as Agriculture, Health and Education, had low priority and were basically managed by Iraqi personnel, with lenient supervision. This enabled the permanent Iraqi servants to have full control of the Department of Education. Al-Husri "a friend and confidant of King Faisal" was asked by the King to follow him from Syria to Iraq, where he, due to the mandatory authority's half measure on the matter of Education, could exert considerable power and influence. Consequently, al-Husri's educational methods were at variance with British advisors' policy.[713]

However, there seemed to be concordance between al-Husri's policy and that of the mandatory power as to the administration in the Kurdish areas. None of the recommendations of the Commission of Enquiry was carried out at the time Iraq was admitted to the League of Nations in 1932, and the policy of ignorance of the Kurdish language and even the Arabization of it continued. Marr argues that despite Husri's opposition to British control in Iraq, there was consensus among them in some policy areas

---

[712] Quotations in Hassanpour, (1992), p. 307.

[713] Slugglett, (2007), p.197. Lionel Smith, a British advisor, resigned several times due to his disagreement with al-Husri's education policy. However, he and many British, had a high regard for al-Husri's work and integrity. At the time of al-Husri's resignation, he wrote that "His unremitting efforts to secure efficiency and a high standard in teachers and pupils naturally aroused opposition and it is deplorable fact that his retirement was largely the result of his failure to obtain even the moral support of those who at heart approved his policy and appreciated his value. No other Iraqi combines his enthusiasm, his experience and knowledge of education system, and his fearlessness." Quoted in Reeva S. Simon., *Iraq Between the Two World Wars: The Creation and Implementation of a Nationalist Ideology*, (New York: Colombia University Press, 1986), p.83.

such as the Arabization of the curriculum; "All vestiges of Turkish language were dropped in favor of Arabic, which became the medium of instruction except for some classes in English."[714] As Director of the General Education between 1921 and 1927, al-Husri had a great influence on the education system in Iraq. A short introduction about al-Husri will hopefully help to gain a deeper insight into his thoughts and increase our understanding of his education policy in Iraq.

Sati al-Husri: An Arab Nationalist Ideologue and Educationalist: His Kurdish Policy

The principal element in Sati al-Husri's nationalist ideology was secularism. Unlike all other Muslim thinkers, he viewed religion and nationalism as two entirely separate entities. He focused on the secular aspects of nationalism and was perhaps more consistent than any other writer on the definition of a comprehensive theory of Arab nationalism.[715] Sati al-Husri was born in Sana'a, Yemen in 1880 into a family of Arab parents from Aleppo, studied in Turkish schools, and learned to speak both Turkish and French. Later when he settled in Arab lands, after the outbreak of World War One, he learned Arabic which he spoke with a slight[716] Turkish accent. In 1900, after he graduated from the Royal Academy, until he left Turkey in 1919, he was appointed as a school teacher by the Turkish government. His interests in the question of secular nationalism began when he experienced different strands of nationalism during his service in the Balkans. He found out that the essential factor, which divided the Christian peoples of the Balkans from the Muslim Turks was not religion but their distinct linguistic and cultural backgrounds.[717]

---

[714] Marr, (1985), p. 92.

[715] Majid kahdduri, *Political Trends in the Arab world: The Role of ideas and Ideals in Politics*, (The Johns Hopkins Press Baltimore and London, 1970), p. 99.

[716] However, Cleveland claims that al-Husri spoke Arabic with a heavy Turkish accent. William L. Cleveland, *The Making of An Arab Nationalist, Ottoman and Arabism in the Life and Thought of Sati Al-Husri*, (Princeton: Princeton University Press, 1971), p.66

[717] Kadduri, (1970), p. 199.

Al-Husri's theory of Arab nationalism derives primarily from the nine-teenth-century German thinkers Herder, Fichte and Arndt. Characteristic for these thinkers was that they completely divorced state from nation, viewing the latter in cultural terms. For the adherents of this enduring leg-acy of the German political philosophy "the *state* is a distinct mechanical and legal construction which is external to the *nation*. The German national thinkers generally considered the *nation* to be something sacred and eter-nal, with a deeper significance than the works of man."[718]

Al-Husri embraced this romantic definition which generated the per-ception that state was separate from nation. He held Germany in high re-gard, where the most significant studies and theories on the subject of na-tionalities were produced and noted that prominent European nationalists have been students of the German philosophers and authors. He was hon-ored that he too had been a student of this German school; he wrote "the two terms *nation* and *state* must be completely separated", especially as the German idea of "the nation ... is effectively corroborated by a long chain of historical events." [719]Based on this harsh distinction between na-tion and state, al-Husri's effort was to develop the idea of the existence of an "Arab nation" by claiming that it was irrelevant if an "all-Arab national state" truly did not exist. He made a historical comparison between the fragmented Germany before 1871 and the disunited Arab world from the Persian Gulf to the Atlantic Ocean. He held the view that the Arabs had a strong desire of an "Arab 1871", and for him it was insignificant by which means this end was to be achieved.

In the war of liberation against Napoleon German Romanticism re-sponded to the revolutionary ideas of the time in that it struggled alongside

---

[718] Tibi, (1997), p. 126. Italic is in the origin. Tibi notes that the reason behind the Arab nationalists' interest in Germany after the First World War, was their hostility against the policy of the colonial powers, such as Great Britain and France in the region. By the 1930s, they cherished hope that the Third Reich, with no colonial intention, would help them in their struggle against those colonialists. Ibid

[719] Ibid., p. 127.

the nationalist movement with the aspiration of a radical change of the society. However, German romanticism could also be considered counterrevolutionary since at the same time it yearned for building a utopian society which only existed in the past. The same was true of Arab nationalists whose aim was the restoration of the "glorious Arab past."

Of all of Fichte's works, al-Husri was only acquainted with his famous work; *Reden an die deutsche Nation* (Addresses to the German Nation), which influenced Arab nationalists through the latter's writing. In this work, Fichte introduced a new means for the emancipation of the German nation and for the unity of a fragmented territory, whose population consisted only of the German people: "In a word" he proposed, "a total change of the present educational system as the only means of maintaining the existence of the German nation." In th German national war against Napoleon, Fichte's intention was not applying practical political strategy *per se,* but basically a strategy of political education. In this sense he was more of an educator than a politician. Tibi points out, "it is perhaps no accident the founders of Germanophile Arab nationalism, al-Husri and Michel Aflaq,[720] never laid any claim to be politicians, and saw themselves, like Fichte, as educators."[721]

Al-Husri's abstinence from involvement in the Iraqi political process can also, to some extent, be related to King Faisal's decision to ensure a sustainable development of the education system of Iraq by granting al-Husri a permanent appointment as Director General of Education. His prestigious position was actually secured regardless of the change of governments or ministers in the vacillated Iraqi politics. However, al-Husri was well aware of the political strategy whose aim was to achieve supreme national objectives such as instilling national sentiments in the Iraqi people. Accordingly, he pursued an education policy in line with this scheme of politics. In this connection he maintained "I will employ every means to

---

[720] A Syrian Arab nationalist intellectual, considered to be the principal founder of the Ba'athist ideology.

[721] Ibid., pp.132-134. Both al-Husri and Aflaq refused involvement in the political life and only accepted to serve in the field of political education. Ibid

strengthen the feelings of nationalism among the sons of Iraq and to spread a belief in the unity of the Arab nation. And I shall do this without joining any of the political parties which will eventually be formed."[722]

During this period he served as Director General of Education and thereafter as a professor at the Higher Teachers Training College until 1937. He attempted to implement his nationalist program, namely propagation for pan-Arabism and assimilation of different ethnic and religious elements of the Iraqi society into a homogeneous whole. Thus, irrespective of the reactions of the Shiites and the Kurds, his aim was "to spread faith in the unity of the Arab nation, and disseminate consciousness of its glorious past, to combat the enemy of Uruba, to teach, to awaken, and to discipline." [723]

Based on German nationalism, al-Husri combined two basic elements, history and language, to constitute an ideal model for Arab nationalism, despite the fact that he dismissed any kind of racial theories. He envisaged an Arab state like Germany's Prussia, which could unite and lead the Arabs.[724]

In line with this nationalist program, al Husri's educational policy was to inculcate "a sense of common identity in the Iraqi people by stressing Arab history and culture, promoting standard Arabic over regional dialects, and trying to suppress particularistic identities such as those of the Shi'is, Kurds, Christians, and Jews." [725]

Al-Husri's educational policy in Iraq was admired and followed by some quarters, but also provoked fierce criticism from others. An Egyptian writer observed al-Husri's increasing influence in Iraq in the 1920s and 1930s and was critical of his attitudes toward non-Arab elements, especially the Kurds.[726]

---

[722] Cleveland, (1971), pp. 61-62.

[723] Hemphill,(1979), p 92.

[724] Simon, (1986), p. 33.

[725] Malik Mufti, *Sovereign Creations: Pan-Arabism and Political Order in Syria and Iraq* (London: Cornell University Press, 1996), p.29.

[726] Cleveland, (1971), p. 67.

He noted:

> We mean by "Husrism" the feeling that to labour for the sake of Arabism requires the adoption of an inimical stance toward non-Arab elements whether these elements are found within the Arab environment or outside it. This Husrism which we have seen in Iraq weakens the Iraqi entity itself since it looks upon the Kurds with some hatred, and does not desire closer relations with the Iranians or other Muslims who neighbor the territories of the Arabic-speaking peoples.[727]

For the pan-Arabs, who glorified the historic achievement of the pre-Islamic Arabs, Kurdistan was part of the geographic unity of the territory which would constitute the modern Arab nation. The boundaries of that territory "were the Taurus Mountains and Kurdistan, Iran, the Arabian Sea, the Indian Ocean, the Gulf of Suez, and the Mediterranean Sea—or, the Arabian Peninsula and the Fertile Crescent. Palestine and Syria were integral parts of this area, but Egypt and North Africa were not included. The Semites were the progenitors of the modern Arabs."[728] In the Iraqi curriculum which was modeled on the French one, the Kurd Salah-al-Din al-Ayyubi was studied as he was a prominent Abbasid or Umayyad caliph, and the curriculum from 1936 to 1940 underlined pan-Arabism and more secular aspects in the study of history. The heroes were "Arab heroes, non-Arabs and North African personalities were replaced by Arab conquerors of Syria and Palestine." [729]

Similar to his German masters, al-Husri believed that language was a vital component of every person. According to him, everyone who speaks the Arabic language is an Arab, and anyone who is affiliated with the Arab people is an Arab. This definition of Arab identity in linguistic terms

---

[727] Simon, (1986), p. 33.

[728] Ibid., p. 100.

[729] Idem, *The Imposition of Nationalism on a No-Nation State: The Case of Iraq During the Interwar Period 1921-1941*. In James Janowski and I. Gershoni (eds.), *Rethinking Nationalism in the Arab Middle East*, (New York: Colombia University Press, 1997), p. 96.

served to ignore or even deny the cultural rights of many other ethnic minorities not only in Iraq but also in the whole Arab world. The Kurds who constituted the greatest ethnic minority in Iraq with a language completely distinct from Arabic claimed their cultural and national rights and were absolutely dissatisfied by al-Husri's Arab nationalism and his education policy.

In his memoirs, al-Husri writes that after the Iraqi government's declaration on July 11, 1923, with respect to the appointment of Kurdish officials and the use of the Kurdish language in the Kurdish areas, he, as the Director of General Education, arranged with the Ministry of Education to prepare the measures necessary for the implementation of that decision. With this end in view, it was decided on the translation of Arabic textbooks into Kurdish, and the ministry formed a committee composed of four Kurdish intellectuals who worked in Baghdad.

These were Tawfiq Wahbi, Abdul Rahaman Saleh, Shukri al-Fadly and Noori al-Barzanji. When al-Husri authorized these individuals to choose translators and supervise and control the translations before they were printed, some of them began to talk about translation of pre-secondary textbooks. Al-Husri opposed this idea and Wahbi, quite frankly, showed his true intentions and basic tendencies, without equivocation: he said things were more complicated than they appeared and that serious matters were in the making, that the British had decided to go the whole hog with the question and that there were millions of Kurds behind the border for whom the British had a plan. Al-Husri protested and replied that the committee was an Iraqi one and was established at the request of the Iraqi government, and therefore, its work should be for the benefit of Iraq and the Kurds without British intrigues. However, Wahbi had a proposal pertaining to printing in Kurdish, which he intended to submit during the second meeting of the committee. [730]

In the meantime, al-Husri met Amin Zaki, the minister of

---

[730] Sati al-Husri, *Muthakerati fi al-Iraq, al-juz al-awal, 1921-1927* (My Memoirs in Iraq, vol. 1, 1921-1927) (Beirut: Dar al-tibaa, 1967), pp.457-458.

communication, "who worked very actively for the Kurdish issue, inside and outside the Cabinet" He told al-Husri that education in Kurdish should comprise all levels of education, including higher education, and a special section for the Kurds should be built in the Faculty of Law for giving lectures in Kurdish, and also at the Military College. However, he emphasized the necessity of starting from the elementary schools. When the second meeting was convened Wahbi put forward his proposal that fifteen new Kurdish characters were necessary to be created and added to the government's printing house in order to be able to translate textbooks into Kurdish. Al-Husri did not agree with this proposal on the grounds that it would render the reading of Kurdish very difficult and doubted that there were any reasonable grounds for such changes and complications, especially considering that Wahbi even proposed adding points and signals to eleven known Arabic characters. Wahbi tried to convince al-Husri that these changes were crucial. Abdul Rahman Saleh supported him by saying "We know the needs of our language." Al-Husri could not express any definite view on this matter and suggested that it should be discussed in a broader committee comprising enlightened scientists from different Kurdish cities to study the issue and make the necessary decision about it. Wahbi replied that the Ministry of Education had chosen them and they had to comply with their opinions. This conversation ended, but no agreement was reached by the committee on the issue.

Together with Saleh, Wahbi conferred with Amin Zaki, who in his turn conferred with al-Saadun on that matter, the latter telephoned al-Husri telling him "you do not know Kurdish, why then do you raise issues related to writing of the Kurdish language?." On the same day al-Husri had a conversation with the Minister of Education Sabih Nashat who told him "is it not enough that you have incurred the hostility of the Ja`fari (Shiite) Why then even make the Kurds your enemies?." Al-Husri told him that he was sure that his position, in that case, was consistent with the true interests of the Kurds. [731]

---

[731] Ibid., pp. 458-461.

Several days later, a meeting was held in the Cabinet office, consisting of al-Husri, al-Saadun, Amin Zaki, Sabih Nashat and Edmonds, who was deputy advisor to the Ministry of Interior, and was considered a specialist in the Kurdish affairs. After some discussions, an agreement was concluded to the effect that the proposal would be sent to the Kurdish educated for consideration.

Wahbi wrote a detailed report in Kurdish explaining his views with respect to the subject, and the committee chose those who would study the report and express their opinions on it. Al-Husri also wrote a draft to be sent with the report, explaining the purpose of that and ending the draft by requesting from those who would give their views on the report to also note how the reading of the Koran could be reconciled with the reading of the Kurdish texts. Having read a copy of the draft, Wahbi became very confused and objected furiously that the committee had not taken such a decision. Al-Husri replied that he did not write that in the name of the committee, but in the capacity of Director of the General Education. Wahbi complained why al-Husri had mixed the Koran in that issue; the latter replied because the teaching of the Koran was in the curriculum prescribed for the Muslims. Upon learning of that matter, Amin Zaki, annoyed, asked al-Saadun to intervene in the conflict. Al -Saadun telephoned al-Husri for an explanation and the latter replied that he wrote that sentence about the Koran since he was Director of General Education and a specialist in education and teaching.

According to al-Husri when the committee members learned that the proposal had been sent, they decided to send people and letters to all those who were chosen for that matter, informing them of his lack of regard for the Koran and that he only wanted to affect them, and warned them not to be deceived by him.[732]

In a letter to the Minister of Education, al-Husri justified his objection to Wahbi's proposal by arguing that the Kurds, evidently, were very concerned that their children would learn the Koran, and since Kurdish was written in Arabic letters and used a variety of Arabic words, it was

---

[732] Ibid., pp. 462-465.

important to consider the fact that if a single word was written in a way which differed from what was said in the Koran that would give rise to a great confusion in the minds of the students. In order to remove that confusion, al-Husri made some suggestions related to the reading and writing of the Koran by Kurdish students. However, his suggestions were rejected primarily by the members of the committee and by Amin Zaki, who approved Wahbi's proposal, and argued that it would not affect the reading of the Koran. The editor of *Bang-i- Kurdistan*, Mustafa Shawqi, also approved Wahbi's proposal and maintained that it was important to translate the Koran into Kurdish.[733]

Many educated Kurds approved Sahib's proposal and, although the votes of Sulaimanya *liwa* were not yet received, which given that it was the stronghold of Kurdish nationalism, and would undoubtedly approve Wahbi's proposal, al-Husri claimed that the majority of the answers were against the proposal.

There is no information or any indication in al-Husri's memoirs as to whether the translations of the Kurdish school textbooks were carried out, either based on his suggestion or someone else's. However, al-Husri managed to stop a proposal whose aim was to facilitate translation of school textbooks into Kurdish for the Kurdish areas according to the Iraqi government recommendation.

Al-Husri was a secular ideologue and the implication of the Koran in the matter of education and school books confirmed just the fact that he tried every possible expedient to impede the realization of Kurdis requests. By1927, the Acting High Commissioner, Bernard Bourdillon, complained to the Prime Minister, Jafar al-Askari, that there was no sign of the establishing of the Kurdish translation bureau which was promised by the government of al-Saadun.[734]

---

[733] Ibid., pp. 569-470.
[734] Sluglett, (2007), p. 127. The bureau was to deal with translation of legal texts and school textbooks.

Toward the Incorporation of Kurdistan into Iraq

*If we pay no attention to our social fragmentation,
how can we hope ever to establish a greater Iraqi society based on a single national ideology and a common goal?*[735]
Jafar al-Askari

Rewarding of the Mosul *Wilayat* to Iraq can be considered as a significant event in the process of forging a nation-state in the country. The unity of the three *Wilayats* of Baghdad, Basra and Mosul, struggled for by the Arab nationalists, King Faisal as well as the British, was achieved. The Iraqis endeavored now to end the mandate regime and be admitted to the League of Nations, and obtain their independence. Yet, the Iraqi and mandatory authorities had to deal with the Kurds who pressed for their national rights, expecting the fulfillment of the recommendations made by the Commission of Enquiry and by the government of al-Saadun. It was also of major importance to these authorities to make the League believe that they implemented or at least had the intention to implement their commitments with respect to the administration of the Kurdish areas. At the same time, they had to come to terms with Shaikh Mahmud, who despite considerable loss of adherents and influence still had enough power to threaten the Anglo-Iraqi authorities in the country.

On September 4, 1926, the advisor of the Ministry of Interior, Cornwallis, the Oriental Secretary to the High Commissioner, Vyvyan Holt, and the British administrative inspector in Sulaimanya met the Shaikh at Khorman, a district to Halabja. They discussed for three hours, the terms which would return law and security to Kurdistan and prevent him from

---

[735] Omar Ziad Al-Askary, *A Soldier's Story: From Ottoman Rule to Independent Iraq . The Memoirs of Jafar Pasha Al-Askary* (1885-1936), (London: Arabian Publishing L td, 2003), p. 237.

intervening in the government's policy there. The meeting resulted in an agreement which was presented to the Shaikh officially on October 9, 1926, which stipulated that the Shaikh and his family remained in Persia and would return only with the permission from the Iraqi government. He would pledge not to interfere in the affairs of the government, nor encourage anyone for such an intervention in Sulaimanya province or elsewhere; additionally, he would be required to abstain from participation in any political activity related to Iraq. The Iraqi government would in return undertake to send his eldest son Baba Ali to Baghdad to study under the auspices of the government, and to return to the Shaikh his estates and a certain number of his followers, in accordance with the conditions set for each of them, with the exception of the defendants of terrible crimes. He would be permitted to appoint one of his agents to manage these estates.[736]

In the middle of January, 1927, the Iraqi government signed the agreement and was returned by his agent Saiyed Ahmad Barzanji who was in Baghdad, to the Shaikh who was back in his headquarters in Persia, to obtain his signature. The Shaikh dispatched a letter, on the 27th of the same month, to the High Commissioner stating that he was prepared to sign the terms, but on condition that the pledge Great Britain made to the League of Nations concerning the legitimate rights of the Kurds should be carried out and that Penjwin sub-district be a place of residence for him and those who shared his opinion regarding Kurdish rights. The High Commissioner rejected the Shaikh's condition and replied that the League did not recognize Kurdish claims for independence and had only made recommendations as to the appointment of Kurdish officials in the Kurdish areas, and that Kurdish should be used as an official language there. Also, that these recommendations were, acceding to the High Commissioner, approved by the Iraqi and British governments and carried out as they had promised.[737] The Shaikh disagreed with the High Commissioner's attitudes and was unyielding in his decision in occupying the town of Penjwin and

---

[736] Abdul Razzaq al-Hasani, *Tarikh al- Wizarat al- Iraqiyah,* Vol.2 (History of the Iraqi Cabinets, Vol.2. Sidon, 1935) , p. 120.
[737] Ibid, p. 121.

its surroundings. This prompted the government to dispatch troops to stave off the Shaikh's approaching to these areas, and to re-establish administrative control there. Two columns participated in the operation; one consisted of Levy forces and the other of units from the Iraqi army and Iraq armed police. On April 23, these troops arrived in Penjwin and the Shaikh and his followers, without offering serious resistance, retreated and crossed the frontier into Persia. The casualties on the Iraqi side were four killed and five wounded; casualties on the Kurdish side were unknown.[738]

During the time this operation was conducted, the two Hamawand guerilla leaders, Sabir and Abdullah, sons of Karim Fattah Beg, who had escaped justice for their implication in the murder of the British officers in 1922, were with their bands busy pillaging in the vicinity of Sulaimanya. In a letter sent to the High Commissioner, however, Shaikh Mahmud dissociated himself from them.

When the reoccupation of Penjwin was accomplished several aerial actions were carried out in order to warn the villagers who had provided the Shaikh with armed contingents, but soon peace was restored to the districts and a normal administration was established there. After suffering a crucial defeat in Penjwin, the Shaikh, early in June, dispatched his representative, Majid Effendi, to Penjwin, to submit a signed copy of the agreement concluded in Baghdad in January. He was accompanied by the Shaikh's son, Baba Ali, who was to be educated at school in Baghdad. On June 17, Shaikh Mahmud himself arrived to Penjwin and met the *Muttasaref* of Sulaimanya to whom he acknowledged that he stuck to the agreement he had signed and requested permission to travel to Baghdad to meet the High Commissioner. This was effortlessly accepted and he came to Baghdad on July 5 where he complained to the High Commissioner that he could not stay in Persia since he was at odds with the Persian authorities. After being offered the choice to either live in Baghdad or in Mosul, in case he wanted to leave Persia, the Shaikh chose the area south of Merivan where he enjoyed huge prestige and influence, and where he finally settled down until

---

[738] Iraq Administration Reports 1914-1932. Vol. 8. 1925-1932, pp.22-23.

the end of the year.[739]

In Sulaimanya, following "the last defeat" that the Iraq army inflicted upon Shaikh Mahmud, peace prevailed and was maintained during 1928. The town which had experienced violent events became a good example of a properly functioning administrative unit for the whole country.[740] The British of course blamed the Shaikh's hostile undertakings and "his persistent clinging to dreams of imperial power" which since 1922, had prevented the establishment of an orderly administration in the Sulaimanya province. By removing the Shaikh, they could declare that:

> Already in the short time which has passed since the settlement of the summer of 1927, there is a marked improvement in general conditions. Confidence has been restored and the highways are once more secured. Agriculture and commercial activities (for Sulaimaniya town has a big trade with north-western Persia) have quickened and fresh optimism has come into the live of the people after the gloom and hardships of the past five years. [741]

Things appeared to develop as the mandatory power and the Iraqi government desired. Their satisfaction with the state of affairs in the country was expressed at the closing of Parliament, in 1927. The King gave a banquet at his Baghdad palace to mark this event. He stated that he was pleased with the competence of the deputies and their efforts to reorganize the life of the country. Addressing the High Commissioner the king pointed out "our relations with our ally, Great Britain, remains as clear as the sky of Iraq, and they will not be disturbed in any circumstances."[742]

---

[739] Ibid, p. 23.According to Col. W.A.Lyon, Shaikh Mahmud's second son Baba Ali had "great charm", he studied at Victoria College for sons of Middle East aristocrats which was then in Alexandria and afterwards he went to a university in the United States. He later entered Iraqi politics and occupied positions in several ministries in the 1940s.The Shaikh's eldest son "had not much personality" and later became a deputy in the Iraqi Parliament. Col.W.A.Lyon, *Kurds, Arabs and Britons*: *The Memoirs of Col.W.A.Loyn in Kurdistan, 1918-1945*, 8 I.B.Trauris, 2002), p. 167.
[740] Iraq Administration Reports, 1914-1932, Vol. 9. 1928-1930, p. 18.
[741] Iraq Administration Reports, 1914-1932. Vol. 8. 1925-1927. P. 23.
[742] Ibid.,p. 354.

The High Commissioner replied:

> I see year by year fresh proofs of the progressive establishment of an independent Government of Iraq. Your frontiers now are fixed; your formerly warring tribes are at peace; you have secured the recognition of nearly all the Great Powers of the world; your forces, which have increased every year both in number and efficiency, undertake every year a larger share of responsibility of the maintenance of internal security; your resources and means of communication are becoming developed; ... If only the leading men of Iraq will exercise a wise patience, you have now all things that we hoped for within our grasp ... For this happy state of affairs the largest share of credit rests, ... with your Majesty ...[743]

Apparently, in his speech the High Commissioner wanted to give the impression that the newborn Iraqi state was now a reality; that it acquired salient components which were imperative for the existence of any nation-state; that after winning Mosul *Wilayat* Iraq's territory became defined and fixed. It had access to an increasingly stronger army, which was capable of putting down movements claiming their rights, Iraq established relationships with foreign powers and was recognized by them. It cultivated relations with its diverse elements resulting in peace and tranquility. However, the fact was that the Iraqi government and the mandatory authority exercised power within a territory which both lacked a unified ethnic identity and any common will among the population to accept the authority of this state. Thus, the Kurds, whose demands for national rights were ignored questioned the legitimacy of this state and challenged its authority. However, despite the British authority's statement about the general improvement of the conditions in the Sulaimanya *liwa*, there was no sign of progress with regards to the administration of the Kurdish areas in accordance with the Kurdish demands. In order to oblige the Residency and the Iraqi government to take measures in this respect, on June 1, 1928, seven Kurdish members of the Chamber of Deputies submitted a petition to the Minister of Education demanding the establishment of a "Translation and Compilation Committee" for the

---

[743] Ibid.,p. 356.

preparation of school textbooks, allotment of funds for the appointment of competent and available teachers for secondary schools, the establishment of a Teacher Training College, the establishment of a single Kurdish education office and inspectorate with the responsibility for the whole of the Kurdish area, completing the building of secondary schools and building new ones, and opening schools for females.[744]

Kurdish protests continued as there were still no indications of implementing the recommendations of the Boundary Commission. Thus, in February, 1929, six Kurdish deputies addressed a memorandum to the Prime Minister, al-Saadun, and the High Commissioner, Gilbert Clayton, in which they complained that the Iraqi authorities were ignoring the recommendations of the frontier commission and outlined proposals such as:

> 1-creation of a new *liwa* with headquarters at Dohuk including the Kurdish *qadhas* of Aqra, Zibar, Amadiya and Zakho of the Mosul *liwa*, and that they should be administered as the rest of the Kurdish areas making Kurdish the official language there. 2-The formation of a special Kurdish administrative unit comprising the four Kurdish *liwas* of Sulaimanya, Kirkuk, Arbil and Dohuk, and that this unit be chaired by a Kurdish inspector general who was to function as a link between this area and the central government
> 3- Increased expenditure on public services in the Kurdish areas. 4- Increased expenditure on Kurdish education.[745]

Both al-Saadun and the High Commissioner were of the opinion that the creation of a new administrative unit was unwise, since such a scheme would create serious administrative difficulties and would contribute to separation rather than unity of the different nationalities and religions in the country, and would finally entail misfortune both for the Kurds and for the Iraqi state.[746]

At the same time, the British government's declaration on September

---

[744] Hassanpour, (1992), p. 309.
[745] Special Report, pp.261-262. The deputies consisted of: Hazim Shamdin Agha (Mosul), Ismail Rawanduzi, Jamal Baba (Arbil), Saif Allah Khandan, Muhammad Salih (Sulaimanya), Muhammad Jaf (Kirkuk). See Qadir,(2007), p. 100.
[746] Special Report, p.262.

14, 1929, for the unconditional support of Iraq's candidature for admission to the League of Nations in 1932 was received with misgiving by the Kurds. They feared that with the withdrawal of the British from Iraq, the Iraqi government would deprive them of the privileges recommended by the League's Commission. Kurdish fear and vexation were expressed by a Kurdish deputy[747] in February 1930, as he asked the Prime Minister whether the Kurdish rights referred to in the report of the Boundary Commission of the League would be safeguarded in the new treaty which was under discussion between the mandatory power and the Iraqi Government. [748]On June 30, 1930, the Treaty of Alliance between the Iraqi Government and Great Britain was signed, preparing for Iraq's independence within a two -year time span, while containing no provisions to guarantee the maintenance of the Kurdish interests, which caused deep resentment in Kurdistan. Consequently, the Kurdsof Sulaimanya organized protest meetings and dispatched petitions and *Madhbatas* (minutes) to the High Commissioner, the King, and the Prime Minister. In one of the petitions dispatched through the High Commissioner [749] to the Secretariat of the League of Nations in Geneva, on July 26, 1930, Kurdish nationalists called the League's attention to the fact that Kurdish national rights recognized by the League were still not implemented, and demanded decentralization since in the new Treaty, Kurdish rights were omitted, and

---

[747] Qadir argues that at a meeting of the Parliament on February 13, 1930, a discussion focused on the question of whether the new Treaty, which was to be concluded, would embody guaranties for the Kurdish rights recommended by the League. At this meeting, the Arbil deputy, Maruf Jiawuuk, asked the Prime Minister, Naji al-Suwaidi, the above mentioned question, and al-Suwaidi replied that Treaty negotiations did not yet start, and that the Iraqi government had decided to implement the recommendations of the League, but they would not be included in the Treaty since it was an international Treaty concluded between two parties on international bases. P. 122.

[748] Iraq Administration Reports, 1914-1932, Vol. 9. 1928-1930.p 25.

[749] Based on a1922 British proposal on Petitions procedure all procedures were to be submitted first to the mandatory power, which would dispatch them within six months, after making observations, to the Secretariat of the League.

that they were subject to constant pressure from preponderant Arab officials in the Kurdish areas to renounce their rights. The Kurds were worried that, after the termination of the mandatory in Iraq, they would be subject to worse treatment by the Iraqi government than they had previously received during Turkish rule, and demanded the establishment of a Kurdish government under the guidance of the League of Nations. They complained that, as a response to their petition, the Iraqi government (Jamil al-Midfa`i) intended to; 1-dismiss the *Mutassaref* of Sulaimanya. 2-dismiss the chief of polis of Sulaimanya and replace him by someone who was proficient in Kurdish.3-displace two governors and chiefs whose opinions opposed that of the central government.4-arrest the most important individuals who demanded a Kurdish government.5- impose a strict legal punishment on those who would advocate separatism. [750]

However, during the period before and after the conclusion of the Treaty of Alliance, Kurdish activities for securing their national rights intensified. The Iraqi government, despite its attempt to show a gesture of goodwill in meeting Kurdish demands, condemned any idea that could be interpreted as separation from Iraq. The Iraqi government's position on that matter was buttressed by Iraqi nationalist papers such as *al-Baghdadiya* which warned the Kurds, in harsh words, of manifesting separatist tendencies, resembling the Armenians' aspirations in Turkey and what the latter did with them. The High Commissioner was also of the opinion that demanding improvements in education and administration in the Kurdish areas should not lead to separation, alluding to the Kurdish suggestion for creating a new *liwa* and the unity of Kurdish *liwas* under the control of a single administrative unit. [751]

The mandatory power believed indeed that "The best was to improve

---

[750] Al-Hasani, Vol. 3. pp. 59-60.

[751] Qadir, (2007), pp.100 -101. Kurdish demand, however, did not confine to creation of a new liwa (Dohok), but another one (Bajlan). This matter was discussed in a meeting of the second parliamentary period, in February, 1930, as a question was posed by Arbil deputy, Jiawuuk, to the Ministry of the Interior, Naji Shawkat, concerning the creation of the two liwas of Dohok and Bajlan which was rejected by Shawkat. Ibid. p.101.

Kurdish confidence seemed to be the Iraqi Government themselves to take such administrative and legislative measures as were possible to establish the existing special regime for the Kurds on a permanent basis." However, the issue was scrutinized by the High Commissioner in consultation with King Faisal, the Prime Minister and British advisors. They would create a program constructive enough to redress Kurdish grievances and make them believe in their future in the Iraqi state. The key to the proposed program was a law to safeguard the use of the Kurdish language in the Kurdish areas. Other issues in the program were:

> That a translation bureau should be set up in the Ministry of Interior in Baghdad to undertake the translation into Kurdish of legislation, regulations and department circulars: that for the purpose of education of Kurdish schools of Arbil, Kirkuk and Sulaimanya *liwas* should be grouped under a suitable Kurdish inspector: and that a Kurdish Assistant-Director General of Administration should be appointed to the Ministry of Interior.[752]

The law came before the Iraqi Parliament in December, 1930; it was not passed, but it was finally promulgated in June 1931.

Actually, during those circumstances, the Kurds had set their hopes primarily on the League of Nations. As an international organization, the League, under Article 22 of the Covenant, was theoretically, responsible for supervising the mandatory power in fulfilling their obligations toward the minorities and redressing their grievances. The exercises of the mandates were supervised by the Permanent Mandate Commission (PMC), which, even if practical, could not impose its will on any mandatory powers, but it was an important body since it was responsible for reading the annual mandatory reports and receiving of petitions. With respect to the entry of Iraq into the League of Nations, the implementation of the recommendations of the League's Commission was therefore of particular importance for Britain, since the League had accepted Iraq to be one of its members in 1932, on the condition that "effective guarantees be secured for the observance of all Treaty obligations in Iraq for the benefit of racial

---

[752] Iraq Administration Reports, 1914-1932. Vol. 9. 1928-1930. P. 25.

and religious minorities."[753] Thus, the League generated academic and legal interest for the question of national minority rights and protection in the Kurdish areas.

As a result of the petitions and telegrams sent by the Kurds to the League of Nations, especially during the month of July, 1930, the League, referring to the recommendations of the Commission of Boundary's decision of December 16, 1925, which were still not carried out, suggested, on the basis of the Permanent Mandatory Commission's recommendation, that the League's Commission reply to the petition of the leading Kurdish citizens, with regards to the establishment of a Kurdish government under the supervision of the League. In addition, it was incumbent on the mandatory power to ensure that the legislative and administrative measures, which guaranteed Kurdish interests were implemented, and that their national rights be safeguarded after the termination of the mandate. The British government assured the League that the Iraqi government was pursuing all of its obligations regarding those issues.[754]

However, despite Kurdish resentment and protests, Iraq and Great Britain, as mentioned previously, agreed to sign the Treaty of Alliance on June 30, 1930, although it was subject to the approval of Parliament. Accordingly, the first Cabinet of the Prime Minister Nuri al-Said (23 Marc, 1930—19 October, 1931) under the pretext of referendum worked to dissolve the Parliament and arrange a general election whereby the new Parliament would guarantee the votes of the majority for ratification of the Treaty. Thus, on July 1, 1930, a Royal Iradeh (decree) was issued to dissolve the Parliament and order a general election:

Whereas Iraq and British negotiators have agreed to sign a Treaty of Alliance and Amity, which shall come into force upon Iraq's being accepted as a member of the League of Nations; and whereas the bases of the Treaty places the country on a new political footing, which necessitates a referendum to the

---

[753] Meeting of Council of the League of Nations, 13 -16 January 1930, League of Nations Official Journal, February 1930. Quoted in Sluglett, (2007), p. 130.
[754] Al-Hasani. p. Vol. 3. 64.

nation in respect to the Treaty, with a view to affording the nation an opportunity of expressing an opinion thereon, ... ordering that the house of Deputy should be dissolved and that the election of a new Majlis should be proceeded with.[755]

The announcement of the parliamentary election was received with exasperation by the Kurds as well as by some Arab quarters.[756] The Kurds in Sulaimanya who were perturbed by the absence of the references in the treaty to the maintenance of the Kurdish interests were encouraged by moderate Kurds to boycott the forthcoming election there. The paper of the Kurdish association *Pushtiwani Kurdistan* (Support of the Kurds), on July 9, 1930, noted that it was the duty of every Kurd to boycott the election and abstain from voting for a decision which ignored their national rights. Another association, *al-Hai'ah al-Wataniyah* (The Nationalist Commission), which was established in Sulaimanya by some Kurdish personalities on July16, 1930, also decided to boycott the election, primarily due to the visit of the Amir Ghazi to Sulaimanya during those days. [757]

Concurrently with the intensified Kurdish grievances against the Anglo-Iraqi Kurdish policy it was rumored in Arab political circles that the British government intended to impede the progress toward Iraq's independence by instigating Kurdish national feelings against the Iraqi government. In order to dissipate the apprehensions of the Kurds, refute rumors among the Arabs and also to underline the Anglo Iraqi unity, it was decided that the Acting High Commissioner, Major H.W.Young, and the Acting Prime Minister, Jafar al-Askari, (in the absence of the High Commissioner and the Prime Minister who were in Europe), make a joint tour in Arbil,

---

[755] Iraq Administration Reports, 1914-1932, Vol. 9. 1928-1930. p. 15.

[756] For example, the party of Jaafar Abu-al-Timman, Hizb Al-Watani, the Nationalist Party, attempted to organize a boycott of the election. The party distributed handbills in Baghdad and attempted to involve the *Mujtahids*, the Shiites priesthood, in the political scene, but they refrained from taking part in boycotting the election. Ibid. See also al-Hasani, Vol.3. pp.67-78.

[757] Qadir, (2007), p. 123.

Kirkuk and Sulaimanya *liwas* and issue a joint declaration on Kurdish policy.[758]

In his meetings with the Kurdish notables in Arbil, Kirkuk and Sulaimanya the Acting High Commissioner stated in August 1930 that the policy of the British and Iraqi governments on all important questions in the whole of Iraq was pursued in perfect harmony. He emphasized the Iraqi government's obligation to recognize the right of the Kurds to use their mother language. He asserted:

> There is no question of a Kurdish child being compelled to take his first lessons in any language than his mother tongue or of any Kurd having to defend himself or hear his case tried in court in a language which he does not understand. Similarly the appointment of Kurdish-speaking officials in various branches of the administration at headquarters shows that the Iraqi Government is ready and willing to make no distinction whatever between the Kurdish and the Arab subjects ...

He also refuted the allegation from certain Arab nationalist groups that it was the deliberate British policy to "encourage Kurdish nationalism" He considered the unity of different communities and making of them "good Iraqis" to be the policy objective of the British and the Iraqi government.[759]

In his statement, Jafar al-Askari, also underscored the importance of satisfying the aspiration of the Kurds. At the same time, he declared the government's and Faisal's determination to "suppress any tendency whatever which is directed against the unity of the Iraqi State or calculated to cloud the atmosphere or affect the neighbourly relations between them and the two friendly Governments of Turkey and Persia."[760] The preservation of the Iraqi unity thus constituted a landmark in the policy of the Anglo-Iraqi governments that they intended to pursue at the expense of depriving the Kurds of their national rights. In a letter, dated August 19, 1930, to Young, al-Askari, again reiterated the significance of the unity between the

---

[758] Iraq Administration Reports, 1914-1932. Vol. 9. 1928-1930. P. 26.
[759] Special Report, p. 328.
[760] Ibid., p. 328.

two peoples, the Kurds and the Arabs, opposing "any proposals which would result in the separation of the Kurdish *liwas* from the rest of the Kingdom." He said that the:

> Kurds have a strong national consciousness of their own, and that success is to be gained, not by trying to stamp this out, but by recognizing it in such a way that the Kurds may feel, in taking part as Iraqi, that their customs, their traditions, and their language are being preserved intact.

However, it was not unfounded that the Kurds mistrusted al-Askary's pledge on preservation of their cultural distinctiveness when he at the same time eagerly endeavored to create a unified Iraq comprising all communities and instilled by an ideology of Iraqi nationhood. Based on this ideology his Kurdish policy was crystallized in notes on the current situation in Iraq, January 15, 1932. In order to confront the threat to Iraq's ideological and national unity he suggested, like al-Husri, introducing "a uniform education system based on a standard curriculum throughout our schools" with preservation of customs and traditions. He simultaneously warned of "activities of haphazard committees or of individuals or other organizations with special interests and objectives", alluding to Kurdish interference in the sphere of the education system. The aim was to prepare "a new and useful young generation, imbued with national pride and devoid of sectarian extremism."

Many of the national differences in Iraq were, according to al-Askary, implanted by foreign interests in order to widen the rifts that divided the people and urged to eliminate these social fragmentations in order to be able to "establish a greater Iraqi society based on a single national ideology and a common national goal." Regarding the Kurds, al-Askary, maintained that he did not agree with the prevailing policy of the government in sub-jugating the Kurds by force, which he deemed as a futile policy. In his opinion, the Turkish extermination of the Armenians had devastating consequences for them since they afterwards suffered from a lack of workers. So to achieve ideological and national unity, his policy toward the Kurds was instead to encourage them to be engaged in the "larger Iraqi project." It was feasible in bringing:

The Arabs and the Kurds closer together: we have to make the Kurds feel they are Iraqis ... if we choose a more appropriate policy that encourage Arabs to live in Kurdish areas, mix with the locals and intermarry with them ... Thus for the purpose of promoting the policy we might conceder transferring the main government centers to the Kurdish region during the summer-to Ruwanduz and Amadiyya for example. These centers would then become much more accessible to larger numbers of people, leading to an increase in transportation, and hence to an increase in mixing of Kurds and Arabs. This would be a factor in accelerating their unification.[761]

In this light, it was not surprising that he anticipated that the government would propose to make the knowledge of the Kurdish language and not ethnicity a condition of employment in the Kurdish districts as soon as the local language law was approved by the Parliament. He believed it would facilitate the employment of the Kurds with knowledge of Arabic in the whole of Iraq, as well as Arabs with knowledge of Kurdish. Although they were not great in number, they could be employed in the Kurdish areas. He argued that the government also considered it to be for the benefit of the Kurds and was in line with the recommendations of the League.[762]

Similar to the British, al-Askary emphasized that the Iraqi government would dismiss any demands for the establishment of a separate administration on the grounds that it was impracticable administratively and financially and would be destructive to the Iraqi government. In addition, he feared that such an administration would put the Iraqi government in a difficult position with the neighboring states of Persia and Turkey since the border areas of these states were inhabited largely by Kurds and, consequently, would put Iraq's relations with these countries at stake unless the Iraqi government itself took responsibility of the administration there. In this connection, he assured Kurdish petitioners that they were mistaken in thinking that the decision of the League of Nations implied that they had the right to establish an independent government under the aegis of the

---

[761] Ziad (2003), pp. 236-238.
[762] Special Report, p. 330.

League after the termination of the British mandate in Iraq.[763]

The Iraqi government would carry out the Kurdish policy outlined in al-Askaty's statement and letter thereby realizing the League's recommendations. This would allay the apprehensions of the Kurds, albeit only the moderate ones, that the government and the mandatory power were serious in accommodating their demands, which at this stage were confined to employment of the Kurdish language, embodied in the local language law, in the Kurdish districts and the appointment of Kurdish officials there.

Indeed, the Kurdish policy that al-Askary and his colleges, such as al-Midfa´j and al-Said, pursued was in symbiosis with that of the British. The statement that al-Askary and Major Young made, in the Sulaimanya tour, left no doubt in this respect. The British, however, wanted the Kurds to be incorporated into the Iraqi state, but with a certain preservation of cultural and linguistic rights stipulated by the council's League. The British, as the mandatory power, were obligated to supervise the implementation of minority rights. It was significant that these rights be fulfilled especially with regards to the question of Iraq's admission into the League of Nations. The Iraqi government, on the other hand, since its formation in 1922, despite their declarations and announced policy to the effect that Kurdish interests would be safeguarded, in practice implemented a nationalist policy, ignoring Kurdish ethnic and cultural distinctiveness. The ultimate goal of this policy was to create a homogeneous nation-state, thereby, forging a sense of Iraqi identity; to simply make the Kurds "good Iraqis." From this perspective, the Sulaimanya uprising should be seen as a logical consequence of a policy of neglect and betrayal toward the Kurds.

The Sulaimanya Uprising of September 6, 1930

As mentioned above, the Sulaimanya associations decided in July to boycott the upcoming election of the inspection committee. In mid-August, the Minister of Interior, Jamil Midfa´i, removed the popular *Mutasarrif,*

---

[763] Ibid., p. 330.

Tawfiq Wahbi, on the grounds that he supported the decision of the leader of the Sulaimanya moderates, Shaikh Qadir, a brother-in-law of Shaikh Mahmud, who also boycotted the election. Shaikh Qadir was also removed and replaced by Ahmad Beg-i-Tawfiq Beg, who decided that the election be carried out.[764]

An mportant factor which contributed to the Sulaimanya uprising, besides the visit of Prince Ghazi on August 6, and the indignation induced by the visit of the Iraqi government's delegates on August 10, was this ill-advised remark by the Prime Minister Nuri al-Said:

> At the beginning the matter concerned acquiring recommended guarantees... then the Kurds manifested their grievances with respect to the existing admin-istration... and then they demanded a quasi-autonomous government, and now it is about secession.[765]

Nuri had, in February 1931, privately assured the Turks that an independ-ent Iraq would firmly oppose Kurdish separatism. Francis Humphrey and the Colonial Office warned Nuri that if these anti-Kurdish attitudes were exposed to the public, Iraq's Kurdish policy would be seen as merely "a facade to impress foreign countries" and its opportunity to become a mem-ber of the League would be "wholly destroyed."[766]

Meanwhile the British government was worried that the explosive situation in Kurdistan would result in the embarrassment of the British government before the League of Nations, particularly with regards to the fact that the Permanent Mandate Commission intended to discuss Kurdish petitions in October 1930. The British feared that the unrest in the Kurdish districts and the punitive measures that the Iraqi government considered to take against the Kurds might portray them as victims in Geneva. The British were cognizant that the PMC's satisfaction was important for the

---

[764] Sluglett, (2007), p.131.

[765] Chris, Kutschera, *Le Mouvement National Kurde.* (Paris: Flammarion, 1979). p. 110. (my translation).

[766] Susan Pedersen, *Getting Out of Iraq in 1932: The League of Nations and the Road to Normative Statehood,* The American Historical Review, Vol.115, (2010), p 994.

admission of Iraq into the League, which was to be discussed at the League in June 1931. Accordingly, the British decided to link its support of Iraq's entry to the League with the Iraqi government's pursuing the policy of reconciliation in Kurdistan. Thus, on August 18, Young warned al-Askary, Nuri al-Said, and Faisal that the British would renounce its responsibility for Iraq's Kurdish policy unless they adhere to Cornwallis' suggestions on that policy, for instance, to exclude the anti-Kurdish ministers, such as al-Midfa'i, from the Parliament and to publish the Local Languages Law. Consequently, the Iraqi government promised to act in accordance with Cornwallis' recommendation and disregard al-Midfa'i 's proposal in taking punitive measures against Kurdish nationalists, and to appoint Salih Zaki (a Kurd) Assistant Director-General in the Minister of the Interior, in charge of Kurdish affairs, and to appoint Nuri Barzanji as inspector of Kurdish schools.[767]

Before long, it became apparent that al-Askary's statements on his Sulaimanya tour, concerning the Local Language Law, justice and appoint-ment of Kurdish officials were meant to be realized in the future. The sit-uation prompted Young to bring petitions to the League, signed by several of Sulaimanya's notables, in which they complained about the Iraqi gov-ernment's reluctance to accommodate Kurdish interests:

> I am telling the Regent and the Acting Prime Minister that unless I am satisfied immediately that policy which I have publicly endorsed on behalf of H.M.Government is carried out in spirit as well as letter I shall be obliged to recommend that in forwarding Sulaimanya petition to the league, H.M.Gov-ernment should explain that my announcement [while on tour in Kurdistan] was made under a misapprehension and that the Iraqi government are not in fact carrying out their programme.[768]

---

[767] Othman Ali, Al *Haraka al-Kurdiya al-Muasira, dirasah Tarikhiya wathaeqiya 1833-1946* (Contemporary Kurdish Movement, Historical Documentary study 1988-1946. (Maktab al-tafsir lilnashr wal Ilan, Arbil, 2011) pp.616-617.Of these promises only the appointments of Zaki, in 24 , and Barzanji in 30 September, were carried out for that year. See Sluglett, (2007), p. 133.

[768] Quoted in Sluglett, (2007), p. 130.

On September 6, 1930, some 30 of the notables as representatives of all parts of Sulaimanya *liwa* were invited to the local government headquarters in the town for the election. As the election of the committee was in progress, about 2000 people crowded outside the government offices to protest against the election. The tension between the crowd and the police who were there to force the holding of the election reached a high pitch and soon turned into clashes. According to British reports the crowd attacked the police and the town jail with stones, which necessitated calling for military assistance. However, the arrival of an infantry detachment proved ineffective in frightening the crowd, therefore a burst of gunfire was ordered to disperse them. The causalities of the riot were; police-10 wounded, Iraqi Army-1 killed, 3 wounded, rioters-14 killed, 23 wounded. Ninety-eight people were brought before the magistrates on various charges connected with the riot. Ninety-five were found innocent and released. Two were committed for trial and acquitted and one was ordered to reside outside the borders of the Sulaimanya *liwa*. [769]

However, Kurdish sources, such as a Kurd who was among the protesters, said that 34 Kurdish protesters were killed and about 100 wounded[770], and the Kurdish paper *Al-Ta'akhi* , on September 6, 1971, reported that 45 civilians were killed, 200 were wounded and around 100 were arrested, among them Shaikh Qadir and some others from the Nationalist Commission. [771]

Owing to the riot in Sulaimanya the election was postponed for more than a week, but then was resumed. The candidates of the Sulaimanya *liwa* were elected and took their seats when the Parliament was opened on November 1st, 1930. It was reported that in Arbil and in the Kurdish districts

---

[769] Iraq Administration Reports, 1914-1932, Vol. 9. 1928-1930, 27.

[770] Qadir, (2007), p. 124.

[771] Al-Hasani, Vol. 3. p. 71.The arrested were: Mirza Tawfiq, Ramzi Afandi, Hama Agha, Azmi Beg Baban, Izzat Beg Uthman pasha, Abd-al-Rahman Ahga Ahmad Pasha, Muhammad Salih Beg, Majid Afandi Kaniskan, Faiq Baban, Shaikh Muhammad Kolani. Ibid.

of Kirkuk and Mosul liwas the general election was held without disturb-ance. [772]

The text of the statements made during the visit of Sulaimanya and the letter of Al-Askary to the High Commissioner on August 19th as well as other documents determining the joint policy of the British and the Iraqi governments with respect to the Kurds, were submitted to the League of Nations. In addition, petitions from certain Kurds on their state of affairs in Iraq were studied by the PMC at their 19th session in November 1930. In its decision, the PMC maintained that there was no decision from the League about the creation of a Kurdish government under the supervision of the League and that such a demand was based on the misunderstanding and misinterpretation of the decision made by the Council on December 16, 1925. The PMC's recommendations to the Council were:

> 1-To reject the petition of the Kurdish notables so far as it aims at the for-mation of a Kurdish Government under the supervision of the League of Na-tions; 2-To request the mandatory power to see that the legislative and admin-istrative measures designed to secure for the Kurds the position to which they are entitled are promptly put into effect and properly enforced; 3-To consider the advisability of providing for measures to guarantee to the Kurds the maintenance of such position, should Iraq be finally emancipated from the trusteeship of Great Britain. [773]

The uprising of Sulaimanya marked a significant change in the character of the Kurdish national movement. Earlier Kurdish nationalist rebellions, especially in Iraq and Turkey, had been exclusively lead by religious shaikhs, although the role of the urban intellectual, of course, had been vital. During the protests against the holding of elections in Sulaimanya on September 6, 1930, the preponderance of the protesters were composed of different urban strata. The emergence of the new urbanized Kurdish na-tionalists in Kurdistan was due to the socio-economic change in Kurdistan,

---

[772] Iraq Administration Reports, 1914-1032, Vol.9. 1928-1930, p. 27.

[773] Special Report, p. 264. See also Luther Harris Evans, *The Emancipation of Iraq from the Mandates System,* The American Political Science Review, Vol. 26, No. 6 (1932), pp. 1024-1049.

particularly after the mid-1920s when a growing professional class in the Kurdish towns became involved in the Kurdish nationalist activities. However, a small group of educated nationalists in Sulaimanya established ko-mala-i-Sarbakhoi Kurdistan (The association for the Independence of Kurdistan) in July 1922. The main principle of the association was the re-nouncement of the Arab rule as well as of that of Shaikh Mahmud and his tribal style.[774] By 1926, Kurdish towns witnessed a remarkable growth of nationalist awareness, especially among the officials and businessmen who formed the club Zanisty, a literary Society, in Sulaimanya. Its aim was the dissemination of secular values among Kurdish circles, but it soon turned into a means of propaganda of national ideas through night classes and the council of Zanisty. The club established branches in other cities such as Mosul, Arbil and Kirkuk, but in 1927, upon learning that the club had been turned to a political megaphone for Kurdish nationalism, the government closed it. [775]

Once the Iraqi Parliament was opened, Kurdish deputies highlighted the Kurdish question and pressed the government to meet Kurdish national demands on many occasions, although they were criticized by educated Kurds that "only the most colourless Kurds" had the opportunity to be members of the Parliament.[776] It was chiefly due to criticism and pressure from some Kurdish urban quarters, and particularly from the Kurdish press [777] that on February 2, 1926, at a secret meeting with prominent Kurdish personalities of Sulaimanya and Kirkuk, six of these deputies submitted a request to the then Prime Minister al-Saadun, offering him their support, on condition that the Kurdish rights stipulated in the decision of the League of Nations with respect to Mosul, be carried out. The request contained the following points:

> 1- That the Kurdish language became the second official language in the Parliament. 2-That all of officials in the Kurdish liwas should be Kurds. 3- That

---

[774] McDowall, (2000), p. 175.

[775] Ali, (1997), p. 580.

[776] McDowall, (2000), p. 175.

[777] Qadir, (2007), p. 100.

one of the three vice-Prime Ministers should be a Kurd. The deputies decided in case the government did not respond to their demands they would leave the party in power (Hizb al-Taqaddum), headed by al-Saadun's block. When the latter met the deputies he assured them that he would give important considerations to their request.[778]

In a similar vein, Kurdish exiles and immigrants from Turkey, Iran and Iraq established Khuybun (Independence), a Kurdish nationalist association in 1926, which in October 1927, was officially announced at a meeting in Beirut. It was headed by Cheladat Bedir Khan and had a close cooperation with (Dashnak) the Armenian Nationalist Party. The activities of the members of the Khuybun were primarily in northern Kurdistan, and among Kurdish immigrants in Istanbul, Aleppo, Tabris, Baghdad, Cairo and Paris. The nationalist activity of Khuybun offered hope for the Iraqi Kurds who harbored deep hate against the Arabs in Iraq, particularly against the Iraqi administration in Kurdistan, which was established after the defeat of the second rebellion of Shaikh Mahmud. Another anti-government association was Zanisty we Peshkawten, (a secret association formed in 1927). Part of its activity was to instigate Kurdish sentiments against the Iraqi government policy of Arabization in Kurdistan. [779]

Kurdish cultural societies, such as the Yanai- Sarkawtin-i-Kurdistan (Kurdish Progress Society) and Jamiati-Zanisti Kurdan, grew in Mosul and Sulaimanya "offered a clear indication of the context in which culture was thereafter to be grasped". The amount of the petitions sent to the League of Nations by the educated Kurds in order to institute the education system in the district, as well as demanding economic and political autonomy, was an obvious manifestation of the impact of the cultural factor at the time.[780]

In addition, two associations- Pushtiwani Kurdan, which was active in Mosul and Baghdad and included several officers and Kurdish nationalist

---

[778] Ali, (2011), p.581.

[779] Ibid., pp.581-585.

[780] Lukitze Liora, Iraq: *The Search for National Identity*, (Frank Cass publishers,1995), p.42.

personalities, and the Nationalist Commission, established for the freedom and independence of the Kurdish people, had a prominent role in the events of the years 1930-1931 in South Kurdistan.[781] By the time of the election in Sulaimanya it had become apparent that "Kurdish national sentiment" had taken a firm hold among the educated classes in the Kurdistan area. [782]

A distinguishing feature of the development of the nationalist movement of educated Kurds was that it differed from previous movements both in terms of its leadership; most of whom were active in highly political bodies such as the parliament and cabinet as well as many literary and political associations and clubs, and in its social basis. In describing the uprising of the 1930 Sulaimanya Jalal Talabani Writes:

> The national uprising of 1930 was a decisive turning point in the Kurdish freedom movement. It accomplished a profound change in leadership, base and the nature of the movement. For the first time in the Modern Kurdish history, a rebellion moved into an urban centre, in which the workers, students and traders participated; for the first time the intelligentsia and the workers, took over the leadership of a national uprising, instead of the Kurdish religious leaders and the tribal princes. After this uprising, the importance of the Kurdish national movement and its leadership shifted from the countryside to the city.[783]

However, despite the fact that nationalism had gained a foothold among the educated Kurds in parts of the urban society, particularly in Sulaimanya, it was not sufficiently entrenched in all social strata in order to organize and lead all forces in Kurdistan. Affiliation and loyalties to the tribal and religious leaders were still strong among the Kurdish public, and a consistent unity or cooperation between these leaders and the educated groups was notable by its absence. Thus, even at this stage the Kurdish national movement could not develop into 'Phase C' according to Hroch's model described previously. This required a mass support of the national

---

[781] Qadir, (2007), p.123.

[782] Sluglett, (2007), p. 131.

[783] Jalal Talabani, 1971. Quoted in Ibrahim, (1983), p. 320. (my translation).

idea, i.e. that the national consciousness became the concern of the majority of the people. After the events in Sulaimanya Shaikh Mahmud thus took the opportunity and resumed his rebellious activities.

Shaikh Mahmud's Third Rebellion, 1930-1931

The Shaikh was not involved in the Sulaimanya incidents since according to his agreement with the Iraqi government in 1927, he undertook to remain aloof from political activities in the Kurdish districts. Early in September 1930, it however became known that the Shaikh was building up an armed tribal force on the Persian border.[784] The Iraqi government was concerned that the Shaikh would become embroiled in the conflict with the Iraqi authorities as a result of the latest incidents. On September 10, 1930, al-Midfai dispatched a letter warning the Shaikh of any activity which could endanger public peace and order in the Kurdish areas and infringe upon the agreement from 1927.[785] Notwithstanding this warning, the Shaikh a few days later crossed the Iranian border into Iraq with a troop of tribal forces. The troop was reinforced by three deserted Kurdish officers[786] in the Iraqi army stationed in Sulaimanya.

In addition, the Shaikh enjoyed the support of the educated Kurds in Sulaimanya as well as several of the Kurdish tribal leaders in Mosul *liwa*.[787] They forwarded a petition, on October 10, to the High Commissioner protesting against the treatment the Kurds were exposed to during the election in Sulaimanya and complained that since the dissolution of the Parliament and the signing of the new Anglo-Iraqi treaty by the Cabinet they realized that their rights were omitted from the treaty. They also realized that they would be put unconditionally under the domination of the Arabs, which conflicted with the decision of the League as well as

---

[784] Iraq Administration Reports, 1914-1932, Vol. 9. 1928-1930. P. 27.

[785] Al-Hasani, Vol. 3. p, 72.

[786] They were: Mahmud Jawdat, Hamid Jawdat and Kamil Hassan. See al-Hasani, Vol.3. p.73.

[787] Qadir, (2007), p. 125.

with the desires of the Kurds. According to the petitioners, this event triggered a riot from Zakho to Khanaqin where the Kurds claimed their rights, but the government answered by committing a massacre in Sulaimanya. They asked the British government to persuade the Arabs in accepting justified Kurdish demands such as; setting up of a Kurdish state stretching from Zakhu to Khanaqin under a British Mandate pending a decision by the League of Nations, evacuation of the Arabs from that region, the immediate release of the detainees and the exiled because of the Sulaimanya event, and moving all Kurdish officers and officials from Arab areas to Kurdish ones.[788]

The Shaikh defied orders to return to Iran and was engaged in spreading propaganda among the chiefs for his benefit in the tribal area north of Sulaimanya. In a letter to the High Commissioner he maintained that the killing in Sulaimanya rendered the unity between the Kurds and the Arabs impossible and demanded complete separation from them. He also repeated the petitioners' demand mentioned above.[789] It seemed that the Shaikh's menacing activities were troubling for the Residency and the Iraqi Government who were preparing for the admission of Iraq to the League of Nations. Consequently, on October 20, 1930, two separate letters were sent by al-Midfai and the High Commissioner Sir Francis Humphreys, to Shaikh Mahmud in which they ordered him: 1-To quit Iraqi territory and return to his headquarters in Piran village with his family, 2-That he could return to Iraq only with the permission of the Iraqi government,3-That he abstain from interfering in the state of affairs of Sulaimanya liwa as well as other liwas in Iraq. In case of infringement of these conditions, the government would take necessary actions against him and his followers and confiscate his properties. He should also return the three deserted Kurdish officers to Iraq.[790]

However, Shaikh Mahmud, who received wide support, particularly in the Sulaimanya and Bashdar regions, launched several attacks against the

---

[788] Al-Hasani, Vol. 3. P. 67.
[789] Special Reports, pp. 265-266. See also Al Hasani ibid
[790] Al-Hasani,Vol. 3. pp. 130-131.

Iraqi army forces. In order to thwart the Shaikh's attacks, 8 army brigades were deployed in Sulaimanya during October 1930.The Shaikh, who waged guerrilla warfare, attempted to seize the town of Halabja but upon a request from the Ministry of Defence they were confronted with the RAF which had been attached to the Iraqi military convoys stationed there.[791] On November 3, a division of the Shaikh forces composed of 200 men attacked Penjwin. A column of the Iraqi army forces with the cooperation of the RAF was sent and it dislodged him from Penjwin. The Shaikh's followers resumed their activities from Sardasht which necessitated sending another military column from Sulaimanya in order to expel them from the town. Several skirmishes were fought and as a result on December 3, four men of the Iraqi troops were killed; two officers and three men were also wounded.[792]

On February 1, 1931, the Iraqi government and the British authority discussed necessary measures that needed to be taken against the Shaikh. The Iraqi side suggested financial assistance to the tribes in conjunction with military support to drive the Shaikh outside the Iraqi border and to implement urgent sanctions after military field trials. The British did not agree on the grounds that these kinds of measures would have negative effects and instead urged using police forces in confronting with the armed movement.[793]

As the guerrilla fighting continued and the Shaikh attempt to gain ground among the Kurds outside Sulaimanya, the Iraqi government tried to deal with the situation by taking new measures. In a meeting on March 24, it was decided to announce martial administration in Sulaimanya under the control of a military commander, capable of reducing acts of lawlessness and restore peace and order. Otherwise the authorities stipulated in the Tribal Criminal and Civil Dispute Regulation would be relegated to the

---

[791] Qadir, (2007), p. 126.
[792] Special Report, p. 266. See also Longrigg (1953), p. 194.
[793] Qadir, (2007), p. 126.

military commander,[794] putting as well all means at his disposal in order to carry out his mission. In case these two arrangements would prove unfeasible the government would be obliged to evacuate the Sulaimanya liwa and withdraw its forces from the area pro tem pending other decisions for restoration of security there. However, none of these decisions were carried out and Faisal accused the cabinet of being inefficient in re-establishing law and order.[795]

In March the uprising reached a critical stage as the Shaikh attempted to expand its scope to reach other liwas in Kurdistan. He called on Kurdish leaders to join the national uprising while moving with his forces toward Qara Dagh, in the southern part of Sulaimanya, and in mid-March, he reached Kifri, and was threatening Khanaqin. He also had intentions to re-cruit from the strong Jaf tribe who was in possession of 2500 fighters and at odds with the government tax policy. In addition, they established a broad-based administration in the territories they controlled, stretching from the Iranian border in the North to districts in South East of Kirkuk in the South. The gravity of the situation forced the British to take quick and decisive military operation against the rebellions. They were determined not to let the rebellions succeed since in that case it would give the impression to the League that Iraq was an unstable country and that the League, as it was decided, would in June 1931 consider Kurdish petitions, as well as the admission of Iraq to the League. Thus, on May 5, a joint operation composed of an infantry column of 400 men backed by the RAF (which had a decisive role) was launched against the Shaikh forcing him to withdraw to the vicinity of Au-i-Barika twenty miles northeast of Tuz

---

[794] "The general principle animating in the Tribal Dispute Regulation was that tribesmen who were (supposedly) accustomed to settling their differences by tribal methods, under the jurisdiction of their shaykh or majlis, should be able to continue to do so, ... The Regulation enhanced the shaykh's position by giving him absolute judicial authority over his tribe ... and had official power to act as judge and jury in civil and criminal matters.... The power conferred by the Tribal Dispute Regulation were extremely wide, a feature presumably judged necessary for wartime condition." See Sluglett, (2007), pp.169-172.

[795] Al-Hasani, Vol. 3. pp. 132-133.

Khurmatu, in Kirkuk liwa leaving 16 dead of the Shaikh's followers dead and the several wounded. The Shaikh was compelled to take refuge in the village of Piran in Iran. He then received a letter from Faisal and Humphrey demanding his surrender and the nassuring him that his life and the lives of his family would be spared. On May 14, 1931, owing to the pressure from the Iranian and Iraqi governments the Shaikh submitted himself to Captain Holt, the British political officer, who was monitoring his movements from Penjwin.[796]

The Shaikh was first brought to Samawa and then transferred to al-Naseria, but upon his protest, the Iraqi authority finally allowed him to reside in Baghdad, and decided to confiscate his properties. Concerning the Kurdish officers surrendered to him, two of them, the brothers Hamid Jawdat and Mahmud Jawdat, repented their act and were submitted to the Iraqi authority which condemned them to imprisonment but then by virtue of a Royal Decree were pardoned and released.[797]

After the victory over Shaikh Mahmud's rebellion and his surrender, the King accompanied by the Minister of Interior paid a visit to Kirkuk and Sulaimanya in order to once again emphasize the importance of Iraq's unity and warn for any separatist attempt. At a banquet hosted by Sulaimanya mutassaref in honor of him on June 11, 1931, the King said that the Iraqi state condemned separation and, as whole, Iraq had become an inseparable entity; he went on further to say that it was impossible for the people of the South to live in security without Sulaimanya liwa being part of their homeland and into their own hands, and that the inhabitants of Sulaimanya could not live a single day away from the situation in the rest of their Iraqi homeland and their Iraqi brothers. He also argued that the platform for the national government since its inception had been and continued to be, to spread justice among the people and to reassure their wishes; among others, it enacted laws under which the freedom of education and local language were granted, as well as freedom of litigation before the court. In addition, the judges should know the language of the litigant in the Iraqi

---

[796] Ali, (2011), pp. 629-633.
[797] Al-Hasani, Vol.3. p 133.

liwas, and that customs, traditions and religions would be fully respected.[798]

The Local Language Law, which the King considered as one of the important achievements of the Iraqi government, was finally passed on May 19, 1931, albeit with considerable limited extent. For example, technical departments were excluded from it; knowledge of the Kurdish language and not race was the condition in employment of officials in the Kurdish areas, in line with al-Askary's wishes, and that the Kurdish qadhas of Mosul liwa were given a year to decide which dialect they preferred. The delay in the legislative process of the law had upset Holt, who blamed the King and the Prime Minister for that:

> My own view is that the King and Nuri are determined to do their utmost to maintain the use of Arabic in these qadhas. If they can delay for a few months implementing the stipulation ascertaining the wishes of the people the Mandate may come to an end before the year is up and then there will be no-one to press them to honour their pledges.[799]

The Kurds became worried when the draft law was published and protested that it was not in accordance with the recommendations of the League. J.C. Edmonds wrote in this respect:

> ... None of my Kurdish visitors has so much as mentioned it spontaneously. When questioned they have manifested no enthusiasm; on the contrary they have been critical of its shortcomings. This is remarkable because it is in many ways the most concrete promise yet made. But the Kurds have reason to know that there is a great gulf between promise and performance.[800]

And on June 25, the king paid another visit to Kirkuk in order to dis ribute awards among those who participated in the operation agains Shiakh Mahmud's uprising.[801]

---

[798] Ibid., pp. 137-139
[799] Sluglett, (2007), pp.143-144.
[800] Quoted in Hassanpour, (1992), p. 116.
[801] Ali, (2011), pp.634-635.

Despite the fact that the military operation against the Shaikh was conducted through coordination and cooperation between the British and Iraqi forces, there was serious dissension in their dealing with that matter. The king and Nuri and his Cabinet advocated a harder line against the Shaikh and were of the opinion that the British impeded the Iraqi army's efforts to crush the Kurdish uprising. Nuri and his Cabinet believed that announcement of martial law in the Kurdish districts was necessary to enable the government to deal with the rebels decisively. The prime minister went so far as to informed the king that the government had two options; either to announce martial law to put an end to the uprising, or to abandon the Kurdish liwas which had become ungovernable and constituted a huge burden for the depleted Iraqi Treasury. Nuri had also complained that in dealing with the rebels they were constrained by employing European methods, such as court, witness etc., rather than imposing collective punishment.[802]

The question of Shaikh Mahmud's latest rebellion was discussed in the Iraqi Parliament, as it was in progress, this time in detail and it was seriously compared with the previous one which only was mentioned in passing. Generally speaking, the deputies assumed antagonistic attitudes toward the Shaikh. The rebellion also provided an opportunity to bring up the question of the capacity of the Iraqi army. Like Nuri al-Said, some deputies such as Naji al-Salih (al-Diwaniya), and Salih Jabr, (al-Muntafik), believed that the war against the Shaikh had a devastating effect on the cabinet's budget, and that despite the enormous amount spent on combating the rebels the Iraqi forces had not yet succeeded to quell the movement. Some other deputies, including Salih Jabr, were very critical of the Iraqi army's incapability in eliminating the rebellion definitely and once for all. The King shared these deputies' perceptions of the Iraqi army. In a note in early 1932, he wrote about his experience and assessment of the situation during the Shaikh rebellion, making an estimation of the amount of forces needed to put down an armed rebellion, telling about the difficulties the Iraqi army experienced during the Shaikh's uprising, and acknowledging

---

[802] Ali, (2011), pp.634-35.

the lack of sufficient troops which became obvious then.[803]

Whilst the Iraqi army had increased from 3,500 in 1922 to about 11,500 at the independence of Iraq in 1932 [804]the king and his closest entourage among the Sharifian officers such as Nuri al-Said, Jasin al-Hashemi and al-Askary, demanded a far larger army, something between 15,000 and 20,000, combined with an Iraqi Air Force. Such an army, in their opinion, was able to safeguard the independence of Iraq, as well as to thwart threats from within and outside the country.[805] The aim of the creation of a strong Iraqi army was also for "the transmission of pan Arab ideology". During the interwar years, "the army became an instrument for the propagation of nationalism in two ways. First by advocating universal military conscription, the Sharifians hoped to make the army a school for the nation, an extension of the education system. Second, the officer corps entered politics." In fact, one might suggest that the Sharifians as ex-Ottoman officers had been involved in politics since 1921.[806]Faisal actually realized that the only way to ensure a substantial state-building was the formation of a strong army. In 1933, there were more than 100,000 rifles in private hands while the government had 15,000 in its possession.[807] For this reason Faisal and other nationalists were against the British policy in hampering the creation of a large and powerful Iraqi army. Thus already in 1922, when al-Askary became the first Minister of Defence, Faisal supported the idea of universal military conscription, and as the issue was debated in the Parliament in 1927, al-Askary, argued:

> We will ... open the door of participation in the defence of the country before all classes of the nation. There is no doubt that an army in which all these classes participate, will be more inclusive of the   racial qualities and national virtues with which the Iraqi nation is graced than an army built on any other

---

[803]Qadir, (2007), pp.128-136.
[804]Hemphill, (1979), p. 95.
[805] Sluglett, (2007), p.95.
[806] Simon , (1986), p. 115.
[807] Hanna Batatu, *The Old Social Classes and the Revolutionary Movements of Iraq* (New Jersey: Princeton University Press, 1978), p. 26.

bases.

No surprise that al-Husri also advocated military conscription; he believed that it would benefit nationalism more than education, since elementary education only prepared one to serve the state.[808]

The British also realized the necessity of forming an Iraqi army, but with restricted size, since the army constituted a crucial component of the Iraqi statehood. After the acquisition of the Mosul *Wilayat* in 1926 the policy of the incorporation of the Kurds into the Iraqi state became clearer than ever. The Kurds were to become good Iraqis in the service of the state. And the Iraqi army would incur responsibility for instilling them with a sense of patriotism. As early as 1926, the British deemed the army as a "valuable means of fostering a true national spirit", which afforded a "degree of homogeneity", a common language, and a "common obedience to the central government."[809]

The universal conscription, was opposed both by the Shiites tribes and the Kurds. They feared that conscription would enable the minority of Sunni officers in the town to preserve their dominance of the illiterate Shiites tribesmen, who would constitute the rank and file of the army. The Kurds were also against the conscription for similar reasons.[810]

In an article in *Baghdad Times* on November 12, 1927, the Arbil deputy, al-Rawanduzi, wrote that the conscription was useless and described it as a "huge bomb" for Iraq, urging the government to disregard the idea. He also maintained that it was not his personal opinion, but the opinions of all Kurds on that subject.[811] Despite the growth of the Iraqi army and the fact that in the operation in 1931 against Shaikh Mahmud's rebellion the Levies were involved in a considerably less degree than in previous operations, the concerns of the king and his close circle on the matter of the inefficiency of the Iraqi army came true as it was manifested in the operations against the Barzanis.

---

[808] Simon, (1986), pp. 117-118.
[809] Ibid, p. 117.
[810] Liora, (1995), pp.15-16.
[811] Al-Hasani, Vol. 2. P. 100.

12

The Barzani Movement, 1931-1932

The victory over Shaikh Mahmud's nationalist movement in 1931, and his subsequent disappearance from Iraq's political scene, soon proved that it by no means implied the end of the Kurdish national movement as the Iraqi government and the Mandatory power had probably foreseen. In fact, the Barzani leaders were as early as 1919 [812] implicated in the Kurdish movement in South Kurdistan headed by Shaikh Mahmud against the British. In that year, when the rebellion of Shaikh Mahmud erupted, Shaikh Ahmad, the leader of the Barzan district supported him, urging chiefs and shaikhs of Badinan to express their solidarity with the rebellion. He also sent fighters from Barzan, among them his brother, Mulla Mustafa, to participate in clashes against the British.[813]

---

[812] Actually the first Barzani revolt occurred during the Ottoman rule as ab-al-Slam II, Shaikh Ahmad's eldest brother, resisted unfavorable rules imposed by the Young Turks, who also accused him of intriguing with Russians. He was hanged in 1914 in Mosul or according to another version in 1916. See Michael M.Gunter, *The Kurds of Iraq:Tragedy and Hope*, (New York, 1992), p. 6. See also Mehrdad R.Izady, who argues that Shaikh Ahmad Barzani provided military assistance to Khyboun, a political party established in 1919 by a group Kurdish aristocratic intellectuals and modernists (comprising tribal leaders, and offsprings of the Kurdish princely houses) living in Paris. Mehrdad R.Izady, *The Kurds: A Concise Handbook*, (Washington, 1992), p. 62.

[813] Masoud al Barzani, *Al-Barzani wa Al-Haraka al-Taharuriya al-Kurdiya,* Vol.1 (Beirut: Kawa, 1997), p. 29.

Then, in the summer of 1931, the rebellion started in Barzan; the center of the gravity of the Kurdish movement shifted from Sulaimanya as the stronghold of Kurdish nationalism to Barzan under the leadership of Shaikh Ahmad. Several factors have been attributed to the armed struggle between the Barzanis and the Iraqi government. Already in 1927, the British reported that the Kurdish chief of Zibar tribe, Shaikh Ahmad, had "a record of continuous and obstinate hostility toward the Government." In June, the Iraqi government dispatched two small columns to the Barzan district to demonstrate its authority, but then they soon withdrew and left a garrison of one company in the village of Bilih some miles south of Barzan, and a police post was built in Barzan Village. Despite Shaikh Ahmad's resentment against the military presence in his area, he refrained from taking any hostile action against them.[814]

The British officials serving in Iraq during the period under the study connected the Barzanis rebellion with Shaikh Ahmad's peculiar mentality and his religious eccentricity. Besides, the British reports indicated that in August a curious incident took place which exhibited the Shaikh's odd mentality and the ferocious fanaticism of his followers. A local Mulla named Abdul Rahman, in the service of Shaikh Ahmad, quite suddenly announced that his master was God, and he himself his prophet. He toured the neighboring villages, preaching the new faith; many accepted his words and put the name of their new God and his prophet in their prayers. On September 1, in the course of his missionary wanderings, Mullah Adbul Rahman endeavored to persuade a village Muazzin to substitute the names of Shaikh Ahmad and Mullah Adbul Rahman for those of Allah and Muhammad in the call to prayer, which he was about to make from the minaret of the mosque. A dispute followed and Shaikh Muhammad Sadiq, a brother of Shaikh Ahmad, and several of his men, murdered the Mullah, two of his converts and the Muazzin.

---

[814] Iraq Administration Reports, 1914-1932, Vol. 8. 1925-1927. P. 25.

The report did not relate the assassinations to any realistic reason and sought the driving force behind the action in the passion brought about by a conflict permeated by fanaticism. As a result of that incident the British reinforced the garrison in Bilih, lest mischief ensue the murders. However, the religion died and no further action occurred in that respect.[815]

As these reports indicated, the Iraqi army was sent to the Barzani district prior to the event to impose its authority. Longrigg, who gives almost a similar account, also refers to the Iraqi army's maneuvering in the Barzini territory in mid-1927, and points out that following the murders at the village the government strengthened the army presence and carried out a police intervention at Bilih.[816]

It seemed that the military activities coupled with the establishment of police posts in Barzan district were deemed by Shaikh Ahmad as governmental policy to expand its jurisdiction in that area. Still, another factor that might have exasperated Shaikh Ahmad was that the new Iraqi government attempted to extract taxes that were unpaid for several years due to the tribal order the British had created.[817] The development appeared disturbing to the Shaikh; consequently in the winter of the same year, he attempted to counteract these kinds of governmental expansion. He therefore established connection with congenial elements and bought arms and ammunition.[818] It was also rumored that in February, of the following year, he had even been in correspondence with Shaikh Mahmud and with Simko, the chieftain of Shekaktribe.[819] However, it was reported that the Shaikh's influence and subversive propaganda created unrest in Baradust (Rawanduz), where false rumors of their evacuation from their villages, and

---

[815] Ibid.
[816] Longrigg (1953), p. 194.
[817] Derk Kinnane, *The Kurds and Kurdistan*, (London New York, 1964), p.40.
[818] Iraq Administration Reports, 1914-1932, Vol. 8. 1925-1927, p. 25.
[819] McDowall, (2000), p. 178.

thereby the Assyrian settlement, had made the tribesmen suspicious and inclined to listen to talks about resistance.[820]

The Assyrian Settlement

One of the Shaikh Ahmad's serious concerns, besides the infringement of the Iraqi army in Barzan territory, was the operation of the Assyrian settlement to be carried out in the northern part of South Kurdistan and the Barzan region. The Council of the League had separated around 20,000 Assyrians from their original homes, situated north of the Brussels line, and scattered in the villages of the Mosul liwas, but a permanent settlement of the majority of them was impractical. On the other hand, the Commission of Enquiry had warned that it was inappropriate to create an Assyrian enclave in Iraqi territory. That was only feasible by forcible evacuation of the Kurds and the Arabs from a wide area. In addition, to entitle the Assyrians such a privilege would certainly "have tended to differentiate between the Assyrians and the Kurds and to cause friction between them." It was also significant in respect to the unity of the new Iraqi state, the British believed, that all communities would be treated indiscriminately and to "emphasize the common citizenship of Assyrians, Kurds, and Arabs in the Iraqi State." The ideal solution to the question of the settlement of the Assyrians was that from that time on, they would be scattered, living in the Kurdish areas, or even as tenants of Kurdish aghas. This solution was regarded to be perfectly practical, since despite the fact that the Kurds and the Assyrians had not infrequently been fighting each other they have been neighbors for centuries. A report from the Commission of the Enquiry stated "We have been able to establish the fact that of all the Moslem races the Kurds live on the most friendly terms with the Christians."[821]

By the end of 1929 the British could consider that the operation of the settlement of the Assyrians was pursued generally in accordance with the established scheme. Nevertheless, there remained about 350 families from

---

[820]Iraq Administration Reports, 1914-1932, Vol.8. 1925-1927, pp. 25-26.

[821] Special Report, pp. 271-274.

the Hakkari mountains who, according to a scheme from autumn 1926, were to be settled in the Baradost area in the north of the Arbil liwa, but it was postponed due to "lack of funds" and particularly to agitation of certain politicians against it. A British report indicated that there was:

> little doubt that irresponsible influences were at work, chiefly in Baghdad, to make trouble between the Assyrians and the Kurds. The object seems to have been to divert against the Assyrians the supposed antipathy of the Kurds to the Arabs and also to weaken both Kurds and Assyrians by applying the maxim divide et impera.

In September, 1930, when the Iraqi government became cognizant of the endeavor of the "trouble-makers" to set the Kurds against the Assyrians, the Ministry of Interior dispatched a memorandum to the Mutasarrifs in the four northern liwas calling upon them to make enquiries on the matter and to hold in check activities of that nature, as well as to maintain that it was the government's obligation to protect all its citizens.[822]

Certainly, the scheme of settling the Baradost area by the Assyrians created a tense situation and it also raised suspicions toward the real intention of the Iraqi government. It seemed that the situation offered a good opportunity for some influential quarters in Baghdad to take advantage of it with the ultimate goal to alienate the Kurds from the Assyrians. It is unknown to what extent they succeeded, but the Iraqi government, which attempted to give the impression of being against the actions of those politicians and to protect the Assyrians against the Kurds, was apparently the main villain of the piece. What reinforced the concern of Shaikh Ahmad, besides his well-founded suspicion around the aim of the settlement, was primarily the penetration of the Iraqi army in Barzan and the government's establishment of an administration there in order to impose its control on the region.

By 1931, the Iraqi army and the Assyrian Levies were, to the resentment

---

[822] Special Report, pp. 277-278. About the Assyrian situation in Iraq see for example Daniel Silverfarb, *Britain's Informal Empire in the Middle East, A Case Study of Iraq, 1929-1941*, (New York, 1986), ch. 4, *The Assyrian Minority.*

of Shaikh Ahmad, still maneuvering within the Barzan territory. Conse-quently, the Shaikh appealed to King Faisal deploring the presence of the garrison in the Barzan district, wondering that if the purpose was to safe-guard security there, they themselves were able to do so, and in case they assisted the settlement of the Assyrians, it was then an unjustified decision. However, the appeal to the King was to no avail.[823]

Prelude to the Rebellion

The prevailing tensions in the Barzan region did not engender any armed conflict between Shaikh Ahman and the Iraqi troops since the onset of the crisis in 1927. However, in 1931 new factors were introduced into the sit-uation forcing the parties involved into heavy fightings. Shaikh Ahmad paid his sheep tax by an annual lump sum to the Iraqi government, irre-spective of the diminishing or increasing of the sheep. The Iraqi govern-ment then attempted to restrain his influence by informing him that he henceforth had to pay a sheep tax per head of sheep each year; a system was created called (Al-code), and was followed all over the country. He was also told, for that reason the government intended to set up govern-mental facilities in the backward Barzani region such as police posts, a clinic, a hospital and schools etc. Shaikh Ahmad agreed principally with the government's demand on the sheep tax, but argued that the establish-ment of stations were unnecessary since neither the Turks nor the British had thought of such measures.

The government considered his answer as disobedience which justified the dispatching of punitive troops, but since Shaikh Mahmud's rebellion was in progress at the time, October 1931 in Sulaimanya, the operation agains him was postponed for the time being. In the meantime, an "extensive propaganda campaign against the Barzanis was organized" the

---

[823] Jwaideh, (2006), p.223.

contents of which were, among others, that Shaikh Ahmad's religion contradicted the beliefs of the Muslims. [824]Since al-Hasani employs passive
voice the agent of the propaganda is not clearly known, but Kurdish
sources indicate that during the deterioration of the states of affairs in Barzan, the rumors against Shaikh Ahmad, particularly from his assailant
Shaikh Rashid Lulan, who distributed anti-Islamic and other novel ideas
among the Barzanis, played a significant role. Shaikh Rashid, who was
pro-government, was involved in a bitter dispute with Shaikh Ahmad on
the question of returning the latter's followers, who had migrated to
Baradost, under the domination of Shaikh Lulan, to Barzan. The government arranged an Arbitration Committee composed of Mutassarif of Mosul
and Arbil and qaimmaqams of Rawanduz and Zibar as well as Shaikh Ahmad and Shaikh Rashid's representatives. The Committee met in Aqara in
October 1931, but the parties failed to come to terms. In December, Mulla
Mustafa acting as his brother's representative, was sent with 600 fighters
to assault the village of Lulan in the Baradost region burning down seven
villages. Consequently, the government warned Shaikh Ahmad to put an
end to his brother's harassment of other tribes. In addition, the government
demanded the stripping of all weapons, except for in the Barzan region,
which was not surprisingly disliked and rejected by Shaikh Ahmad. This
move was to provoke the tribes which were hostile to Shaikh Ahmad, especially Shaikh Rashid who was supplied with funds and arms.[825]

In the light of these facts, then, it is not difficult to conclude that between the Iraqi government and Shaikh Rashid there was frequent cooperation against their common enemy, Shaikh Ahmad. It is also not unwar-
ranted to suggest that Shaikh Rashid's rumors against Shaikh Ahmad and
the Barzanis occurred in symbiosis with the government. Furthermore, it
seems that Longrigg, who attributed the conflict between Shaikh Rashid
and Shaikh Ahmad to the latter's alleged religious eccentricity, was inclined to embrace such rumors and propaganda as he wrote that the Shaikh,

---

[824] Al-Hasani, Vol.3. p. 188.
[825] Qadir, (2007), pp.139-140.

in 1931:

> Again lost his wits, accepted and imposed Christianity, and ordered his scared
> followers to conform to his new faith by roasting and eating pork. A number
> of the horrified retinue obeyed; but a neighbor, Sheikh Rashid of Baradost,
> expressed his disapproval by raids which kindled all the fires of tribal warfare.
> Sheikh Ahmad's brother, Mulla Mudtafa, and other well-wishers, tried in vain
> by diplomacy to extinguish them: but he himself, restored to the Muslim faith,
> led forays of unusual savagery into Baradost country.[826]

The Outbreak of the Rebellion and Military Actions
Against Shaikh Ahmad, 1931

The event in Baradost apparently triggered the first armed clash between
the Iraqi army and Shaikh Ahmad's forces in December 1931. An Iraqi
force penetrated deep into Barzan Mountains, up to Shaikh Ahmad's village, but was severely beaten and only saved from the fiasco by the intervention of the RAF. Owing to the intensive bombing of the Shaikh's position, he released the prisoners he had taken during the operation and protested obedience to the government. He then withdrew from the Baradost
territory, but still was unvanquished.[827]

The failure of the operation against the Shaikh concerned the government officials. On February 12, 1932, the cabinet issued a decree on launch-
ing a wider attack on Barzan region, but it was postponed to the spring
season due to the cold winter.[828]

On March 10, the Minister of Interior issued a warning to Shaikh Ahmad, urging him to appear before the Zibar qaimmaqam no later than
March 14, in order to pledge allegiance to the government. A similar note
was sent from the High Commissioner to the Shaikh, but the   warnings

---

[826]Longrigg, (1953), p.195.
[827] Ibid.
[828] Qadir, (2007), p.140.

went unheeded since he was fully aware that the objective of the government was his arrest.[829] The second time the Minister of Interior sent Nuri al-Berifkani, a prominent Kurd, to explain to the Shaikh that the Iraqi government did not intend to cause him any harm and would guarantee the security of his property and life, but even this attempt proved futile.[830]

The government, thus, dispatched punitive troops to the Barzan region in order to consolidate security as well as to establish a government administration there. Concurrently, the Ministry of Defence initiated its work in coordination with the Ministry of Interior in setting out military operations, which were carried out on March 15 and composed of a military column backed by the British RAF. They gained control of Mirkesur the following day. The column was attacked by Kurdish rebels, but they were able to repel them.[831]

Although there was a consensus regarding the subjugation of Shaikh Ahmed and control of the Barzani district, the Iraqi government was inclined to pursue a more aggressive military policy than the British. As early as April 1931, the Iraqi Prime Minister Nuri al-Said, informed the Turkish government, which complained about Shaikh Ahmad's support of the Ararat rebellion in Turkey by sending armed fighters, that the Iraqi government had laid down a military plan for eliminating the Shaikh.[832] In addition, the Iraqi politicians, particularly the military leaders such as al-Askary, were critical toward the British for preventing them from employing severe methods in the treatment of the tribes and imposing collective punishment on the villagers as well as conducting indiscriminate bombings. Without the interference of the British, the military leaders claimed, they would have been able to end the battles within only a few weeks.[833]

On March 23, 1931, at the ordinary session of the Iraqi Parliament,

---

[829] Barzani, (1997), p. 40.
[830] Al-Hasani, Vol. 3. p. 190.
[831] Qadir, (2007), p. 141.
[832] Ali, (2011), p. 647.
[833] Ibid, p. 657.

when the question of the rebellion in the Barzan region was brought up for discussion, al-Askary explained that the government's aim in sending troops to the Barzan area was to maintain the security of the roads in order to enable the establishment of an administration there. He emphasized that Shaikh Ahmad was mistaken in thinking that he was detached from the Iraqi government, and could refuse submission to any authority. According to al-Askary, Shaikh Ahmad challenged the authority of the Iraqi state by not heeding their warnings and proceeding with his subversive deeds, which were insupportable and justified punitive actions. [834]

However, despite the Iraqi government's constant and tremendous pressure on Shaikh Ahmad to compel him to abide by its requirements, there was no sign of compliance from the Shaikh at the beginning of Spring. Consequently, the government was obliged to dispatch troops, which advanced into the Barzan territory, occupied Markesur and threatened Barzan. The Barzanis answered the troop movement with a sudden attack, inflicted heavy losses and a second defeat on them. For the second time the RAF came to the rescue of the troops, and covered a second Iraqi column, which then could occupy Barzan and much of its surrounding countryside.[835] An intermission was thought to be necessary in order to release a pilot captured on April 26 and to also negotiate with Shaikh Ahmad to end the fighting. During the negotiation, which lasted until May 23, the Shaikh and his brother were offered generous terms, but this was in vain.[836]

At the end of May 1932, the RAF resumed its operations, conducting perpetual and heavy air bombing against the Barzani rebels. At the same time, the Iraqi army had advanced as far as Shirwan Mazen in the heart of the rebellious territory, while Shaikh Ahmad and his close followers were forced, under massive air bombardment and threat from all sides, to surrender to the Turkish soldiers at the border on June 22. It is worth noting that Shaikh Ahmad's disdain toward the Iraqi government was, to an extent,

---

[834]Qadir, (2007), pp. 142-143.
[835]Longrigg, (1953), p. 195.
[836]Al-Hasani, Vol.3. p. 190.

as he told Captain Holt, that he preferred to go to the Turks, his overt enemy, a hundred times than to surrender to the British slaves.[837] The Turkish government transferred the Barzanis to Ardine on the Turkish-Bulgarian border, but the Iraqi government wanted them to be extradited to Iraq as disobedient subjects. Turkey, however, returned them to Iraq after receiving assurance that they would be pardoned. Shaikh Ahmad and his brother first dwelled in al-Naseria, then were moved into al-Hilla and al-Diwaniya and finally to Sulaimanya where they remained until the outbreak of the rebellion of Mulla Mustafa in 1943.[838]

---

[837]Basile Nikitine, *Les Kurdes, Etudes sociologique et Historique*, (Paris, 1956), p. 200."Je préfère cent fois me rendre aux les Turcs, mes ennemis ouverts, que de me livrer aux esclaves Anglais."
[838] Al-Hasani, Vol.3. pp.190-191.

Conclusion

In a memorandum submitted in 1933, Faisal deplored:

> In Iraq, is still- and I say this with a heart full of sorrow- no Iraqi people but un-imaginable masses of human beings, devoid of any patriotic idea, imbued with religious traditions and absurdities, connected by no common tie, giving ear to evil, prone to anarchy, and perpetually ready to rise against any government whatever. Out of these masses we want to fashion a people, which we would train, educate, and refine ....[839]

The failure of the project of nation-state formation in Iraq is evidently illustrated by the above-mentioned quote by Faisal, who himself together with the Anglo-Iraqi authorities, was ardent exponents of the creation of a homogeneous nation from an ethnically and religiously heterogeneous population. This policy starkly contrasted with the promises and pledges made to the Kurds with respect to their national rights. Following the abolition of the Sèvres Treaty, which provided for creation of a Kurdish national state, and the awarding of the Mosul *Wilayat* to Iraq in 1926, the ground was well prepared for consolidation of the Iraqi state, which had been initiated with the establishment of the first government of al-Naqib in 1921, and for integrating the Kurds into the structure of the nation-state. Despite the fact that after the determination of the Mosul dispute Kurdish national rights were limited to cultural rights embodied in the recommendation of the commission of enquiry, the Anglo-Iraqi authorities were reluctant to even realize these recommendations and instead pursued a policy with the ultimate goal to suppress Kurdish ethnic particularity and make

---

[839]Quoted in Batatu, (1978), pp. 25-26.

the Kurds good Iraqis. Consequently, the Kurds intensified their activities and advanced their cause for political and cultural rights. Owing to this development, the British faced a delicate situation. As mandatory power they had incurred obligations toward the League of Nations and Iraq and had to reconcile between the accommodation of Kurdish desires, which was necessary for the admission of Iraq into the League of Nations, and the Iraqi government's negligence to carry out the same rights. However, at the final analyses the British concurred with the Iraqi government's Kurdish policy to a degree that, at the end of the mandate, the recommendations of the Commission of Enquiry were not yet implemented. The policy might have derived from the perception that it was the only feasible way to forge an Iraqi identity, or as Majid khadduri puts it:

> The British seem to have believed that Arabs and Kurds, as well as other minorities, might eventually be welded together to create a new national identity based on the territorial concept of the newly established Iraqi state and sustained by their common interests.[840]

And the Iraqi Government believed that by denying the minorities their political and cultural rights they could be able to transcend ethnic and religious barriers and to build a state where these minorities would finally identify with it, i.e. to create a common identity and ideology, which are key aspects of a nation-state. Iraq, nevertheless, just experienced the opposite. The Kurds, not being satisfied with the Anglo-Iraqi Kurdish policy, defied the authority of the Iraqi government and challenged its legitimacy.

In other words, and according to Gellner's theory, there should be congruence between the national unit, i.e. the different groups of population and the political unit i.e. the government as precondition for nation building. In Iraq, there was no such congruence between these two units. Gellner's view on this conflicting situation is:

> In brief, nationalism is a theory of political legitimacy, which requires that ethnic boundaries should not cut across political ones, and in particular, that ethnic

---

[840]Majid Khadduri, *Iraq: A study in Iraq's Politics since the Revolution of 1958*, (London: Oxford University Press, (1969),p.173.

boundaries within a given state -a contingency already formally excluded by the principle in its general formulation–should not separate the power-holders from the rest.[841]

---

[841]Gellner, (1983), p. 1.

Bibliography

Unpublished Primary Sources:

Colonial Office, 730/5 No. 503, 23 September, 1921 Cox to *Churchill*.
Colonial Office, 730/6 No. 616, 25 October, 1921, *Cox to Churchill*.

Published Primary Sources:

League of Nations: *The Mandates System: Origins-Principles-Application*, (Geneva, 1945)
British Documents on Foreign Affairs: Reports and Papers from the Foreign Office Confidential Print.
Part 2, *From the First to Second World War*. Series B. *Turkey, Iran and the Middle East, 1918-1939*:
Vol. 1, *The End of the War, 1918-1920.*
Vol. 2, *The Allies Take Control, 1920-1921*. Vol. 3, *The Turkish Revival, 1921-1923.*
Vol. 29. *Turkey, August 1922-July 1923.*
Vol. 30, *Turkey, July 1923-March 1927.*
Document on British Foreign Policy 1919-1939, (ed.), Rohan Butler, M.A. First Series Vol. X111.
Great Britain, Colonial Office: *Iraq Administration Reports*, April 1922-March 1923.
*Reports by His Britannic Majesty's Government on the Administrations of Iraq for the Period, April, 1923-*Decdember, 1924. *Iraq Administration Reports 1914-1932*, Vol. 8, 1925-1927.
Iraq Administration Reports 1914-1932, Vol. 9, 1928-1930. *Iraq Administration Reports 1914-19332*, Vol. 10, 1920-1931.
Special Report by His Majesty's Government in the United Kingdom of Great Britain and Northern Ireland to the Council of the League of Nations

on the Progress of Iraq during the Period 1920-1931.

Books in Arabic, Kurdish and Persian

Abd Alla, Lutfi Jafar Faraj, *Abd al- Muhsen al-Sadun, dawrahu Fi Tarikh al Iraq al Syiasi al Muaaser*, (Abd al Musen al Saadun and his Role in the History of Iraq's Contemporary politics (Baghdad: Al-Khuld. 1988).

Al-Barghawi, Ahmad Rafiq. *Al-Ilaqat al-Syiasyiah Bain al-Iraq wa Baritania 1922-1932.* (The political Relations between Iraq and Britain 1922- 1932), (Baghdad: Dar al-Rashid, 1980).

Al-Barzani, Masoud . *Al- Barzani wa Al- Haraka al- Taharuriya al-Kurdiyay.* Vol.1 (Beirut: Kawa, 1997).

Al-Haj, Aziz, *Al- Qadiyah al-Kurdiya fi- al- Ishriniyat.* (Beirut: Al-Muasasa al-Arabiya lildirasah wa al Nashr, 1984).

Al-Hasani, Abdul Razzaq, *Tarikh al- Wizarat al Iraqiya.* 3 vols (History of Iraqi Cabinets), (Sidon, Libanon, 1933-1940).

Al-Husri, Sati, *Muthakerati fi al-Iraq, al-juz al- awal, 1921-1927.* (My Momoirs in Iraq,vol.1,1921-1927) (Beirut: Dar al-tibaa, 1967).

Ali, Othman, *Al Haraka al-Kurdiya al-Muasira, dirasah Tarikhiya wathaeqiya 1833-1946*, (Contemporary Kurdish Movement, Historical Documentary study 1988-1946, (Arbil: Maktab al-tafsir lilnashr wal Ilan, 2011).

Bitlisi, Sharaf Khan, *Sharafname: Tarik -e Mofassa l-e Kordestan.* (Tehran: Elmi Press, 1964).

Fadil, Husayn, *Mushkilat al-Mawsil, dirasah fi-al- diblumasiyah al-Iraqiyah- al-Injiliziyah-al -Turkiyah wa-fi al-ray al-amm.* (Beirut, 2015).

Nadmi, W.J.O., *Al -Judhuor al- siyasiyya wal fikriyya wal Ijtimayya lil-haraka al-Istighlaliyya fi -Iragh 1920.* (The Political, Social and Intellectual Roots of the Iraqi Independence Movement of 1920) .(Beirut: Markaz Dirasat al-Wahda al- Arabiya, Ph.D.Thesis, 1984).

Qadir, Ahmad Muhammad Amin, *Mawqif-Majlis al-nuwwab al-Iraqi Min al- qadiyah al- Kurdiyah fi al- Iraq, 1925- 1945*. (The Position of the Iraqi Parliament toward the Kurdish Question in Iraq, 1925- 1945. (Al- Sulaimaniya: Bnkaizhin, 2007).

Zaki, Muhammah Amin, *Kholaseh Tarikh- i-Kurd u Kurdistan, Barg-i-yakem u Duwam*. (A Concise History of the Kurds and Kurdistan Vol. 1 &2) (Slemani: Sardam, 2000).

Books and Articles in European Languages

Ali, Othman, (1997) *South Kurdistan during the Last Phase of Ottoman Control: 1839- 1914*, Journal of Muslim Minority Affairs, 17:2, 283-291.

Allawi, Ali A., *Faisal 1 of Iraq*. (New Haven: Press. 2014).

Aloian, Zorabe Bud., *The Image of the Kurds in Hungary: Hungarian Material on the Kurds from the Ottoman Times until the End of the Twentieth Century*. (Spånga, 2008).

Anderson, Benedict, *Imagined Communities: Reflections on the Origin and Spread of Nationalism*. (London: Verso, 2006).

Anker, Peter Martin, *The Mandates System: Origin - Principles-Application*. (Geneva: League of Nations. April 1945).

Antonius, Georg, *The Arab Awakening: The Story of The Arab National Movement*. (London: H. Hamilton, 1938)

Armstrong, John A., *Nations before Nationalism*. (Chapel Hill, University of Northern Carolina Press, 1982).

Arno, J. Mayer, *Political Origins of the New Diplomacy, 1917-1918*. (New Haven: Yale University Press, 1959).

Bailey, Thomas A., *Woodrow Wilson and the Lost Peace*. (New York: The MacMillan Campany,1944).

Batatu, Hanna, *The Old Social Classes and the Revolutionary Movements of Iraq*. (Princeton N.J. Press, 1978).

Beck, Peter J., *A Tedious and Perilous Controversy: Britain and the Settlement of the Mosul Dispute, 1918- 1926*. Middle Eastern Studies, Vol. 17, No. 2. (April, 1981). pp. 256-276.

Bibliography

Bell, Gertrude, *The letters of Gertrude Bell*. Vol. 2 (New York, 1927).

Brownlie, Ian, *An Essay in the History of the Principle of Self-Determination*. In C.H. Alexendrowicz, (ed.) Grotian Society Papers, Studies in the History of the Law of Nations, 1968, (The Hague,1970), pp.90-99.

Bruinessen, Martin van, *Kurdish Society, Ethnicity, Nationalism and Refugee Problem* , in Philip G. Kreyenbroek and Stefan Sprel (eds.)The Kurds:A Contemporary Overview, (London: Routledge 1992), pp.33-68.

Bruinessen, Martin van, *Agha, Shaikh and the State: The Social and Political Structures of Kurdistan* (London: Zed Books, 1992).

Bruinessen, Martin van, *Nationalismus und religiöser Konflikt: Der Kurdische Wiederstand im Iran*. Collected Articles. In Kurdis Ethno-Nationalism versus Nation-Building States (Istanbul: Isis Press, 2000), pp.43-66.

Bruinessen, Martin van, *Ehmdi Xanis Men u Zin and Its Role in the Emergence of Kurdish National Awareness*. In Abbas Vali (ed.) *Essays on the Origins of Kurdish Nationalism*. (Costa Mesa: California Mazda, 2003), pp.40-57.

Burgoyne, Elizabeth, *Getrude Bell: From Her Personal Papers, 1914-1926*. (London 1961).

Busch, Briton Cooper, *Mudros to Lausanne: Britain's Frontier in West Asia, 1918 -1923*. (New York: State University of New York Press, 1976).

Chaliand, Gerard, *Le Malheur Kurde*. (Paris: Editions du Seuil,1992).

Cobban, Alfred, *National Self- Determination*. (London: Oxford University Press, 1945).

Choueiri, Yousef M., *Arab Nationalism: A History, Nation and State in the Arab World*. (Oxford: Blackwell Publishers, 2000).

Cleveland, William L., *The Making of An Arab Nationalist: Ottomanism and Arabism in the Life and Thought of Sati Al-Husri*. (New Jersey: Princeton, 1971).

Cleveland, William, *A History of the Modern Middle East*. (Boulder

Colo: Westview Press, 1994).

Cohen, Stuart, *British policy in Mesopotamia, 1903-1914.* (Ithaca Press, 228).

Cohen, S.A., *The Genesis of the British Campaign in Mesopotamia, 1914.* Middle East Studies, Vol. 12, No. 2, (May, 1976), pp. 119-132.

Coshar, Nevin and Sevtap Demirci, *The Mosul Question and the Turkish Republic, Before and After the Frontier Treaty,* 1926. Middle East Studies, Vol. 42, No. 1, (2006), pp.123- 132.

Cumming, Henry H., *Franco- British Rivalry in the Post-War Near East: The Decline of French Influence.* (London, New York, Toronto, 1938).

Day, A.J., (ed.) *Border and Territorial Disputes.* (London: Longman,1982).

Davidson, Roderic H., *Reform in the Ottoman Empire 1856-1976* (Princeton: Princeton University Press, 1963).

Dawisha, Adeed, *Arab Nationalism in the Twentieth Century: From Triumph to Despair.* (Princeton: Princeton University Press, 2003).

Dawisha, Adeed, *Iraq: A Political History from Independence to Occupation.* (Princeton: Princeton University Press, 2009).

Dawn, C. Ernest, *From Ottomanism to Arabism: Essay on Origins of Arab Nationalism.* (University of Illinois Press, 1973).

Demirci, Sevtap (2010) *Turco- British Diplomactic Manoeuvres on the Mosul Question in the Lausanne Conference, 1922-1923.* British Journal of Middle Eastern Studies, 37:1, 57-71.

DeNovo, John A., *American Interests and Policies in the Middle East 1900- 1939.* (Minnesota: Minnesota University Press, 1963).

Deutch, Karl W., *Nationalism and Social Communication: An Inquiry into the Foundation of the Nationality.* (Cambridge: Mass.: The M.I.T.Press, 1966).

Dodge, Toby, *Inventing Iraq: The Failure of National Building and a History Denied.* (London: C. Hurst & Co. 2003).

Drijvers, Jan Willen, *The Limits of Empire in the Res Gestae of*

Bibliography

Ammianus Marcellinus. In Oliver Hekster and T ed Kaizer
(eds.)*The Frontier in the Roman World. Proceedings of the
Ninth Workshop of the International Network, Impact of
Empire,* (Durham, 16- 19 April, 2009), (Leiden and Boston,
Brill, 2011), pp.13-31.

Dundar, Fuat, *Statisquo: British Use of Statistics in the Iraq Kurdish
Question 1919- 1932.* (Brandies University, 2012), pp.1-62.

Earle Edward Mead, *Turkey, the Great Powers and the Baghdad
Railway: A Study in Imperialism.* (New York, 1923).

Edmonds, C. J., *Kurds, Turks and Arabs: Politic, Travel, and
Research in North-Eastern Iraq, 1919-1925.* (London: Oxford
U.P.1957).

Edmonds, C. J., *Kurdish Nationalism,* Journal of Contemporary
History, Vol.6.1, Nationalism and Separatism (1971)
pp.87-107

Evans, R. J. W., *Essay and Reflections: Frontiers and National
Identities in Central Europe,* (The International Review Vol.14.
No. 3, (Augusti, 1992), pp. 480-502.

Evans, Laurence. *United States Policy and the Partition of Turkey,
1914-1924.* (Baltimore: The John Hopkins Press, 1965)

Evans, Luther Harris, *The Emancipation of Iraq from the Mandate
System.* American Political Science Association,Vol.26, No. 6
(1932), 1024-1049.

Foster, Henry A., *The Making of Modern Iraq: A Product of
World Forces.* (London, 1936).

Fowler, W.B., *British- American Relations 1917-191: The Role of Sir
William Wiseman.* (New Jersey, 1969).

Fromkin, David, *A Peace to End all Peace: The Fall of the Ottoman
Empire and the Creation of the Modern Middle East.* (New
York: Avon Books, 1990).

Gabrieli, Francesco, *The Arab Revival.* (London: Thames and
Hudson, 1961).

Gayim, Eyassu, *The principle of self-Determination: A Philosophical,
Historical and Legal Approach.* (Uppsala Universitet, 1987)

Gelner, Ernest, *Thought and Change* (London: Weidenfeld & Nicilson, 1964).

Gellner, Ernest, *Nation and Nationalism.* (New York: Cornell University Press, 1983).

George Lloyed, *The Truth about the Peace Treaties.* Vol. 2 (London, 1938)

Gerig, Benjamin, *The Open Door and the Mandates System: A Study of Economic Equality before and since the Establishment the Mandates System.* (London: Allen & Unwin, 1930)

Ghareeb, Edmund, *The Kurdish Question in Iraq* (Syracuse N.Y: Syracuse U.P, 1981).

Goldstein, Erik, *The Foreign Office and Political Intelligence 1918-1920,* Review of International Studies, Vol.14, No. 4. October 1988, pp.275-288.

Goldstein, Erik (1998), *The Round Table and the New Europe.* The Round Table: The Commonwealth Journal of International Affairs, Vol. 87, 346,177-189,

Goldstein, Erik, *Winning the Peace: British Diplomatic Strategy, Peace Planning, and the Paris Peace Conference 1916-1920.* (Oxford: Clarendon, 1991)

Goldstein, Erik, *The Eastern Question: The Last Phase.* In Dockrill, M.L. and Fisher John (eds.) *Paris Peace Conference 1919: Peace Without victory?* (New York, N.Y: Palgrave, 2001) pp. 141-157

Goldstein, Erik (2003) *The British Official mind at the Lausanne Conference, 1922-1923*, Diplomacy and Statecraft, 14:2,185-206.

Gorgas, Jordi Tejel (2008) *Urban Mobilization in Iraqi Kurdistan During the British Mandate: Sulaimaniya 1919-30*, Middle Eastern Studies, 44,4,537-552

Gottmann, Jean, *The Significance of Territory.* (Charlottesville: The University Press of Virginia, 1973).

Gottlieb, W.W., *Studies in the Secret Diplomacy during the First World War* (London: Allen & Unwin, 1957).

Bibliography

Gunter, Michael M., *The Kurds of Iraq: Tragedy and Hope*. (New York, 1992)

Haraldsson, Erlendur. *Land im Aufstand... Kurdistan* (Hamburg: Martari-VLg, 1966).

Hassanpour, Amir, *Nationalism and Language in Kurdistan, 1918-1985* (San Francisco: Mellen Research University Press,1992)

Hassanpour, Amir, *The Making of Kurdish Identity: Pre-20th Century Historical and Literary Sources*. In Abbas Vali (ed.) *Essays on the Origins of Kurdish Nationalism*. (Costa Mesa: California Mazda, 2003), pp. 106-162.

Hay W.R., *Two Years in Kurdistan:Experience of a Political Officer 1918-1920*. (London, 1921).

Heller, Joseph, *British Policy toward the Ottoman Empire, 1908-1914*. (London: Cass, 1983).

Helmreich, Paul C., *From Paris to Sèvres: The Partition of the Ottoman Empire at the Peace Conference of 1919-1920*. (Columbus, Co. 1974).

Hemphil, Paul P.J., *The Formation of the Iraqi Army, 1921-1933*. In Abbas Kelidar (ed.) *The Integration of Modern Iraq*. (London: Croom Helm, 1979), pp. 88-110.

Henderson W.O., *German Economic Penetration in the Middle East, 1870- 1914*. The Economic History Review, Vol. 18, No. ½ (1948), pp.54-64.

Hobsbawm , E, J.and T. Ranger (eds.) *The Invention of Traditions*. (Cambridge: Cambridge University Press, 1983)

Hobsbawm, J., *Nation and Nationalism since 1780: Programme, Myth and Reality*. (Cambridge: University Press, 1990).

Hoepli, Henrry U., *England im Nahen Osten Das Königreich Iraq und die Mossulfrage*. (Erlangen,1931).

Howard, Hary N., *An American Inquiry in the Midddle East: the King-Crane Commission*. (Beirut, 1963).

Hroch, Miroslav, *Social Preconditions of National Revival in Europe*. (Cambridge: Cambridge University Press, 1985).

Hroch, Miroslav, *From National Movement to the Fully-Formed*

Nation: The Nation -building Process in Europe, New Left Review, (1/198, 1993), pp. 1-13.

Hroch Miroslav, *National Self- Determination from a Historical Perspective*, Canadian Slavinic Papers/ Revue Canadienne des Slavistes, Vol. 37, (1995), pp.83-99.

Hroch, Miroslav, *The Nation- forming Process under Conditions of the Ottoman and Habsburg Empires.* In Tuuli Forsgren, Martin Peterson (eds.), *Cultural Crossroads in Europe.* (Uppsala: Ord och Form AB,1997), pp. 42-51.

Hroch Miroslav, *Real and Constructed: The Nature of the Nation*, in J.A.Hall (ed.), *The State of the Nation: Ernest Gellner and the Theory of Nationalism*, (Cambridge: Cambridge University Press, 1998), pp. 91-106.

Ibrahim, Ferhad, *Die kurdische Nationalbewegung im Irak: Eine Fallstudie zur problematic ethnischer konflikte in der Dritte Welt.*(Berlin: Klaus Schwarz, 1983).

Ireland, Philip Willard, *Iraq: A Study in Political Development.* (London: Alden Press, 1937)

Izady, Mehrdad R., *The Kurds: A Concise Handbook.* (Washington, Crane Russak, 1992).

Joffé, George, *Territory, State and Nation in the Middle East and North Africa.* In Clive H. Schofield and Richard N. Schofield (eds.)*The Middle East and North Africa.* World Boundaries Volume 2, (London and New York: Routledge, 1944) pp.1-20

Jwaideh, Wadie, *Kurdish National Movement: Its Origins and Development.* (Syracuse N.Y.:Syracuse University Press 2006).

Kadhim, Abbas K., *Reclaming Iraq: The 1920 Revolution and the Founding of the Modern State.* (Austin:University of Texas Press, 2012).

Kedourie, Elie, *England and the Middle East: The Destruction of the Ottoman Empire 1914-1921.* (London:Dowes & Dowes,1956).

Kedourie, Elie, *Nationalism.* (London: Hutchinson, 1960).

Kedourie, Elie (ed.), *Nationalism in Asia and Africa.* (London, 1970).

Khadduri, Majid, *Iraq: A study in Iraq's Politics since the Revolution of 1958.* (London: Oxford University Press, 1969).

Khadduri, Majid, *Political Trends in the Arab World: The Role of Ideas and Ideals in Politics*. (Baltimore and London: The Johns Hopkins Press, 1970).

Kent, Maria, *Oil and Empire: British Policy and Mesopotamian Oil 1900-1920.* (London: Macmillan, 1976).

Kent, Maria, *Great Britain and the End of the Ottoman Empire 1900-1923.* In Maria Kent (ed.) *The Great Powers and the End of the Ottoman Empire*. (London: George Allen and Unwin, 1984), pp.172-206.

keynes, John Maynard, C.B., *The Economic Consequences of the Peace.* (London, 1919).

Khalidi, Rashid, Lisa Anderson, Muhammad Muslih, and Reeva S., (eds.), *The Origins of Arab Nationalism.* (New York: Columbia University Press, 1991).

Kinnane, Derk, *The Kurds and Kurdistan.* (London, New York,1964).

Klieaman, Aron S., *Foundations of British policy in the Arab World: The Cairo Conference of 1921.* (Baltimore and London, 1970).

Kohn, Hans (1958), *The United Nations and National self-Determination.* The Review of Politics, Vol.20, No. 4. Twentieth Anniversary Issue, pp.275-288.

Kohn, Hans, *The Age of Nationalism: The First Era of Global History* (New York: Harpers & Brothers, 1962)

Kristof, Ladis, K.D., *The Nature of Frontiers and Boundaries.* AAG, (Association), of American Geography), Vol. 49. No. 3 1959. pp. 269-282.

Kuchler, Hannelore, *Öffentliche Meinung: Eine theoretisch-methodologische Betrachtung und eine exemplarische Undesuchung zum Selbstverständnis der Kurden.* (Berlin,1978)

Kutschera,Chris, *Le Mouvement National Kurde.* (Paris: Flammarion, 1979).

Laurance, Evans, *United States Policy and the Partition of Turkey 1914-1924.* (Baltimore: Johns Hopkins Univsity Press, 1965)

Laurence, W. Martin, *Peace without Victory: Woodrow Wilson and the British Liberals* (New Haven: Yale University, 1958).

Lawrence, T.E., *Seven Pillars of Wisdom: A Triumph* (New York, 1935).

Lawson, Fred H., *Constructing International Relations in the Arab World.* (Standford,California:Standford University Press, 2006)

Lees, G.M., *Two Years in South Kurdistan.* Journal of the Royal Central Asia Society, Vol. 15, Issue 31, (1928), pp. 253-277.

Lewis, Bernard. *The Emergence of Modern Turkey.* (London: Oxford University Press, 1961).

Lewis, Bernard. *The Middle East and the West.* (London,Weidenfeld and Nicolson, 1964).

Liora, Lukitz. *Iraq: The Search for National Identity.* (London: Frank Cass publishers, 1995).

Longrigg, Stephen Hemsley, *Iraq, 1900 to 1950: A political, Social, and Economical History.* (London:Oxford University Press,1953)

Longrigg, Stephen Hemsley and Frank Stoakes. *Iraq.* (London: E. Benn, 1958).

Longrigg, Stephen Hemsley, *Oil in The Middle East: Its Discovery and Devolopment.* (London, New York, Toronto, Oxford University Press, 1968).

Lynch, Allen, *Woodrow Wilson and the Principle of `National Self-Determination`: A Reconsideration.* Review of international Studies, Vol. 28, No.2, (April, 2002), pp. 419-436

Lyon,W.A., *Kurds, Arabs and Britons: The Memoir of Col.W.A.Loyn in Kurdistan, 1918-1945.* (London: I.B.Trauris, 2002)

Macfie, A. L., *The End of the Ottoman Empire, 1908-1923.* (London and New York: Longman, 1989).

Macfie, A: L., *The Straits Question 1908-36.* (Thessaloniki: Institute for Balkan Studies, 1993).

Makko, Aryo, *Arbitration in a World of Wars: The League of Nations And the Mosul Dispute, 1924-1925.* (2010). Diplomacy and Statecraft, Vol.21, issu, 4. pp.631-649.

Bibliography

Manela, Erez, *Wilsonian Moment: Self Determination and the International Origins of Anti-Colonial Nationalism* (Oxford, Oxford University Press, 2007).

Margaret, McMillan, *Peacemakers: Six Months that Changed the World.* (New York: Random House, 2003)

Marr, Phebe, *The Development of a Nationalist Ideology in Iraq 1920-1941.* The Muslim World, Vol. 75, (1985), pp.85-101.

McDowall, David, *A Modern History of the Kurds*, (London, I.B. Tauris, 2000).

Mello, Roy E . H., *Nation, State, and Territory: A Political Geography.* (London and New York: Routledge, 1989)

Miller, David Hunter, *The Origin of the Mandates System*, Foreign Affairs. Council of Foreign Relations, (1928), pp.277-289.

Montgomery A.E.,*The Making of the Treaty o f Secret of 10 August 1920.* The historical Journal, vol. 15, No. 4. (1972), pp.775-787.

Mufti, Malik, *Sovereign Creations: Pan-Arabism and Political Order in Syria and Iraq.* (Ithaca and London: Cornell University Press, 1996).

Nezan, Kendal, *The Kurds under the Ottoman Empire. In Gerard Chaliand* (ed.) *A People Without A Country, The Kurds and Kurdistan.* (London, 1980).

Nielson, Jonathan M., *American Historians in War and Peace, Patriotism, Diplomacy, and the Paris Peace Conference, 1918-1919.* (Dublin, 2012).

Nikitine, Basile., *Les Kurdes, Etudes Sociologique et Historique.* (Paris, 1956)

Olson, Robert, *The Emergence of Kurdish Nationalism and The Sheikh Said Rebellion, 1880-1925.* (Austin: University Texaspress, (1989).

Omar, Ziad, Al-Askary, *A Soldier's Story: From Ottoman Rule to Independent Iraq, The Memoirs of Jafar Pasha Al-Askary (1885- 1936)*, (London. Arabian Publishing L td, 2003).

Passi , Anssi (1998*) Boundaries as Social Process: Territoriality in the World of Flows*, Geopolitics, 3:1, 69-88, pp. 69-85

Pedersen, Susan, *Getting Out of Iraq in 1932: The League of Nation and the Road to Normative Statehood*. The American Historical Review, Vol.115

Pomerance, Michla, *Self- Determination in Law and Practice, The New Doctrine in the United Nations*.(The Hague: Nijhoff, 1982)

Pool, David, *From Elit to Class: The Transformation of Iraqi political Leadership*, in Abbas Kelidar (ed.) *The Integration of Modern Iraq*. (London: Croom Helm, 1979), pp. 63-87.

Prescott, R. V., *The Geography of Frontiers and Boundaries*. (London: Hutchinson University Library, 1965).

Prescott, R.V., *Political Frontiers and Boundaries*. (London, 1987).

Preston, Zoe, *The Crystallization of the Iraqi State: Geopolitical Function and Form*. (Bern: Peter Lang, 2006).

Rogan, Eugene L., *The Fall of the Ottomans: the Great War in the Middle East 1914-1920*. (London: Allen Lane, 2015).

Rogers, John, (2007). *The Foreign Policy of Small States: Sweden and the Mosul Crisis, 1924-1925*,Contemporary European History,16, pp 349-369.

Rothwell, V. H., *Mesopotamian in British War Aims, 1914-1918*. The Historical Journal, Vol.13, No.2. (1970), pp.273-294.

Sabine,George H., *A History of Political Theory*. (London, 1964).

Samuel, Annie Trac, *The Open Door and U.S. Policy in Iraq between the World Wars*. Diplomatic History. (2014) 38 (5) 926-952 DOI: 10.1093/dh/dhu033

Scazzieri, Luigi (2015) *Britain, France, and Mesopotamian Oil, 1916-1920*, Diplomacy and Statecraft, 26:1, 25-45,

Schwabe, Klause, *Woodrow Wilson and the Revolutionary Germany, and peacemaking 1918-1919:Missionary Diplomacy and Realities of Power* (Chapel Hill: University of North Carolina 1985).

Shakely, Ferhad, *Kurdish Nationalism in Mam u Zin of Ahmad-I Khani*. (Brussels: Kurdish institute of Brussels, 1992).

Sharabi, Hisham B., *Nationalism and Revolution in the Arab World*: (The Middle East and North Africa) (New York, 1966).

Shields, Sarah, *Mosul Questions: Economy, Identity, and Annexation.* In R. Spector Simon and E.H.Tejirian (eds.) The Creation of Iraq 1914-1922, (New York, 2004), pp.51-60

Silverfarb, Daniel, *Britain's Informal Empire in the Middle East: A Case Study of Iraq, 1929-1941.* (New York, 1986)

Sluglett, Peter, *Britain in Iraq: Contriving King and* Country. (London, 2007).

Simon,Reeva S., *Iraq between the two World Wars:The Creation and Implementation of a Nationalist Ideology.*(New York:C, 1986).

Simon, Reeva S., *The Imposition of Nationalism on a Non-Nation State: The Case of Iraq During the Interwar Period, 1921-1941.* In Jankowski ,James and I. Gershoni (eds.), *Rethinking Nationalism in the Arab Middle East.* (New York.:Columbia University Press, 1997).

Smith, Anthony D., *The Ethnic Origin of Nations.* (Oxford, 1986)

Smith, Anthony D., *Nationalism and Modernism: A Critical Survey of Recent Theories of Nations and Nationalism.* (London:Routledge,1998

Smith, Anthony D., *National Identity.* (London: Penguin, 1991).

Smith, Anthony D., *Nations and Nationalism in a Global Era.* (Oxford: Blackwell, 1995).

Smith, Anthony D., *Nationalism: Theory, Ideology, History.* (Cambridge: Polity, 2001).

Smith, Leonard V., *Empires at the Paris Peace Conference,* in Robert Gerwarth and Erez Manela (eds.), *Empires at War: 1911.1923.* (Oxford: Oxford University Press, 2004).

Steiner, Zara, *Lights that Failed: European International History 1919-1933.* (Oxford: Oxford University Press, 2005).

Stivers, William, *International Politics and Iraqi Oil, 1918-1928: A Study in Anglo- American Diplomacy,* The Business History Review, Vol. 55, No. 4 (1981), pp. 517-540.

Stivers, William, *Supremacy and Oil: Iraq, Turkey , and the Anglo-American World Order, 1918-1930.* (Ithaca and London: Cornell University Press, 1982).

Strohmeier, Martin, *Crucial Images in the Representation of a Kurdish National Identity: Heroes and Patriots, Traitors and Foes.*(Berlin, 2003).

Taha, Mai, *Self- Determiniation, Oil and Islam in the Face of the League of Nations: The Mosul Dispute and the "non-European, Legal Terrain"*, in Duncan French (ed.) *Statehood and Self-Determination, Reconciling Tradition and Modernity in International Law.* (Cambridge University Press, 2013)

Taspinar, Omar, *Kurdish Nationalism and Political Islam in Turkey: Kemalist Identity in Transition.* (New York: Routledge, 2005).

Tauber, Elieze, *The Formation of Modern Iraq and Syria.* (Ilford : Frank Cass, 1995).

Tibi, Bassam, *Arab Nationalism: Between Islam and the Nation-State.*(New York: St. Martin Press,1997).

Tillman, Seth P., *Anglo-American Relation at the Peace Conference of 1919.* (Princeton, New Jersey, 1961).

Temperley, H.W.V., *A History of the Peace Conference of Paris*, vol.V1, (London: H. Frowde, 1924).

Townshend, Charle, *When God Made Hell: The British Invasion of Mesopotamia and the Creation of Iraq 1914-1921.*(London:Faber and Faber,2000).

Tripp, Charles., *A History of Iraq.* (Cambridge: Cambridge University Press, 2000).

Trygvne, Throntveit, (2011) *The Faible if the Fourteen Points*: *Woodrow Wilson and National Self-Determination*, Diplomatic History 35 (3), pp. 445-481.

Vali, Abbas, *Nationalism and the Question of Origins.* In Abbas Vali (ed.) *Essays on the Origins of Kurdish Nationalism.* (Costa Mesa: California Mazda, 2003).

Vali, Abbas, *Genealogies of the Kurds: Constructions of Nation and National Identity in Kurdish Historical Writing.* In Abbas Vali (ed.) *Essays on the Origins on Kurdish Nationalism,*(Costa Mesa: California Mazda, 2003).

Venn, Fiona (2009*), Oleaginous Diplomacy: Oil, Anglo-American*

Relations and the Lausanne Conference, 1922-1923, Diplomacy and Statecraft, 20:3, 414-433.

Wien, Peter, *Iraqi Arab Nationalism, Authoritarian, Totalitarian, and Pro-Fascist Inclinations, 1932-1941*.(London: Routledge, 2006).

Wimmer, Andreas, *Nationalist Exclusion and Ethnic Conflict: Shadows of Modernity.* (Cambridge: Cambridge University Press, 2002)

Westrate, Bruce, *The Arab Bureau, British Policy in the Middle East, 1916-1920*, (University Park: Pennsylvania State University Press,1992).

Wilson, A.T., *Loyalties, Mesopotamia 1914-1917.* (London, 1930)

Wilson, A.T., *Mesopotamia 1917-1920: A Clash of Loyalty.* (London, 1931).

William, Spencer, *The Mosul Question in International Relations.* (Ann Arbor Michigan, 1988).

Wright, Quincy, *The Mosul Dispute: The American Journal of International Law*, Vol. 20, No.3 (Jul., 1926) pp.453-464, (American Society of International Law)

Yapp M. E., *The Making of the Modern Near East 1792-1923*, (London: Longman, 1978).

Yapp M. E., *The Near East Since the First World War: A History to 1995.* (London: Longman, 1997).

Zeine N. Zeine, *The Emergence of Arab Nationalism, With a Background Study of Arab-Turkish Relations in the Near East.* (New York: Karavan Books, 1966).

Zeine N. Zein, *The Struggle for Arab Independence: Western Diplomacy and the Rise and Fall of Faisal's Kingdom in Syria.* (New York: Caravan Books, 1977).

Özoglu, Hakan, *Kurdish Notables and the Ottoman State: Evolving Identities, Competing Loyalties and Shifting Boundaries.* (New York: State University Press, 2004.

Index